JEANNE CHEZARD DE MATEL
COMPLETE WORKS
VOLUME 2

ROUGH DRAFT OF THE AUTOGRAPHIC LIFE

PRAISED BE THE INCARNATE WORD, NOW AND FOREVER. AMEN.

Commemorative edition of the 400th Anniversary of the Birth
of Venerable Jeanne Chezard de Matel Roanne, France

We gratefully acknowledge all who have assisted in making this second volume a reality: His Excellency, Bishop David Fellhauer, D. D.; Rev. Eustace Hermes; Sister M. Andrea Hubnik, IWBS; and everyone else.

AUTOGRAPHIC LIFE

OF

JEANNE CHEZARD DE MATEL

FOUNDRESS OF THE ORDER OF THE
INCARNATE WORD AND
BLESSED SACRAMENT

ORIGINAL MANUSCRIPT IN FRENCH
IN THE ARCHIVES OF
THE SISTERS OF THE INCARNATE WORD AND BLESSED SACRAMENT
LYONS, FRANCE

VICTORIA, TEXAS, 1997

PREFACE

Part II of the *Autobiography* of our beloved Mother Foundress, Venerable Jeanne Chezard de Matel, has now been completed and made available to our readers. It is being released as Volume 2 of her *Complete Works*. It is not heavily footnoted as was Part I in which an effort was made to compare her original expression with what her secretary, Sister Françoise Gravier, penned thereafter, although what the latter did was always with the approval of Mother de Matel. As is generally known, the Foundress suffered from an eye condition that prevented her from preparing the final copy recounting her prayer experiences in obedience to Cardinal Alphonse Richelieu and, later, to her spiritual directors. She did personally write out her original inspiration which Sister Françoise then neatly copied.

Canon Leon Cristiani states: *"The Spiritual Journal,* begun in 1633, ended in fact with the removal of Jeanne's *Writings* by order of the Archbishop. What was to replace it a little later would be the continuation of the *Autobiography* until 1660. Beginning now, it is permitted to us to formulate a judgment about the ensemble of this collection that we believe to be unique in the history of spirituality." (Eng. Trans., Vol. II, *Historical-Critical Study of the Writings of Jeanne de Matel,* p. 82.)

It is with deep joy that this milestone has been attained on the Feast of St. Augustine. Mother Jeanne de Matel selected his Rule for her Order, because she felt it was the closest to the spirit of the Gospel.

Sister M. Carmelita Casso, IWBS
Feast of St. Augustine
August 28, 1997
Victoria, Texas

JEANNE'S ORIGINAL DRAFT

CHAPTER 91

Cardinal Richelieu returned from Narbonne to Lyons (1642) and what God allowed me to understand about the deaths of Monsieur de Thou and Monsieur le Grand. How Providence allowed the Chancellor to arrive there for the establishment of our Order in France, according to the Blessed Virgin's plans, and about Saint Michael's victory. (650)

Adorable Trinity, after I prayed to You to continue the effusions and profusions of your graces within my soul, I reflected that I ought to receive them from You and return them to You by remaining in You and that their origin would be their end. I did not think that I would write any more, but remain in the adoration that your divine love has taught me. I would visit with You, the Blessed Virgin and all the saints during the twenty-four hours of the day and night.

I offered You three novenas: the first through Saint Michael; the second through the Blessed Virgin, our wonderful Mother; and the third through the Incarnate Word for the relief of the arm of His Ducal Eminence, for I had learned that it was gravely infected. O Divine Savior, I know that the Wise Man warned me that there is no evil or pain in the city that your most equitable justice does not ordain or at least permit. You wound in order to heal. I pray that the one You have wounded may not die so soon, and that he may return from Narbonne according to your word. My desire or prayer was answered, for he returned to Lyons where he stayed a while, during which time the trial of Messieurs le Grand and de Thou was held. From the temporal ignominy of all this, You had their eternal glory spring forth.

Monsieur le Grand had not honored You during the height of his fame in this life. Heaped with disgrace and near death, he came to acknowledge You. During his lifetime, vanity and sensuality had blinded him, but your truth enlightened him at the point of death. (651)

JEANNE'S ORIGINAL DRAFT

Madame de Pontal, Monsieur de Thou's sister, arrived in Lyons shortly before her brother. She honored me by her visit to our Congregation to ask me to pray for her brother whom she loved unutterably, affecting me by her sorrow. Confidently I prayed to You, and, according to your usual goodness, You told me the secret of this brother: *ita stultum est semel mori; it is foolish to die in this way.* I said to You: "Lord, I well know the words of the Apostle, that it is decreed that all men will die once." "My daughter, those who are dead and then die the second death, die twice. This *semel* that I am telling you about means that you will not die the second death, which is the death of the wicked. He will die only once: the blessed moment of his eternal happiness will occur soon afterward. I reported this to Father Gibalin on September 7th, the day after You had assured me about it. I asked the priest not to upset Madame de Pontal beforehand, because, like all those who were in Lyons, she hoped that he would not be condemned to death. Her friends also entertained this hope until Friday the 17th, a few hours before noon.

On the birthday of your Blessed Mother, I was enraptured by a very sublime contemplation, during which You explained Psalm 23 to me: *Domini est terra, et plenitudo eius; The earth is the Lord's and the fullness thereof.* She belongs to You and You to her. You had filled her with graces and (652) glory, and, when she conceived You within her womb, divinity enclosed Him whom the heaven of heavens cannot contain: *Quia ipse super maria fundavit eum, et super flumina præparavit eum; For he hath founded it upon the seas; and hath prepared it upon the rivers.* (Ps 23:2) Represented by the rivers, the saints are beneath her; they receive a share of grace and glory, but your Blessed Mother received its plenitude. She is seated at your right side so as to communicate your favors to the Church Triumphant, Militant and Suffering. From her come waters which are, first of all, *usque ad talos, up to the ankles;* secondly, *usque ad genua, up to the knees;* (358) and thirdly, *usque ad renes, up to the loins.* (Ezech. 47:3-5)

For beginners, she purifies their feet of all earthly affections. Those who profit from this, she forms into adorers of your great attributes. The perfect she strengthens that they may fly to You and be stable in your love. For those

JEANNE'S ORIGINAL DRAFT

in glory, she is a torrent whom they cannot pass without being submerged in her adorable, marvelous waters as the Prophet says: *Torrentem quem non potui pertransire, quoniam intumuerant aquae profundi torrentis, qui non potest transvadari; A torrent which I could not pass over: for the waters were risen so as to make a deep torrent which could not be passed over.* (Ez. 47:5) (653)

Only the One who came from the Orient and is the Orient within the divinity, can measure these waters that are the perfections of this incomparable Virgin, the Blessed Mother. When I saw myself engulfed in these grandeurs, I abandoned myself to his goodness, losing myself in this blessed shipwreck and dying to all things visible. My whole life was orientated to adoring the Invisible One, who invited me to mount the waves of this torrent through innocent desires. He offered me the merits of his Mother so that from her I might receive an abundant blessing which filled my soul with joy. I seemed to be participating in the delight of this Virgin, who contemplates the face of the God of Jacob and who transmitted to me her splendor as well as her joy. Marveling at this, Father Gibalin ordered me to tell the Abbé de Cérisy what I had just told him. The Abbé marveled at Mary's incomparable qualities which I described and which appeared to me to be a source of splendor. I saw God in her and her in God. The mystery of the Incarnation was explained to me through lights that were so resplendent that they illuminated my face. My shining spirit made it obvious that my Love granted me a share in the happiness of those wonderful animals who drew the chariot of God's glory: *Et animalia ibant et revertebantur, in similitudinem fulguris coruscantis. And the living creatures ran and returned like flashes of lightning.* (Ez. 1:14)

Accompanied by Monsieur de Boissac, Madame de Pontat came to visit me in the afternoon. He had assured her that Monsieur de Thou, her brother, would not be condemned to death. This was the widespread expectation of everyone and even of most of his judges, but You, O my Oracle of truth who cannot deceive, told me that he would die in a few days and that he would be one of those to participate in the first resurrection. I could not conceal that from them.

JEANNE'S ORIGINAL DRAFT

It was clear that You were his salvation, support, and interior light. (655) While he was on the scaffold to be deprived of exterior life by the sword, You not only strengthened him to persevere to the end, but You gave strength and courage to the executioner assigned to decapitate him. You increased his faith, strengthened his hope, and perfected his charity so that he loved those who were depriving him of life. Humbling himself, he paraphrased that admirable Psalm: *Credidi propter quod locutus sum. I believed, therefore have I spoken.* (Ps. 115:1.

Yet, from the depths of the abundance of his heart from which he spoke and knowing that the thoughts of men are vain and that truth is to be found only in God, since in himself he did not find anything worthy of offering You, he presented to You the chalice of his salvation for all the good that You had done for him. He praised You for loosening the bonds that bound him to creatures, as well as those which joined his soul to his body. To You he made his vows in the presence of all those who were spectators at his beautiful death whereby he would enter eternal life. There his soul would make his vows to You before all the citizens of the heavenly Jerusalem. There, through an election beyond my understanding, your mercy gave him a place, saying with the Apostle: *Qui dilexit me tradidit semetipsum pro me; Who loved me and delivered himself for me.* (Gal.2:20)

The next day—September 13, 1642—his sister, Madame de Pontat, came to see me, inconsolably distressed. "Oh, Mother," she said to me, "you knew very well that my brother would die, and you did not tell me! Father Gibalin told me that you had informed him on the seventh of this month that Our Lord had revealed it to you."

I replied: "Madame, when you came to see me on the Feast of the Birth of Our Lady, 1642, Divine Providence made me fearful of anticipating your sorrow. You were in the parlor with Monsieur de Boissac, who accompanied you to your residence. (657) That left me with the Abbé de Cérisy to whom I recommended your brother's case so that he might speak to the Chancellor on your behalf. He did so with all the zeal that could possibly be called forth by

JEANNE'S ORIGINAL DRAFT

his own goodness and your great sorrow. He was not aware of the decree of the Incarnate Word who willed this death so as to raise him to a very high place in glory. Father Gibalin has told you that I had learned of this favorable end to his life by our Savior who wanted him to share in his own glory on the day of his ignominy. I do not want to conceal from you, Madame, the sentiments of my soul because of his happiness—a happiness ln which my soul shared through the charity of our adorable Incarnate Word, who wanted me to console you with the happy news that your brother would not die the second death, but that he would possess eternal life."

A few days later, the Chancellor told the Abbé de Cérisy that he desired to come visit me. This brought no small joy to the Abbé who had developed such a strong affection for me that his soul and mine were united by a charity that was similar to the love between Jonathan and David. (658) He answered him: "Monsigneur, Father Gibalin, the Jesuit, had assured me that, at the beginning of the year 1633, Mother de Matel informed him that the Incarnate Word, through Saint Michael, would give you the Seals attached to the blue cord. He also assured her that you would be the Chancellor of France."

Your wisdom, that disposes all things strongly and gently, caused the Chancellor, whom I had seen only in a vision, to come see me. At the moment I met him, I experienced such an intense fear that I could hardly answer him. The words that he addressed to me were full of gentleness, sincerity and charity. This fear did not leave me even after he had departed. Therefore, I complained about it to your kindness which removed it, saying: *"Descendit in hortus; She went down into the garden."* (Cant 6:10).

"My daughter, externally, the Chancellor of France is like the shell of a hard walnut which, at first, seems very severe; but internally, he is gentle, anointed with the oil of my grace and mercy which are very great in him. (659) When he returns to see you, you will not be afraid of him. I want you and him to be like the two Cherubim accompanying the Ark of the Covenant that you may gaze perpetually at Me with a pure intention. Through my ordinance and choice, he judges exterior matters and you, those that are interior. It is I and

JEANNE'S ORIGINAL DRAFT

not men (who are simply ministers of my will) who gave him the Seals and established him as Chancellor. Rest assured, my daughter, that he will promote the establishment of my Order in France. He will have you go to Paris, and you will see the coat-of-arms of France united with that of the Holy See. Thus will be fulfilled the vision that you had while you were still in Roanne. You will see a mystical extension of my Incarnation through a spiritual generation which is very well described by these words found in St. Matthew: *Jacob autem genuit Joseph virum Mariae, de qua natus est Jesus, qui vocatur Christus. Jacob begot Joseph, the husband of Mary, of whom was born Jesus, who is called Christ.* (Mt. 1:16)

Through my pure election, he is the father of the Abbé de Cérisy whom you think of as Joseph, because he takes care of my household. (660) Joseph will be the spiritual father and superior of my family and the man whom I have chosen to assist you; and you will be like my Blessed Mother, since it was she who gave Me birth. He will be like the foster father, and you, my mother. From you, through this Order, I have already been born in Avignon, and I will be born again in France from you and through you who extend my Incarnation.

"O, my daughter! Was it not the Blessed Virgin who produced the vision which our daughter, Elizabeth Grasseteau, experienced of the forty days that I remained in the stable at Bethlehem? This sword that was carried by my Mother symbolized the happy death of the two who were beheaded on September 22nd. One was De Thou, who was devoted to her when he was a student and who had joined her Congregation. She remembered what he had done then and brought about this death which caused him to act in a Christian manner. She assisted him to perceive the vanity of the world—he might have been lost had he lived any longer.

"This young woman did not understand the vision, and I explained it to you. I informed you about the whole secret and how my Blessed Mother had obtained their salvation through this temporal death. (661) She had the judgment and decision given in Lyons so that the Chancellor of France might go there to see you and so that you would give birth to my Order in France. You see how she directed several angels to bring judges from different places to assist

JEANNE'S ORIGINAL DRAFT

in the judgment of these two persons in order to make known the great graces that I have given you, that I now give you, and that I will give you purely out of my goodness." Dearest Love, blessed may You be with every blessing, as well as your saints and your most worthy Mother, my beautiful Noemi, who arranges all for Your glory and my benefit.

On the Feast of Saint Michael, You wanted to show me the glory with which You honored him. It was a glory which I would have thought belonged to You alone had You not told me that what is yours by nature and acquisition was, by your goodness, given to this first among the faithful who had driven from the heavens the first being who rebelled against your law and his duties, as well as all his followers: *Et factum est praelius magnum in caelo: Michael et angeli ejus præliabantur cum dracone, et draco pugnabat, et angeli ejus: et non valuerunt neque locus inventus est eorum amplius in cælo. Et ipsi vicerunt eum propter sanguinem Agni. And there was a great battle in heaven: Michael and his angels fought with the dragon, and the dragon fought and his angels. And they did not prevail ; neither was their place found any more in heaven.* (Apoc 12:7-8, 11) (662) All these angels were triumphant under him. After this victory, I understood great marvels about this magnificent prince: *Multa magnalia de Michaele Archangelo, qui, fortis in prælio, fecit victoriam. Many wondrous deeds are recounted about the Archangel Michael, who because of his bravery in battle, obtained the victory. (Office* for Sept 29)

It pleased You, my Savior, to have this conqueror for your glory appear to me in a triumphant chariot, all shining with splendor, elevated by light: *Ascendentem ab ortu solis habentem signum Dei vivi. Ascending from the rising of the sun, having the sign of the living God.* (Apoc 7:2) But the marvel of your goodness was that, after You had raised him up to You through your glory, he bent toward me by your grace, inviting me in an angelic way to ascend in the same triumphant chariot through your Order. I was more embarrassed than I can explain, and I humbled and abased myself in my nothingness. During this self-emptying, the assisting angels, who were participants in this triumph, raised themselves up with such magnificence that eye has not seen, ear has not heard, nor has human heart conceived of it.

JEANNE'S ORIGINAL DRAFT

These favors exceed the senses and the thoughts of the human heart. (663) I do not know how the soul can animate the body while it is so occupied in loving, admiring and adoring your divine glory in itself and in your angels, all flame and splendor. I can only repeat the words of the Apostle after he was taken up in rapture to the third heaven: *Sive in corpore, sive [...] etc. Whether in the body, whether [...] etc.* (2 Cor. 12:2)

CHAPTER XCII

The Incarnate Word told me that He wanted to lower the hills of the world by removing Cardinal de Richelieu; that He wanted his Order to be established in France and that He would have the Chancellor retain the Seals.

On the Feast of Saint Francis, 1642, the Abbé de Cerisy gave us a homily which many of those who had accompanied the Chancellor and were still in Lyons desired to hear. Among them was Monsieur de Laubardemont, a Councillor of Parliament in Paris, who went to visit the Cardinal of Lyons when he left our chapel. The Cardinal inquired where he had been, and he replied: "I have just come from hearing a homily given by the Abbé de Cerisy." "Where?" "At the Incarnate Word Convent." (664) To explain himself better, Monsieur de Laubardemont declared: "At Mother de Matel's." His Eminence replied: "I don't want to hear anying about Mother de Matel." Monsieur de Laubardemont said nothing more, knowing that His Eminence was not at all favorable toward your Order nor toward me who was unaware of these scathing replies at the time. But You were not unaware of all this, my Divine Love, who as God are present everywhere by essence, presence and power, and, as the Apostle St. Paul states: *Jesus Christus heri, et hodie: ipse et in sæcula. Jesus Christ, yesterday, and today: and the same for*

JEANNE'S ORIGINAL DRAFT

ever. (Heb 13:8)

You waited for me to be alone before the Blessed Sacrament in the evening, as was my custom, to show me your displeasure. By a deep rapture, You elevated my spirit. I was indeed surprised when I heard You emphatically pronounce these words: *Quare fremuerunt gentes, et populi meditati sunt inania? Why have Gentiles raged: and the people devised vain things?* (Ps 2:1)

Lord, who caused You to have this just anger? "The one who opposes my Order. Do not restrain my arm by your prayers. I want my Order to be established in France; do not pray to Me to leave Cardinal de Richelieu on earth any longer. I want him to die so as to abase and bring down the hills of the world along the route of my eternity. Some years ago, I told you that I would strike down the first-born of Egypt in possession of the See, who is as hard-hearted as Pharaoh. Cardinal de Richelieu is not the first-born by nature, but he belongs to the Court which is well symbolized by Egypt. He was a bishop when the Cardinal of Lyons became a Chartreux (Benedictine monk). My daughter, I want to break this earthen vessel and laugh at those who depend upon his authority: *Qui habitat in cælis, irridebit eos, et Dominus subsannabit eos. He that dwelleth in heaven shall laugh at them: and the Lord shall deride them.* (Ps 2:4) You explained this entire Psalm to me, scorning apparent earthly powers.

Dear Love, You know how astounded and afflicted I was by your resolve to take away the temporal life of the one whom You had before said would guide France at your command as Moses did the people of Israel. "My daughter, this has been determined to overthrow the ones who have worked together to prevent the establishment my Order. His Eminence is the one who came to visit you incognito, saying that he was Cardinal Richelieu's confessor."

Because I was sad, my Divine Consoler, your goodness favored me with indescribable delights, telling me that You no longer cared to endure allowing the powerful on earth cause me to suffer too much as we awaited your foundation. (666) Also, I was being afflicted by what was beneficial for me.

JEANNE'S ORIGINAL DRAFT

Dear Love, I was not upset that You wished to remove the obstacle to your glory by this Order. However, a good that is for a special case does not affect me as much as one that is for the general good. Pardon, dearest Love, but France will be deprived of a great deal; your Church will not gain thereby. This Cardinal promotes the glory of each of them. But, Lord, I who am dust and ashes, how dare I answer You? Not my will, but yours, Lord, that You show me with so much delight when I am caught up by a gentle rapture.

I addressed St. Bruno, whose feast was the following day: "Great saint, can't you touch the heart of him who is still your son, even though he does not live in your monastery? Why did you allow him to leave your deserts in order to oppose the Order of our love, the Incarnate Word? Oh! you tell me nothing! You are are on the side of the One who allows this for good reasons." (667) From that evening on, I could no longer pray as I had been doing for the prolongation of Cardinal Richelieu's life. His death made me fear that the seals would be taken from the Chancellor to whom I reported what You had given me to know, as well as to the Abbé de Cerisy. The latter recalled the death of the Duke de Lesdiguière's little girl that I had predicted to them would occur on the day that it did. They saw that You are my veritable Oracle. You lovingly favored me, telling me that You would fulfill all your promises and those of your Blessed Mother.

During my repose on the night of November 17-18, 1642, I was led to a suburb of Paris where I saw a multitude of people following Saint Denis, who was dressed in pontifical robes. Beside him were a number of saints in attendance, among whom I saw Saint Peter, Saint Paul and Saint Martin. St. Paul was informing St. Denis about what he should do during this great solemnity and how he should act in the presence of the vast multitude. (668) The real Bishop and Prelate of Paris let me know that I was to follow him and that he was making this magnificent and pontifical entrance for your glory. Blessed Incarnate Word, who let me know that the time for your establishment in the St. Germain suburb of Paris was approaching, You did not oppose my conversing familiarly with St. Paul to whom I said: "Great Apostle, now I understand what you meant when, prompted by humility, you said that your

JEANNE'S ORIGINAL DRAFT

letters are solemn and that your person is lowly. However, you are Saint Denis's teacher in theology and famed for your sacred mysteries." On the left side, I saw Saint Martin who also possessed a humble appearance; yet each one seemed to me to be a very great saint.

After I had this dream, I received a letter from the Abbé de Cerisy who wrote me from Paris that on that particular day a devout woman had come to the Chancellor's hotel. In the Chancellors's chapel, she had attended holy Mass during which she had become enraptured . Her confessor informed her of what she had been heard to say during that time: that Your Majesty wanted the Chancellor to have me go to Paris to establish your Order there and that the Abbé de Cerisy was destined to be involved in it. He alluded to himself with great modesty, humbling himself while You wanted to exalt him. (669)

On the eve of the Feast of Saint Andrew, You set a raging fire in my heart, prompting me to ask You for the establishment of your Order in France. On the same day, Cardinal Richelieu felt worse, and from that day until Thursday, December 4, 1642—the day he died—I prayed to You for him and begged You to alleviate his soul. You did not reject my prayer. Even now, I ask You to do so, my Divine Love. The Chancellor took every possible means to have me go to Paris and promote the establishment of your Order in France. As for me, I can only be prompted by your Spirit; I remained in a tranquillity that I cannot express. Your love impelled me to love You with greater fidelity than in the past, telling me that You delight in fulfilling your promises for which I thanked You with humble gratitude. (670)

On January 4, 1643, while I was at prayer, You showed me how your loving breast blazed with the fire of your love. You told me: "My daughter, my zeal for the glory of the divinity and the salvation of souls has thus consumed Me." Dear Love, I see your Sacred Body, this holy Temple, so burnt that I cannot detect your breast, stomach, ribs, heart nor intestines. Speaking in your Name, David said: *Factum est cor meum tamquam cera. Liquescit in medio ventris mei. Aruit tamquam testa virtus mea. My heart is become like wax melting in the midst of my bowels. My strength is dried*

JEANNE'S ORIGINAL DRAFT

up like a potsherd. (Ps 21:15b-16a)

O, my Jesus, can I see You that way without fainting? God of my heart, why do You leave it in my bosom, since yours is consumed with love. Is it that You have deprived Yourself of it to place mine there (which belongs to You)? Do so, dear Love, and all your saints will proclaim: *Et factus est in pace locus eius, et habitatio eius in Sion. And his place is in peace: and his abode in Sion.* (Ps 75:3)

What, Lord, do You abide among the shadows of death, for all I see in You is darkness, since You resemble a burnt tree trunk to me. Through your Prophet Ezechiel, You said: *Ossa arida, audite verbum Domini. Ye dry bones, hear the word of the Lord.* (Ez 37:4b) (671) Otherwise, I would think that I were dreaming or seeing a ghost and not the Incarnate Word, the Word of Life. You retain the marks of death on your Body, a proof to me of the condition to which love and sin have reduced You.

Dear Love, You step into the Jordan River and there offer Yourself as a holocaust. Not even this entire river could extinguish the flame of your deep love. Understandably, Elias and all the people thought they saw a great miracle when fire descended from heaven to consume their sacrifice upon and around which he had poured water, but it was not an entire river like the Jordan. You invited me to see these marvels. I adore You, my wonderful One. I know very well that You can make two contrary conditions subsist in one same subject, that You were showing me your love and the sins of mankind, that You are a perfect holocaust and a living God, a river of grace, a sea of blazing glory and a consuming fire. (672)

During my Communion on January 18th, I fervently prayed for the Chancellor, recalling that his name was Pierre. You deigned to assure me of your special protection for him to retain the seals for a number of years. I prayed to Saints Peter and Michael to obtain a confirmation of this from your goodness, and they did not keep it from me. As a sign that my request was ratified, a strong perfume filled my room and the places where I passed. Without asking my

JEANNE'S ORIGINAL DRAFT

permission, one of my daughters led all our Sisters and boarders, one after another and then altogether, to share doubly in this sweet perfume that was so profuse. My divine Savior, I ask that he and I may in all truth say: *Christi bonus odor sumus. We are the good odor of Christ.* (2 Cor 2:15) (673)

CHAPTER XCIII

Different states and indescribable interior suffering in which God placed my soul; the foundation of the monastery in Grenoble. My return to Lyons and journey to Paris.

On the Feast of the Purification of your Blessed Mother in 1643, I was favored according to your goodness. You had told me: *Inveni quem diligit anima me. Tenui eum, nec dimittam, Donec introducam illum in domum matris meæ. I held him: and I will not let him go, till I bring him into my mother's house and into the chamber of her that bore me.* (Cant 3:4b) Could I let You go after your Blessed Mother and mine had ransomed You for me without accompanying You everywhere, even to Egypt, waiting with her to be recalled and return to Israel. Dear Love, the Evangelists say nothing about what happened to You, your Blessed Mother and Saint Joseph in Egypt. I do not really know how many years You remained there, but I well recall that seven years ago when I wrote this I left Lyons to go to Avignon. That was by order of your Providence, prompted by Fathers Gibalin and Arnoulx, who told me that he would pray to You to treat me differently from what You had done ever since my childhood. Alas! how can I express how my soul suffered at the time? You are aware of it, Divine Love. (674)

On Wednesday, after the Feast of the Purification, You allowed me to

JEANNE'S ORIGINAL DRAFT

have inexpressible troubles. That day I saw my spirit constantly shifting in different states. At one moment, I found myself in Limbo in the shadow of death, yearning for my redemption. Later, I seemed to descend further down, and I was in palpable darkness, overwhelmed by despair for my salvation. I could say with Job: *Elegit suspendium anima mea; Desperavi, nequequam ultra iam vivam. So that my soul rather chooseth hanging; I have done with hope, I shall live no longer.* (Job 7:15a-16a)

I felt without order or support and was convinced that I deserved every suffering. My sins were against me, and, more than I can say, all creatures had the right to avenge their Creator offended by my multiple crimes. At another moment, I experienced a purgatory by suffering that I found to be truly just. I could not complain of divine justice. Although I wanted to be freed from these sufferings, I did not want to be delivered from them unless reparation had been made for them according to his will. I was resigned to it, complaining of myself, my lax behavior and other failures. (675) At another moment, You filled my spirit with delight, but this happiness lasted only a short while so that I enjoyed it only momentarily. Soon I was back in my suffering, saying to You: *Quare posuisti me contrarium tibi, Et factus sum mihimetipsi gravis? Cur non tollis peccatum meum, Et quare non aufers iniquitatem meam? Why hast thou set me opposite to thee, and I am become burdensome to myself? Why dost thou not remove my sin, and why dost thou not take away my iniquity?* (Job 7:20b-21)

Lord, my God, how unhappy my soul was to find itself, by your just rigor, in a condition that seemed contrary to my obligations and your love, since love is all afire for the object loved. Alas, why do You not deliver me from the burdens to which my own heaviness has reduced me? You are the one who takes away the sins of the world. Through grace, save me from mine. *Quis det ut veniat petitio mea. Et quod expecto tribuat mihi Deus? Et qui coepit, ipse me conterat; Solvat manum suam, et succidat me? Et hæc mihi sit consolatio, ut affligens me dolore, non parcat. Nec contradicam sermonibus Sancti. Who will grant that my request may come: and that God may give me what I look for? And that he that hath begun may*

JEANNE'S ORIGINAL DRAFT

destroy me: that he may let loose his hand, and cut me off? And that this may be my comfort, that afflicting me with sorrow, he spare not: nor I contradict the words of the Holy One. (Job 6:8-10)

In 1643, on the Thursday before Lent, Madame de Revel, the Attorney General's wife, arrived in Lyons with Priors de Croixil and St. Robert. They had a letter and an order from Father Arnoulx to take me to Grenoble, for which I felt an indescribable repugnance, but Father Gibalin took every means to convince me to make this voyage. (676) I said to him: "Father, who will provide the foundation? What will the Cardinal of Lyons say when he learns that I departed without requesting his permission to do so? I would not go to Grenoble, because the foundation in Paris is urgently awaiting me." Yet none of my reasons served to make Father Gibalin change his mind. He wanted me to leave Lyons, saying that he would offer my excuses to His Eminence when the latter returned from Marseille and that he would defer the establishment in Paris until the one in Grenoble was made. I could not resist his determination, although I thought it would be better to establish the one in Paris first.

On Quinquagesima Sunday, I resolved to leave Lyons after having told him: "Father, this night I saw a furnace into which I was being forced to enter." Neither did my frankness allow me to conceal my reservations from the two Priors and Madame de Revel. I said to them: "Your zeal is obligating me to go beyond all the difficulties that my spirit anticipates. (677) I know that neither storm, hail nor the extreme cold in which you came could influence your charity: *Nescit tarda molimina Spiritus Sancti gratia; The grace of the Holy Spirit knows no delay.* Let us say with St. Thomas that we wish to die for the Incarnate Word. Let us get into our carriages, Madame, and leave Lyons without notifying anyone about our departure."

The next day, between three and four o'clock, we arrived at the monastery of the Prior of St. Robert who zealously took care of our needs. Then, between seven and eight o'clock in the evening in Grenoble, the Countess de Rochefort, wife of President de Chevrière; her mother, Madame de Semiane and other women of high society came to meet us. They told me that we had

JEANNE'S ORIGINAL DRAFT

to remain several days incognito in Grenoble. President de Chaune and his wife would provide me with accommodations. With great kindness, they welcomed me and my dear Sister Grasseteau (my faithful companion). We remained there until Holy Thursday, for which we were very grateful. A relative of Madame de Revel, Monsieur de Miribert, kindly offered me a part of his home that faced that of the Capuchin Fathers, where we might begin the foundation. (678)

President de Chaune admired the writings that Father Gibalin had requested me to give Madame de Revel and the two above-mentioned priors to whom she had lent them. They inquired if I had others and, if so, to let them see them. I would have been ungrateful for the kindnesses of such a gentleman and host had I refused. Besides, they were no longer secret, since His Eminence of Lyons had taken them away, and Father Gibalin had given the ones still in his room to whomever he thought it appropriate to do so, knowing that some were already in different provinces. I told You: "My Divine Love, my writings are like the apples of Jerusalem. Whoever can take them away, does so: *Posuerunt Jerusalem in pomorum custodiam. They have made Jerusalem as a place to keep fruit.* (Ps 78:1c) May this be for you glory and my confusion."

When the Bishop of Grenoble had seen them in the hands of President de Chaune, he asked the latter to tell his wife to go visit him and take me with her. As soon as he saw me, he offered me his protection and permission to set up an establishment in Grenoble. (679) No one offered to defray the expenses as founder. He said that he was of the opinion that I was able to endow it, that I should submit a request to him and another one to the city. I did so and obtained from both him and the city all that I requested.

The gentlemen from Parliament informed me that I had to petition for Patent Letters from His Majesty. The Chancellor took the trouble to write two or three letters on my behalf to recommend to them the establishment of our monastery. They came to see me with great civility. However, some were resolved to oppose this establishment, saying that there were already

JEANNE'S ORIGINAL DRAFT

enough religious houses in Grenoble.

While at prayer, around the Feast of your Incarnation, I saw a cross similar to that of Saint Andrew's that seemed to extend to the four corners of the earth. I was ready to suffer everything and everywhere if I could only spread the message of the Cross that worldly ones do not love: *Verbum enim crucis pereuntibus quidem stultitia est. For the word of the cross, to them indeed that perish, is foolishness.* (1 Cor 1:18a) Chosen ones deem it to be wisdom and power: *Iis autem qui salvi fiunt, id est nobis, Dei virtus est. But to them that are saved, that is, to us, it is the power of God.* (1 Cor 1:18b) (680)

The day before the Feast of Saint James and Saint Philip, Monsieur Le Roux, the Councillor, who was the chairman, came to visit me, saying that we had to wait, because he feared the resistance of opponents to our project who were determined to militate against it. I wanted to write to the one who was determined to resist, thinking that your Spirit was prompting me to write this letter. Human prudence thought that it had influenced this Spirit to dissolve everything, but, instead, your providence arranged that things become consolidated, saying that I had made it firmer by calling him both judge and party. He did not want to participate in the matter; he was followed by three others who shared his views. These went outside, leaving only those who favored the establishment in distress because of my letter. However, O divine wisdom, You reminded them about what the Church chants on [Holy] Saturday, *O felix culpa, O happy fault* contrary to all human prudence. It caused those who were opposed to depart so that there might be but one accord among us, numbering more than the opponents. (681)

Meanwhile, I was in the church of the Capuchin fathers, where I received Communion, while weeping a torrent of tears. I remembered hearing one night that I was to have a great cross during the month of May, the 2nd, and that it was the Feast of St. Athanasius to whom I said: "Against all hope, I want to imitate you. Have the Incarnate Word triumph today through a young woman. He is the same Incarnate Word whose divine equality with his Eternal

JEANNE'S ORIGINAL DRAFT

Father you had upheld."

A few days later, the Councillor from St. Germain, who was related to Madame de Lessin, who was opposed to us, came to visit me. He asked my pardon for having been against me and said that in the future he would be at my service. I replied: "Sir, you must imitate Saul when he was converted. The glorious Incarnate Word appeared to him and told him secrets that He told no one else. Here, Monsieur, I am entrusting to you the story of my life that I have written by order of the Cardinal-Archbishop of Lyons. Through prudence, you will not tell anyone, please. Here it is, and know that God has accomplished these marvels all by Himself. (682) He witnesses to Himself, and his testimony is true. I am also informing you that our King Louis XIII will die in a few days, because I have understood these words of the angels written in Daniel: *In sententia vigilum decretum est; He was sentenced according to the decree of the sentinels.* I told him this, because it was being said in Grenoble that a devout woman from Provence had predicted that he would live another thirteen years.

On the eve of May 17th, he came to see me with Madame de Lessain to know which day I would be leaving for Avignon to get four Sisters. I told him: "Tomorrow, please God." While we were speaking together in a parlor, Madame de Lessain, he and I saw a large chair fall over that no visible person had touched. This astounded them deeply.

The next day, May 17th, dedicated to Blessed Felix of Cantalicia, Monsieur Bernardon, Prior of Denicé; my dear Sister Grasseteau and I left Grenoble going by the river that enters the Rhone to get to Avignon. We arrived at our monastery at seven o'clock on Saturday morning, May 20th. (683) My Sisters came in procession to welcome me at the convent door. So great was my joy upon seeing them that I forgot all the sufferings I had had, which it would be inappropriate to specify.

After my arrival in this dear city, I was told that our King had died. This did not surprise me at all, for I had been notified by heaven and by the

JEANNE'S ORIGINAL DRAFT

overturning of the chair, reminding me that the sees and thrones of this world are not permanent. With signs of joy, the men and women of Avignon came to visit me. They wanted me to remain in our monastery. However, the Bishop of Grenoble had told me to return there as soon as possible. This made me hasten my return.

On Saturday, the eve of the Most Blessed Trinity, I bade farewell to my daughters. This departure was accompanied by tears; I felt my heart cut in two. (684) Those who remained in this monastery kept half of it, if I may so speak. I took with me three of the first ones I had assigned there: Sister Marie of the Holy Spirit Nallard, Sister Therese of Jesus Gibalin, Sister Jeanne of the Passion Fiot and Sister Pierre of the Conception, a native of Villeneuve and a turn Sister from Avignon. Thus, together with my very dear Sister Grasseteau, we numbered seven in the carriage for our journey. She was my faithful companion par excellence whose bodily infirmities and weakness caused me deep compassion.

There had been such heavy rains that the rivers were flooded over, the roads inundated and broken up and looking like torrents and rivers from the sea. We could hardly find land for fording. Only the heads of the horses could be seen. The water came up to our carriage seats. All seven of us had to remain standing. (685) In addition, the carriage was so rickety that we thought it could not take us three leagues without falling apart, because it also carried three chests and many other items. The coachman and his valet were in danger of their lives. The Prior and our Sisters looked like fear itself, afraid of perishing in this deluge. They did not dare express their dread, for they saw that I was as confident as in my oratory, recalling what the Prophet said: *In mari via tua, et semitæ tuæ in aquis multi. Tu es Deus qui facis mirabilia. Thy way is in the sea, and thy paths in many waters. Thou art the God that dost wonders.* (Ps 76:20a,15a)

You work them, my God, not only upon and in the water, but also on earth. Our carriage was transported a long time and suspended by your divine power, about which I was not thinking. (686) Since my companions saw that I

JEANNE'S ORIGINAL DRAFT

was recollected, they insisted that I pray to You to help us in this imminent peril. So as not to seem insensible, I prayed to You and your Blessed Mother to look upon us with the eyes of your benignity. I said to You: *De vultu tuo judicium meum prodeat; perfice gressus meos in semitis tuis, ut non moveantur vestigia mea; mirifica misericordias tuas, qui salvos facit sperantes in te. Let my judgment come forth from thy countenance. Perfect thou my goings in thy paths: that my footsteps be not moved. Show forth thy wonderful mercies; thou who savest them that trust in thee.* (Ps 16:2, 5, 7)

When all these dangers and precipices were past, the Prior and our Sisters marveled at your providence over us. They thought that all your angels, together with Saint Raphael, had miraculously guided us. In thanksgiving, they chanted the *Te Deum*. We arrived in Grenoble on June 2, 1643, at about eight or nine o'clock in the evening, on the eve of the Feast of your most precious and Sacred Body. The Bishop of Grenoble wanted us to obtain his blessing before we went to the home of Madame de Vitalieu that was prepared as a monastery. The next day, your holy feast, at about eight o'clock, the Prior of Croixil offered Mass and exposed the Blessed Sacrament. Our Sisters recited aloud the Office in choir. After Vespers, Father Arnoulx gave us a homily. A large number of ladies and gentlemen of Grenoble were present to their own satisfaction. The Bishop of Grenoble sent me his carriage in the evening on the same day to go visit him, since he was unable to come to his new monastery of the Incarnate Word, for he had to leave for Paris the next day at four o'clock in the morning.

It did not take long for him to urge me to go there and establish the third monastery of your Order, my most amiable Incarnate Word. All my friends encouraged me to hasten the foundation of the monastery in Paris, fearing that the seals might be taken from the Chancellor at the beginning of the regency. (688) Monsieur de Servien, presently the ambassador in Piedmont and next to the Duchesse of Savoy, told me that Monsieur Seguier was no longer Keeper of the Seals nor Chancellor. Instead, Monsieur de Chateauneuf held both positions. I told her: "Monsieur Seguier is both, or Our Lord has not heard

JEANNE'S ORIGINAL DRAFT

my prayers. I trust that, even though I am unworthy, Our Lord will hear my prayer, just as He did when I prayed for the health of your two children. I was so deeply moved when I saw you weeping in fear of their death after thirteen days of continual fever. You told me that God had healed them in answer to my prayer. This son and daughter were not prayed for with greater confidence than that with which I confidently request that the Chancellor continue to retain the seals." He told me: "It is true, Madame, that I owe the health of my two children to your prayers and that I certainly believe that Monsieur Seguier will continue to be the Keeper of the Seals." (689)

Dearest Love, who are pleased to answer the prayers of your beloved and cannot leave her in trouble. By the odor of very light perfume the next day, You confirmed for me that Monsieur Seguier again possessed the Seals of little King Louis XIV: *Testimonia tua credibilia facta sunt nimis. Thy testimonies are become exceedingly credible.* (Ps 92:5a)

The heat was so excessive that the doctors feared that it might cause me to succumb. They said I should not travel so much without being refreshed by the waters and baths. They would not be responsible for my life unless I were made to rest because of my sufferings from gallstones. I departed from Grenoble on the 30th, and then, on July 2nd—the Feast of the Visitation of your Blessed Mother—I arrived in Lyons where I took the treatment provided by the waters and baths through obedience.

The Abbé de Cerisy and the Chancellor's wife prompted me to advance my journey to Paris. The Bishop of Grenoble ordered his official to send me two Sisters to Lyons for Paris of the four I had taken from Avignon. I asked the Prior of Denicé to return to Grenoble to request the official for my Sister of the Holy Spirit and Sister of the Conception, thus sharing with Grenoble. (690) However, your providence allowed this sharing to take place cautiously, due to the plague that had forced them to interrupt their journey to go stay in the home of the Baron of Bouffin, the Prior of Croixil's father.

Prior Bernardon arrived in Lyons with my two Sisters on the Feast of the

JEANNE'S ORIGINAL DRAFT

discovery of the relics of St. Stephen, the first martyr. This was on August 3rd, and I replaced them with Sister Elie of the Cross and Lucrecia de Bely. On the sixth day of August, they arrived at the gate of Grenoble, but could not enter because of the plague. They departed to join the Sisters who were in Uriage with the Baron of Bouffin, father of the Prior of Croixil.

On Friday, the 7th of the same month, the Prior, our two Sisters, my dear Sister Grasseteau, Sister Gravier and I left Lyons for Paris. Dearest Love, you could see that I was sad, fearing the great world, but I desired nothing more than to sacrifice myself for your glory and my neighbor's salvation. I recalled that Saint Paul said in his Letter to the Romans: *Unusquisque vestrum proximos suos placeat in bonum ad œdificationem. Etenim Christus non sibi placuit. Let every one of you please his neighbor unto good, to edification. For Christ did not please himself.* (Rom 15:2-3a)

I renounced all my delight in the solitude of Lyons and the consolations my soul received upon the holy mountain there. Dear Love, I yearned to have the blood that flowed so freely upon this holy mountain of Gourguillon during the time of so many martyrs to follow me, as it is declared that the water of the rock followed the people of Israel. (691) Dearest Love, my repugnance for leaving Lyons did not cause me to loiter along the way. By my desires, I deeply implored heaven, earth and the waters, praying to your angels to guide us diligently in health so that we might arrive in Paris on the Feast of the triumphant Assumption of your glorious Mother. I wanted to dedicate our entrance to her, as well as everything we would do thereafter. My desire was fulfilled despite the opinion of the bargemen. The Loire River was so low that they feared we would be held fast in the sand. However, O marvel, your holy angels caused the water to increase so abundantly that the bargemen were astounded that it happened without there having been any rain in the surrounding areas, not even an indication of it.

We remained about two days in Orleans. The coachman who took us from Orleans to Paris was astonished to arrive shortly before noon on the Feast of the Assumption in 1643. It was a Saturday, and we had departed late on Friday. He feared being reproved for going too fast. He took us almost all around Paris, for we entered by the gate of St. Honoré, and there was no bridge close to the Louvre. (692)

CHAPTER XCIV

Our arrival at the faubourg Saint Germain; how divine providence gave us lodging that night. The next day at Holy Mass, the Incarnate Word appeared to me in the arms of his Blessed Mother; and everything that occurred until the Feast of All Saints.

King of kings, Lord of lords and sovereign Monarch of heaven and earth, although a number of people of high status would have liked to provide accommodations for your daughters, your prudence chose to have us arrive in Paris without our having found a single place. Thus, we could say to a certain degree: *Non erat ei locus in diversorio. There was no room for them in the inn.* (Luke 2:7) Through blessed necessity, we were lodged in a small room lower than the pavement of the street. Had it not possessed a fireplace, it could have been better termed a stable, for it was really a place for a number of domestic animals.

With inexpressible joy, I entered, recalling that your Blessed Mother and her beloved spouse, Saint Joseph, had lived in worse quarters on the night of your blessed birth. That drew the angels there from heaven to chant the triumphs that You brought rather than the glory of the world or the vain, perpetual riches of earth. They praised the true glory of your Divine Father in heaven, marveling at the peace that You had caused your Blessed Mother, Saint Joseph and all people of good will on earth. (693) As for me, Lord,

JEANNE'S ORIGINAL DRAFT

with delight and truth, I could sing: *Regnum mundi et ornatum sæculi contempsi propter amorem Domini mei Jesu Christi. I have despised the reign and pomp of the world for the love of my Lord Jesus Christ.* (Ceremonial for the Investiture of Novices, p. 28)

Father Carré, prior of the novitiate of St. Dominic, promptly came to visit us and had supper sent us. An hour later by torchlight, the Abbé de Cerisy arrived, accompanied by Monsieur Gurlat. Since it was late, they could not remain very long, especially since the Chancellor's home where they lived was about a half league away. Our place is far within the St. Germain suburb. Since Your Majesty had let me know that that is where You wanted your monastery established, I had requested the Abbé de Cerisy to rent us a good house there in which to establish it. He did so in my name for the price of eight hundred pounds. I considered this to be expensive for a young woman, but I trusted in your magnificent generosity, Lord, for You had told me: *Meum est argentum, et meum est aurem. The silver is mine, and the gold is mine.* (Hag 2:9)

The next day, August 16th, the Abbé de Cerisy came with the Treasurer of the Abbey in the name of Father Brachet, the Vicar General of the Bishop of Metz, Duke of Verneuil, Abbé of St. Germain, lord of this suburb and superior of our monastery. (694) They came to present me the King's Patent Letters and decree. Likewise, they assured me of his good will toward me and the joy experienced by many because of our foundation. As soon as possible, a small chapel was prepared with an altar upon which the Abbé de Cerisy offered Holy Mass. We received Communion, thanking You for so many favors. My Divine Savior, You appeared to me in the arms of your august Mother, holding two golden keys which You presented me in such a delightful way that they filled my heart with rejoicing. You told me: "My daughter, here are the keys with which to open hearts. Just as, through a miracle of loving confidence, St. Hyacinth carried Me and my Blessed Mother and preserved us from our enemies, save Me from those who persecute Me by their bad will and the torrent of their excesses."

JEANNE'S ORIGINAL DRAFT

In the afternoon, Father Carré arrived to tell me that the Duchess of Rocheguyon was sending for me in her carriage until the place rented for our accommodations would be ready. He said that I would offend her should I refuse to accept. Being already so obligated to her for her many kindness to me during my first sojourn in Paris, I did not wish to delay going with her, although I knew, through You and your angels, that she would not do all that the superiors of the monastery wished and that You wanted me to be the foundress of the temporal part, as well as the institutrix of the spiritual.

On Wednesday, the 19th, she sent for our two Sisters and my dear Sister Elizabeth Grasseteau. She provided us with lodging and treated us with great charity. My Divine Love, please repay her for this, we beg You in all humility. (695) I am grateful for what she has done to the least of your daughters, according to your promise. You knew what mortification my soul endured because of her dissatisfaction. She had decided to bring two girls in perpetuity to a foundation that was too small for the clauses she requested in her document. I had prayed to the saints for her to enjoy the privileges of a foundress accorded to me when I provided the foundation. She did not want to accept my payment for anything she had spent for the bulls or the accommodations for my companion and myself for about three years nor for any other expenses we might have caused her. Again, my Divine Lord, I beg You to grant her a hundredfold and life eternal.

We remained at the Rocheguyon hotel until All Saints Eve when we returned to our own home. A small church had been built and many efforts made to make it appropriate and spacious. Before I had left Lyons, your providence, my Divine Love, had provided me with the funds to defray all these expenses. I thank You with humble gratitude, my adorable Benefactor. I acknowledge to You my hurt or repugnance when I learned that a young woman, through charity, had told others who had helped me with this foundation that the excessive cost of our little church and the furnishings of the house was too extreme. (696) Therefore, I could not possibly feed my daughters nor maintain the monastery unless I would be given alms. I told those who had informed me about this: "Although she obligates me by her plan, I did not request her

JEANNE'S ORIGINAL DRAFT

charity. I have not placed my confidence in people, but in the providence of the Incarnate Word, my Love, and his care for me. When we entered the house, we had spent six thousand pounds for furnishings and accommodations."

CHAPTER XCV

The Incarnate Word told me not to hasten in assuming the obligation of the cloister. The graces He gave me on the Feasts of Saint Martin and Saint Cecilia, the first Sunday of Advent and about the cross erected in the monastery after benediction on January 1, 1644.

On the evening of the Feast of All Saints, I told You: "My Divine Oracle, what do You think about what is being proposed to me: that I should take the holy habit and become a religious right away?" You told me: "My daughter, do nothing in haste. You can tell those that are rushing you that Saul, who did not wait for my Prophet Samuel, did something that displeased me, despite his attempt to persuade Me to accept his prayer because of his sacrifice. The Prophet told him: "*Stulte egisti; Thou hast done foolishly.* (1 Kings 13:13b) Your kingdom will be given to another who will be more faithful and punctual in obeying the divine will, being according to my heart. He will fulfill them all." Tell this to your director. My daughter, wait for my orders and do nothing through human respect: *Homo enim vidit ea quæ parent, Dominus autem intuetur cor. Man seeth those things that appear; but the Lord beholdeth the heart.* (1 Kings 16:7)

Your Apostle said: "If I am pleasing to men, I am not a servant of my Divine Master." O Savior, dear Love, I want only your glory. Whatever is

JEANNE'S ORIGINAL DRAFT

not You means nothing to me. I will do whatever my director commands me according to your will. (697) "My daughter, you are there in solitude. Sustained by two large wings, my glory and the salvation of souls, together with two other wings that seem large by their dignity on earth, you will arrive sooner. You will be nurtured by God, who has delivered you from the dragon that vomited forth a river of anger against you. The land of my Sacred Humanity receives you, and He will never harm you. I have provided for all the needs of my establishment and of your own." Your goodness granted me many graces that I have recorded in other notebooks. I do not want to include them here so as to avoid being too voluble.

The Feasts of Saint Bartholomew, of our Father Saint Augustine, of the Exaltation of the Holy Cross, of the Apostles St. Simon and Jude, of St. Martin, of St. Cecilia were days of favors, illumination and most beneficial blessing for me. Yet, O my Divine Savior, I noted that You were not satisfied with two persons whom I commended to You, to whom I felt obligated for having desired your foundation in Paris. During the month of September in 1643, I saw You turn your face away from the first; and regarding the other one, You told me on the Feast of the holy Apostles Saints Simon and Jude: *Penitet me; I deeply regret* having done them the favor I showed you. Since then, You have shown me nothing whereby to rejoice for them, despite my prayers on their behalf. Dear Love, I beg You to enlighten them so that each of them may please You, my Lord and my God.

My Divine Love, I recall that on the Eve of the Feast of St. Luke in 1625, when I left my father's home, You promised that I would not be called "the abandoned one". (698) Although at the present time, it seems that those who persuaded me to come have abandoned me, I do not fear destitution. Your angels are very faithful observers of your commands. Just knowing that You commissioned them to take care of me calms me. I beg your pardon for my extreme repugnance to remain outside of Lyons. Paris is a troublesome dwelling-place for me. "My daughter, you will glorify Me there despite any aversion you may feel. Take courage; you will be my glorious repose: *Dum non facis vias tuas, et non invenitur voluntas tua. While thou dost not thy own ways and thy own will is not found.* (Is 58:13c) I will raise you

JEANNE'S ORIGINAL DRAFT

above the heights of earth *et cibabo te hæreditate Jacob; I will feed thee with the inheritance of Jacob.* (Is 58:14c) I have personally promised and am promising you this."

On the Feast of St. Martin, You permitted me to share in the understanding and ardor of this fervent prelate and most worthy Pontiff. You told me that, just as, in the presence of your angels, You praised the alms he gave as a catechumen, You would not remain silent before your Divine Father and these very angels about how I was investing You by doing so to your spouses, besides nurturing and maintaining them. Divine Love, these are favors You have given me and continue to do so daily. Your goodness caused me indescribable confusion, telling me that I dressed them with lovely garments, but that I used the worst I could possibly have.

Lord of my heart, who dwells in the highest heavens, deign to look upon the weakest of your servants when she dresses in these patched garment. The Prophet-King assures me of this loving goodness when he says: *Quis sicut Dominus Deus noster, qui in altis habitat, et humilia respicit in cælo et in terra? Who is as the Lord our God, who dwelleth on high, and looketh down on the low things in heaven and in earth?* (Ps 112:5) You told me a number of other things that I recorded in a separate notebook. That is the reason I did not add that part here. (699)

On the Feast of the glorious virgin and martyr, Saint Cecilia, You were amused about dealing with this matter with me, telling me that from my poverty, You had built a new Church wherein You would dwell with your friends, just as You had dwelt with your saints in this saint's home that became a church. You added: "My daughter, my spouse, your clothes bear my good odor. You deprive yourself so as to give to Me; you humble yourself to exalt Me." "Lord, my God, can nothingness become lowered, or sovereign and divine grandeur be exalted? In my astonishment, allow me to tell You: *Deus meus es tu, quoniam honorum meorum non eges. Thou art my God, for thou hast no need of my goods.* (Ps 15:2) How fortunate I would be if I could live and die for You and were You to favor me by having your Gospel of light

JEANNE'S ORIGINAL DRAFT

and love brought to my mind and allow it repose in my heart, as is said of Saint Cecilia.

On the first Sunday of Advent, I felt an inexplicable depression. I asked my dear Sister Grasseteau to pray for me, as I went down to the church. Approaching the altar, I said to You: "Dear Love, I cannot go on any longer. My soul is overcome by weakness and anxiety. Sustain me by grace, and pray to your Father for the weakest of your loved ones. I abandon myself to your charity. I would lose courage if You did not sustain me." Dearest Love, You received me upon your bosom, holding me in your arms in such a way that I could entrust myself to the care of your love. In this condition, I received the strength and consolation of a most faithful Lover who is as powerful as He is loving. (700) You placed me in your arms and upon your heart, as You told your spouse in the Canticle that she should do, (Cant 8) showing me that your love is stronger than death, for it is the death of my death and the sting of my hell. I call this sadness my hell, because my soul was desolate, and it seemed to be enveloped by the pains of death and almost overcome by the pains of hell, because it did not see You, You who are its paradise. I rose from prayer like someone who had withdrawn from darkness into a marvelous light. With Anne, the mother of Samuel, I could declare: *Dominus mortificat et vivificat, deducit ad inferos et reducit. The Lord killeth and maketh alive: he bringeth down to hell and bringeth back again.* (1 Kings 2:6)

I met my dear Sister Grasseteau whom I asked if she had prayed for me. She replied: "I did so with great compassion at the beginning of my prayer and great wonder at the end." I asked which prayer she had made and the reason for these two different sentiments. She said: "Mother, as soon as I knelt down, in spirit I saw you really overwhelmed and harrassed by problems, but, after a moment, the Incarnate Word, at the age of thirty-three, appeared near you as you were seated. He was kneeling, looking at you with eyes of pity and love. He gave you faithful confidence by which you could draw even closer to Him. With both arms, He held you close to his breast, so as to sustain and uphold you with his own heart. He raised his eyes to his Divine

JEANNE'S ORIGINAL DRAFT

Father, praying for you in an ineffable way. During his prayer, I had no understanding and in great astonishment, I saw you elevated from earth to heaven upon a glorious throne in your ordinary clothes. I could not perceive your having passed through anything in between." From this daughter, I learned what I already knew from my own experience, but not about being elevated or seated upon a throne where she had seen me. (701) She saw the visible sign of the invisible fact. This mystery or Sacrament of Love is inexpressible to someone still in the flesh. It could be better declared by those assistant forms who go from beginning to end without passing through any center. They are pure spirits, having no antecedents or consequences.

On December 18, the day of the expectation of the incomparable birth of your Virgin Mother, my spirit was so profoundly elevated that it felt more in heaven than on earth. Elsewhere, I will record only what I deem appropriate about this experience for my inventory of your graces. In a way I consider ineffable, I understood: *Urbs Jerusalem beata dicta pacis visio. City of Jerusalem, lovely vision of peace.* (Hymn: *Coelestis urbs*, Primitive Ceremonial for Temporal Profession) May your goodness make a new dedication of your new Jerusalem, where you allowed me to to enjoy a peace somewhat like that of the blessed. But this is just in passing, because in this valley of tears, the soul experiences happiness only *per modum transeuntis; in a transitory manner.*

On the Feast of the Holy Innocents, You appeared to me with a number of tubes in your breast through which You wanted to communicate Yourself to your daughters. I understood that You had suffered intensely in order to give these communications of your merits to us. It seemed to me that your love had made a number of little, painful openings in your breast so that, through your distress, we might receive health and holiness. Afterward, You showed Yourself to me with a number of crowns acquired by your sufferings. Thus, my Divine Lover, You showed me that these were from generous souls in your Order who would suffer as You did, for love of You: *Et livore eius santi sumus. By his bruises we are healed.* (Is 53:5c) (702)

On the first day of the year 1644, Father Brachet, Prior of the Abbey and

JEANNE'S ORIGINAL DRAFT

Vicar General of the Illustrious Bishop Demest (de Metz), superior of the monastery, arrived, accompanied by the Procurator General of the Abbey, to bless the different parts of the monastery and inaugurate the cloister there. The day before, he had accepted the thousand pounds in funds that I gave for the foundation of the said monastery. With great devotion, he offered Mass and formally initiated the establishment, set up the Cross and performed all the ceremonies required for such a foundation, even though there were only two Sisters, my dear Sister Grasseteau, Sister Françoise Graver and I. Dear Love, your blessing was given, not to many, but apparently to one Sister, because one of the two had to return to her monastery in Avignon. Alluding to the blessing You gave Abraham's seed, his only son Isaac, the Apostle declared: *Non dicit: Et seminibus, quasi in multis; sed quasi in uno: Et semini tuo, qui est Christus. He saith not: And to his seeds, as of many. But as of one: And to thy seed, which is Christ.* (Gal 3:16)

You consoled me by saying: "My daughter, do not be disturbed if you do not see a prompt multiplication in your monastery in Paris as you did in the one in Avignon. In the latter, my saints told you: *Soror nostra es, crescas in mille millia, et possideat semen tuum portas inimicorum tuorum. Thou art our sister: Mayst thou increase to thousands of thousands, and may thy seed possess the gates of their enemies.* (Gen 24: 60b)

Now I am forming your first daughters and will continue to do so. Let them be careful to avoid presumption, for this comes from my love for you. You prayed to Me that they might live in my presence, and I have granted your request. I have multiplied the monastery in Avignon and will continue to do so. *Ecce, benedicam ei, et augebo, et multiplicabo eum valde. Behold, I will bless him, and increase, and multiply him exceedingly.* (Gen 17:20b) I will call young women from important homes to enter there: *Et faciam illum in gentem magnam. Pactum vero meum statuam ad Isaac. And I will make him a great nation. But my covenant I will establish with Isaac.* (Gen 17:20e-21a) (703)

Dearest Love, while the Father Prior was setting up the cross on the chapel door, my Sister Elizabeth Grasseteau could see You setting it up in my heart

JEANNE'S ORIGINAL DRAFT

as a New Year's gift on this first day of the year. There You established an interior monastery by the cross that I adore in your hands. I accepted it as a most precious gift: the cross that has crucified me, not only on one day, but for many years. I cannot express the pain of this cross, nor can I describe how delightful it is at the same time, since it unites me to You.

The Abbé de Cérisy, who was appointed to be the substitute superior, and Father Carré, superior of the Dominican novitiate, realized that I could not be externally invested with the liveries of my Divine Spouse. Like a number of other priests, they did not judge it appropriate to allow me to do so. Thus, they blessed a red and white habit, together with the veil, and gave this to me in the sacristy to wear as a religious underneath my secular clothing, until such time as I could embrace the cloister, together with my two daughters. Present for all this were my two daughters, Sisters Grasseteau and Gravier, besides several little boarders.

CHAPTER XCVI

The Incarnate Word allowed me to rest upon his breast, making a bed, a cabinet and a marvelous ornament for me with his Precious Blood. He immediately told me not to hasten to obligate myself by the cloister, even though some priests were urging me to do so. He invited me to the virginal nuptials of Saints Agatha and Dorothy. (704)

On the Feast of the Conversion of St. Paul, as I was descending the stairs to go to choir, I fell in such a way that one might think I had hurt my head with the bumps I had on the steps. This alarmed our confessor, the Prior of Denicé, when my Sister Françoise Gravier informed him about it. Dear Love,

JEANNE'S ORIGINAL DRAFT

did You not act like the Angel who extended the hands of your protection so that I might not be hurt? After I received You, I offered You redoubled thanks and gratitude. Fearing that I ought not remain kneeling, my Sister Gravier came to sustain me from behind. But, O marvel of your providence, while she held my head upon her stomach, You gave me your breast whereon to repose my spirit. You said to me: "My beloved spouse, come use my breast for your nuptial bed. *Benjamin amantissimus Domini habitabit confidenter in eo: quasi in thalamo tota die morabitur, et inter humeros illius requiescet. Benjamin, the best beloved of the Lord shall dwell confidently in him. As in a bride chamber shall he dwell all day long: and between his shoulders shall be rest.* (Deut 33:12)

"My little Benjamin, beloved daughter of your Father and cherished bride of your Divine Spouse, confidently rest upon my breast, not my shoulders. The latter is for the Law of Moses whom I told that he would see my shoulders, but after coming into the world and giving Myself to my loved ones, I allow them to rest upon my bosom, placing them upon my very heart." O dearest Love! A Cherubim would have to express the deep thoughts with which You entertained my spirit and a Seraphim to show the impact of the flame that burned your heart, my adorable altar as well as my delightful bed. I can utter this only by silence. (705) *Te decet hymnus, Deus, in Sion. A hymn, O God, becometh thee in Sion.* (Ps 64:2a)

Nor will I utter any word, my Spouse and my God, as I adore You through a loving and respectful silence. You told me: "My daughter, to keep you in peace and at rest, I offer you a bed with my own Blood. Since I want you to see how it is made, I show it to you in the form of a bed covered with crimson velvet, fringed curtains, but large curtains like an alcove that serves also as your cabinet where you will hear my secrets and receive my orders. Right now they are that you should not make profession, regardless of what others tell you about the matter. I envelop you with my Precious Blood. Thus, you are invested with the garments that my love gives you through a totally incomprehensible excess of goodness." Let your Prophet speak. I can only marvel: *Quam magna multitudo dulcedinis tuæ, Domine, quam abscondisti timentibus te! Perfecisti eos qui sperant in te, in conspectu filiorum*

JEANNE'S ORIGINAL DRAFT

hominum. O how great is the multitude of thy sweetness, O Lord, which thou hast hidden for them that fear thee! Which thou hast wrought for them that hope in thee, in the sight of the sons of men! (Ps 30:21)

You conceal them under the holy hiding-place of your adorable face so that people may not disturb them: *Proteges eos in tabernaculo tuo, a contradictione linguarum. Thou shalt protect them in thy tabernacle from the contradiction of tongues.* (Ps 30:21b)

Lord, my God, how wonderful is your wisdom! Had it not taught me your will, could I have remained at rest while so many others were troubled, even I myself, about the fact that I did not have the external religious habit of your Order although I conferred it upon your daughters. Dear Love, this is a deep mortification for me which I offer You for your greater glory. (706) I am embarrassed by it, accepting it whole-heartedly for as many years as will please You, since a number of experienced and upright persons are of the opinion that I should deprive myself of this satisfaction. Lord, with the bride of the Canticle, I tell You: *Filii matris meæ pugnaverunt contra me; Posuerunt me custodem in vineis, Vineam meam non custodivi. The sons of my mother have fought against me. They have made me the keeper in the vineyards: my vineyard I have not kept.* (Cant 1:5)

With care for my daughters, who are vines that You have planted in your Church so as to produce flowers and fruit there, it appears that I have forgotten to take care of my own: *Indica mihi, quem diligit anima mea, ubi pascas. Ubi cubes in meridie. Shew me, O thou whom my soul loveth, where thou feedest, where thou liest in the midday.* (Cant 1:6a)

Dearest Love who loves my soul, do not permit me to stray nor to fall back. Everywhere and in all things, I want only You. Let no creature distract my thoughts; they would be vagabonds. In them there is no stability: *Vanitati enim creatura subiecta est non volens. For the creature was made subject to vanity: not willingly.* (Rom 8:20a)

JEANNE'S ORIGINAL DRAFT

Dearest Love, in humility and confidence, I pray that wherever You may repose at midday, may your divine illumination be the light of my understanding and your ardent charity the flame of my will. In gentle repose, there I shall be satisfied with You, my Lord and my All.

You did not spurn my prayer, but invited me to your nuptials with the two holy virgins, Agatha and Dorothy. You told me that, since I was their sister and your spouse, I could freely enter your nuptial chamber, that You are my lamp as well as my Spouse. In these nuptials, I would experience holy delight. There I would see the chaste, pure and virginal generation. (707) Your breast was the bed whose curtains are brilliant lights. Since your word does what it says, You led me there with such majesty and gentleness that I seemed to be another Esther, crowned with your glory, leaning upon your loving dilection. I was followed by your merciful clemency. I languished because of the abundance of holy delights communicated to me by your lovingly gentle spirit: You were the very wonderful grace that You spread upon my lips. My soul seemed to become totally one with You. And, as in a corporal marriage it is said: *erant duo in carne una; they shall be two in one flesh,* (Gen 2:24c) we were two persons in one love, or in one Spirit. Your most pure simplicity imparted an innocent candor to me that enabled me to kiss you virginally along life's journey, as do those virgins who are in heaven. However, they remain in their glory in their eternal, happy dwelling-place, while I, as a pilgrim, am still on life's way.

JEANNE'S ORIGINAL DRAFT

CHAPTER XCVII

My joy was troubled when I learned that the love of the Incarnate Word did not reign in the hearts of those whom I had offered Him; and about my weighty distress.

Dearest Love, You allowed me to receive a note that troubled me and changed my joy to sadness, because therein I noted inclinations which I could not approve. They were produced by the spirit of flesh and blood. I wanted your Spirit to be the bond of these persons and have grace prevail over imperfect nature in them. Alas, I would have thought that my desires were fulfilled except that they committed a fault against your Majesty that caused me to weep bitterly and suffer intensely. Your Wisdom allowed this note, that was not addressed to me, to be sent to me from a hundred leagues away. It was innocently handed to me, just as I accepted it with simplicity, being caught up in the delights You had given me at our adorable nuptials. I would have remained inconsolable; in fact, I would have disturbed a celebration that I could call *Sabbatum* or *Sabbatho* (Is 66) had I unexpectedly intercepted this note and other letters brought me from three hundred leagues away. Through them, I became aware of ingratitude of persons You had made dear to me and whom I fully pardoned. I had and still have only thoughts of peace that caused the flame of charity to be intensified for them. I wanted them to possess the peace and joy that surpasses all feeling and experience the delightful, glorious Sabbath which they had troubled by inexpressibly afflicting me. I wish to suffer, my Lord and my God, while adoring You in spirit and in truth. (709)

A number of your Machabees were killed on the Sabbath, who were the holy victims acceptable to You. Mathathias resolved to fight to uphold your law during this solemnity. Lord, my resolve was to resist those who were unfaithful to You. This resolution caused me suffering due to every kind of

JEANNE'S ORIGINAL DRAFT

struggle. It was opportune that in one hand I held the trowel and in the other the sword, as is declared in Esdras: *Una manu sua faciebat opus et altera tenebat gladium. With one of his hands he did the work, and with the other he held a sword.* (2 Esd 4:17) But, what could a young woman accomplish against so many enemies unless she said to You: "Stay by me, Lord of Armies, and fight for me"? No, let it be for your glory. *In te inimicos nostros ventilabimus cornu, et in nomine tuo sperabo, et gladius meus non salvabit me. Through thee we will push down our enemies with the horn; neither shall my sword save me.* (Ps 43:6a; 7b)

My pen, that is the pen of the winds as it records the delights of your right hand when You treat me as Benjamin, the youngest child, seems to be leaden when I have to describe my sadness. Then You place it in the left hand, and it seems to be Benoni, the child of sorrow. One would think that death had abandoned me in this life to be its image and that I was to abide in its shadows. I have also told you several times: *Collocavit me in obscuris, sicut mortuos sæculi, et anxiatus est super me spiritus meus. He hath made me dwell in darkness as those that have been dead of old: and my spirit is in anguish within me.* (Ps 142:3c-4a)

Lord, my God, what a difference there is between your treatment of me at my father's house and in Lyons and that of the present. It seems entire ages that I have not enjoyed your delights. Your hands used to shower me with delight, together with an abundance of joy. It was a continual outpouring of your graces. (710) You sprinkled my soul; indeed, You engulfed me in your delightful waters. Together with David, it exclaimed: *Dominus regit me et nihil mihi deerit: in loco pascuæ ibi me collocavit. Super aquam refectionis educavit me. The Lord ruleth me: and I shall want nothing. He hath set me in a place of pasture.* (Ps 22:1-2)

Now with outstretched hand, it says to You: Lord, I am like earth without water: *Velociter exaudi me, Domine, defecit spiritus meus. Hear me speedily, O Lord: my spirit hath fainted away.* (Ps 142:7a) Do not turn away your face from me, for I would almost be like those who have already

JEANNE'S ORIGINAL DRAFT

descended into the lake. The difference is that they are in the other life and without hope, and I still possess the consolation along life's journey that I trust in your mercy.

CHAPTER XCVIII

The Incarnate Word consoled me by his goodness, which He abundantly showered upon Monsieur de la Piardière, to whom He had alluded as Jacob while I was still in Lyons. He had given him to me as a son, just as He had given me to him for a mother.

The Prophet Habacuc assures me that, even in your deepest wrath, You remember your mercy which motivates your charity, represented by midday, to come and remove our sins (that comprise the mountain of Pharan; meaning division), thus filling us with your glory and changing our troubles into jubilation. You did this, my Savior, when you saw me in affliction and sorrow. You filled me with joy and sorrow, not only for myself, but for those who visited me. Among them was Monsieur de la Piardière, whom, when I was still in Lyons, You had called Jacob, that is the same as Jacques. You told me: "He is busy with finances." (711) Having filled me with your holy blessing which could be called grace, You showered it into his heart, as I told him about your profusions and sacred unions. Delighted by your marvels, he no longer belonged to himself, but entirely to You; yet he did not dare aspire to possess these sublime favors. Without informing him that a long time ago it was he about whom You had spoken to me, I encouraged him, assuring him that You would grant him the gift of prayer and that your most gentle Spirit would anoint him. Your Holy Spirit prompted me to speak in that way. When he returned home, his coach carried his body, but your love elevated his spirit higher than

JEANNE'S ORIGINAL DRAFT

the Empyrean, because he lifted it up to You who are the supreme heaven. He experienced what David had declared: After having tasted, he saw that You are most gentle, indeed gentleness itself. He began to receive Communion more often, overcoming all human respect. A short time later, he received Communion four times weekly. By the power of this divine food and heavenly bread, he rose to the very height of your holy mountain, my Lord and my God, and by your holy anointing, You consecrated all the powers of his soul, setting your Holy of Holies in the superior part of his spirit. In less than six months, I saw him elevated gradually to the sixth dwelling-place indicated in *The Mansion of the Soul* by your beloved Saint Teresa.

God of love who fills heaven and earth, You entertained his spirit with sublime thoughts, through a marvelous economy, enabling him to find the time and means to carry out his work in finances. What is marvelous is that I saw that this man was more detached from gold and silver than a number of religious who have made the vow of poverty. He could say: *Beatus dives qui post aurum non abiit, nec speravit in pecunia et thesauris. Blessed is the rich man that hath not gone after gold nor put his trust in money nor in treasures.* (Eccl 31:8) Add to this all the rest, including: *Ideo stabilita sunt bona illius in Domino, et eleemosynas illius enarrabit omnis Ecclesia sanctorum. Therefore are his goods established in the Lord: and all the church of the saints shall declare his alms.* (Eccl 31:11)

Dearest Love, had You not designated this man to me when I was in Lyons, I would fear to be mistaken, in view of all that I have said, and that all this was but the invention of the one who incites a person to see imaginary kingdoms. That is meant to attach us to persons we admire and who can assist us in the pursuit of our plans so as to remove distrust in ourselves and have confidence in You, my Lord and my God.

But You told me: "My daughter, there is no illusion in my knowledge. Remember that I have told you repeatedly that I will glorify Myself in you, whenever you set aside your will, not following your own ideas or inclinations: *Et non invenitur voluntas tua, ut loquaris sermonem: Tunc delectaberis*

JEANNE'S ORIGINAL DRAFT

super Domino; Et sustollam te super altitudines terræ, Et cibabo te hæreditate Iacob, patris tui; Os enim Domini locutum est. While thou dost not thy own ways and thy own will is not found, to speak a word: Then shalt thou be delighted in the Lord, and I will lift thee up above the high places of the earth and will feed thee with the inheritance of Jacob thy father. For the mouth of the Lord hath spoken it. (Is 58:13f-14)

Your Blood upon me is always marvelous, and your surprises unceasingly enrapture me. I could find no one who agreed to do what You wanted for our Order unless I begged him to do so. When he offered me money, that others might have pursued with avidity or dexterity, I blushed and caused him great pain; but I willingly made use of him as the one You had given me to assist us in our temporal affairs.

One day he told me: "Mother, give me the receipts with which to withdraw your rents," and, through plans inspired by charity, he enabled me to receive what God had sent me. He said I had no obligation to him, that your goodness blessed him and increased his spiritual and temporal goods during the time that he took care of my business that was yours. (713) He added that my generosity caused him pain and admiration, adding that I was as skilled at avoiding gaining interest as others were to obtain it. He said that ever since his youth, he had yearned to find someone gratified by your favors to whom he could entrust himself so as, through that person, to follow your will completely and advance in perfection. He maintained that your providence had found the one he wanted, with advantages he had never dared to aspire to have. Since your goodness was magnificently liberal toward me and with me, he could say: *Venerunt autem mihi omnia bona pariter cum illa. For thou didst admonish and try them as a father.* (Wis 7:11a)

Around the Feast of Saint John the Baptist, as I spoke to him about your goodness, I told him that You would not leave him in the state he was in for long years. On hearing this, he was seized by such a trembling that he could hardly sustain this assault. I wanted to reprimand myself for being outspoken, but, when he could speak, he said to me: "Mother don't regret what you have

JEANNE'S ORIGINAL DRAFT

told me. I had wanted to be a religious before I married. Celibacy is no less agreeable to me than the state I am in now. I will follow the will of our Divine Savior in everything. I trust that, through you, He will make it known to me, since He has chosen you to lead me to Him."

On the eve of the Feast of Saint John the Baptist, your Precursor and my holy patron, when I went up to the choir to pray to You through him, You did not answer my prayer, but, in an ineffable way, You made a sacred union with me, the like of which I had never had with any creature. Through the holy freedom your love gave me, it seemed that I had the right to complain about You (714) to You personally. I said: "You have not allowed any of your Seraphim to be united to me in such a way." "My daughter, this union is divine. It is I, my dearest, who bring it about. It is all-pure; it is supernatural." You told me everything You wanted to, and my spirit remained suspended until your wisdom, which extends from one end to the other, gently but firmly directed me. I could not be satisfied, a fact that did not displease You. On the contrary, your Spirit appeared gentler and kindlier because of this. He made me know that, detached from everything to belong to You alone, my love would even give You up unless You were the Supreme Being and the One who is essentially what You said to Moses: *EGO SUM QUI SUM.* Sic dices filiis Israel: *QUI EST*, misit me ad vos. *I AM WHO AM.* Thus shalt thou say to the children of Israel: *HE WHO IS*, hath sent me to you. (Ex 3:14)

The next day, he (Monsieur de la Piardière) came to see me and told me: "Mother, while at Matins in the evening with the Oratorian priests, Our Lord let me know that He wants me to obey you. Prompted by the power of his gentle force, I vowed to obey you in everything that my profession and my state can allow. Your wise prudence will judge all this." I was somewhat reticent, but, lest I resist your orders, I submitted my spirit, trusting that You would enlighten me in the matter. That is what You have done, my brilliant Sun, with so much light that You seemed to be my mid-day. I saw no one else but You and will never do so, if You please, my Divine Beloved. Anything that is not You means nothing to me. Whoever loves anything together with You, loves You less, unless that love is for You and through love of You.

JEANNE'S ORIGINAL DRAFT

You assured me that this is perfect charity. You are love. Whoever abides in love, abides in You, my Lord and my God. I thank You for (715) making him grow in charity, having given him to me as a son, just as You gave your beloved disciple to your Blessed Mother. I have accepted him from You; through You, he has accepted me as his mother. This bond will be indissoluble. Your Father placed a seal on our love: *Hunc enim pater signavit Deus. God the Father gave this one his seal of approval.* And this Beloved told us: *Si diligamus invicem, Deus in nobis manet, et charitas eius in nobis perfecta est. If we love one another, God abideth in us: and his charity is perfected in us.* (1 Jn 4:12b)

CHAPTER XCIX

Divine Wisdom allowed sorrow and trouble so that we might be united to it; how it fulfilled all its promises for the common and particular well-being.

Had I been the mother of only children of rejoicing, I would experience but joy and satisfaction. Just as You prepare your kingdom for us, as your Father prepared one for You, You have made me the mother of other children who have caused me great affliction: *Filios enutrivi, et exaltavi; ipsi autem spreverunt me. I have brought up children and exalted them: but they have despised me.* (Is 1:2b)

I complained to You about our spiritual children in the way that Rebecca did about her corporal ones: *Si sic mihi futurum est. If it were to be so with me.* (Gen 25:22b) Dear Spouse, who knows all things, You knew that I was not yet strong enough to endure the sufferings that the Order I had

JEANNE'S ORIGINAL DRAFT

conceived through your inspiration unceasingly caused me: *quid necesse fuit concipere; what need was there to conceive?* (Gen 25:22b) Lord, were there not enough Congregations of women in the Church without this one, setting aside the vision I had had in Lyons about the tiara (716) lacking a precious stone that You made me understand represented our Order. You said to me: "My daughter, this Order is the missing precious stone. The Church is the queen seated at my right hand, embellished by different Orders. Embroidered in different colors, her golden robe is charity; the different Orders emphasize her beauty."

Dear Love, You pardoned my weaknesses and consoled me in my troubles, adding that these children were more yours than mine and that You put up with their faults. Indeed, these You concealed because of repentance and for other reasons. Those who came later would surpass the first through the practice of charity. A number of our spiritual children seemed to make great strides toward perfection.

I spent the year 1644 and the following 1645 in inexpressible sorrow, weeping a part of the night. I felt an inexpressible aversion for living in Paris. Adorable Providence, how wise You are in all your ways. Had I liked Paris, I might have become involved in a number of intrigues of devotion. My forthrightness might not have allowed me to reject those who came to me for advice through curiosity as well as pity. I might have been urged to pray to You for things that appeared to pertain to devotion but were not really so in effect. They would have pressed me had You given or allowed a little light in their darkness. What began with charitable intentions perhaps might have ended in self-interested actions. I would not have wanted to displease anyone, thinking to do everything for You and winning them all. (717) My natural tendency to satisfy all who strove to have confidence in me might have overburdened me with external cares and taken me away from the domestic ones. I would not have been able to refuse Madame de Cressay about going to the hotel of Orleans to pay my respects to the Duchess for whom, ever since 1638, You had given me a high regard. While I was still in Lyons, You assured me that her marriage to the Duke of Orleans, only brother of the late

JEANNE'S ORIGINAL DRAFT

King, would not be dissolved. In writing to someone involved in trying to break this up by order of eminently-placed persons, I said: "You will never succeed in your undertaking. I am confident that God wants Madame to be honored in Paris, together with the Duke, and that I will no longer live in Lyons when she arrives there. One of these nights I saw her give birth to a daughter, who had a fall, and someone scorned this blessed child. Our Lord wanted me to take special care to pray for her. I have done so to make her more pleasing."

Dear Love, this was fulfilled, as well as the other matters You have promised or shown me. My secretary, who knew what You had done for me, has often urged me to tell my secret to Madame de Cressay who loves me as much as I honor her; that is, a great deal. She has often urged me to go to the royal palace, insisting that I am delaying the glory of your establishment by not telling the Queen what You have told me about her, our King and the Duke of Anjou. (718) These words failed to convince me to leave my retreat. She said to me: "Your enemies are giving the Queen a bad impression of you by saying that you confer the habit on your Sisters and do not receive it yourself. In her presence, they blame you for what they do not understand. You possess the key to hearts and do not use it. Aren't you afraid of burying the talents that God has so freely given you?" The more she insisted, the more I felt determined not to do what she suggested. My only joy was and is to be hidden from all that is visible so as to be seen by You alone, dear Love, the image of the invisible God. Almost constantly weeping, I said to You: *Tibi dixit cor meum, exquisivit te facies mea. My heart hath said to thee: My face hath sought thee.* (Ps 26:8) Or this other verse: *Tibi derelictus est pauper; orphano tu eris adjutor. To thee is the poor man left: thou wilt be a helper to the orphan.* (Ps 9:14)

Lord, my God, You see me in this place like a poor orphan, for I have neither father nor mother. I can trust no one here, as I did in Roanne and Lyons with my directors whom I could see often. At this end of the faubourg, I find myself almost in exile. *Pater meus et mater mea dereliquerunt me. For my father and my mother have left me.* (Ps 26:10)

JEANNE'S ORIGINAL DRAFT

My former and present directors can see me very little because of the great distance between Saint Louis and this place. My former directors are there, and I do not want to do anything without their advice. Thus, only rarely do I see the priests of your Society, my sweet Jesus. I have always considered them to be my fathers and the Society my mother. I am so far from their residences that I do not dare ask them to visit me often. (719)

Your goodness consoled me like a flash that passed in a moment. Then the thunder of those who murmured or grumbled that I did not take our holy habit crashed like lightning; that is, from my friends, parents and all those who were upset that they still did not see me living the state they desired for me. They were unaware that, with respect, I wore it under my external clothes ever since 1644, as I declared above. I saw myself the aim of all the arrows: *et in signum cui contradicetur; a sign which shall be contradicted.* (Lk 2:34) I recalled that on February 4, 1641, You had appeared to me on the Cross, telling me: *Tuam ipsius animam pertransibit gladius ut revelentur ex multis cordibus cogitationes. And thy own soul a sword shall pierce, that, out of many hearts thoughts may be revealed.* (Lk 2:35)

I offered You my sufferings and the contradictions caused by those who thought they were offering You a sacrifice, because they did not know the will of your Father which is yours. Those who belonged to me contradicted me; that is to say, my daughters of Avignon, Grenoble and Lyons. They contended that I ought to increase my glory together with that of my Divine Spouse by multiplying the monasteries and thus promoting his glory. But, O Lord, through David, You told me: *Dominus scit cogitationes hominum, quoniam vanæ sunt. The Lord knoweth the thoughts of men, that they are vain.* (Ps 93:11) And in Isaias: *Non enim cogitationes meæ, cogitationes vestræ; neque viæ vestræ viæ meæ. For my thoughts are not your thoughts: nor your ways my ways, saith the Lord.* (Is 55:8)

My daughter, the thoughts of men are not my thoughts, nor their ways, my ways. Trust in my goodness. All the words I tell you are words effective of my will. They will do what I wish and will be beneficial to you. (720)

JEANNE'S ORIGINAL DRAFT

Whoever thinks that you will make no progress for my establishment in Paris will be astounded when they see the eternal and temporal goods I now give and will give you and how I enable you to prosper without your being attached to that. Lord, You are everything to me.

CHAPTER C

The death of my dearest, virtuous daughter, Sister Elizabeth Grasseteau, and how it caused me inexpressible sadness for which God alone could console me.

Half of the year 1646 seemed less distressing than the preceding ones, but the Feast of St. Barnabas, that means son of consolation, was a day of extreme desolation for me. Your justice took my dearest Elizabeth Grasseteau from me. This death was most bitter to my soul which I saw separated and deprived of the person it truly considered to be my faithful one par excellence. All the virtues she had practiced so efficaciously since leaving her home, her relatives and herself in order to follow You, my Divine Word made flesh, caused me deep confusion, for I saw myself far from this perfection. She imitated You to the extent that she could know your wishes for which she constantly mortified herself. She was humble of heart. (721) Although she was considered to be ascetic, far from the amiability and affability that others desired her to have, she feared that sweetness would possibly cause her to be amiable, sociable or satisfied and that these qualities, that creatures regard as pleasant, might turn her away from or distract her from the continual conversation she could have with You, our Divine Creator and Savior.

Dear Love, I would never have thought that this daughter would be so dear

JEANNE'S ORIGINAL DRAFT

to me, except that I felt her loss as the most profound one I could endure in this life, excepting your grace. By your permission, my sadness was so extreme that it seemed to end my life. For two whole years, I had a heart murmur that caused my daughters continual fear that I would soon end my days and that they would be left orphans. I repeated a number of times day and night as I wept: "Did I have to ask you to go to Lyons, to show me that you loved me more than yourself and to maintain my authority there? You gave up your life there. O dear daughter, how well you deserved your mother's love for you. Remember her, since you are in your kingdom with our Divine King for love of whom you deprived yourself of everything that could console you on earth."

Together with the regret for having allowed her to be so far away, grief filled my soul that seemed unable to employ its powers. Often I told You, together with the sorrowful Prophet: *Vide, Domine, afflictionem meam. Behold, O Lord, for I am in trouble.* (Lam 1:20) Dear Love, my Lord and my God, consider my affliction; this is the favor I ask of You. Your heart was never insensible toward the afflicted. (722) I know well that no sorrow exists in the city unless You permit it, not to say that You cause it.

The Royal Prophet declared that one abyss calls another. I invoke You through my tears. My eyes seem to be cataracts that cause a deluge, whose waters are like oceans that engulf me alive, like the whale that swallowed up Jonas. His prison enclosed him only three days and three nights, but, for a number of months, I have been engulfed in the abyss of my overpowering afflictions. Long ago, Rebecca told Isaac: *Tædet me vitæ meæ propter filias Heth: si acceperit Iacob uxorem de stirpe huius terræ, nolo vivere. I am weary of my life because of the daughters of Heth. If Jacob takes a wife of the stock of this land, I choose not to live.* (Gen 27:46)

Divine Spouse, will I remain a long time in this anguish? Paris is a prison to me, even though it seems a delightful place to others. Were I in Lyons, on the holy mountain that is my Jerusalem, I think I would be filled with joy. The blood of your martyrs would be a chalice of benediction for me, with which I

JEANNE'S ORIGINAL DRAFT

would become inebriated to the extent that I would not feel the tortures that affect me inwardly and the troubles surrounding me externally. What is most distressing is that I want no consolation from any creature whatsoever. I do not wish to see nor speak to anyone: *Renuit consolari anima mea; My soul refused to be comforted.* (Ps 76:3c)

I refused to be consoled. I could not express my afflictions without intensifying them, because I understood that (723) I would be complaining about what You allowed for good reasons, although unknown to me. Thus, I often said: *Justus es, Domine, et rectum judicium tuum. Thou art just, O Lord: and thy judgment is right.* (Ps 118:137) I awaited your help, for I could expect it from nowhere else. It consoled me fleetingly, because my prayers lacked unction, it seemed to me, and I could see no door open to your operation within my soul. I said to You: "Oh! Oh! Lord, You certainly entered the Cenacle when the doors were closed. Gloriously did You leave the sepulchre that the Jews, your enemies, had sealed and ordered to be guarded."

Dear Love, could I dare call You by this name, not knowing whether or not I am your beloved. I do not deserve it, but I cannot truly love anyone except You alone, and, if I am rejected by your goodness, where could I go? With Job, I say to You: When You would have punished me through your justice, I trusted in your mercy. Through You, I called upon You personally. Magdalen could not be consoled by your angels, for, thinking that You were among the dead, she asked for You in the same condition she had seen You placed in the tomb.

I spent the year 1647 like that of 1646, sick in body and languishing in spirit. All my actions were displeasing to me. I was somewhat unbearable to myself. Passive visits were inexpressibly tedious for me. (724) I undertook no active ones, not leaving our monastery at all. Early morning comforted me, because I had more time to pour out my soul through my eyes, staying away from the community so that no one would notice my sobs and sighs, which would have been considered unreasonable, since their source was unknown.

JEANNE'S ORIGINAL DRAFT

No one in Paris caused me any displeasure; every effort was made to please me. Everything was provided me in abundance. Without caressing me, Your Majesty caused everything I said to be successful in imitation of your Blessed Mother at the Wedding in Cana. I was confident that You would do whatever I prayed for if I so desired, but I wanted nothing. I felt empty. I was astounded at how others put up with and conversed with me. I adored your wise goodness that allowed me to be in this condition.

CHAPTER CI

As Monsieur du Bousquet was saying Holy Mass in a chapel, I saw a cloud over the paten; my conviction that he would become the Bishop of Lodève, despite any opposition to this.

Monsieur du Bousquet came to offer Holy Mass for us one morning, during which I saw something like a cloud on the paten wherein the blue and white were nicely blended; from then on I felt convinced that You wanted to consecrate and elevate him to a dignity he did not yet possess. A short time later, You gave me a firm assurance that You would elevate him to the bishopric by a heavenly grace, just as the cloud had symbolized it for me. The same day, I expressed something about this to him. (725) He often came to offer Holy Mass in a small chapel with a devotion that seemed extraordinary. With great frankness, he spoke to me about his interior life, deeming himself very unworthy in your presence. At other times, he spoke about me as though to convince me that your illuminations were my own thoughts. He said that my spirit was naturally sharp, my judgment quite good and that I had a facility for explaining to myself whatever You concealed from me if I thought that You had withdrawn three-fourths of the lovely thoughts You had given me in Lyons

JEANNE'S ORIGINAL DRAFT

and blunted the sharp spirit that many had admired. These admirers could not convince me that I deserved their praises or that your caresses could ever keep from me the idea of my nothingness or make me think that I had merited your favors. I have always acknowledged that they proceeded from your goodness which is self-communicating.

On the Feast of the Exaltation of your Holy Cross, he sent me a very lengthy letter, telling me many things that might have astounded someone whom You had not assured, as You did me. He told me that You were my Lord, my God and my all, to whom I rendered thanks the best I could. Adorable Savior, at the very time that You were favoring me, he was offering Holy Mass, (I do not know in which church) during which You allowed him to see that your love brought about a marvelous union; that is, the unity of your heart and mine to which You gave wings, commanding your angels to take it up to repose on your own breast. It was as though I were the eagle that You allowed to repose there, allowing it to see the splendors of your glory as it slept. (726)

This vision astounded him, convincing him that your thoughts are not those of men and that they are further from their understanding than heaven is from earth. The soul that accepts your loving words is nurtured, fortified, elevated and almost divinized by them, seeming to be one with You. Also, I could say: that whoever adheres to God becomes one same spirit with God: *Mihi autem adherere Deo bonum est, ponere in Domino Deo meo spem meam: ut annuntiem omnes predicationes tuas in portis filiæ Sion. But it is good for me to adhere to my God, to put my hope in the Lord God: That I may declare all thy praises in the gates of the daughter of Sion.* (Ps 72:28)

A few days later, he visited me. His deep gravity, yielding to your kindness toward me, prompted him to say what he had seen, saying that You do all You wish in heaven and on earth. He added that You are Lord of all and the God who alone does marvels. Also, You had made him a bishop contrary to the expectations of his friends and enemies. The former had lost

JEANNE'S ORIGINAL DRAFT

hope for it, and the latter were determined to prevent it. All had reason to say that no council is victorious over You, my Lord and my God.

Monsieur de Priesac, his faithful friend, wrote me the following words on the day he received the decree: "It had to be that Monsieur du Bousquet would become bishop, since the oracle of the Incarnate Word had predicted this to him." Your goodness made me understand: "You see, my daughter, how I fulfill all that my Spirit made you know, although you did not assure him that it was a prediction, but a confidence you have in Me who love you and do not want to abandon or leave you in embarrassment when you hope for something good." (727)

CHAPTER CII

Assuring me that He would provide abundant illuminations, the Incarnate Word prompted me to encourage Monsieur de Priesac who, through humility, would not dare write about the privileges of your miraculous Mother.

It is You, dear Love, who promised me to provide special assistance and abundant illuminations for Monsieur de Priesac, who, through humility and modesty, did not dare write about the privileges of your miraculous Mother. These illuminations were so multiple and brilliant that the doctors who have seen the three volumes he wrote about her are and will always be filled with admiration. They acknowledged that, although his spirit seemed excellent in moral and political science and purity of language, that it far outstripped itself by dealing with your highest and most profound mysteries without his even having studied theology and having read Sacred Scripture very little. He

JEANNE'S ORIGINAL DRAFT

explained its meaning so clearly and a propos that it seemed that your Spirit had dictated it to him and that, through this Spirit of goodness, science and theology had been divinely infused into him. These books possess almost as much brilliance in word and eloquence as intelligence.

Mother of beautiful dilection, I beg you to accept the praises he offers you, just as you accepted those presented you by the great lights of the Church. These saints have deserved the title, not only of being your devotees, but your favorites as well. (728) Let him be numbered among those whom the Prophet Daniel, his patron, saw as shining and brilliant as stars for all eternity: *Qui autem docti fuerint, fulgebunt quasi splendor firmamenti; et qui ad justitiam erudiunt multos, quasi stellæ in perpetuas eternitates. But they that are learned shall shine as the brightness of the firmament: and they that instruct many to justice, as stars for all eternity.* (Dan 12:3)

Inspired by your Spirit, Deborah encouraged Baruch to fight, which he did not want to do without her, so as to dedicate to her the glory of the victory. Being too modest, Monsieur de Priesac would not have dared write about the privileges of your incomparable Mother if a simple young woman had not promised to pray to You to assist him with your light and if she had not read everything he wrote to give him the glory of this victory that she had won over his distrust of his spirit and learning. Blessed Virgin, I offer this to you; it belongs to you. You have always been seated under the victorious palm tree of all your enemies. God acknowledges Himself to be vanquished and declares Himself to be your subject for all eternity, for He is your Son, although equal to his Divine Father.

JEANNE'S ORIGINAL DRAFT

CHAPTER CIII

My heart murmur ceased after I had had two annual Masses offered for the soul of my dear daughter, Elizabeth Grasseteau. She obtained for me the grace to undertake the kitchen, a charge that humility had prompted her choose.

Toward the end of the year 1648, my heart murmur ceased, as well as my tears at the deprivation of my dearest daughter, Elizabeth Grasseteau. I had had two (729) annual Masses offered so that she might give these treasures to the Suffering Church, just as she had given everything she could to the Militant Church. I trusted that so many good works, alms and constant suffering, together with an innocent and laborious life that I had admired in this daughter, through your mercy, had delivered her from Purgatory if she had gone there. This was because on the Saturday after her death she had appeared to me in a dream with a happy expression like someone who did not suffer any more. She did not tell me anything. At the moment, I did not understand that she thus appeared to me to tell me not to be afflicted about her condition. She did not speak as You do, my Lord and my God, as your Prophet assures us, inviting the heaven of heavens to praise the name of the Lord who made them by saying: *Fiat quia ipse dixit, et facta sunt; ipse mandavit, et creata sunt. For he spoke, and they were made: he commanded, and they were created.* (Ps 148:5b)

This holy soul had no command from You to tell me not to weep any more nor the power to change my sadness into joy, a joy that she possessed as her portion, leaving me with sobs, sighs and tears for mine. Also, I was to remain in this valley of misery that gives rise to them and where they abound, even when one receives the Bread of Angels which is You Yourself, O my dear Spouse, who are a hidden God as well as the Savior. The Wise Man

JEANNE'S ORIGINAL DRAFT

declared: *Aquæ multæ non potuerunt extinguere charitatem. Many waters cannot quench charity.* (Cant 8:7)

Although imperfect, these tears could not extinguish the charity that this faithful soul possessed for me. She obtained a grace for me (730) that was inconceivable to me or anyone else, even those who had visited me for a number of years during the time that I was constrained to take the baths and waters every summer. It was to take charge of the kitchen, a work she preferred to any dignity or other responsibility. While I was in Lyons, I could not enter it without feeling suffocated by the odor of food and almost fainting from the heat of the fire.

On the eve of the Feast of St. Michael, the Sister in charge of the kitchen had such a large and inflamed swelling in one eye that she had to remain in bed. Mother Marie of the Holy Spirit Nallard, who was to substitute for her, was sick with a bad cold and was also in bed with a cyst on her knee that she had endured in silence for fourteen years. It brought about such a high fever with an inflammation of her entire knee which was terribly swollen that the doctors who treated her, seeing her in peril, told me that they would not be responsible for her life after the operation they had to do. But, my Divine Physician, my trust in your goodness assured me that she would not die from it and that the other Sister would not lose her eye. Seeing that she was most anxious to be relieved of her pain, I exhorted her and told her that she ought to endure whatever God willed and that I would take care of the kitchen. I might have considered it to be like recreation had I not applied myself to this work.

On the Feast of St. Michael, not thinking about prayer nor of St. Raphael for the relief of this daughter's eye, she spent the entire night in complaining so loudly that, prompted by my ordinary compassion for the pains of my daughters, I prayed for her. At about four o'clock in the morning, my idea changed. (731) I said to this saint who is called God's Physician: "This daughter prevented me from sleeping until now. I beg you to relieve her so that she may have repose and me, too." At the same moment, this heavenly physician punctured the swollen tumor so skillfully that the surgeon who came to lance it

JEANNE'S ORIGINAL DRAFT

at seven or eight o'clock in the morning found the eye no longer swollen. There was an incision made for this purpose better than any he might have made. He put a dressing there to withdraw all the pus and prevent the incision from closing. A few days later, he sent me a message asking if I wanted him to cauterize it to arrest the abcess that this daughter had had as a result of smallpox at an early age, that is to say, almost her entire life. Upon seeing the fire, she feared suffering a great deal, but, O marvel, she felt nothing when the surgeon applied it to the incision. The angelic spirit did what he had done in the furnace of Babylon wherein the three holy young men were cast. Seeing that she was in health, she begged me to let her return to her charge, but I could not consent to giving it up nor prevent the one I had called to assist me from continuing either. The latter had no knowledge of preparing a broth, an egg or anything else, although for more than two years she had been occupied in this with me. This humiliated her continually, because she possessed good will but very little patience, although she would have liked to satisfy the entire community. (732)

CHAPTER CIV

The blockade of Paris and the way we had to enter the city limits where Divine Providence favored us in both corporal and spiritual matters. I was blessed to be able to consult Fathers de Lingendes, Decret and de Condé. The illness and healing of our Sister Jeanne de Jesus.

In 1649, the blockade of Paris made us leave the St. Germain suburb and enter the city, because our monastery was outside the barrier. We could not get bread nor other necessities, due to the ditches torn into the passageways,

JEANNE'S ORIGINAL DRAFT

besides the danger of being exposed to those engaged in war. Your providence, that governs all things, took special care in accommodating your daughters well, reserving five domestic rooms and a chapel, on Vivient Street at the home of Monsieur de Laubardement, in the appartment that Monsieur de Rossignol had rented. The former, together with his wife, received them with great kindness. They could thus observe their religious obligations and attend Holy Mass daily. Besides, they could go to confession and receive Communion in the chapel without being obliged to go out as many religious were forced to do in order to attend Mass and receive the sacraments. We were grateful to the pastor of Saint Eustachius' Church for the above graces. He also allowed us to have the Blessed Sacrament there on Holy Thursday and perform the services as though we were in our own monastery.

Dear Love, please give him a place in your Heart. (733) Let these two verses from the Prophet King be applicable to him: *Beatus qui intelligit super egenum et pauperem: In die mala liberabit eum Dominus. Dominus conservet eum, et vivificet eum, Et beatum faciat eum in terra, Et non tradat eum in animas inimicorum eius.* Blessed is he that understandeth concerning the needy and the poor: the Lord will deliver him in the evil day. The Lord preserve him and give him life, and make him blessed upon the earth: and deliver him not up to the will of his enemies. (Ps 40:2-3) This is because your daughters were satisfied with the Heavenly Bread as though they were in your house. As for the other bread that sustains the body, I did not allow them to lack anything. We even had a surplus of flour, as I had often assured them would happen.

Your providence allowed Monsieur de Langlade to be in Paris the entire time of the blockade. He was delighted to offer Holy Mass for your daughters and hear their confession. Although he told me that he would do so gratis, I did not want to allow this, for it is understandable that whoever serves at the altar should be nurtured by the altar.

Father Morin, a priest of the Oratory, gave the exhortations and conferences in the room downstairs where an oratory had been prepared, since the

JEANNE'S ORIGINAL DRAFT

chapel was very small and could not accommodate everyone. Father de Condé and other religious visited them. They lacked no spiritual aid nor anything required for their corporal well-being. One thing grieved me: it is that the parents of four of our boarders had withdrawn them and had removed the little habit from two of them. As your justice has always allowed my soul to be afflicted, due to my tenderness and their gratitude, when my boarders are taken away, despite my resignation to whatever You allow, I felt deeply grieved. (734) This occurred especially when on Easter Sunday, during Father de Condé's sermon, I was informed that one of my little ones, de Beauvais, had died. Since she had no name, I feared that she had died without baptism, keeping her two days without allowing her to be buried until her mother sent me a message that she had been conditionally baptized and that she was a little angel in heaven. She added that my care had kept her on earth since the beginning of December when the chest infection, together with fever, threatened her with death at that time. I had inexpressibly obligated her by having accepted the child in this extremity, showing that I loved her more than myself. As I was weeping for this blessed child in the Dominican church, that is of St. Thomas, I saw Seraphim who came to console me, but this was for the death of my Sister Catherine de Jesus, called Richardon in the world, who had died in our monastery in Avignon on Holy Thursday.

I did not stay at Monsieur de Laubardement's home with my daughters, because Monsieur de la Piardière wanted me to be at his home. He and his wife begged me to grant them this consolation. She was so kind that she helped me obtain the provisions needed by my daughters for whom I served as a turn Sister. I performed all the charges and work, and your providence had placed me there to be able to attend the sermons in Saint Eustachius' Church, where the Jesuit priest preached during Lent. (735) I also had the blessing of conferring with him about my soul and visiting the priests of the Society, namely, Father de Lingendes, to whom I gave an account of everything I could recall since my first voyage to Paris in 1632.

It was no mediocre consolation to hear from the lips of this devout and educated priest that You wanted me in my present state. He assured me that,

JEANNE'S ORIGINAL DRAFT

were I obliged to observe the cloister by profession, I could not maintain your monastery in Paris and that Grenoble and the Congregation in Lyons could exist no longer, because I would be powerless to act and aid them in their need. Father Decret told me the same thing, aware of the fact that those who had written him from Lyons and elsewhere that I was not doing your will, my Divine Governor, were ignorant of this. They had all erroneously blamed me, insisting that I invested the Sisters with the habit and did not take it externally. They added that I was like the bell or like those who built the ark during Noah's day but did not enter it themselves. I was like the notaries who obligate others, but not themselves. These discussions were not held only among the ordinary people. (736) It formed part of the conversations of their Majesties and Eminences. Thus, the contempt heaped upon me by these important ones of earth made me resolve to satisfy them against your orders. I would not discuss extensively with them, thinking I ought not do so, since I was restrained by modesty. Those who did not know me interpreted my frankness to be vanity. They contended that I spoke too freely about the illuminations You are pleased to communicate to me, my adorable Benefactor.

When the blockade was over, we discovered that our monastery had not yet been repaired. Because the masons and other laborers worked there for three weeks, we had to remain in the city until Ascension Day. Added to this was a necessity due to the illness of our Sister Jeanne de Jesus, daughter of Monsieur de Belly of Avignon. She was at death's door, unable to be transferred without endangering her life. Monsieur de la Chambre, the King's physician, did not think he could cure her, saying that her body had no more reserves. On the Feast of All Saints, she had come from Grenoble with a consuming fever that had caused her to waste away ever since the month of September. Two Sisters of the said monastery had died from it. She would have undoubtedly succumbed, as they did, had I not ordered her to be brought to Paris close to me.

Dear Love, You know how many tears I shed to obtain from You the health of this child and how I begged You that she might become a religious. I beg your pardon for what I told Monsieur de Priesac, who came to visit me in

JEANNE'S ORIGINAL DRAFT

accordance with your will about the death of this child. (737) He considered it inevitable, because, beside the continual fever and terrible chest infection, she was visibly swollen for two days. "Monsieur," I said to him, "I know very well that according to the knowledge of the doctors, my daughter is in danger, but not according to my trust. I will weep in front of the Incarnate Word until He heals her." I did this and You dried my tears, miraculously healing her. You gave her the grace of receiving the holy habit on the thirty-first of May, Feast of Saint Petronilla, the Monday between the Feast of the Blessed Trinity and Corpus Christi, my Lord and my God.

On May 31, 1649, after I had invited Monsieur de la Chambre to attend an investiture, he was inexpressibly astounded when he heard the voice of this young girl and said: "It is death come to life!" He marveled at her bodily strength and presence of mind during the entire ceremony which in this Order is very long, but it is so lovely and mysterious that it is not tiring. It is your Spirit who dictated it, O my Divine Love. (738)

CHAPTER CV

Our return to the monastery. What the divine goodness allowed with regard to the vocation of two novices. Their investiture and profession.

I cannot express the satisfaction our community has had of being in a monastery far from visits that importune good religious because of being close to the city. Many lay people, who have nothing to do, look for entertainment in parlors, and unfortunate are the religious who enjoy keeping company with them. Unless they are there through obedience and mortification, they them-

JEANNE'S ORIGINAL DRAFT

selves become corrupt, because the Heavenly Spouse, who stands by the wall of their cloister, regards them through the grill with indescribable jealousy. He tells them to leave promptly and come to their heavenly exercises and holy meditation. There they will see the ravishing beauty of the flowers in the sacred garden. Also, they will enjoy the fruit of the marvelous orchard of this Divine Spouse that wisdom has planted for their recreation. *Surge, amica mea, columba mea, formosa mea, et veni, Iam hiems transiit. Arise, make haste, my love, my dove, my beautiful one, and come. For winter is now past.* (Cant 2:10c-11) (739)

Do not think about anything that is of the world. It is a winter without fruit and brings troublesome rains. Let them retire to their cisterns. Let them flow in their rivulets that have their course below. Our garden possesses fountains whose sources are divine. The Father and I are the sources of the Holy Spirit who emanates from Us. He regards us and has a relationship with Us, for He possesses equality with our one principle: *Surge, propera, colomba mea. Flores apparuerunt in terra nostra. Arise, my beloved, my dove. The flowers have appeared in our land.* (Cant 2:10; 12a)

He shows flowers and fruit to all of them in general and tells each one in particular: "Arise, my Sister, and come into my garden to rejoice innocently with Me. Come, my dove without guile. Leave it to the worldly. Come to your cell which is like a honeycomb. It is well symbolized by the niches in the rock and by a poor dwelling. This poverty contains all the riches of heaven. I dwell there with you; I, in whom are contained all my Divine Father's treasures of understanding and knowledge. Meditate upon the profound mysteries of our unique being and the plurality of our Divine Persons. Meditate on the marvels that are corporeally contained in my Sacred Humanity. (740) I do not call you from the parlor to occupy yourself in the monastery, with the vain images you have experienced. Let them vanish the moment you leave it. Do not turn your thought back as did Lot's wife to see the burning of Sodom: *Surge, amica mea, speciosa mea, et veni: Colomba mea, in caverna maceri. Ostende mihi faciem tuam, sonet vox tua in auribus meis: vox enim tua dulcis, et facies tua decora. Arise, my love, my beautiful one,*

JEANNE'S ORIGINAL DRAFT

and come. My dove in the clefts of the rock, in the hollow places of the wall, show me thy face. Let thy face sound in my ears: for thy voice is sweet and thy face comely. (Cant 2:13c-14)

"I want to hear your voice which is my sweet, melodious music. You should neither sing nor speak except to praise Me. Your face should be concealed from all in the world so as not to be unveiled except in my presence. My Apostle, who has perceived my jealousy, has declared that women should be veiled in church in consideration of the angels, more so than men. Job, who was not enlightened by the Gospel, stated that he had made a pact with his eyes never to look at a virgin. My virgins owe Me more fidelity, not seeing nor being seen by any man except through constraint that causes them a suffering inexpressible to creatures."

I have made a digression. I beg You, my Divine Love, to let it be a lesson to all religious who read it or hear it read. (741) I stated that our community felt an indescribable satisfaction in its location, but, since every general rule has exceptions, I want to add that one or two of your daughters, who still had not received virtue from on high because they had not withdrawn like the others, did not find your flowers and did not taste your honey. They possessed only gall and apparent leaves, which fell because of their lack of devotion.

One of them shrewdly had herself removed by her nurse, and the other, with great effort to lose her vocation, had her parents and others informed that she had lost it. Who would believe that these two daughters would become separated from and rejected by your community, having made themselves unworthy of the happiness You had prepared for them? Everyone despaired for their perseverance, except the one who hoped against all hope and tried to imitate your faithful Abraham in all things by believing in God; and this was justified. I hoped in your goodness that your great mercy would not totally abandon your daughters. (742) It brought them back to their mother, who presented them to You, convincing their parents that their frailties would not bring them eternal death. Certainly, it demonstrated your sovereign goodness and power and the truth of the words I have declared: that they would belong

JEANNE'S ORIGINAL DRAFT

to the period when I chose the religious. They showed so much fervor that they asked me, my daughter, the Assistant and the Mistress of novices, for the holy habit. More than forty days later, with sighs and tears, they seemed impelled by your Holy Spirit: *Flabit Spiritus eius, et fuent aquœ. Qui annunciat verbum tuum Jacob, justitias et judicia sua Israel. His wind shall blow, and the waters shall run. Who declareth his word to Jacob: his justices and his judgments to Israel.* (Ps 147:18-19)

May they and all who read this bear in mind that your Holy Spirit does not grant this favor to all who resist his graces and their vocation as He did them. He obligates them doubly to make good use of this intensified grace received: *Non fecit taliter omni nationi, et iudicia sua non manifestavit eis. Alleluia, Alleluia. He hath not done in like manner to every nation: and his judgments he hath not made manifest to them. Alleluia.* (Ps 147:20)

On the Feast of Kings in 1650, the first one received the holy habit. I pray You, my Divine Savior, that she may hear from your mercy what your Father told You through your justice: "Behold, this is my beloved Son, in whom I am well pleased. May your Holy Spirit conduct her to the desert of holy religious life where your grace will assist her. Thus, she will be victorious over all her enemies. At the end of her mortal life, which is the being set free from this desert, may she be worthy of being accompanied by your holy angels. May they present her to You, purified of every impurity so that You may receive her as your beloved spouse, saying to her: *Sponsabo te mihi in sempiternum. I will espouse thee to me for ever.* (Hos 2:19a) (743)

The other, seeing that she had chosen to do by her will what the Prodigal Son had done in effect—that is, that she had requested being sent somewhere far from your house where your love produces holiness which is appropriate for your daughters who are your temples—began weeping, sobbing, sighing and wailing aloud. She took hold of my feet while, prompted by your love in the maternal loving way, I bent to embrace and kiss her. With a tenderness that was most urgent and inexplicable to me, I raised her up. I begged the angels to praise You with their angelical motets, and I invited all my Sisters,

JEANNE'S ORIGINAL DRAFT

your daughters, to share in the joy that I thought belonged to all to see their sisters return to the happiness they had chosen to lose. They were unaware of the precipices wherein they were going to cast themselves, because one abyss calls to another, whenever one leaves the vocation to which Your Spirit has called one.

She received the holy habit on Thursday during the Octave of your glorious Resurrection, being a novitiate companion of the one who had received it on the Octave of Kings, as well as Sister Jeanne of Jesus whom You had so providentially and miraculously healed. All three made their profession when their years of probation or novitiate ended, each according to the time she had received the habit. Lord, may they be invested with power and grace, which is the beauty You love in your spouse, and may they rejoice on the Last Day. (744)

CHAPTER CV

Our Lord let me understand that the time He had set for raising Monsieur de la Piardière to the priesthood was approaching. The illness, death and glory that God gave his wife.

On the Feast of Saint Joachim 1650, your goodness elevated me by your sublime contemplation. You spoke the words recorded in Haggai 2(:7c) : *et mare, et aridam; the sea and the dry land.* My daughter, wait a little while, and you will see what I will accomplish in you and in your dear son, whom I have chosen to serve Me in the dignity of a priest. I will remove his worldly habits and invest him with priestly ones. Neither Satan nor any contradiction of men can prevent my plans for him. He will receive my Spirit and the seven

JEANNE'S ORIGINAL DRAFT

gifts that will shine upon his head like brilliant, shining lamps. You will be two olive trees in my dwelling. A number of years ago, I told you that you are my dear Zorobabel, that all grandeur is but a mountain of presumption before you. I will bring down this mountain and have you establish and perfect my house with the means that I will place at your disposal. Your hands will establish it, and we will perfect it: *Manus Zorobabel fundaverunt domum istam, et manus eius perficient eam. The hands of Zorobabel have laid the foundations of this house, and his hands shall finish it.* (Zach 4:9)

Your wisdom, that knows all things wisely and has counted the number of our days, made known that those of Madame de la Piardière had come to an end. She took to her bed with a fever that consumed her mortal life to give her the possession of a blessed eternity. (745) All who knew her could say that her humility and charity had attained the highest perfection. The former prompted her always to have a lowly opinion of herself, considering herself to be nothing; that is, imperfect in everything she did. The latter made her sacrifice her life by her care of the poor in St. Eustachius' parish. She could be regarded as the holocaust of both corporal and spiritual charity. Her zeal in encouraging all the poor of the parish to go to Confession and Communion at Easter caused her to overlook her own need for repose, food and refreshment. Indescribably afflicted, her husband begged me to pray to You to leave her still longer. Feeling obliged to visit her, I went to the church of the discalced Augustinian fathers to hear Mass and receive Holy Communion. Then You told me: "For a number of years, you have known that she must die before her husband. If not, the Holy Spirit will not descend upon him. He will not become a priest unless she dies. Tell her that she will die from this illness." Heaven, that wanted her, did not choose to leave her on earth for a long time. The world was unworthy of this daughter of heaven who no longer thought of what she was leaving on earth. A few hours prior to her death, I asked if she wanted to see her husband and four children. She made me understand that it was not necessary, and thus, by these words, she did not want to see what she was leaving behind her. With the Apostle, she could say: *Unum autem, quæ quidem retro sunt obliviscens, ad ea vero quæ sunt priora, extendens meipsum, ad destinatum persequor, ad bravium supernæ vocationis Dei*

JEANNE'S ORIGINAL DRAFT

in Christo Jesu. But one thing I do: Forgetting the things that are behind, and stretching forth myself to those that are before, I press towards the mark, to the prize of the supernal vocation of God in Christ Jesus. (Phil 3:13-14)

No longer should I have any other love or thought except for God." By a holy donation, she entrusted me with the care of her husband and her children, then being able to say as did the Prophet-King: *Domine, probasti me, et cognovisti me; tu cognovisti sessionem meam et resurrectionem meam. Lord, thou hast proved me, and known me: thou hast known my sitting down, and my rising up.* (Ps 138:1-2) Detached from all visible things, this soul was attached to You, my Divine Love, the image of the invisible God. At this moment, on your behalf, I said to her: *Veni, electa mea, et ponam in te thronum meum. Come, my chosen one, and I will establish my throne in you.* (Office, Common of Virgins)

She expired on Friday, May 13, 1650, at 5:00 o'clock in the evening. You received her in a way inexplicable to me. She had told her husband, as soon as she took to her bed, that she wanted to see me, but that she feared I would be upset upon seeing her ill. Your Spirit of truth had let her know that I loved her. After this dove-like soul left her body, I told the one who accompanied me (Sister Gravier): "Behold, a saint!" "Mother," she said to me, "you make saints very soon!" In no way did this reply diminish the esteem You had given me for this holy soul of your Divine Father whose providence ordained that the next morning the very same person came with me to the church of the Oratorian Fathers on Saint Honoré Street. (747)

Upon seeing me go to Confession and Communion, she wished to do the same thing, but, O marvel of your divinity, You chose to convert this person for the glory of this soul whom You had glorified, allowing her to see her in glory, filled and ornamented with the splendor with which your Majesty had invested her. It resembled a white diamond-covered robe embroidered with diamonds that divinely revealed and concealed her, just as by your marvelous light, she was hidden from her own eyes. She was dressed in a long robe that

JEANNE'S ORIGINAL DRAFT

went past her feet. The person was unable to determine the material of this marvelous robe or the crown that was set upon her hair and elevated it in a heavenly way. Upon seeing her face, she recognized her, but her beauty and girth made her unrecognizable. Divinely adorned, this soul ascended, and the one who contemplated these marvels perceived that she did not walk on earth or fly, but ascended into heaven. It seemed to her that this cherished soul came from the place where I was kneeling. The same person, whom You allowed to see this glorious soul, said that the latter was followed by a multitude of souls or glorified spirits. She was unable to distinguish the saints from the angels. (748) She said to herself: "This glory is too magnificent for a woman who is neither virgin nor martyr. This would be more appropriate for the one who is here," alluding to your most unworthy servant. At this moment, she heard: "God does not exhaust the immense riches of his glory by adorning this soul. He possesses infinite ones for whomever He wants to sanctify through his goodness and the correspondence with grace that He gives."

Dear Love, the one to whom You chose to manifest this glory thought that I had had the same visions and that I had prayed to You to convert her by that manifestation. She told me that this soul and all her retinue had departed from the place where I was located. When I spoke to Father Menam of the Oratory, he made me give a brief account of my thanksgiving so as to tell him about the precious death of the deceased. When the priest had left me, I was surprised to see this person waiting by the railing. She was in a state of astonishment and asked me: "Mother, did you see Madame de la Piardière in glory?" At this, I told her that she was too curious in asking about something that she had so completely repelled the preceding evening. At my rejection, she was even more curious. This prompted me to look at her intently and perceive by her face that she had an extraordinary attitude of recollection. The more I looked at her, the more her modesty increased, and, what is a sign of real visions, she seemed increasingly immersed in profound embarrassment. Having authority over her, I asked her to speak openly to me and not to conceal anything that had caused her condition. (749) She begged me not to name her should I wish to repeat what she had seen, that I should indicate it as part of my own experience, as though I had witnessed these things. She felt it

JEANNE'S ORIGINAL DRAFT

would be more authentic than coming from her and that I would be telling the truth, since I had seen these marvels before she did. She added that this vision began to appear to her near me and concluded near herself and that it had lasted a long time. They were so indelibly imprinted in her memory that she had remained attached to these sublime understandings. It was like the Apostles upon the Mount of Olives when your Humanity ascended above the heavens on the day of your glorious Ascension. When the angels saw them, in order to withdraw them from their admiration, they told them: *Viri Galilee, quid statis aspicientes in cælum?   Ye men of Galilee, why stand you looking up to heaven?* (Acts 1:11)

In this vision, she received the healing of an incurable malady of a certain faintness and weakness in all her limbs that was often extreme. By this experience, she had been perfectly healed. I asked her to record what she had told me. It was evident that she had felt a very deep repugnance. She obeyed me, but wrote with her left hand so that her writing would not be recognized. I took this to Monsieur de la Piardière, assisting him to read it. Monsieur D'Archambaut, an ordinary assistant of the King, brother of the deceased woman and who was in the room, said to Monsieur de la Piardière and me when he had learned about the glory his sister possessed: "In the evening, a half hour before my sister expired, I withdrew from beside her bed, because I just could not see her die. I went into her room, because she died in the living-room. (750) I sat down in a chair, momentarily overcome by grief. I was suddenly awakened to see an angel dressed in an ornate yellow-gold robe who was leading a woman dressed in a flowing white robe that resembled the habit of a religious. I quickly got up to go into the living-room where I found her already dead."

Divine Wisdom, how admirable You are in your chosen ones who live holily! Oh, how true it is that the torments of death do no touch them. In the evening of life, You have them presented to You by your angels with their justice, and then You personally crown them with your mercy, adorning them with majestic splendors at life's end. As I have said, she expired at 5:00 o'clock in the evening on Friday, May 13th, and was presented to Your

JEANNE'S ORIGINAL DRAFT

Majesty by her angel who had accompanied her during her works of charity. This was represented by the golden yellow, and on Saturday, at ten o'clock in the morning, You demonstrated that You had led her to your own glory with the adornment of a holy spouse. Thus I can apply to her the words of your beloved disciple: *Vidi sanctam civitatem Ierusalem novam descendentem de cælo a Deo, paratam, sicut sponsam ornatam viro suo. I saw the holy city, the new Jerusalem, coming down out of heaven from God, prepared as a bride adorned for her husband.* (Apoc 21:2)

I must not omit what the priest who kept wake with her told me on Sunday morning; that is, that he had been looking at her face that seemed beautiful to him and that he was not at all perturbed by keeping wake for this blessed body for the two following nights. (751) This was due to the fact that it was kept in her bed after death until Sunday afternoon without the length of time or the exceptional heat during these May days causing any bad odor. The man who prepared her leaden coffin marveled that, when, on Sunday evening, he picked up her remains to place them inside, it was as pliable as soft wax even though three entire days had passed that her soul, which had inhabited it, had departed. I can say that, by a divine marvel, this soul had been allowed to visit it as though assisting at her own funeral, since she had spurned it so much during life. She was buried at Saint Innocent on Monday after the service conducted at Saint Eustachius. I can declare and certify that I could visit it only as a body that filled me with respect and veneration. I had to kneel, and, so as not to astound those present, I took the asperges and knelt before the Cross, hardly able to pray for the soul of the deceased one, except to thank God and pray for those in need of spiritual help. Thank You, my Divine Love, for what You have done in your servant. The Sister (Sister Gravier) who accompanied me the entire time I remained in this place, descended the great stairway during the night. She was amazed not to be afraid, saying to herself: "There is a dead person here, and I am descending alone!" As she made this reflection, she interiorly heard: *Beati mortui qui in Domino moriuntur. Blessed are the dead who die in the Lord.* (Apoc 14:13b) (752)

JEANNE'S ORIGINAL DRAFT

CHAPTER CVII

The Incarnate Word allowed me to marvel at his glory and allowed me to share in it. The favors He gave me during the month of July. His love for me. The part that his august Mother gave me on the Feast of her Assumption. The birth of Monseigneur d'Orlean's son. About Saint Matthew. The things that Saint Michael and his angels told me on their feast day. The visions I had on the Feast of the holy Apostles Simon and Jude.

A few days before your triumphant Ascension Day in 1650, as my soul became elevated by your holy delights, You had me marvel at your glory and the happiness of your saints to share in it. You invited me to this common rejoicing with favors that I cannot express. Whenever I could be in solitude, I forgot everything visible so as to contemplate the beauty of the invisible God that is You, my Love and my weight, who bear me up and elevate me to the very bosom of your Divine Father. I did not ask to make a tabernacle there, recalling that You had told your Apostles to draw them after You and to detach them from every earthly affection: *In domo Patris mei mansiones multæ sunt. In my Father's house, there are many mansions.* (Jn 14:2)

During the month of July, my soul enjoyed the company of your beloved Saint Magdalen who had chosen the better part when she remained with You, after You had delivered her by your strong love from the obstacle of domestic occupations. She poured perfume upon your feet and head. My soul adored your wounds and self-emptying, as well as your sovereign, holy attributes. It considered You to be in her, as in the lower parts of the earth and yet, simultaneously elevated above the heavens, You were the supreme heaven. (753) It argued about your mercies toward this fortunate sinner, saying to her: "Holy beloved, you were called the sinner of a city, but as for me, I am the sinner of the universe. Jesus, our Love, has pardoned me more sins than you. Thus, He has shown me more mercy. Just as soon as you came to

JEANNE'S ORIGINAL DRAFT

know Him, you loved Him and never again offended Him. As for me, I have continued my offenses. Because of this, one can say about this unfaithful spouse whom He deigns to love and whom his goodness had lodged in his house: *Quid est, quod dilecta mea in domo mea facit scelera multa? What is the meaning that my beloved hath wrought much wickedness in my house?* (Jer 11:15)

For so many years through his love, He has daily given me the most holy flesh of this divine Lover. He has prepared a new life for me and left me his Precious Blood in the sacrament of Penance. He has provided me with an inexpressible and continual confidence in it, granting my body and spirit a grace that can be described only by Him: *Quam initiavit nobis viam novam, et viventem per velamen, id est, carnem suam. A new and living way which he hath dedicated for us through the veil, that is to say, his flesh.* (Heb 10:20)

Great saint, in the desert the angels elevated you seven times daily to join them in praising their King, our same Love, but we are not told that You received Communion every day. Certain contemplatives believe that their General, Saint Michael, brought you a cross so that you might recall the Passion of our adorable Spouse, as well as fight and overcome the temptations of your enemies. (754) Through love that surmounts all things, you were always victorious. Pray to Him that I may never be ungrateful for his favors and that He may not allow me ever to stray, since He is my straight path; nor to wander, for He is my truth. May I die in possession of this divine life. For any offenses I may have committed, I trust in his mercy and declare to all the powers of my soul: *Accedamus cum vero corde in plenitudine fidei, aspersit corda a concientia mala et abluti corpus acqua munda: teneamus spei nostræ confessionem indeclinabilem (fidelis enim est qui repromisit). Let us draw near with a true heart, in fullness of faith, having our hearts sprinkled from an evil conscience and our bodies washed with clean water. Let us hold fast the confession of our hope without wavering (for he is faithful that hath promised).* (Heb 10:22-23) And let us not abandon our divine refreshment. Let us not deprive ourselves of daily Communion,

JEANNE'S ORIGINAL DRAFT

which is our Viaticum, to pass from the pilgrimage of this world—that is a dark night—into the day of eternity, a day that You make, my Lord and my God.

Dear Love, without a crime deserving your greatest punishment through the justice of your most ardent love for me, could I possibly withdraw from your table where You nurture and have me so delightfully repose. You tell me that whoever loves the most will suffer the most and that, were You able to suffer, this deprivation would make you feel pains incomprehensible to me. As for what pertains to your fidelity toward me, just as You will not die again and that death will never eliminate You, so, too, You would not deprive me of this holy collation. (755) I should highly esteem your Precious Blood with which You cleanse and inebriate me. Then You would take delight in my requests. With patience, for a time, You endure those who stamp on this adorable Blood of the Testament of Love. The punishment for such a crime toward a God who died for us will be ordained by a living God: *Horrendum est incidere in manus Dei viventis. Iustus autem meus ex fide vivit: quod si subtraxerit se, non placebit animæ meæ. It is a fearful thing to fall into the hands of the living God. My just man liveth by faith: but if he withdraw himself, he shall not please my soul.* (Heb 10:31; 38)

Divine Savior, may I be justified by your justification and that of all your saints together with You. By your testament, You ordained this to surpass any sacrifice. My gentle Redeemer, You tell me that You prefer your mercy toward me to all the ancient sacrifices: *Immola Deo sacrificium laudis, et redde altissimo vota tua. Et invoca me in dei tribulationis; eruam te, et honorificabis me. Offer to God the sacrifice of praise: and pay thy vows to the Most High. And call upon me in the day of trouble: I will deliver thee, and thou shalt glorify me.* (Ps 49:14-15)

Around the Feast of the triumphant Assumption of your august Mother, You let me participate in her glory. You elevated me so high that it certainly seemed that your love was my support and that it drew me near the one who is your love. (756) This marvelous Mother, who alone comprises your choir at

JEANNE'S ORIGINAL DRAFT

your right hand, accepted me in the distribution of graces that she made of her throne of glory to those whom You love. She gave me a generous portion, so that I may say: *Funes ceciderunt mihi in præclaris; etenim hereditas mea præclara est mihi. The lines are fallen unto me in goodly places: for my inheritance is goodly to me.* (Ps 15:6)

On August 17th at 5:00 o'clock in the morning, the portress came to tell me that the Duchess of Orleans had given birth to a son, according to my prediction which she called prophecy. Your goodness always fulfills what it prompts me to say a long while in advance. I rejoiced in the excitement of this fine Duchess, who had undergone trials for a number of years in affliction and half-consolations, because she had had only daughters. In the midst of my joy, I was troubled, since You let me see a pit that was almost filled with the blood spilled and shed by women. This vision troubled me. I felt obliged to share it the same day with Monsieur de la Piardière and my daughters, who recall it as does he. Your goodness strengthened me, calming my spirit near the great Saint Michael on his feast day. As I praised and admired him, with his faithful angels, I told him that he had triumphed over the dragon and all his rebel angels, expelling them from the Empyrean heaven by his glorious victory, through the power of your Blood: (757) *Ipsi vicerunt eum propter sanguinem Agni, et propter verbum testimonii sui. And they overcame him by the blood of the Lamb and by the word of the testimony.* (Apoc 12:11a)

The word of their witness is the word that Saint Michael uttered, the first that acquired for him his name "Who is like God?": *Michael, quis sicut Deus; Michael, who is like God.* I admired this marvelous declaration, praising this first faithful one and repeating: *Michael, quis ut Deus?* This magnificent prince, through an ineffable courtesy, together with all his angels, replied: *Jesus amor meus, Jesus amor meus; Jesus, my love, Jesus, my love.* By a profound self-emptying or evacuation, they were like echoes, for they replied: *Jesus amor meus.* Since I was astounded by their repeated response, Saint Michael told me: "Just as the Divine Word has honored me with this holy name whose repetition is acceptable to Him, He wants you to be honored and praised by all his chosen ones, wearing upon your heart: *Jesus amor meus,*

JEANNE'S ORIGINAL DRAFT

which is as great and as adorable as these words: *Quis sicut Deus.*

Enraptured by these repetitions by all your chosen ones and the saints who pronounced them for the honor and glory of the Saint of saints, my soul desired to take up its abode with them and leave external occupations; namely, the care of the kitchen. I told this Prince of the angels that I had fulfilled this charge for a number of years and that certainly I could be discharged from this taxing duty to be occupied in contemplating the divine mysteries with greater ease. (758) Assembling as though in a chapter and consultation, they all concluded, together with the opinion of the saints, that I should still be left and confirmed in this charge as cook in the Incarnate Word's house. He said that, with his angels, he had prepared and given manna to the people of Israel for forty years in the desert.

On the eve of the Feast of the holy Apostles Saint Simon and Saint Jude, when I went to our chapel to adore You in your most august Sacrament, You were pleased to favor me with ineffable graces. You appeared to me with a triple crown of diamonds, letting me see heaven open, whose vaults shone like your crown. I was fascinated by these marvelous spectacles. Your benignity invited me to draw near your loving Majesty, saying to me: Come closer, my spouse. Have no fear of the persecution by your enemies: *Multæ filiæ congregaverut, divitias; Tu supergressa es universas. Many daughters have gathered together riches: thou hast surpassed them all.* (Pro 31:29)

JEANNE'S ORIGINAL DRAFT

CHAPTER CVIII

On the Feast of All Saints, they accepted me into the participation of their happiness. It pleased the Divine Savior to gratify me on the Feast of the Octave of the Saints and its dedication. What I understood for his Order. His protection over and dispensations toward me.

On the Feast of All Saints, You were pleased to have them welcome me, having me share in their happiness, but, since I was a pilgrim, my soul saw that it was engaged in responsibilities from which they had been delivered; that is, being obliged to inform a body that retained it on life's journey and occupied in very lowly matters, since it had to take care of what concerned the senses. It declared: *Infelix ego; Unhappy am I.* (759)

To distract me from my troubles, these charitable courtiers allowed me to hear that along life's journey I was gratified by many favors that were not ordinary to all its travelers. As the Foundress of an Order, I was ranked with the Patriarchs of the Old and New Testament; with the Prophets, since You had given me the gift of knowing and predicting a number of things that You had fulfilled; with the Apostles, being sent into the world to bear your Name and your glory by your Father, You and the Holy Spirit, O my Divine Redeemer; with the martyrs, witnessing by word, writings and action that I am ready, by your grace, to seal with my blood the faith and belief that the Catholic, Apostolic and Roman Church professes, as a daughter of this holy Church, of which You are the most holy Head. You had invited me to die for love of You, for proclaiming your adorable truths in the way You expected of my fidelity. (760) I ranked with the Doctors by teaching about your mysteries, for You commanded me to write about them, either interiorly by You Yourself, or externally by my Prelate, and my directors and superiors; with the

JEANNE'S ORIGINAL DRAFT

Confessors, telling me that for many years your Spirit inspired and led me in your piety; with the Virgins, for sharing in their roses as well as their lilies. You had commanded me to establish your Order with its white and red liveries, since these are your colors.

Divine Love, You chose to honor me by your marvelous marriage, espousing me in the presence of your heavenly courtiers, leaving me like a widow on earth to guide our children ever since the eve of the Ascension 1617 when You told me to remain for love of You. When I saw that I was abandoned by those who could have assisted me in promoting your glory, You prompted me to describe your Divine Paraclete, your Love, the Holy Spirit from whom I receive all graces and possessions. You told me to recall that, since the year 1619, I was accepted by the Holy Innocents into their company on Mount Sion. I then received from your goodness the impression of your Father's Name and yours with a delightful kiss from your Father, and yours with a sweet kiss from your most sacred and divine lips. All your holy angels received me into their nine choirs, elevating me up to their heavenly hierarchies by marvelous impressions. Your august Mother cherished me as your august bride and her daughter, although most unworthy of either of these favors. I humbled myself more than I can say. You shed your graces abundantly and superabundantly within me, there where sin had abounded. (761)

I spent the Octave of All Saints, just like the Feast, with ineffable daily favors, because of your new blessings. On the Feast of your Dedication, O my Divine Savior, you gave me no less grace than You did Solomon at the dedication of your former Temple. You had me recall that, in the presence of all your saints, You had called me "a miracle of love." I told You that You were obligated to make me what You had called me, that I ought not bear this title in vain. Your words give reality to what they signify, and, above all, regarding your graces and favors, You tend to give me grace for grace. The law had been given by Moses: *Quia lex per Moysen data est,Gratia et veritas per Jesus Christum facta est. For the law was given by Moses: grace and truth came by Jesus Christ.* (Jn 1:17)

JEANNE'S ORIGINAL DRAFT

Your goodness allowed me to tell You confidently that it could justify and protect me from the contradictions of tongues that criticized my conferring the habit without apparently wearing it myself. You told me: "My daughter, I have brought you into the world as a proverb for many and an enigma that men cannot understand by feeble reason." (762) You added that You had been unknown among your own who never understood your qualities, that You were the wisdom in mysteries concealed from men who presumed themselves to be wise and prudent. The princes of the era did not know You; they were unaware of your divine filiation with your Divine Father, who had sanctified You before sending You into the world. You possess substantial grace. They considered it blasphemy when You called Yourself the Son of God. When they crucified You, they scoffed at You, saying that You should come down if You were the Son of God. They regarded You to be an imaginary God and King who saved others, but could not save Himself. To John the Baptist, whom they considered crude and mortified, they attributed the quality of Messias, which pertains to You and is essentially due to You. Men consider the exterior. You are the Eternal Priest who did not receive your priesthood from men, but, with an oath worthy of Him, from your Father. They should tell and show me from whom Moses had received the priesthood, he who consecrated and made Aaron and his children priests, investing them with priestly attire. "My daughter, what would they reply to these words?" Lord, You Yourself had anointed them as sacred and invested them in your tabernacle in the presence of your angels. Eminently and augustly, they received from You the anointing and priestly robes, just as You had let me understand that You gave me, the most unworthy of your creatures. (763)

The Prophet-King calls him a priest, together with Aaron, when he says: *Moyses et Aaron in sacerdotibus eius; Moses and Aaron among his priests.* (Ps 98:6) "My daughter, whoever knows about the marvelous mercies I have worked in you will not doubt that I have eminently and marvelously given you the Order and the habit that you have given and do give your daughters. I have imparted to you the power to accomplish what he has achieved and the requisite mission.

JEANNE'S ORIGINAL DRAFT

"The Holy Father, the Archbishop of Avignon, the Bishop of Grenoble, the Vicar General and the Priors of Saint Germain have been only following my orders in this. Then, let people talk. I have chosen you for great things. You are the mother and nurse of this Order which is, it seems, endangered upon the waters, as was Moses. To nourish him, his mother was called, after Pharaoh's daughter had withdrawn him from the water. My providence had this plan that surpasses men's orders. There is no rule so general that it cannot have an exception. I have often told you that all the laws given to others are not meant for you, because I am pleased to favor you due to the dispositions of my goodness and wisdom. I am the Lord; I do what I wish in heaven and on earth." (764)

CHAPTER CIX

The Incarnate Word invited me to ask Him for a New Year's gift; what He told me on the Feast of the Kings while my daughters were renewing their vows; and what I understood on the Feast of the Incarnation, Good Friday, Easter Sunday and Ascension Day.

On the Feast of the Circumcision in 1651, my Divine Love, You were pleased to elevate my spirit by a loving confidence, inviting me to ask You personally for my New Year's gift. You told me: "I am the One by whom my Father made the ages and everything that is created. I am the universal Heir of all his possessions, the figure of his substance and the splendor of his glory. I belong to You as a New Year's gift and as everything."

On the Feast of Kings, while my daughters were renewing their vows, I humbled myself in your presence, because I did not possess the entire external

JEANNE'S ORIGINAL DRAFT

habit nor had I made religious profession. By your royal and divine benignity, You bent toward me and said to me: "Why are you upset, my only one, my dove, whom I consider beautiful. All the daughters are symbolized by the sixty queens, the eighty concubines and the innumerable young women, but she alone is the unique dove, the one whom my divine goodness has engendered, whom I prefer to ten thousand. He addressed the words of Elcana to Anna, his wife, to me: *Anna, cur fles? et quare non comedis? et quam ob rem affligitur cor tuum? numquid non ego melior tibi sum, quam decem filii? Anna, why weepest thou? And why dost thou not eat? And why dost thou afflict thy heart? Am not I better to thee than ten children?* (1 Sam 1:8) (765)

"Jeanne, my spouse, why do you afflict my heart? Am I not all goodness and love to you? Am I not more beneficial to you than ten thousand daughters? Be consoled, and do not be disturbed by the torture of your unhappy considerations. Know that, were I able to suffer, you would make Me sad. You are my heart's delight, and I am your loving Conqueror."

On the Feast of your loving, marvelous Incarnation, I received great favors from your gracious Mother, who again invited me to enter her virginal bosom. It was a wonderful cloister to me, where this Queen of Virgins accepted me as a cherished spouse and a sister in her adorable bosom, where, in spirit and in truth, I adored your Father, together with You and the Holy Spirit. She deigned to consider me as her sister, because I have been devoted to Saint Anne, her holy mother, even before I came into being, that is, before my birth. I offered myself to be her servant and her slave of love, subjugated by the chains of her desires. These gently bound me to her Divine Son and to Her. I asked them to let the virginal heart be our sacred altar, at which those who served at the ancient tabernacles, which have passed like the shadows of these divine truth, could not participate.

On Good Friday, as I contemplated You nailed to the Cross, drawing all things to You, O Love of loves, You let me understand that You gave magnificent gifts upon your Cross. (766) You gave your Spirit to your Divine Father, your Blessed Mother and Saint John, and your Paradise to the good thief.

JEANNE'S ORIGINAL DRAFT

Also, You were giving me all these gifts. Bowing your Head toward me, You gave me an outpouring of your Spirit, seeing me standing by your Cross together with your Blessed Mother, whom the disciple of grace, Saint John, had received for himself. By your inclination and loving goodness, she was mine. I received her with most humble, loving gratitude.

On Easter Sunday, upon offering me your victories, You made me understand that You were victorious over the world, the devil and the flesh. Although this was done through your merit, your most courteous goodness and civility did not want to enjoy it without having me share in it. You said to me: "You are my Deborah, seated, standing and progressing along life's journey. With Me, you fight the battle for the palm that is assuredly mine, for I finish as the Conqueror. I entreat you, in all your circumstances, my beloved, then, consider what glory I have merited. I overcame my enemies who hoped to get the spoils, whereas in the meantime I distributed them to my chosen ones in Limbo, the tomb and upon Calvary, where, through her strong fidelity, my wonderful Mother attached Sisara to the wood of my Cross.

"She is the wonderful Jahel who caused the leader of the condemned and his followers to be thrown into confusion while she was victorious upon Calvary. (767) Even more, she is the incomparable Deborah. I did not want to ascend there without her, because she was present at the battle by which the victory over infernal powers was won.

By a tree, the first Eve and the first Adam received the punishment of disgrace and death, leaving death for their entire unfortunate posterity. Due to another tree, the second Eve and the second Adam gave life to all the elect who are their blessed posterity. Calvary became a Tabor, because, through the power of my voice, I was there acknowledged to be the Son of God: *Videns autem centurio, qui ex adverso stabat quia sic clamens expirasset, ait: vere hic homo filius Dei erat. Now, the centurion, seeing what was done, glorified God, saying: Indeed this was a just man.* (Lk 23:47)

On the Feast of your triumphant Ascension, when I awoke at three o'clock

JEANNE'S ORIGINAL DRAFT

in the morning, I heard: *Terribilis est locus iste, non est hic alius nisi domus Dei et porta cæli. How terrible is this place! This is no other but the house of God, and the gate of heaven.* (Gen 28:17b)

After seeing a ladder extending from heaven to earth, Jacob declared: "Truly this place is terrible; it is the house of God and the gate of heaven." He saw that the Lord sat at the top and that the angels ascended and descended the steps. Rejoice today, my daughter, for you see Me ascend from the Mount of Olives above the heavens. I am the Angel of the Great Council. I am God and Man, the glory of heaven and earth, the victor and triumphant One par excellence, who takes away my chosen ones who were captives so as to give them the glory I have acquired for them. (768) Thus the declaration of the Royal Prophet is fulfilled: Ascending above the heavens, I lead captivity captive. I am their glorious Assumption, giving a donation among the living to all my chosen ones. The day of the Last Supper was none other than a testament to assure my death. Draw near, my beloved; in abundance receive the anointing that flows from my Sacred Wounds. Consider the path of heaven and of earth: *Lætentur cæli, exultet terra; Let heaven rejoice and earth exult.* (1 Par 16:11) Marvel at my elevation, how I ascend by my own power and that all the angels in acclamation tell my Divine Father: "Behold Him who ascends in jubilation and to the sound of trumpets! He is your Son, *Iste venit saliens in montibus; He cometh, leaping over the mountains.*" (Cant 2:8)

On the Sunday of the Octave of this admirable Ascension, You raised my spirit straight to your right hand, saying to me: "Come, my beloved, above the heavens to be near me and my spouses, the virgins. Take up your harp and psalterium. All of you, entone a lovely canticle. Consider that, due to my Incarnation, I made a wonderful covenant with all the saints of the Old Testament who were married, hoping to be born in time from their marriage. Eye has not seen, nor ear heard, neither has the heart of man been able to conceive of these marvels. (769) Like the royal eagle, my favorite disciple contemplated it and spoke more clearly to you about it in his Gospel and first Epistle than any of the others: *Quod fuit ab initio, quod audivimus, quod vidimus*

JEANNE'S ORIGINAL DRAFT

oculis nostris, quod perspeximus, et manus nostræ contrectaverunt de Verbo vitæ; et vita manifestata est, et vidimus, et testamur, et annunciamus vobis vitam æternam, quæ erat apud Patrem, et qui apparuit nobis. That which was from the beginning, which we have heard, which we have seen with our eyes, which we have looked upon and our hands have handled, of the word of life. For the life was manifested: and we have seen and do bear witness and declare unto you the life eternal, which was with the Father and hath appeared to us. (1 Jn 1:1-2) "My daughter, what do you think about all these delights?" O, Lord, how could I express all this? I am enraptured with admiration, for, through your wisdom, You have opened a door for me to the Word, making my tongue childlike and eloquent to proclaim your divine marvels. I maintain that silence would help me understand better. Who am I, Lord, to speak about what is ineffable to me: *Mirabilis facta est scientia tua ex me; Confortata est, et non potero ad eam.* Thy knowledge is become wonderful to me: it is high, and I cannot reach to it. (Ps 138:6)

Page added and glued to Page 766 of the Manuscript

"When I came across this small fragment of paper written personally by our devout Mother Jeanne Chezard de Matel, Foundress and Institutrix of our Congregation of the Incarnate Word, I was prompted to place it in this book of her works, fearing that it might become lost among the other papers. What induced me to do so was my respect for this worthy Mother and the veneration I have always had for her solid virtue, besides my esteem for her *Writings*. All persons of merit and others, likewise, have valued them. It will be easy to remove it from this location if the ten lines of the other part are found marked in her own book."

Sister Jeanne de Jesus de Bely, Secretary of our
Incarnate Word Convent in Paris

JEANNE'S ORIGINAL DRAFT

March 1635

On Good Friday, as I was lovingly complaining to my Spouse that He went to his death without me, as did Saint Lawrence and Pope Saint Sixtus, I asked if I might assist at his sacrifice. I wanted to share in it by the immolation of myself and of my own death. The reply given me was that I would be left to endure a longer death, to be interiorly placed on the gridiron, like Saint Lawrence, and to distribute the treasures of the Church as he did. What comprises this is the understanding of God's word that David valued more than gold, silver or any jewels on earth: *Super aurum et topazion; Above gold and the topaz.* (Ps 118:127b)

CHAPTER CX

The Blessed Virgin's glory and grandeur; the graces God gave me during her entire Octave. The Feast of Saint *Ennemond*. The Seraphim are closest to the Incarnate Word's sacrifice. He is the immortal Victim. He is the sacrifice of peace. He is the Eternal Priest who accepts the prayers of his faithful beloved. (770)

A few days around the Feast of the Assumption of your radiant Mother, whom You have crowned with twelve stars, dressed with the sun, shod with the moon, I was blinded by her prodigious splendors. My dazzled spirit declared: *Et nox sicut dies illuminabitur; sicut tenebræ eius, ita et lumen eius. And night shall be light as the day: the darkness thereof, and the light thereof are alike to thee.* (Ps 138:12b)

"My daughter, I have chosen you to let you understand my marvelous,

JEANNE'S ORIGINAL DRAFT

mysterious wisdom. I want to match you against the woman described by my beloved disciple in his Apocalypse, whose name is a mystery: *Et in fronte eius nomen scriptum: Mysterium; On her forehead a name was written: A mystery.* (Apoc 17:5a) Just as, by my powerful light, I have destroyed the works of the devil and gathered the dispersed children of Israel, I want you to destroy his evil works and reunite the doctors to me. They are my Israelites who have wandered away. By their vanity, they have been prompted by their presumption. Knowing that I deserve all praise and glory, they have been governed by their senses. They do not give it to me." Lord, my God, what are You saying? Is it to mortify me by the thoughts they will have of me, but, what am I saying! You are the Lord of all. You told your Apostles to untie the ass and her foal so as to bring them You. Using both of them, You deigned to enter Jerusalem in triumph where the children at the breast sang your praises, blessing You and praying that You would take them from the earthly Jerusalem up to (771) the palace of the heavenly one. They exclaimed: *Hosanna Filio David: benedictus qui venit in nomine Domini: Hosanna in excelsis. Hosanna to the son of David: Blessed is he that cometh in the name of the Lord: Hosanna in the highest.* (Mt 21:9)

One day during this Octave, after Holy Communion, I was marveling at your goodness toward me. You let me understand that it was as wonderful as that of all the saints in heaven, who in suspense considered these outpourings upon me. I puzzled them, as well as people on earth, because all could see my imperfections, for which I felt and always feel great embarrassment in the presence of your Divine Majesty. With ineffable tenderness, You told me: *"Babylon dilecta mea posita est mihi in miraculum. Babylon, my beloved, is become a wonder to me.* (Is 21:4b)

"My daughter, a number of years ago, I told you that you are my miracle of love. Now I am telling you that you are the book sealed with seven seals, which cannot be opened nor known except by the Lamb whom you have heard. He is a Lamb that is the lion of the tribe of Juda, conqueror of all his enemies, a book in which my wisdom has written. He is all mystery. It is a mysterious Apocalypse that I make with you and within you. It is written

JEANNE'S ORIGINAL DRAFT

externally by your exterior actions which ordinary persons can neither read nor interpret. A Daniel is required who possesses and is the Spirit of the Father and of the Son, our Holy Spirit. (772) My dearest daughter, I am also the interpreter of our mysteries." Blessed may You be, my God, my ordinary and extraordinary Physician, who distill your dew upon me morning and evening. You make me your peaceful Sion and Jerusalem in all your locations. I will praise You: *In Deo laudabo Verbum; in Domino laudabo sermonem. In me sunt, Deus, vota tua, quæ reddam, laudationes tibi. In God will I praise the word, in the Lord will I praise his speech. In me, O God, are vows to thee, which I will pay, praises to thee.* (Ps 55:11a, 12a)

In God, I will praise the Word; in our Lord Jesus Christ, I will praise the Word in the bosom and mind of the Heavenly Father. I adore the Word who is his divine praise in the humanity, supported by the divine hypostasis of this Word made flesh. I will praise the Eternal Word. Could I keep silent when You command me to speak about your marvels? Without being guilty, could I withdraw from life and go far from Him who made me live? Lord, all the powers of my soul tell You with Saint Peter, the acme of theology: *Domine, ad quem ibimus? Verba vitæ æternæ habes: et nos credidimus, et cognovimus quia tu es Christus Filius Dei. Lord, to whom shall we go? Thou hast the words of eternal life. And we have believed and have known that thou art the Christ, the Son of God.* (Jn 6:69-70)

On the Feast of Saint *Ennemond*, November 16, 1651, I was recalling that You had appeared to him at Pré-aux-Clercs of this faubourg Saint Germain to assure him that You were pleased by his modest seclusion, leaving his companions to contemplate your mysteries. (773) While they were assembled together, this saint found his delight in You, who are the eternal Wisdom. Imitating him, I told You that I find my joy and my peace in You alone. By a most sublime suspension, You were pleased to elevate my spirit up to the Empyrean where You were like an adorable holocaust, continually burning in your love and delightful flames in the presence of your Father, the Holy Spirit, your most august Mother and all the saints. I perceived that the Seraphim were the closest to You in your condition as holocaust. They adored and marveled at the state to which love had reduced You. You were not prom-

JEANNE'S ORIGINAL DRAFT

ised to be relieved of this, because it was there that You found all your delight.

The Eternal Father is pleased that You are the Eternal Priest and immortal Victim in your glorious, loving life. All the saints are enraptured with admiration and joy at sight of the excess of this love that is impenetrable to all of them. Setting aside all that is not God, my soul entered the divinity through Him and in Him to see this wonderful marvel that your wisdom and incomprehensible goodness had invented so as to offer an eternal holocaust to your Heavenly Father. He took a holy, delectable delight in it, declaring to all the heavenly citizens: "Behold my Son in whom I am well pleased. Contemplate Him by adoring Him, and adore Him by contemplating Him." Have you ever thought about this sacred, loving invention of the powerful, gentle and eternal dilection, a sacred love that consumes Him and makes Him live in this state as an endless Victim of glory, for He is the Eternal Priest. (774) He desires to be an eternal Victim, in gratitude for the eternal, immense divinity and to maintain the cult of the most august, most devout religion that a loving God could have invented. For all eternity, men and angels will be delighted about this. As I have said, elevated in this sublime suspension, my soul exclaimed to itself: Lord, *Introibo in domum tuam in holocaustis: reddam tibi vota mea quæ distinxerunt labia mea. I will go into thy house with burnt offerings: I will pay thee my vows, which my lips have uttered.* (Ps 65:13-14a)

Divine Savior, You invited me to enter your heavenly city to visit You, You who are the adorable temple as well as the infinite holocaust. You called me so gently that I did not reply what the people of Bethlehem said to Samuel: *Pacificusne est ingressus tuus? Is thy coming hither peaceable?* (1 Kg 16:44) It was, because You gave me your peace by becoming mine, assuring me that You are a sacrifice of peace for me and a holocaust of infinite, immense love. I was to offer You to your Father through You, the Eternal Priest; I should make my vows to You in the presence of all your saints. My lips have distinctly pronounced them to You with ardent words that stemmed from the abundant source or furnace You had set in my heart. You deigned Yourself to maintain this sacred fire, personally fulfilling what You had commanded the priests. (775) Through your grace, I offer them to You in the

JEANNE'S ORIGINAL DRAFT

Militant Church and, by your glory, You offer them in the Triumphant one, for You asked me for them with ineffable goodness. You do so, even though I am most unworthy because of my sins and imperfections which You despise to the extent that You love your essence. I do indeed dare address You with my own lips, acknowledging my iniquities which trouble and afflict me because You are good. I offer You sacrifices: *Et locutum est os meum, in tribulatione mea. Holocausta medulata offeram tibi, cum incenso arietum; Offeram tibi boves cum hircis. And my mouth hath spoken, when I was in trouble. I will offer up to thee holocausts full of marrow, with burnt offerings of rams: I will offer to thee bullocks with goats.* (Ps 65:14b-15)

CHAPTER CXI

What I understood about Saint Andrew's faithful humility; Saint Xavier's zeal; Saint Nicolas' innocence and abstinence; Saint Ambrose's gentle, yet powerful eloquence.

On the Feast of Saint Andrew, You were pleased to elevate my spirit by a sublime light which enlightened me that Your Majesty had chosen Saint Andrew to be your first disciple and to elevate him to be with You. He left Saint John the Baptist as soon as He came to know You. (776) No sooner did he belong to You than he drew his own brother to You by telling him about the One whom he took to be the true Messias. Like another Moses, he was withdrawn from the waters to deliver the peoples still in servitude to the world, the flesh and the devil.

Saint John, the favorite disciple—who described his vocation to us, adding circumstances that show that he was the unnamed disciple–proclaimed Love through love, declaring that You told them: "What seek you?" Thus, informed

JEANNE'S ORIGINAL DRAFT

by this loving questioning and having discovered You, they asked You: "Where dwellest thou?" Impelled and pressed Love replied: "Come and see," and they stayed with Him that day: *Hæc dies quam fecit Dominus; exultemus, et lætemur in ea. This is the day which the Lord hath made: let us be glad and rejoice therein.* (Ps 117:24)

It is a day which You made, my Lord, enlightening these two disciples with your own light. They saw the burning bush aflame without being consumed; their feet were unshod of any other affection. They were delighted to see the Holy Land, yes, this Land of Promise seen only from afar by Abraham, all the Patriarchs and all the Prophets except for Zacharias and Saint John the Baptist. Saint Andrew spoke personally to your Majesty made Man, thereby receiving sacred oracles which he was to reveal to the whole world: *In omnem terram exivit sonus eorum, et in fines orbis terræ verba eorum. Their sound hath gone forth into all the earth: and their words unto the ends of the world.* (Ps 18:5) (777)

He said them to the one You had chosen to be high priest, that is to say, his brother Simon. Your choice in this did not offend Saint Andrew, although, by age and vocation, he was the elder and had been called before his brother. He conceived such perfect love for your sacrifice that he did not want to aspire to anything more than to sacrifice himself for You, for he sacrificed You daily as the Lamb of God offered for the salvation of the world. He wanted to be at the right hand of your Father, living by your glorious life, after all Christians had partaken, do partake and will partake of You in this Holy Sacrifice, adorable Sacrament and your pleasing Sacrifice. His joy was complete when he saw his altar that symbolized yours for him. He greeted it with the words of an impassioned lover: *O bona crux diu desiderata, et iam concupiscenti animo præparata: securus et gaudens venio ad te, ita et tu exultans suscipias me discipulum eius, qui pependit in te. O good Cross, so long desired and now set up for my longing soul! Confident and rejoicing, I come to you; exultingly receive me, a disciple of Him who hung upon you.* (Ant. II: Vespers, St. Andrew)

JEANNE'S ORIGINAL DRAFT

After being raised upon it, he did not want to descend. There he confounded Lucifer, for, through love of the Cross, he became like the Son of the Most High upon the mountain of the Testament, where he beheld the whole Trinity who came to him and suspended him in the air. There They made a sacred victory by which the angels adored, together with Saint Andrew, the Living One of the ages upon ages. (778) They allowed Saint Andrew to see the glory of their unique deity and the marvels of their adorable society. He saw You, Divine Lamb, seated at the right hand of your Father. He saw You full of glory and truth. He adored You in your marvelous light and, together with him, all your saints. As a sweet odor, You received him in a sacred holocaust. With David, he said to You: *Introibo in domum tuam in holocaustis; Reddam tibi vota mea quæ distinxerunt labia mea. I will go into thy house with burnt offerings: I will pay thee my vows, which my lips have uttered.* (Ps 65:13-14a) Sanctified by the Divine Sacrifice, his lips offered their vows with a holy eloquence upon seeing the most unique essence and distinction among the Three Divine supports. He entered your glory for all eternity.

On the Feast of the ardent and most fervent Apostle of the Indies, Saint Francis Xavier, I felt humiliated at the sight of my sins. Through justice, I was impelled and prompted to make honorable reparation to You, not only for myself in particular, but for all sinners. With a zeal inexplicable to me that You produced, I offered myself to receive the punishment and suffering for everyone even to enduring the pains of hell to make reparation for all to your Divine Majesty offended by all. This was on condition that, due to your indignation, I were not to be deprived of your grace or of loving You perfectly, adoring You in spirit and in truth.

Unable to leave me a long time in this pain, Your goodness inclined toward me (if I may so speak), allowing me to see a luminous ray by which I saw this word in blue letters: *Justus; the Just One.* (779) Thereby I understood that my sins and those of all men had been immersed in You, my Divine Savior, the Just One par excellence and the source of all justification. You made me recall what your favorite disciple had said: *Advocatum habemus apud Patrem, Jesum Christum Justum; et ipse est propitiatio pro peccatis*

AUTOBIOGRAPHY

JEANNE'S ORIGINAL DRAFT

nostris: non pro nostris autem tantum, sed etiam pro totius mundi. We have an advocate with the Father, Jesus Christ the just. And he is the propitiation for our sins: and not for ours only, but also for those of the whole world. (1 Jn 2 :1b-2)

I was filled with loving confidence that You had remitted and pardoned my sins which, with humble contrition, I had confessed, and that You had cleansed and purged me of all my iniquities. Elevated above itself by a divine attraction, my soul withdrew from the cleansing-place and was united to You by a powerful, gentle inclination. Instructing me about the glory that You had imparted to this great saint, You told me that You had made him like those who witnessed your Transfiguration. These he had imitated, baptizing your Indian people, not symbolically by the cloud, but by a true Baptism. Delivering them from the slavery of sin, You had them pass through these salutary waters to the very possession of grace and glory that is the Land of Promise. The Holy Spirit had hovered over these waters to warm them with his loving ardors. (780) You gave him the fervor of Elias. You made him your Apostle, as zealous as the Sons of Thunder, Saint James and Saint John, who remained a virgin. Like Saint Peter, he had converted thousands of people by his preaching. This great Saint Xavier was elevated by You to such a marvelous glory that it would enrapture us with admiration for your goodness were it known to us.

In 1651, on December 6th, the Feast of Saint Nicolas, Monsieur de Priesac came to visit me, together with the Bishop of Coserant whom I had become acquainted with in the year 1642. Since I retained my esteem for his knowledge and merit, the presence of this Prelate convinced me that I had not been mistaken. Upon seeing him, my soul was very satisfied. I understood: *Inveni David virum secundum cor meum. I have found David, a man according to my own heart.* (Acts 13:22)

You wanted me to pray for two things for him: that he might perfectly possess the kindness of Saint Nicolas and the eloquence of Saint Ambrose. I treated him as though You had already granted him what You wanted me to wish for him, together with the dignity as the Archbishop of Toulouse.

JEANNE'S ORIGINAL DRAFT

This is what I told Monsieur de Priesac who, as soon as he saw him, informed him about my wish for him. It intensified the latter's affection for me that he had had ever since 1642. He said: "I want to maintain this friendship to the extent that I am able to go to the Incarnate Word." After he left the parlor, I conversed with You and your saints. I wanted to imitate the humility of Saint Nicolas. (781) He considered himself to be a great sinner, although a number of people believe that he was sanctified in his mother's womb and that the history of his life declares that, from the time he was born, he fasted twice a week, feeding at his nurse's breast only once a day.

The great Archbishop of Milan enraptured my spirit as much by his devotion as by his eloquence. Could I not possess a most profound love for the one who, symbolically speaking, begot a father for us by converting our Father, Saint Augustine, and by giving him to us after his regeneration by baptism. We ought to sing the *Te Deum* with a universal devotion, for we are especially obligated to thank the Holy Spirit who dictated this marvelous hymn by a divine union for the glory of the Most Adorable Trinity, the Most Sacred Humanity, and the entire Church. As daughters of the latter, we should rejoice in the holiness of each of these saints, recalling that this holy, totally-ardent Prelate told us that we have a good Lord. Let us feel his goodness and look for it in simplicity of heart, loving our Divine Savior, who became our food. Not content with having created heaven and earth for us and of having given us blessings and the Sacraments, which are the channels of his graces, He chose to give us Himself, He who is the Giver and Author of our wonderful sacraments in the adorable Sacrament of the Eucharist. It is marvelous grace and divine thanksgiving. He is God of God, Light of light, the source of gentleness, through whom we draw abundantly from the fountains of his Wounds. (782) Thereby we are satisfied; indeed, inebriated, saying to Him in total ecstasy: "Lord, what generosity toward mankind: *Inebriabuntur ab ubertate domus tuæ, et torrente voluptatis tuæ potabis eos; quoniam apud te est fons vitæ, et in lumine tuo videbimus lumen. They shall be inebriated with the plenty of thy house: and thou shalt make them drink of the torrent of thy pleasure. For with thee is the fountain of life: and in thy light we shall see light.* (Ps 35:9-10)

JEANNE'S ORIGINAL DRAFT

CHAPTER CXII

My sufferings caused by a homilist who preached against the Immaculate Conception of the always Most Pure Virgin Mother of God Incarnate; and the illuminations I received.

In 1651, on the Feast of the Immaculate Conception of your all-beautiful and all-pure Mother, I was joyful until the moment that the preacher, who is indeed well-known, went up to our pulpit where he upset me by these words of the Canticle: *Nigra sum, sed formosa. I am black but beautiful.* (Cant 1:4) I foresaw that he was going to relegate to the darkness the one who had conceived and given birth to You, You who are the Light that illuminates every person who comes into this world. (783)

Dear Love, to what a state was my soul reduced! O, You knew this when his indiscreet lips uttered several times that your all-pure and radiant Mother was black, and, through an inexplicable contempt, he dwelt on these words: *that she had had original sin*! He told his listeners that it had been for a short time. O, my Heart, what a wound received through our ears! My pen cannot express my feelings when I heard this insult to the Mother of Beautiful Love. This tongue that cut with a double-edge (without being the sword which Saint John alludes to in his Apocalypse) pierced me totally. I felt as desolate as your lamenting Prophet explaining the anguish and affliction of the Daughter of Jerusalem and the Daughter of Sion. If all your creatures were reduced to one, they still could not say, by the pen of this Prophet in his Lamentations: *Cui comparabo te, vel cui assimilabo te, Filia Jerusalem? Cui exæquabo te, et consolabor te, Virgo, filia Sion?* (784) *Magna est enim velut mare contritio tua; Quis modebitur tui? Defuerunt præ lacrymis oculi mei. To what shall I compare thee, or to what shall I liken thee, O daughter of Jerusalem? To what shall I equal thee, that I may comfort*

JEANNE'S ORIGINAL DRAFT

thee, O virgin daughter of Sion? For great as the sea is thy destruction: Who shall heal thee? My eyes have failed from weeping. (Lam 2:13; 11a)

My daughters, what can I say! I am indescribably troubled: *Conturbata sunt viscera mea; My bowels are troubled.* (Lam 2:11b) My daughters came to see me when he had finished his sermon that was injurious to Her who never had, never could have and never will ever have any stain; who has been, who is, and who for all eternity will be the all-pure creature to receive the Divine Word. Unable to speak, they surrounded me, as had Job's friends, being reduced to affliction itself. When I could finally express my pain, my spirit was afflicted and supercharged beyond measure: *Quasi arena maris hæc gravior appareret; Unde et verba mea dolore sunt plena. As the sand of the sea this would appear heavier: therefore my words are full of sorrow.* (Job 6:3) These mournful words pierced me like arrows: *Quarum indignatio ebibit spiritum meum. The rage whereof drinketh up my spirit.* (Job 6:4b)

I said things to them that caused them the same sufferings as mine, asking all to undertake all kinds of pain to make reparation to our all-pure and all-august Princess, in general and in particular, for all the insults he had pronounced from our pulpit in our church. (785) We renewed the vows we had made a number of years even before our foundation to uphold by our very lives the honor of her Immaculate Conception. I recalled that this Virgin, on the same day in the year 1619, had promised me to have the Order of the Incarnate Word, her Son, be established if I wrote and loudly sustained the truth of this most Immaculate Conception. I can firmly attest that the Holy Spirit explained it to me and told me, from this day in 1619, that I would not come out of the rapture I had, with mouth open, in Saint Stephen's parish church in Roanne unless I promised to write about what He had informed me concerning it through pure locution, explaining this marvel to me through Holy Scripture that I did not have, nor had I read it at during that time.

Upon hearing your admirable Mother spoken about with such contempt, Monsieur de la Piardière felt the same pain that I did. He told me that I had to

JEANNE'S ORIGINAL DRAFT

complain about this preacher who had scandalized his listeners. He added that not everyone in his Order would have dared utter the least word to anyone in particular about what he had publicly preached. As for him, he felt obliged to make honorable reparation to your Blessed Mother. I addressed her with indescribable cries, tears and groans, presenting my breast and heart whereon to receive all those words like sharp arrows to cause me to die in reparation for the fault committed against my Blessed Mother: *Arcum suum tetendit, et paravit illum. Et in eo paravit vasa mortis, sagittas suas ardentibus effecit. He hath bent his bow, and made it ready. And in it he hath prepared the instruments of death: he hath made ready his arrows for them that burn.* (Ps 7:13b-14)

The next day, after having made my confession to him as I ordinarily did and acknowledged my pain at receiving Communion at his hand, for he came to offer our daily Mass, I told the Sister sacristan to convey to him the displeasure he had caused all of us by his sermon and that all the Sisters of the Order of the Incarnate Word had vowed to honor the Immaculate Conception of your most pure Mother. (787) When he heard this, he raised his voice and, with intolerable contempt for this vow and for the learned, ecclesiastical and religious persons who had been consulted before making it, he declared that all those priests were ignorant and that a number of the Fathers had opposed this idea. Fearing that he might affect the esteem that this daughter should have for the purity of the Immaculate Conception, I returned to the confessional grill. There I begged him not to turn my daughters away from the observance of their vows, that those who had directed them were learned, devout and holy religious men. He told me nothing less than he had to the daughter, with a scorn that I offered up for love of You. I replied that I was ready to die a thousand misfortunes to uphold the honor of the Immaculate Conception of your most Blessed Mother and that our devotion to this Immaculate Conception had obtained a promise from your august Mother to promote the establishment of the Order and that this great and holy Princess had influenced our Holy Father, Pope Urban VIII, in Rome to grant the first Bull on August 13th, 1631, in the church of Saint Mary Major. (788)

JEANNE'S ORIGINAL DRAFT

These realities made him snap and utter words that I will not repeat, nor should I record them here through modesty, a modesty that enabled me to endure all his wrath which astonished me greatly. I said to him: "Father, I would never have thought that your Reverence would become so angry, because our sacristan had convinced me some years ago that you strive to live in the continual presence of God, not saying any useless words. (789) This fact gave me special esteem for you, besides the respect I have for your religious profession and veneration for your character." If I am not mistaken, these words and others might have appeased anyone else except him. On the contrary, he presumed all the more on his authority, saying many things, that must be kept quiet through charity. With very piercing bitterness, he added that he would not come any more. Nonetheless, I held that he would change his mind and make us obligated to him. Should he not take the trouble to come administer the Sacraments to us, I would notify the Prior. I strove to appease him so as to win him over by your words, my Divine Savior, who are sweeter than honey, begging him to go up to the altar so as to offer You in Sacrifice, for You are the Lamb of God who eradicates and takes away the sins of the world. (790) I received You from his hands, as though doing so from your own, with so much tranquillity and peace because of this talk that I could say: *In pace in idipsum dormiam, et requiescam. In peace in the selfsame I will sleep, and I will rest.* (Ps 4:9)

Dear Love, You know that I continued with the sentiments of respect I possessed for him and that I banished from my thoughts all upsetting things that he had told me and my entire community in order not to diminish the regard I wanted to have for his virtue, except for the above-declared idea regarding my holy Queen. They well understood that the charity I exercised toward him and my simplicity like that of a dove led me to be influenced by the account the sacristan had made me of his mortification. The latter was resolved to converse with him. She did so, being also the portress, but unknown to me, discussing many topics with him. The result would be embarrassment for her and inexpressible suffering for the Order and for me. (791)

Dear Love, I do not know if I were Jonas asleep while so many pilots

JEANNE'S ORIGINAL DRAFT

were in torment caused by the storm that they wished to calm by throwing me out of the monastery, aspiring to take possession of all that your Providence had magnificently and angelically given in my own name to follow your intentions. Ignoring all the tempests aroused by this priest and a number of others, I lived in peace.

During the Octave of the Immaculate Conception of your most august Mother, I reflected on the exceptional favors which your Father, You and the Holy Spirit had given her. Interiorly apologizing to this wonderful Empress, the most beautiful among the beautiful, I said to her: "You are black, my holy Princess, in the eyes of those who cannot detect your whiteness. (792) They are owls who despise the light. You are black, my all-beautiful one, in the abysmal depths of the one who hides you in his darkness: *Posuit tenebras latibulum suum; in circuitu eius tabernaculum eius, tenebrosa aqua in nubibus æris. And he made darkness his covert, his pavilion round about him: dark waters in the clouds of the air.* (Ps 17:12)

Short-sighted eyes cannot gaze at You while the sun is at its brilliant zenith in You, its dazzling tabernacle, unless He sends clouds there to shade your light by marvelous shadows that conceal your splendors. By these, He makes you beautiful like Himself by participation. (793) The eagle, Saint John, could contemplate you, surrounded by the source of light. However, to be seen by those whose sight is poor, Eternal Wisdom has to dim and temper your brilliant rays, O most beautiful one, not only among women, but among all creatures. Come out, *Alma*, Virgin concealed by God's camouflage; come, follow the steps of your flocks. Remember, my holy Queen, that you are our Shepherdess and that we are your wayward sheep. Take us close to the living quarters of the shepherds. Lead us to the Three Divine Persons. Let the Father draw and attract the Son to us, for He is the great Shepherd of our souls. The Father's love for Him is the Holy Spirit. Let us enter these lodgings, the Wounds of our Divine Savior. They are the Wounds He received in the house of those whom He loved.

The convent to which this preacher claims he belongs does love you, even

JEANNE'S ORIGINAL DRAFT

though his tongue has wounded you. (794) I still receive and suffer from the after-effects that cruelly grieve me. But, Lady, I am drawn to die for your Immaculate Conception. At the moment of my death, I will say, if I can, for an entire eternity: *Tota pulchra es, et macula non est in te. Thou art all fair, and there is not a spot in thee.* (Cant 4:7)

In God's mind, before your conception, you were all-pure; totally pure in your conception at the moment when Saint Anne, your mother, conceived you, Daughter of Jerusalem. Once again, our august Queen is black within the soul of those who cannot see her brilliant whiteness, but she is beautiful in the eyes of those who see with their own eyes. They have been blinded by the order that the Prophet Isaias received from this God who is upon his high throne. (795) Their ears are offended. They judge according to their reasonings. They do not understand the mystery which the Oracle reveals to the little ones, in which your Son, O my August One, rejoices. He declared: *Confiteor tibi, Pater, Domine cœli et terræ, quia abscondisti hæc a sapientibus, et prudentibus, et revelasti ea parvulis. Ita Pater: quoniam sic fuit placitum ante te. I confess to thee, O Father, Lord of heaven and earth, because thou hast hid these things from the wise and prudent and hast revealed them to little ones. Yea, Father: for so hath it seemed good in thy sight.* (Matt 11:25b-26) (796)

JEANNE'S ORIGINAL DRAFT

CHAPTER CXXIII

Divine Wisdom allowed Saint Thomas' doubt to affirm and enlighten our faith. His love which is an abyss. The blessings I received on Christmas Day, the Feast of Saint John and the Feast of the Royal Prophet David.

On the Feast of Saint Thomas, while I was praying for my soul to be your Majesty's herald, I received many favors. You like to enlighten those who languish in darkness. You are the living Son who comes to us through the charity of your Divine Father. He is the Father of mercies and the God of all consolation. His providence governs all things and can draw forth good from whatever people consider to be evil. You had me understand that from St. Thomas' incredulity, your Church had been strengthened, because the Synagogue, that had not believed You to be a living God, strove to make You known as a deceitful Man after your death. They paid false witnesses to say that your disciples had gone to your tomb to remove You; misinforming the people by declaring that You had not risen. Your Wisdom, who knows and can do all things, allowed one of your disciples to doubt your Resurrection so that You might personally come to raise him up by showing him your Wounds. At sight of them, he believed in your humanized divinity and your divinized humanity. He believed You to be God and Man and acknowledged You to be his Lord and his God. Had You not made known your Resurrection by this disciple who had doubted it, many would still be in doubt. In vain would there be preaching about all your preceding miracles unless there were an authentic premise of your Resurrection. Saint Paul declares this loudly, referring to the General Resurrection: *Si autem Christus non resurrexit, inanis est ergo predicatio nostra, inanis est fides vestra. And if Christ be not risen again, then is our preaching vain: and your faith is also vain.* (1Cor 15:14) (797)

JEANNE'S ORIGINAL DRAFT

However, because You have risen for the glory of your Father and for our salvation, our religion is veritably accepted and acknowledged to be the true religion. Saint Thomas' error was a blessing for us. I dare call it a happy fault that has provided us with a moving demonstration of our Divine Redeemer. Many had contended that You indeed did appear in a scarred Body, but that, since no one had touched You, You were only a ghostly Body. Added to this, they maintained that You had enchanted the eyes of your disciples who were simple persons; that, when You forebade Magdalen to touch You, it sufficiently proved that the pain must be real.

Great Saint Thomas, I could well apply the following words of the Prophet to you: *Qui ascendit super occasum: Laudabile nomen eius. Who ascendeth upon the west. Praise ye his name.* (Ps 67:5; 99:4) You were elevated higher by your fall than before it; you have prevented us from falling into doubt about the most important mystery of the Incarnate Word. The First-Born has risen from among the dead: *Et omnia in ipso constant. Et ipse est caput corporis Ecclesiæ, qui est principium, primogenitus ex mortuis. And by him all things consist. And he is the head of the body, the Church: who is the beginning, the firstborn from the dead.* (Col 1:17b-18a)

Thomas, He is our Lord and our God. He is the One who loved you so much even though you would not be convinced of his Resurrection except through your eyes and hands. You would have crucified Him anew without this trial causing Him any suffering. Love thus transported you. (798) Your heart could not trust except through your senses; your spirit became immersed in your sorrow. You yourself were an abyss of disbelief, unable to be called to the knowledge of this mystery except through the abyss of love who, being the Author of the faith, had to produce it in you so as to transmit it to us. According to what the Prophet King declared, God's judgments are immense abysses. Thomas, I have always considered you to be an abyss wherein God concealed great mysteries. Never have I been able to blame you, together with the preachers who rant against you. Your Master gently reprimanded you to teach us to believe without desiring to see, because He would not

JEANNE'S ORIGINAL DRAFT

manifest Himself, as He did to you, to everyone who doubts his Resurrection. Such doubt would not stem from the abyss of love to which your poor heart was reduced.

Magdalen did not dry her tears at the fiery, brilliant sight of the angels who are blazing flames, even though they spoke angelically to her. Also, had Love not called her by name, she would have continued the flood, even though the Incarnate Word had told her as they did: *Mulier, quid ploras? quem quæris? Woman, why weepest thou? Whom seekest thou?* (Jn 20:15) She is looking for You, Love of loves. Where have You hidden? Why do You allow her to languish? Tell her just one word so that she will know that it is You; You will certainly then see if, more than any of your other creatures, she loves You alone. She loves only You. Call her by name, and she will know You by yours. Possessing You, she wants nothing else. (799) Thomas wanted to see You so as to possess You: *Abyssus abyssum invocat, in voce cataractarum tuarum. Deep calleth on deep, at the noise of thy flood-gates.* (Ps 41:8a)

You showered on him your love, which is a sea whose waters rose above his head and engulfed him. He exclaimed: *Omnia excelsa tua, et fluctus tui super me transierunt. All thy heights and thy billows have passed over me.* (Ps 41:8b) On the day of your holy birth, since it found no lodging for your Majesty in the inns, my soul could find no place to stop, even to maintain itself. Everything was monotonous and sterile for it until after Midnight Mass. Then, when it reported its misery to You, You took pity on it. Drawing me by your sweet favors, You had me understand: *Domini est terra, et plenitudo eius; orbis terrarum, et universi qui habitant in eo. The earth is the Lord's and the fulness thereof: the world and all they that dwell therein.* (Ps 23:1b)

My beloved, I am the Lord to whom belongs its entire circumference and plenitude. Do you not believe that my Sacred Humanity is the sublime land that corporeally encloses the fullness of the divinity? Also, within Me, I possess all the treasures of my Divine Father's knowledge and wisdom? I am

JEANNE'S ORIGINAL DRAFT

consubstantial with Him. Through the *communication of idioms* and based upon my divine support, this Sacred Humanity owns the attributes that appertain to the God-Man alone, who, without any infringement is elevated as high as the Father. The Father engenders Him in the splendor of holiness. At the moment that I am placed in this manger, I am radiant and resplendent in the heavens. (800)

Dear Love, I certainly experience the declaration of the Prophet King: *In terra deserta, et invia, et inaquosa, sic in sancto apparui tibi, ut viderem virtutem tuam et gloriam tuam. In a desert land, and where there is no way and no water: so in the sanctuary have I come before thee, to see thy power and thy glory.* (Ps 62:3) My soul was this land, this way without water and sterility itself, for I could not produce any good thought when your Goodness appeared to it with holy rejoicing, manifesting to it your glory. You are your Father's universal Heir, bearing his total word and power. You personally spoke to me; through You, the Father made the ages. You are the splendor of his glory, the figure of his substance and yet You deign to give Yourself to me with the ineffable delights of a torrential river that rejoices your city Bethlehem, the city of David, your father according to the flesh. This city belongs to You. You are the real Son of David and the true Son of God. You are the God-Man who was born in this city. You are the open fountain in David's house, by which my soul is cleansed of its iniquities and made fruitful. You are my temporal and eternal life. You are my grace and my glory. You are my peace and my Savior who was born for me in the city of David. (801) It is the great joy announced by your angels to the shepherds of Juda, that You personally proclaim with so much rejoicing: that through your mercy I possess the happiness of those called blessed by the same Prophet-King: *Beatus populus qui scit jubilationem. Blessed is the people that knoweth jubilation.* (Ps 88:16a)

Increated and Incarnate Word, my Love and my All, on the Feast of Saint John, your beloved disciple, You let me share in your dilection for him while You were passible on earth. This dilection is anticipated eternal life, although You communicate it only in passing to those who are still on life's journey. We

JEANNE'S ORIGINAL DRAFT

can say: *Domine in lumine vultus tui ambulabunt et in nomine tuo exultabunt tota die et in justitia exaltabuntur. Quoniam gloria virtutis eorum tu es: et in beneplacito tuo exaltabitur cornunostrum, quia Domini est assumptio nostra et sancti Israel regis nostri. They shall walk, O Lord, in the light of thy countenance and in thy name they shall rejoice all the day: and in thy justice they shall be exalted. For thou art the glory of their strength: and in thy good pleasure shall our horn be exalted. For our protection is of the Lord, and of our king the holy one of Israel.* (Ps 88:16b-19)

The light You impart to my spirit and body comes from the rays of your face that enable me to advance along your paths with a holy rejoicing that your Name produces through your justice. This sacred Name elevates your loved ones, because You are their glory and their power. You raise them up personally, associating them with your kingdom. You are their crown, as well as their King, and You are pleased to grant me all these graces. You elevate me above the clouds which You have chosen as your throne, and in these clouds You allow me to see your spouse, whom You glorify with a crown of clouds. (802) While I marveled at this wonder, You made me understand that You will show your goodness and greatness through the cloud. Through benignity, your goodness grants crowns; your greatness elevates your loved ones above the earth, distilling favors through them while the rays of your charity are pleased to grant your generous gifts. *Rorate, cæli, desuper et nubes pluant justum; Apariatur terra, et germinet Salvatorem. Drop down dew, ye heavens, from above: and let the clouds rain the just. Let the earth be opened and bud forth a Savior.* (Is 45:8)

On the Feast of David, the holy royal Prophet, as I was thanking You for all the graces given me by your bounty during the year, your loving Majesty allowed me to hear these words: *In finem dilexit eos; He loved them unto the end.* (Jn 13:1d) Through love You wanted to redouble your divine graces in me, raising me up by a sublime light. Thus, You allowed me to see a collar from which shone rays of light that flashed lightly. You told me that this collar represented your Blessed Mother who is the neck of the Triumphant Church

JEANNE'S ORIGINAL DRAFT

of which You are the Head. Through her, You grant glory to all your happy, heavenly citizens. Your benignity delighted in using me in the Militant Church, humbling me before your Majesty. Goodness prompted You to incline toward me. You told me that I was Ruth who gleaned after your holy harvesters whom You had commanded to scatter the ears of your graces along the path where You have me walk. (803) This was so that without embarrassment, I would become enriched by the outpourings of your inexhaustible treasures they leave at your command.

CHAPTER CXIV

The New Year's gifts that divine goodness granted me on the Feast of the Circumcision. The illuminations and graces I received on the Feast of the Kings and during its Octave.

On the Feast of the Circumcision in 1652, I was preparing to receive You as my New Year's gift. Your benignity drew me to You in the Crib. There I received You, my Lord, my God and my All, after which nothing else could please me. You were my Spouse of blood. The fountain was open in the city of David. Your linens, which were your clothes, were stained with the blood of your circumcision. You burned with love to have me as your spouse, offering Yourself to your Divine Father for it during the days of your flesh, not waiting for the evening of the Supper to be our nourishment nor the midday of Calvary on which to pay my ransom. You became a slave to free me. To be my food and drink, You did what means everything to me. (804) I understood the following words: *Et vestimentum mistum sanguine, erit in combustionem, et cibus ignis. Parvulus enim natus est nobis, et filius*

JEANNE'S ORIGINAL DRAFT

datus est nobis; et factus est principatus super humerum eius; et vocabitur nomen eius; admirabilis Consiliarius. And garment mingled with blood, shall be burnt and be fuel for the fire. FOR A CHILD IS BORN to us, and a son is given to us, and the government is upon his shoulder: and his name shall be called, Wonderful, Counsellor. (Is 9:5b-6)

I adored You, *Deus fortis, Pater futuri sæculi, Princeps pacis; God the Mighty, the Father of the world to come, the Prince of Peace,* (Is 9:6) knowing that through your Precious Blood You will grant peace to heaven and earth. You began to shed it during your circumcision. You arranged a new path in your flesh, passing under the veil of the law, You who are the Author and Light of the faith. You assumed the burden of the sinner without knowing sin; becoming similar to sinful flesh and tricked the devil who thought You were subject to sin. He found nothing of his there, nor himself in You. Thus, You could declare: "Sin and the prince of this world have been expelled, finding nothing in Me except their own ignominy: *Venit enim princeps mundi hujus, et in me non habet quidquam. For the prince of this world cometh: and in me he hath not any thing.* (Jn 14:30b) I will be the death of sin and the sting of hell: *Ero mors tua, o mors! Morsus tuus ero, inferne! O death, I will be thy death; O hell, I will be thy bite!*" (Os 13:14c)

On the Feast of Kings, I humbled myself before your Majesty, offering You all the mortifications of the saints together with your own, all their acts of charity with yours, all their prayers with yours. (805) Filled with confidence, my soul could not think of being rejected by your Crib where your kindness draws the most frightened souls through gentleness. *Dicite pusillanimis: Confortamini; Say to the fainthearted: Take courage, and fear not.* (Is 35:4) There your grace was shown to all mankind for their eternal salvation. I considered myself to be rich in your mercies which I prize above all your other works. I present them to You, as well as to your Father and to the Holy Spirit. Through Him, You offer Yourself as a holocaust, for You are the Lamb slain from the beginning of the world, and not for only one year. I contemplate and adore You, acknowledging You to be my Creator and my Savior and the male Child whom this wonderful Woman dressed with the sun

JEANNE'S ORIGINAL DRAFT

gave birth to in the stable. There You lie while the angels adore You, resplendent in the heavens: *Jacebat in præsepio et fulgebat in cælo. While lying in the manger, He shone brightly in heaven.*

Divine Word made Flesh, my King and my God, accept the perfect holocaust that You personally present. Solomon answered all the questions and solved all the riddles which the Queen of Sheba proposed to him. Since she was in the shadows, this sufficed to astound her, but not me, for I live in the light of the newborn Sun where everything is new, a God-Man, a Virgin Mother. Solomon had not witnessed this when he declared that there was nothing new under the sun. (806)

Jeremias said something referring to this marvelous novelty, calling the People of Israel by the name of a virgin who was somewhat vagabond: *Revertere, virgo Israel, revertere ad civitates istas. Usquequo delicis dissolveris, filia vaga? Quia creavit Dominus novum super terram: Femina circumdabit virum. Hæc dicit Dominus exercituum, Deus Israel. Return, O virgin of Israel, return to these thy cities. How long wilt thou be dissolute in deliciousness, O wandering daughter? For the Lord hath created a new thing upon the earth:* A WOMAN SHALL COMPASS A MAN. (Jer 31:21-23a)

Today's kings are more blessed and enlightened than was Solomon. They see Him who created the happiness of the heavens and those who contemplate it: *Beati oculi qui vident quæ vos videtis; Blessed are the eyes that see the things which you see.* (Lk 10:23) Our love intensifies, and we exclaim: *Dominus meus et Deus meus; My Lord and my God.* (Jn 20:28b)

The Queen of Sheba languished at seeing Solomon with such great wisdom, and I, I am not astonished at seeing You, for You are more than Solomon. (807) You are the sun of justice; You are the Man from the Orient; You are the Orient from on high who has come to visit us through the depths of your divine mercy. During the entire Octave, You treated me royally and

JEANNE'S ORIGINAL DRAFT

divinely, making my heart your censer. You wanted to be my King and my little Pontiff with a marvelous grace that my pen cannot record. My spirit admired it and still marvels at it: *Non est sermo in lingua mea; There is no speech in my tongue.* (Ps 138:4b) Tell it, dear Love, that angels and mankind acknowledge that You alone are eloquent and eloquence itself. Intending to advance your death, the Scribes and Pharisees sent ministers (stopped by your eloquence), saying to them: "We could not capture Him. His words enraptured us: *Nunquam sic locutus est homo, sicut hic homo. Never did man speak like this man.*" (Jn 7:46)

Guided by the Holy Spirit, the Church which You produced together with your Divine Father, represents or solemnizes your marvelous baptism where everything is amazing. The heavens open so as to see the most beautiful among the children of men, upon whom the Holy Spirit descends in the form of a dove: *Spiritu sancto misso de cælo, in quem desiderant angeli prospicere. The Holy Spirit being sent down from heaven, on whom the angels desire to look.* (1 Pt 1:12) They desired to see the plenitude that this Spirit poured out upon You; You are the Nazarean par excellence. *Descendit super eam omnis fons Spiritus Sancti. All the riches of the Holy Spirit descended upon her.* He is a fountain that covered You, filling You and enrapturing all the heavenly spirits who contemplate You. (808)

Adorable Ark in this sacred, protected, overshadowed, ornamented, crowned, engulfed river without being damaged, say to your Divine Father: *Omnia excelsa tua, et fluctus tui super me transierunt; All thy heights and thy billows have passed over me,* (Ps 41:8) without smothering me by their immensity. All this divine plenitude abides corporeally in Me. These are the desires of your Eternal Father who speaks from the heights of heaven. Referring to your attributes, your Father's delight, the Apostle who contemplated this during his rapture told us: *Hic est filius meus dilectus, in quo mihi bene complacui. This is my beloved Son, in whom I am well pleased.* (Matt 3:17)

Saint Jerome said: *Quia in ipso inhabitat, omnis plenitudino divinitatis*

JEANNE'S ORIGINAL DRAFT

corporaliter. Nequaquam per partes ut in ceteris sanctis. For in him dwelleth all the fulness of the Godhead corporeally. (Col 2:9) *You do not receive these divine favors in parts as did the saints.* You do not receive these divine favors in fragments as did all the saints. He communicates all his divine plenitude to You. Comprised in You are all the treasures of eternal and infinite knowledge and wisdom. (809)

CHAPTER CXV

The understandings by which the Holy Spirit illuminated me about my Savior's baptism. The nuptials of Saint Agnes. The joy I felt on the Feast of the Purification and the Feast of Saint Matthew. Monsieur de la Piardière received the ecclesiastical garb. [1652]

From the open heavens, the voice of the Divine Father declares before angels and mankind that the Savior is his Beloved Son and holy delight. The Holy Spirit, all love, hovers over Him. Who would not think that these prodigies occurred to have Him declared King of heaven and earth and from this moment on, command both angels and men to offer Him homage by adoring Him as their Lord and their God? *Non enim cogitationes meæ, cogitationes vestræ; Neque viæ vestræ, viæ meæ, dicit Dominus. Et statim Spiritus expulit eum in desertum. Et erat in deserto quadriginta diebus, et quadraginta noctibus: et tentabatur a satana: eratque cum bestiis. For my thoughts are not your thoughts: nor your ways my ways, saith the Lord.* (Is 55:8) *And immediately the Spirit drove him out into the desert. And he was in the desert forty days and forty nights, and was tempted by Satan. And he was with beasts.* (Mark 1:12-13)

JEANNE'S ORIGINAL DRAFT

Having hovered over this Nazarean, the Holy One of God, the Holy Spirit drove Him into the desert to fast for forty days and forty nights, to be tempted by Satan and to reflect in solitude upon the marvels that had occurred at the Jordan. He set Him there with the animals for forty days and forty nights. The angels do not appear until after this fast and these victories to act as table servers. Their angelic music is not heard; they do not utter a word. Although He was with an ox and an ass, they do not sing *Gloria* as they did at his birth in the stable. This is because there are no shepherds in the desert watching over their flocks to invite them to see this Lamb who is the Good Shepherd. (810) The desert was the testing-place of the Savior's fidelity toward his Father. It was the site where He fought the rebel spirits whom He had to conquer after having tested their strengths, ruses and malice. The desert is rough and terrifying; only Divine Love can alleviate it. The love that this Son of prayer possessed for his Father's glory and the salvation of mankind prompted Him to do everything possible and endure all things in the fullest reparation required by justice for offended Justice and to acquire happiness for us through these sufferings (although it was essentially due to Him).

The blessings given me by the Holy Spirit at the baptism of my Love, the favors I received during the forty days and nights in the stable, the Feasts of Saint Agnes, the Purification of Our Lady, Saint Agatha, Saint Dorothy and Saint Apolonia were moving demonstrations of happiness and joy. By this, one would think that I was the beloved daughter of the Divine Father who took his delight in me.

On the Feast of Saint Agnes, I assisted at the feast in honor of the Lamb, sharing in his happiness, *per modum transeuntis; in a transitory way. Beati qui ad cœnam nuptiarum Agni vocati sunt; Blessed are those called to the nuptial supper of the Lamb.*

On the Feast of the Purification, I thrilled with joy upon seeing the Light of the Gentiles and the glory of the people of Israel. I considered myself to be a Christ-bearer, as I called Saint Ignatius. (811) When I had received You in the Sacrament of Love, I told You, together with the fine, elderly Saint Simeon:

JEANNE'S ORIGINAL DRAFT

"*Nunc dimitis; Now You can dismiss.* The eyes of my spirit see You, my Divine Redeemer." I offered You Yourself for everything I might owe your Divine Father and in thanksgiving for the favors granted me by your wonderful Mother. With Saint Agatha, I wanted to honor You by my substance and to deliver all France, my country on earth, so as to serve You and voluntarily suffer there. Begging You to sanctify me, I cast myself into the fire of your ardent love, in imitation of Saint Apolonia. I reflected on a sacred river flowing from her holy jaws. I thought about her teeth, broken and wrenched out for the living faith, animated by love. I saw a fountain of blood that gushed forth even to eternal life. Her ivory teeth were more appropriate to make your throne lovelier than Solomon's; and her jaws overcame more enemies than Samson's did when he taunted the Philistines. They overcame the demons, vanquished tyrants and sensuality. This fountain, that seemed to me to be afire, relieved and inflamed me. Burning with the desire to drink from the torrent of the divine delights, I no longer thirsted for the water of earth. (812)

Did it not seem that I was in the joy of my Lord, even though I possessed so little fidelity in serving Him? However, since He wants us to pass through suffering, and He tests us by contradictions even from good persons, He allowed, even though He did not ordain, that certain individuals bearing the sacred mark, who are elevated in dignity, and others made commendable by devotion, called an assembly to correct matters that they thought needed attention. They expected thus to be making a great sacrifice in the eyes of your Divine Father whose designs they did not know. They wanted to demoralize and destroy the one You sustain by your mercies. You have destined her to show forth the height of your glory in her lowliness and your power in her weakness and that she has forgotten her own people and her father's house, together with all her relatives according to flesh and blood. She had been betrayed by daughters whom she had given birth to through your Spirit. What she did not want to know, despite the signs given her about the matter, she clearly understood that the demons were playing their games which almost always are tragedies.

Dear Love, Abel and Zacharias were overcome between the temple and

JEANNE'S ORIGINAL DRAFT

the altar. Others wanted to sacrifice them and prevent them from making a sacrifice or from receiving their daily Bread or perpetual Guest. In all this, they were prompted by the idea that they should have this dedication and zeal for sacred matters. (In my opinion), these considerations were as devout for them, as they were oppressive for the victims they immolated as best they could. (813) The victims could say to You: *Quoniam propter te mortificabimur tota die; æstimati sumus sicut oves occisiones. Because for thy sake we are killed all the day long: we are counted as sheep for the slaughter.* (Ps 43:22b)

You had me understand that the time determined by your wisdom was approaching, and You wanted to show the one You had chosen, who did not choose to place herself there: *Sed qui vocatur a Deo, tanquam Aaron; He that is called by God, as Aaron was* (Heb 5:4) to offer You the incense and sacrifice, despite the contradiction of many whom I will not name. I pray that Saint Jude may not hold them to their vow.

On the Feast of Saint Matthew, Monsieur de la Piardière received the investiture of the Church at the hands of Monsieur Vincent, distinguished Founder of the Mission, fundamental rock for many holy priests who shine in their Congregation and in many dioceses. This is your holy day, Incarnate Word, on which You command your angels to rejoice anew, showing them the rock that had been rejected and similarly reproved by those who lead edifying lives. This was so that You might personally show forth your marvels by your own power. You had me share in this joy, although others had planned crosses for me. You made me understand that the lot of the saints in light had come upon us, but that You would fulfill the promises You had made. I was not to be astounded about whatever people told me, that You would not allow the councils held against your plans for me to last. (814) I was to be your Zorobabel. Monsieur de la Piardière was your sacrificer as was Jesus, the high priest, son of Josedec. He remarked that, when he was in the refectory at the Saint Lazare, the reading was on the chapter from Zacharias that You had let me understand on the Feast of Saint Joachim, as is indicated above.

JEANNE'S ORIGINAL DRAFT

After this election, had all these persons been in prayer through zeal and common charity, your Spirit of love would have given each a tongue of fire with which to proclaim your marvels. Instead, on the contrary—I would dare say—a number of them saddened your Spirit, who sustained me in the joy of my divine Savior, that is, You, my Love and my All.

On the Sunday of the five barley loaves, You elevated me to your greatness, telling me that You are the God of breasts filled with delightful milk for me and that they were my towers and fortresses. When You saw me at prayer, contemplating your Blood flowing from your pores in the Garden of Olives, You let me understand that these streams falling to the earth were more delightful for me than milk, wine, nectar or ambrosia. (815) All your open pores were meant to serve me as channels by which to shed upon me the torrents of your delights. I had already received them in a marvelous way like delicacies on the lips of my desires.

Dear Love, was I not lovingly impelled to tell You: *Satis est, Domine; It is enough, Lord.* I am dying from delights, wishing to expire from desolation in memory of yours in the Garden of sorrow where an angel was sent to comfort You. When You were in agony, You combatted death and all hell, and You delighted me with life and the entire Paradise. Oh, Jesus, how wonderful You are! You mortify and vivify at the same time. You lead one to hell and back again. My soul is more in You whom it loves than in its body that it animates. In You, it suffers; take your delight in me.

The Prophet Isaias declared that You chose to be attached so as to free us and that through your distress we are healed and regain our health. Your Apostle stated that You had impoverished Yourself to enrich us, that You are the Pontiff who chose to assume our infirmities and were tempted in all kinds of things, exempting Yourself only from ignorance and sin, for You are holy and free from uncleanness, separated from sinners by your essential holiness. (816) Being substantial grace, You chose to taste death for all mankind to be its death and the sting of hell.

JEANNE'S ORIGINAL DRAFT

Divine Savior, You are the Victory that has conquered the world. You are the Author of faith, divine charity. You do not look for what makes You rejoice. It is to delight Me that You were afflicted. I do not want my ways and my desires, but yours that are thoughts of peace for me. You will be glorified in me when I no longer follow my own ways. I want to follow yours along the trail of your own Blood which is shed, not to demand vengeance as did that of Abel, but mercy from your Eternal Father and to purify our consciences from all sin. Also, it was therein to cleanse and whiten the nuptial robe with which You invest your spouses. Inviting me to approach this precious river, You urged me by sweet, loving words to plunge into it lovingly and confidently. There I would be clothed in your own vestment; that is, the royal purple. You told me that it was my royal ornament and that all my thoughts, represented by my hair, would enter your open pores by a mystical penetration so that I might experience what is declared in Canticles: *Caput tuum ut Carmelus; et comæ capitis tui sicut purpura regis vincta canalibus.* (817) *Thy head is like Carmel: and the hairs of thy head as the purple of the kin bound in the channels.* (Cant 7:5)

This Precious Blood was my cleansing-place and my fountain of grace at which I drank deep drafts, even to becoming inebriated as your very dearest one. Through your utter bounty that delights in its abundant communications, You are my true, useful and delightful happiness, and I am your beloved. You repeated these words: *Quam pulchra es, et quam decora, charissima, in deliciis. How beautiful art thou, and how comely, my dearest in delights!* (Cant 7:6)

My daughter, the water and blood I shed for you make you acceptable in my eyes: cleansed, ornamented and covered with this Precious Blood. Are you not clothed in Jesus, your Spouse of blood, that your daughters exteriorly wear? Is He holier when you receive Him from visible hands because He is seen by bodily eyes? The One I give you, invisible to mortals, is seen and admired by immortal spirits. In the eyes of the divinity who had invested him in the tabernacle of his own understandings and covered with the cloud to conceal him from men, Moses was as acceptable as Aaron who was conse-

JEANNE'S ORIGINAL DRAFT

crated and invested with priestly vestments at the hands of Moses who did not have them nor even a miter crafted by mortals. The rays from his face were more august and brilliant. (818) Was he not a priest in the presence of God who had chosen him and of the angels who accompanied him in the Taber- nacle? Did not David acknowledge this when he said: *Moyses et Aaron in sacerdotibus eius. Moses and Aaron among his priests.* (Ps 98:6)

Passion Sunday was not less delightful to me. I almost feared that the delights I experienced at sight of your sufferings might be the illusions of the one who often attempts to transform himself into an angel of light except that I knew that, through them, You have given birth to our happiness. Also, your Passion is a subject of joy to your loved ones, since You will no longer die. Instead, You have conquered death by causing sin to die. As the risen God, You live and will live forever. The soul that loves You and is loved by You should not become afflicted even when You appear to it as the slain Lamb with the marks and stigmata of your Passion. They are signs of your jubilation and the trophies of your glory. They are fountains of rejoicing from which the Evangelical Prophet invites us to drink with joy and delight: *Haurietis aquas in gaudio de fontibus salvatoris. Et dicetis in die illa: Confitemini Domino, et invocate nomen eius; Notas facite in populis ad inventiones eius, Mementote quoniam excelsum est nomen eius.* (819) *Cantate Domino, quoniam magnifice fecit; Annunciate hoc in universa terra. Exulta et lauda, habitatio Sion, Quia magnus in medio tui Sanctus Israel. You shall draw waters with joy out of the savior's fountains. And you shall say in that day: Praise ye the Lord, and call upon his name. Make his works known among the people: remember that his name is high. Sing ye to the Lord, for he hath done great things: shew this forth in all the earth. Rejoice, and praise, O thou habitation of Sion: for great is he that is in the midst of thee, the Holy One of Israel.* (Is 12:3-6)

Who among mortals could invent these marvels! Who would not feel strong against any opposition made by a number of persons to prevent Mon- sieur de la Piardière from receiving sacred Orders, especially that of the priesthood which they thought would prompt him to resolve to serve You in

JEANNE'S ORIGINAL DRAFT

your house, Divine Incarnate Word He offered his First Mass there and the rest for your glory and the sanctification of your spouses, abandoned by all who could have assisted them. Added to this was that the one You had chosen to be the foundress did not measure up to their ideas (for men abound therein). They thought up ways to repel, rebuff and remove her under the guise of God's glory by bringing down the one You had made as she is. Their plans seemed to be as judicious as their charitable discourses so as ardently to motivate the most fervent pastors, pious prelates and a number of seculars who seemed zealous; all this to prevent imaginary disorders. The preacher for the Feast of the Conception (the last one, as I have said) (820) had ever since then striven to turn away from me whomever he could persuade so as to elevate the one he secretly visited in the parlor. She could not know his purpose, for he came daily to offer Holy Mass for us, and I gave him a hundred *ecus* [five-franc pieces] annually.

Dear Love, You continued your favors during the time that these persons engaged in negative, harmful discourses about your beloved. They thought that this proceeded from holy zeal. It served as the devotional topic during such a holy time of the year. Certain devout persons came to inform me that a resolution had been taken to have the last Order refused to Monsieur de la Piardière. Also, the instigators wanted to speak to the Bishop of Perigueux (who had conferred the other Orders upon him) to propose that he should oblige him to choose a parish or a Congregation of priests or missionaries and not dedicate himself to that of your daughters. You had called him for this purpose a number of years before and had let me know this so that I might accordingly inform him, without this knowledge urging me to force him. He had personally requested me to beg You to advance the time, but I awaited your hour in hope and silence, O my Divine Redeemer. Whoever believes does not act in haste. (821)

JEANNE'S ORIGINAL DRAFT

CHAPTER CXVI

The ineffable graces I received on the Feast of Saint Joseph. Monsieur de la Piardière offered his First Mass in our church in the Saint Germain suburb.

When the morning You had arranged for me arrived, your goodness awakened me to invite me to an ineffable joy. You sent me a heavenly spirit to tell me three times in a majestically gentle, delightful tone: *Ecce virgo concipiet, et pariet; Behold a virgin shall conceive and bear.* (Is 7:14c) These words astounded me the first and second times, for I feared that the spirit who tries to imitate, could be using the words of Holy Scripture which You have told me would be the code by which I would hear You. However, at the third time, I felt assured that it was a good spirit that uttered these marvelous words with admiration for your goodness toward and within me. You have made me the mother of a new priest to whom, for You, I had spiritually and virginally conceived and given birth. It was not in the way that the incomparable Virgin conceived and gave birth to You, but also in a most spiritual, most pure way. The purity he received is a hidden manna obtained for him from your goodness by the virgin, evangelical Apostle. (822) He had possessed this purity ever since the feast of this saint in 1646. (As for me, You had gratified me with it from the beginning on a feast of your Circumcision in a way that I cannot express).

Elevated by your spirit in a sublime contemplation, I said to You: Since You assure me of your grace: *Ecce ancilla Domini, fiat mihi secundum verbum tuum; Behold the handmaid of the Lord; be it done to me according to thy word.* (Lk 1:38) It is through your goodness that I am virginally the mother of a priest. You let me know that Monsieur de la Piardière would not have been called to the priesthood had he not been my

JEANNE'S ORIGINAL DRAFT

spiritual son and had your wisdom not led me to Paris so as there to establish a house of your Order. *Behold the handmaid of the Lord; be it done to me according to thy word.* Great Saint Joseph, you granted me so many favors during the First Mass of the one who had selected your feast, that they are indescribable. The rain intensified my attention and the repose allowed me during this delightful Mass. I enjoyed a peace and joy that surpassed all feeling. I invited all the heavenly court to descend with their Pontiff and King, who desired to be present upon this altar of grace during the time that the lips, tongue and intention of this new priest, produced the adorable Body and Blood. (823)

Lord, my Love and my All, could I possibly describe the marvel that enraptured my spirit! It is You, divine Savior, produced upon your altar. In a small chapel, I asked You for all heaven with its glory. It was an immense reduction to one point. You produced an ocean of delight which You arrested at the presence of a grain of sand that said to You: Lord: *Usque huc venies, et non procedes amplius, et hic confringes tumentes fluctus tuos. Hitherto thou shalt come, and shalt go no further. And here thou shalt break thy swelling waves.* (Job 38:11)

O inexplicable goodness, You heard my prayer, not allowing me to be carried away by either an assault nor an ecstasy. Your wisdom disposes of all things gently and powerfully, leading me after Mass to the parlor. I considered myself to be like Aaron's child, who was nourished with holy food, because the Communion was still recent that I had received at the hands of our new priest and son, and You could well preserve this heavenly Bread within my breast without my natural heat consuming it all. You wanted the manna in the Ark, that in the desert lasted only a few days, kept in a crock. I can state that on the eve and the feast of the Sabbath, nothing is impossible to You. You delight in being the light in the little world that loves You, while the day of your goodness enlightens it with your rays that are as ardent as they are brilliant. Blessed may You be with all benedictions. (824) Also, You are the blessed Son of God.

JEANNE'S ORIGINAL DRAFT

CHAPTER CXVII

The great qualities of Saint Joachim and Saint Anne who, after Jesus and Mary, are the glory of the People of Israel through whom they have supereminently honored God.

The next day, the Feast of Saint Joachim, your wonderful Mother's blessed father, I prayed to him to offer this adorable sacrament to your Divine Father, honoring Him with his own substance which he had given his daughter when he begot her. The entire Trinity showed that he had been favored with more blessings than You had given Moses. You had commanded the latter to die with these holy kisses to reward the delightful services he had rendered You, after resuming them following the two blows he gave the rock contrary to your order which was that he should speak, and it would yield its waters. He saw the Promised Land, but he did not enter there because he had not glorified You in the waters of contradiction.

The favor granted Saint Joachim and Saint Anne, who glorified You, is incomparable. (825) They have produced the ocean of graces, the sublime land, the blessed land, the land that You chose to base upon your hypostasis. It was a land promised by all the Prophets, a priestly land exempt from all tribute, from all original and actual sin. By divine dispensation, Saint Joachim and Saint Anne were elevated in a suspension or most marvelous contemplation. The whole Trinity ordained that their union should produce Mary's most blessed body, which was suddenly organized, and in it, It infused the soul that informed it. This blessed body and soul were not subject to sin or corruption. Neither could demons approach them any more than sin: *Nec dabis sanctum tuum videre corruptionem; Nor wilt thou give thy holy one to see corruption.* (Ps 15:10b) From this holy body would be formed the one for the Holy One of God, the Word who would thereby become incarnate. At the moment

JEANNE'S ORIGINAL DRAFT

that this Virgin was conceived, she lived and progressed along the paths of life. She was filled with rejoicing by the face and eyes of God, who destined her to be the Queen, invested with all virtue, seated at his right hand forever. At the moment of her Conception, she possessed the happiness of seeing the Unity of the essence and the Trinity of Persons, as well as what You let me understand on the last Feast of her Immaculate Conception which I will explain in its due place.

As I admired Saint Joachim's greatness, my soul became elevated in a most profound contemplation, repeating a number of times: (827)[1] *Tu autem in sancto habitas, laus Israel. But thou dwellest in the holy place, the praise of Israel.* (Ps 21:4) Since Mary's body came from the substance of her father, Saint Joachim; and that of the Incarnate Word from the substance of Mary, his true Mother; Saint Joachim dwells in the source of holiness in the bosom of the Father in Jesus Christ. This dwelling is divine; it is the praise of Israel and the greatness of his glory. I maintain the same thing about Saint Anne. Both honored God with their own substance, perfectly fulfilling the counsel of the Holy Spirit, recorded in the third proverb: *Honora Dominum de tua substantia; Honor the Lord with thy substance.* (Prov 3:9) The Virgin by herself honors God more than all other creatures together. Saint Joachim and Saint Anne gave God everything they possessed by giving of themselves. The gifts and offerings they made to the Temple, their alms to the poor, and the third part which they used to nourish and maintain themselves and their family, all belonged to God by a marvelous relationship.

They become the temple of God. They are the poor of heart par excellence. Jesus Christ, the Poor One through anthonomacy, is their Grandson whom their daughter has conceived, carried, given birth to and nurtured. He has declared that Mary, the sister of Lazarus, did a good deed by preparing Him for his tomb, that the world would never lack having the poor nor

---

[1]Note: The Manuscript skips from page 825 to 827, and from 824 to 829.

JEANNE'S ORIGINAL DRAFT

poverty. The latter refers to the ordinary poor, but He would not always be there, for He would ascend into heaven to dwell. This declaration was not meant for Saint Joachim or Saint Anne. Wherever He may be, He will always belong to them and they to Him. (829) He is their temple. He is their Poor One. He is they, and they are He. He is their dearest, adorable Son, and they are his dearest, kindest relatives through their only offspring, who is Mary of whom He was born through the operation of the Holy Spirit who took from her the substance she had received from Saint Joachim and Saint Anne so as to inform a Body for the Eternal Word become incarnate within her.

Divine Savior, what a maze I have placed myself in by speaking of your human generation, while I began my narration centered on Saint Joachim and Saint Anne, so as not to go out on a tangent! If, after Abraham, I consider him to be like Saint Matthew, Joachim—that means preparation for the Lord— entails everything, for this most pure matter is worthy to receive the form of God, who bases it on his own support at the moment of the Incarnation, being able to be equal to his Divine Father without any infringement, assuming and possessing by every right the same glory: *Qui cum in forma Dei esset, non rapinam arbitratus est esse se æqualem Deo. Who being in the form of God, thought it not robbery to be equal with God.* (Phil 2:6) He emptied Himself, taking the form of a Servant: *In similitudinem hominum factus, et habitu inventus ut homo. Being made in the likeness of men, and in habit found as a man.* (Phil 2:7b-11)

He made Himself like the most humble Saint Joachim whom Holy Scripture never names, as though he did not exist, so much had he concealed and engulfed himself in his nothingness with his wife, Saint Anne. (830) It is a great mystery that had been hidden for ages in God, because during the final times, He wanted it to be declared to the saints for them to proclaim to and notify both earthly and heavenly principalities and powers the inexhaustible riches of Jesus Christ according to the flesh, according to his human birth. Thereby He: *Humiliavit semetipsum factus obediens usque ad mortem, mortem autem crucis. Propter quod Deus exaltavit illum, et donavit illi nomen, quod est super omne nomen: ut in nomine Jesu omne genu flectatur cælestium,*

JEANNE'S ORIGINAL DRAFT

terrestrium et infernorum et omnis lingua confiteatur, quia Dominus Jesus Christus in gloria est Dei Patris. He humbled himself, becoming obedient unto death, even to the death of the cross. For which cause, God also hath exalted him and hath given him a name which is above all names: That in the name of Jesus every knee should bow, of those that are in heaven, on earth, and under the earth. And that every tongue should confess that the Lord Jesus Christ is in the glory of God the Father. (Phil 2:8-11)

He elevated Saint Joachim and Saint Anne to sublime thrones near their august daughter. Their humility and relationship to Jesus and Mary merited this elevation. Saint Joseph honors them with a reverence that I cannot describe, treating them as Raguel and his wife recommended to their daughter, Sara: *Monentes eam honorare soceros. Admonishing her to honor her father and mother-in-law.* (Tob 10:13a) An irreproachable just man, Saint Joseph knew the inclinations of the Incarnate Word whom he nurtured and brought up on earth. He loved Saint Joachim and Saint Anne with the same love that this divine Child loved them, honoring them in imitation of his spouse, their daughter, with more respect and tenderness than Solomon had for Bathsheba, his mother. (831)

Could any request have been refused them by this worthy Mother of God, their wonderful daughter who is all-powerful with the eternal Father, all-powerful with the Son of the Most High, all-ardent with the Most Holy Spirit, most holy love and one unique God with Them, offering the Sacrifice of the Altar to this holy Joachim! I recalled that he had appeared to me a number of years before, bearing or holding Jesus Christ on the Cross in the way artists represent Him being carried by his Eternal Father. I understood that this vision was but a faint representation of the part Saint Joachim took in You, my sweet Crucified Jesus, and that he would have been the most afflicted of all mankind had he been on Calvary at the death of his Grandson, present when his only daughter, your Mother, received in her soul the blow of the lance that opened your side. At your death, You no longer felt any pain, but your Mother was transpierced because of it. Saint Joachim would have suffered a number of

JEANNE'S ORIGINAL DRAFT

deaths in this case: yours and that of his daughter whom love allowed to live after your death, because her body and soul were transpierced. Her life was an unparalleled miracle. Saint Ignatius called her a heavenly prodigy, declaring something about this miraculous Mother who remained firm beneath the Cross, when all other creatures were shaken, and the Eternal Father had abandoned his own Son. (832) Just before expiring, the latter complained personally about this with the complaint of a Son who was keenly aware of his Blessed Mother and who did not surprise her at all; miracle upon miracle.

Saint Joachim could not have suffered so many deaths when he left Limbo unless he had been glorious. In the tomb, he would have fainted upon seeing your body torn, wounded and bruised from head to toe, resembling that of a leper. His glory spared him his reactions, but not from embracing You with admiration, adoration and tenderness, nor considering your sorrows which, in his glorious state, he could not keenly feel. Instead, they were marvelous by promoting his own glory because You are his Grandson.

Great saint, forgive me if I so poorly explain what I was shown during sublime and profound elevations. I was an eagle elevated up to the rays of the sun. Now, I am certainly the same eagle, but I have descended to Limbo, where the Body is which the powers of darkness have so disfigured that He is a hidden God: *Non est species ei, neque decor. There is no beauty in him, nor comeliness.* (Is 53:2) (833) All who beheld Him in this pitiful condition exclaimed: *Vidimos eum, et non erat aspectus, et desideravimus eum; despectum, et novissimum virorum, virum dolorum, et scientem infirmitatem; et quasi absconditus vultus eius et despectus. We have seen him and there was no sightliness, that we should be desirous of him: Despised and the most abject of men, a man of sorrows and acquainted with infirmity: and his look was as it were hidden and despised.* (Is 53:2c-3)

In this Divine Son and his most admirable Mother, your only daughter, you have suffered what no one else has endured. Jesus is without equal; Mary is incomparable. I must draw the curtain so as not to depict on paper the vision

JEANNE'S ORIGINAL DRAFT

I was shown and that was exposed to my spirit that had not been deprived of its body, but had experienced this illumination. He informs spirits in the way the angels communicate their understanding and illuminations to one another. They admired the excellence of Saint Joachim who is a great sacrament (for the ages) hidden in God, who created him so as one day to produce the first among his pure creatures, the Mother of the beginning of his ways, the Incarnate Word. From all eternity, He is the splendor of his divine Father's glory for eternal generation. In time, He was the image of his marvelous Mother, the most beautiful among the children of men.

Saint Joachim and Saint Anne are the abridgment of God's marvels. (834) In them, God has chosen a Daughter, a Mother and a Spouse. Therefore, I may declare: *Dominator Domine ex omni silva terræ et ex omnibus arboribus eius eligisti vineam unicam: et ex omnis terræ orbis elegisti tibi foveam unam, et ex omnibus floribus orbis elegisti lilium unum: et ex omnibus abyssis maris repleti tibi rivum unum, et ex omnibus ædificatis civitatibus sanctificasti tibimetipsi Sion, et ex omnibus creatis volatilibus nominasti columbam unam, et ex omnibus plasmatis pecoribus providisti ovem unam. O Lord, owner of all the forests from whose trees You chose one only vine. From the entire globe of the world, You chose for Yourself one only cave, and from all the flowers of the universe, You selected one only lily. From all the abysses that fill the oceans, You chose one only river, and from all the cities built, You sanctified Sion for Yourself. From among all the birds created, You named only one dove, and from all the herds, You prepared and provided for Yourself one only sheep!*

Lord, Universal Ruler of all creatures, in Saint Joachim, You have chosen a vine from among all and above all from which your Son is the grape for all the world. Saint Joachim and Saint Anne have been a deep moat. From their most humble Daughter was born the One who made Himself the last among men and who humbled Himself. From among the flowers, a lily; from all the seas, an abyss, a stream that You have corporeally filled with the plenitude of your divinity. From their Daughter, You built your city that You have sanctified through your Son, divine holiness. (835) He is one God with You and the

JEANNE'S ORIGINAL DRAFT

Holy Spirit, who in Her made his unique dove and marvelous ewe of whom You were born, most holy Lamb who takes away the sins of the world. Joachim was with his shepherds when he received the good news of having been chosen to beget your holy Mother. In her garden, Saint Anne learned that she would produce the flower of Jesse upon whom the Holy Spirit would repose. Whoever possesses God, possesses everything. By the term "everything", no exception is allowed. All the other Patriarchs have greeted and seen from afar the promise of the Messias, but Saint Joachim and Saint Anne have brought into the world the Flesh of his flesh; his beginning according to his human nature on the day of his power. The (Holy Spirit) overshadowed her when she conceived the Orient Sun, the God-Man, You Yourself, my Love and my All. While I marveled at the great qualities of this saint manifested by your own, You made me understand: "My daughter, you will be a sharer, for you are my spouse. He is your father, and Saint Anne, your mother: *Adhuc unum modicum est, et ego commovebo cælum, et terram, et mare, et aridam. Et movebo omnes gentes. Yet one little while, and I will move the heaven and the earth and the sea and the dry land. And I will move all nations.* (Hag 2:7c-8)

"As for Me, I, who am the desired One of all the nations, will come to establish the houses that I have told you must be established for my glory. I will make them magnificent. Trust in Me." (836)

JEANNE'S ORIGINAL DRAFT

CHAPTER CXVIII

God wanted to be everything to me as He was for Saint Benedict, allowing me to see the world under his feet. The Savior's delightful favors to me on Palm Sunday. Saint John's excess of love at the Last Supper. On Good Friday, I was on Calvary, and the favors I received on Easter Sunday.

On the Feast of Saint Benedict 1652, through your goodness my heart became your censer for which You were both fire and incense. What is even more marvelous, You wanted to be the Pontiff to incense the surrounding area and the *Sancta Sanctorum; the Holy of Holies*, in my body and spirit. You made them your exterior and interior temple, your palace, your Louvre, your city and your world. Therein You are the light, operating as long as the day of your splendors endures, showing me that You had been all things to Saint Benedict. Furthermore, You had placed the world under his feet by his spurning anything there that is not You. Later, You had me understand these words: *Videntis Creatorem angusta est omnis creatura. It is the anguish of every creature that sees the Creator.*

I felt the same as this great Patriarch, recalling that, beginning in the year 1617, You had shown me, as You did him that the world and its vanities are but one point. (837) You lodged me within Yourself, You who are immense, deigning to recreate, guide and govern me as a little child. I saw You as my God, Triune and One, in a sublime and intellectual perception which did not put me in ecstasy, but strengthened my body and elevated my spirit.

On Palm Sunday, You came to me as to the daughter of Sion, full of gentleness. You filled me with your loving profusions while I did my utmost to speak about You with the two Sisters in the little Bethany of your monastery, Divine and Royal Spouse. I wanted the hearts of all mankind to be filled with the perfume of Mary, your dear beloved. I would pour this upon your sacred

JEANNE'S ORIGINAL DRAFT

head and feet. I would shatter them as this loved one did her alabaster container, so that the perfume thereof might spread over the entire earth where your Gospel has been, is and will be proclaimed for your glory and the salvation of all.

On Holy Thursday, You let me experience this infinite love with which You love your own who are in the world. You let me repose upon your breast, even though I was far from the perfections of Saint John who, You told me, was a replica of You. (838) This was through the omnipotence of your adorable transubstantiation, fulfilling in him these loving, holy words: "Whoever eats my flesh and drinks my blood abides in Me, and I in him." You assured me that You had preserved in this saint the manna that your Father, the Holy Spirit and You had given mankind on the evening of the Last Supper. Also, this saint was the marvelous Ark of the Covenant wherein, with your divine and sacred hands, You placed the Living Bread that has come down from heaven: *Panis enim Dei est, qui de cælo descendit, et dat vitam mundo. For the bread of God is that which cometh down from heaven and giveth life to the world.* (Jn 6:33)

By giving him your own life, changing him into You, You made him the Son of your Mother through the power of your word which You want to remain stable. You said to me: "If the manna was preserved for a number of years through the divine power, which was only the figure of this supersubstantial Bread, with greater reason have I desired to preserve this true Manna from the time of the evening when I gave it to my Apostles. (839)

"Heaven and earth were shaken and troubled, but my word remains firm in Saint John. My gift was without regret. I did not want his natural warmth to use up all the Species. The fire in the furnace was not effective, for the three Hebrews were preserved, without even their clothes becoming blackened: *Et odor ignis non transisset per eos; Nor the smell of the fire had passed on them,* (Dan 3:94g) because my omnipotence ordained it so.

"If all-powerful Love wanted to perform a miracle within my favorite and

JEANNE'S ORIGINAL DRAFT

made my favorite the son of the fruitful Virgin, can I not do so? And who would contradict my desires when they are absolute? When my Angel Gabriel announced my Incarnation to my Mother, assuring her of this miraculous marvel and of the fruitfulness of her sterile cousin Elizabeth, he told her: *Quia non erit impossibile apud Deum omne verbum. Because no word shall be impossible with God.* (Lk 1:37)

"My daughter, when, in astonishment, my angels saw what I wrought in this favorite one, they could declare in heaven what the Church says on earth: *Stupendum supra omnia miraculum, domum transcendens omnem plenitudinem, spiritualis dulcedo in propria fonte degustata. The spiritual sweetness tasted in its own source, is a miracle excelling all others, a gift transcending all fullness.*

"This gracious, beloved disciple received the gift and was filled with the divine Humanity. From the fountain itself, he drank and received in himself the source and the very fountain. (840) Reclining upon my breast, he was changed into Me by the power of this bread and drink. He ascended up to the very mountain of God and became God in a miraculous way. By virtue of the Bread of Life, he remained standing on Mount Calvary without fearing death that struggled against life and numbered Me among its own. I had submitted to its empire for a while, then subjected it to mine forever. I knew very well that I would be its death and the sting of hell: *Ero mors tua, o mors! Morsus tuus ero, inferne! O death, I will be thy death; O hell, I will be thy bite.* (Hos 13:14c)

"This favorite disciple always remained in the light that shone through him, while the whole earth was covered by darkness. He was the true Israelite who enjoyed heavenly light. Also, did he not speak about the eclipse that the other Evangelists remarked: *Et tenebræ factæ sunt in universa terra; There was darkness over the whole earth* (Matt 27:45b) from the hour of Sext until that of None: *Et obscuratus est sol; And the sun was darkened.* (Lk 23:45) In him, I was the abridgment of the miracles of all law: the law of nature, the written law and the law of grace. At the Last Supper, I made him

JEANNE'S ORIGINAL DRAFT

the miracle of love. This marvel occurred upon my own breast, when I consecrated him with greater magnificence than Moses did when he consecrated Aaron. I, who am the Creator, the Redeemer, the Glorifier and God of heaven and earth, I served as his ornament, nourishment and everything. (841)

"Since my Father placed all things at my disposal, I subjected Myself to that of Saint John. Love, which leaves the soul it animates to be in the one it loves, enabled me to enter this precious person who preserved in himself what I was going to leave behind and give for the salvation of mankind: my own life and Precious Blood. He fell asleep amid the lot of the saints in the Holy of Holies. I showed the angels the marvelous high priest like a host of love consumed and preserved by my flames, maintaining my life and all my marvels in him. Upon Calvary, I declared him to be my Mother's son after having declared him to be my brother and, as I have told you, I had borne her son upon my breast.

"The words I uttered upon the Cross declared him to be the son of this Virgin who would lose Me through death. I addressed my Mother: *Cum vidisset ergo Jesus matrem, et discipulum stantem, quem diligebat, dici matri suæ: Mulier, ecce filius tuus. Deinde dici discipulo: Ecce mater tua. When Jesus therefore had seen his mother and the disciple standing whom he loved, he saith to his mother: Woman, behold thy son. After that, he saith to the disciple: Behold thy mother.* (Jn 19:26-27a) I did not say: 'I make you,' but, 'Behold your son' and to John, 'Behold your Mother.' This had occurred through my word at the Supper on the preceding evening."

Madame, allow me to address You, saying that your Son did not forget you when He made his will and gave Himself to his Apostles. (842) Samuel reserved the shoulder for the king whom he was to consecrate. While preparing his banquet and testament of love, Jesus remained impassible and immortal. Through his mystical death, He foresaw his physical death, through this real sacrifice and true sacrament. He concealed Himself and remained in Saint John, making him your true son through his divine power. The furnace wherein this identity was made by this divine Worker is his adorable breast. His all-

JEANNE'S ORIGINAL DRAFT

powerful word brought about this marvel for you. Behold your son, miraculous Mother. Behold your Mother, prodigious son; receive her now, she belongs entirely to you. The time has come for you to accept her. She does the same for you by her admirable silence.

Jesus, my Love, after this declaration, You had consummated everything. But in order to fulfill the Scriptures, You said that You were thirsty and accepted the vinegar so as to consummate the bitterness of the sins of mankind. You thus left us your lovability, bowing your head and giving up your spirit for your Church, after having commended it to your Divine Father.

The next day, which was Good Friday, I disposed myself to die with You, my Spouse and my King. I went up to Calvary, acknowledging my sins before heaven and in the presence of the earth. My soul felt outraged with sorrow and engulfed in an ocean of bitterness. This astonished my confessor to whom I made my confession, so that he was surprised by this, never until that moment having heard anything like it. I do not know whether, with his learning and eloquence, he could express and determine this extreme pain that You demonstrated by a marvelous locution, deepest contrition and marvelous delight, sweetness, love, joy and sadness. For a moment, I was lost in exterior darkness. (843) At another time, I found myself to be in interior illumination. The sorrows of death enveloped me like a vise. Constantly pursuing me, the pains of hell entered my soul, causing it to be engulfed in silt and mire, unable to find itself. I exclaimed: *Infixus sum in limo profundi et non est substantia. Veni in altitudinum maris; et tempestas demersit me. Laboravi clamans, raucæ factæ sunt fauces me; defecerunt oculi mei, dum spero in Deum meum. I stick fast in the mire of the deep: and there is no sure standing. I am come into the depth of the sea: and a tempest hath overwhelmed me. I have labored with crying; my jaws are become hoarse: my eyes have failed, whilst I hope in my God.* (Ps 68:3-4)

Noting the different states I experienced and the unheard of changes in my spirit that remained in the instability of its love which was its weight, my confessor was in suspense, awaiting the end of these different movements.

JEANNE'S ORIGINAL DRAFT

Raising and lowering me by the power of his will, this holy Love, that apparently wished to have earth and heaven play before Him to give him delight, gave wings to my superior part. It became an eagle, contemplating the sun (if I may dare say so) in its source set amid its lights. It became enlightened, and, by a reverberation, it caused the light to explode though its luminous discourse, declaring the mysteries of our faith as though I had read them in a book where everything is recorded. The Lamb who was slain opened the seals and spoke through my lips. I was possessed by this God who belonged entirely to me so as to be all things to me, thus causing two contraries to reign simultaneously in one subject, acting in equilibrium. With its seven horns, this Lamb showered upon me the seven gifts of his Spirit of Love. (844) By ineffable irradiations, He enlightened me seven times more than the sun does the air during its zenith, as though He had placed the seven eyes in me with which He illuminates the entire earth. He was accompanied by all his saints, contemplating the prodigies He wrought within me through pure goodness, offering all their merits for my sanctification.

This most gentle Lamb removed from me all the sins of the world which I had assumed so as to present them to Him on this Good Friday that He might once again make them die in a mystical manner. He commanded all the saints to sing a canticle during which he had me pass from death to life. He brought about this divine marvel in me which I can call my Easter and which was his own: *Phase (id est transitus) Domini; The Phase (that is the Passage) of the Lord.* (Ex 12:11) His love prompted Him to resurrect within me, who was almost dead from the participation in or communication of his loving death.

On Easter Sunday, I saw myself in life, transiently adorned with his glorious dowries, because I was still not at life's end. I was illuminated and also enlightened those to whom I spoke, who marveled at the depth of understanding and the facility with which I expressed divine mysteries. I possessed a body that did not weigh down my spirit, but seemed already to share in impassibility, in the light of the glorious Body of my Divine Spouse. I saw myself united to Him by a marvelous union which could be called the unity He

JEANNE'S ORIGINAL DRAFT

had requested of his Divine Father in his prayer at the Last Supper. (845) Although I did not perceive that I was as faithful as such prodigious favors required, He did not allow his unworthy spouse to remain in a state of confusion. He urged me to accept the entire portion of his glory that Love imparted to me. Without waiting for me to be rid of this mortal body in order to see Him glorious, such as He is, He told me that I was glorious, a mirror of his light, an image of his goodness and a representation of his candor. Just as, when He was in the world, He procured the glory of his Divine Father, never seeking his own but that of the One who had sent him into the world after having sanctified Him, I was not to claim mine, no matter what a number of people thought of my naïveté and the openness with which I speak. (846)

CHAPTER CXIX

The warning God gave me about the plans that others had to deprive me of the happiness his goodness had granted me; how He protected me, confounding my enemies and dissipating their decisions.

Certain visitors informed me about a council that was being held in order to humiliate me. You let me understand that I was not to be upset, that You were my Advocate with your Father. These persons, who imagined themselves to be prompted by zeal for his glory, thought that they would be doing Him a great service if they embarrassed me, without knowing my plans that are yours. Since You had assured me of your divine protection, ought I fear people? You told me: *Intonuit de cælo Dominus et Altissimus dedit vocem suam. And the Lord thundered from heaven, and the Highest*

JEANNE'S ORIGINAL DRAFT

gave his voice. (Ps 17:14)

My daughter, I will make this council to be fruitless, like that of Achitophel against David. Remain tranquil amid this commotion. It is your blessing to be tested by those who are thought to be devout. The disciple is not above the master. If the Scribes and Pharisees mistreated Me, should you not joyously or patiently endure the present threats of mistreatment? Sleep among the situations that my goodness has allowed you to have. Fear not, I am and will be with you." (847)

On April 9th or 10th, 1652, when my confessor arrived to hear my confession, I heard the bell ringing that announced that You, my gentle Savior, were being taken to a sick person. I adored You and told him: "Monsieur, behold God's visions, alluded to by the Prophet Ezechiel and whom the Martyrology represents to us by today's feast. It is the Word through whom the Father has created the ages, who contains the entire word of divine power. It is the marvelous coach which the hand of a man takes to the lips of a poor sick person. There this God of greatness wants to enter and, from there, to his stomach which will still contain the flesh of his glory, if his soul is pure when he receives this God of purity, who became the chariot and carrier of those who are true Israelites in whom there is no dissimulation. Their power is their naiveté and simplicity by which they are the dwelling-place of God, the eternal light, a light that elevates my mind in a most sublime elevation and inflames my will in a most ardent blaze.

Divine Love, You caressed me and let me repose in your lights as did Saint John at the Last Supper. You did so to draw me near Calvary and to show me how to imitate You by sustaining the efforts of those prompted by the powers of darkness. Their powers last a few days, but this weighed upon me for only three hours. You reminded me that I had requested You to suffer from contempt, sorrow and poverty and that the fervor that your Spirit gave me had impelled me even to desire and ask for all torments like another Saint Ignatius. Although I did not possess his virtue, by possessing the same God, I felt that I could do all things in Him who strengthened me. (848)

JEANNE'S ORIGINAL DRAFT

Your magnificent goodness made me understand that my desire to please You were acceptable to You and that, were I to ask for half of your kingdom, You would tend to give it to me. Induced by this loving inclination, I told You that I requested sufferings on earth. You replied that they had been your kingdom during your mortal life, at the end of which You received the crown which penetrated the forward part of your precious head. You shared it with me, since I yearned to do so in this life. Because this request was pleasing to You, through inexcusable sentiments, You allowed a number of others to afflict me, including some of my daughters. However, I do not wish to condemn, because I do not want to be the judge in my own case. Pardon them, Lord.

During my prayer on April 21, 1652, the third Sunday after Easter, I understood: "The daughter of Juda is condemned." I said to You: "Lord, who will be my Daniel?" You deigned to reply: "My daughter, it is I." Trusting in your goodness, I went to confession and received Holy Communion with the devotion You intensified so as to strengthen me. After dinner, I sent a message to Father Morin of the Oratory to come see me. He complied, inquiring about the reason I had sent for him on Sunday, since it was unusual for me to do so. I said to him: "Father, while at prayer this morning, I understood: 'The daughter of Juda is condemned.' (849) I do not know by whom. I have certainly heard the news that certain devout persons assembled to make Monsieur de la Piardière give up the plans God had given him to assist our Order by offering Holy Mass for us. They wanted to prevent him from doing this and instead to go celebrate in other churches. They are determined to aim their batteries against me, declaring that the said Monsieur de la Piardière was too greatly attached to my guidance and that I was deceiving him. They do not know me at all; I am too outspoken to deceive anyone."

The said priest did not want to deny completely the effort being made against me by the confessor of our community who is a religious by profession. He acted like an anchorite as far as I was concerned, for, in my presence, he observed an affected silence. To influence me to esteem him and think well of

JEANNE'S ORIGINAL DRAFT

him, one of my daughters, who conversed with him, recounted marvels to me about him so as to prevent me from perceiving her dealings with him and for him. For this reason, I put up with him, despite the sermon on the Immaculate Conception about which he had scandalized us.

While I was speaking, a gentleman servant sent me a three-line note telling me that, when he passed in front of Saint Sulpice, he had learned that a rector of Paris and two clergymen had formally arranged for a visitation regarding me. He wanted to know if I had requested this or who had decided the matter. No time was left for me to reply, because the rector with two clergymen asked the portress for me. She came to inform me as they were going up to the parlor. I said to Father Morin of the Oratory: "Behold the reality of what was told me this morning during my prayer." (850) I received them politely and respectfully and listened to the reason for this visitation to which I submitted. I remembered that, even though You were innocent, You had chosen to endure the interrogations made by your own enemies without being obliged to do so. You told the one who judged You that he had no power over You except what was given him from on high: *Non haberes potestatem adversum me ullam, nisi tibi datum esset de super. Thou shouldst not have any power against me, unless it were given thee from above.* (Jn 19:11b)

Divine Protector of those whom others try to oppress, I told You that in your hands was and is my lot. I placed my trust in You; I would willingly undergo all the rigors You would allow. While I was at prayer, You gave me many favors for two whole hours. I immediately abandoned myself to your will for me and was resigned to endure anything, knowing well that, unknown to the Prior Vicar General, this visitation had been prompted by envy. I considered You in your Passion to be my model, expecting one of my daughters to do as did Saint Peter, as well as the one who had imitated Judas. I had shown the latter more cordiality from the beginning of Lent than at other times. I saw that she was ill, almost dropsical, ever since she had listened to this priest and thereby subjected me to contempt, sorrow and poverty. Those who were more sensible than she protested that I was too good toward this

JEANNE'S ORIGINAL DRAFT

person who did not love me as she should. After You, my Lord, she had only me to assist her, for she had been abandoned by everyone when I accepted her as a child. I had served her in every way, and since then she had a number of times offended me as much as one can offend a benefactress. (851) Recalling that the "Golden Lips" [St. John Chrysostom] had stated that no one is offended except through himself, I did not give her any indication that I believed what I was told about the matter. I always left her in the most outstanding offices or charges of the monastery except that of assistant.

The day that the visitation commenced was Tuesday, April 23rd. I asked for no delay, although on reading the commission submitted I noticed that this was to last an entire year, and this was followed by things that I saw were false persuasions of my enemies. I prepared to receive these visitors, praying with more fervor or assiduity than customary, applying myself to prepare everything. I had to speak to all those who asked for me and to all my daughters, to show them my love, even those who had offended me. I found that I was extremely weak and all afire with fervor, recalling, Divine Savior, that You lengthened your prayer in the Garden. Saint Luke declares about You: *Et factus in agonia, prolixus orabat. And being in agony, he prayed the longer.* (Lk 22:43b) I drew strength from my weakness. No angel appeared to comfort me. Rather, I was a heifer that awaited a blow from a man who was not a butcher, but exhibited the rigor of one, raising his arm with the ax. He seemed ready to deprive this poor heifer of life. I did not stop to consider what this vision symbolized for me, but, continuing to pray as I dressed, I said to You: "O Lord! Am I the heifer that will be put to death? (852) I offer myself for the sacrifice, but the vision has disappeared before I could see its death. It was neither killed nor skinned. I do not deserve to suffer or die for You, my Divine Love."

As I prepared to receive You, Divine Savior, You were a hidden God. After Communion, You left me in my inferior part to my weaknesses, terrors and fear. The superior one You used as the dungeon where You were lodged and appeared to your angels, my Sovereign Protector and my strength, although hidden from me. Thus, in some way, I experienced what your Prophet

JEANNE'S ORIGINAL DRAFT

said of You: *Virum dolorem, scientem infirmitatem; et quasi absconditus vultus eius et despectus; Et percussum a Deo et humiliatum. A man of sorrows and acquainted with infirmity: and his look was as it were hidden and despised. As one struck by God and afflicted.* (Is 53:3b; 4d)

In the afternoon, You allowed me to know the one that I had refused to consider to be as others had depicted for me. Embracing her with a more than motherly love, full of love and sorrow, I told her: "Too many witnesses have led me to believe what I have tried to elude, that you had betrayed me, but they cannot prevent me from protecting you. You will not undergo any punishment." Filled with sadness, I felt deep compassion. My tears signified my deep pain. I experienced the words of David: *Terra mota est etenim cæli distillaverunt a facie Dei Sinai, a facie Dei Israel; pluviam volontariam segregabis Deus hereditati tuæ: et infirmata est, tu vero perfecisti eam. Animalia tua habitabunt in ea: parasti in dulcedine tua pauperi Deus. The earth was moved, and the heavens dropped at the presence of the God of Sina, at the presence of the God of Israel. Thou shalt set aside for thy inheritance a free rain, O God: and it was weakened, but thou hast made it perfect. In it shall thy animals dwell; in thy sweetness, O God, thou hast provided for the poor.* (Ps 67:9-11) (853)

The visitors arrived. The main one offered Holy Mass during which, at my command, canticles were chanted as though it were a day of joy and a solemn feast. After this, they commenced the visitation by opening the tabernacle to see how You were kept, my Divine Sacrament, my Love and my Weight. From there, they went up to the parlor where You remained with me. After I had knelt to inquire of the one who presided how he wanted me to proceed, whether through respect or silence, I was to listen to everything he had to tell me or, through candor and confidence, I should speak to him as I do to You, regarding him as my judge, although I was not obliged to do so for a number of reasons that it would take too long to record here. The interrogation was more detailed than that of an ordinary visitation, even for someone obligated by religious profession. I strove to satisfy them with a peace surpassing natural feeling. It came from You, my peaceful King, who made me your

JEANNE'S ORIGINAL DRAFT

Sulamitess, saying to me: *Revertere, revertere, Sulamitis! Revertere, revertere ut intueamur te. Return, return, O Sulamitess: return, return, that we may behold thee.* (Cant 6:12) My daughter, Aminadab's chariots have troubled you for three hours. Our Three Divine Persons summon you through the three powers of your soul and my quadrupled Sacred Humanity to behold your interior and your exterior. *Judica me, Deus, et dicerne causam meam. Judge me, O God, and distinguish my cause.* (Ps 42:1) You are my strength. I hope in You alone. What can men do against me? (854) *Ego autem semper sperabo, et adiiciam super omnem laudem tuam. But I will always hope, and will add to all thy praise.* (Ps 70:14)

These men departed without having spoken to any of my religious. This visitation was meant for me alone. The daughter who had been blind about the plans that the aforementioned father confessor, who pretended to have the well-being of all at heart, acknowledged her fault. She loudly protested that she had offended You by adhering to the advice of this priest against me and Monsieur de la Piardière, which was against You, my Lord and my God.[1]

---

[1]Note after the text by Lucretia de Bely:

The priest spoken of here was highly esteemed for his virtue and depth of spirit. Shortly after the above-mentioned visit, he was afflicted by a paralysis of his entire body for a period of seven years. He attributed it to the results of the problems he had caused Mother de Matel for having too readily believed the reports given him about her. Regarding this, he asked her pardon through the medium of a priest called Gautery, from whom I learned this detail in 1655.

Sister Jeanne de Jesus de B(ely), unworthy superioress, was then in charge of our monastery in Paris, where he had brought two of our Sisters from Grenoble whom our Mother Foundress had sent us. In Lyons, she had asked him to greet Monsieur Olier in her name, a great servant of God, who admired the goodness and generosity of this humble Foundress, according to the kind director of our Sisters, Grenat des Anges and Saint Pierre, who were present there. I considered myself obliged to witness to this.

Sister Lucrecia de Bely,
called Jeanne de Jesus.

JEANNE'S ORIGINAL DRAFT

CHAPTER CXX

The second war in Paris caused us to leave our monastery in the Saint Germain suburb to enter the city. The graces God gave me on the Feasts of Pentecost, Trinity Sunday, Corpus Christi, Saint John the Baptist, Saints John and Paul and the Visitation.

The next Tuesday, May 7th, due to the war, we had to leave our monastery in the Saint Germain suburb, because it was too distant, and enter the city. (855) Monsieur de la Piardiëre received us in his home where the official and pastor of Saint Eustachius Parish allowed us to have a chapel for Holy Mass and Holy Communion. Monsieur de la Piardière offered it for us there, and we received Communion. Your goodness showered a thousand favors upon me which I will not relate at length. He has written extensively about them, and this is to be found among my writings at his home and elsewhere.

On the Feast of Pentecost, You showered me with favors. Your Holy Spirit was all fire and love for me. The ardors which assailed my heart induced such loving raptures that my daughters thought I needed refreshment. This Holy Spirit—called the living fountain and fire of love, unction and Spirit of goodness—was my host and gentlest coolness in the fire of love and the water of my tears. He seemed to draw and burn me incessantly. Devotion and envy caused different feelings in those who witnessed these various states of mine. With my Father, Saint Augustine, I could declare: *Da amantem, et sentit quod dico: da desiderantem, da esurientem, da in ista solitudine peregrinantem, atque sitientem, et fontem æternæ patriæ suspirantem: da talem, et scit quid dicam. Give me one who loves, and he will understand what I say. Give me a person who longs, give me one who hungers, give me one who is wandering in this desert and thirsting after the fountains of his eternal home; give me such a person, and he will*

JEANNE'S ORIGINAL DRAFT

understand what I am saying. (St. Augustine, Breviary: *Wednesday of Pentecost)*

On the Feast of your Most August Trinity, which is the ineffable mystery, I had no words with which to express the descent that your adorable Society chose to make in me. (856) I exclaimed to myself: "Triune and One God, I am neither worthy nor capable of having You enter my littleness with your greatness. What are You doing by coming to me? The heaven of heavens cannot contain You, and You make your dwelling-place within a young woman. I perceive You to be total light and the center of light that illuminates my little mind by your power. I receive You within myself, and I become lost in You. It is not even proper for your glory to stop within me. Raise me up to You, through You. A simple shepherdess would suffer great embarrassment were the king to establish his Louvre in her home wherein to dwell with all his court. Upon seeing her King and Beloved inebriated with the wine of her love, with his throat and lips sated, the holy loved one exclaims: *Ego dilecto meo, et ad me conversio eius. I to my beloved, and his turning is toward me.* (Cant 7:10)

I belong entirely to my Beloved through duty, since I am his subject, and I belong to Him for every reason. Through his divine Passion, his love transformed and made Him totally mine. I am completely overwhelmed by his self-emptying. What must his entire court say referring to the covenant He makes with his spouse? *Dominus est; It is the Lord!* (Jn 21:7) It is the Lord who wills it so. *Veni, dilecte mi, egrediamur in agrum, commoremur in villis. Come, my beloved, let us go forth into the field, let us abide in the villages.* (Cant 7:11)

Since You have raised me up by your goodness, come and spread it throughout our spacious fields: Let us dwell in the village. I am delighted to see the love that transports You. Let us arise early in the morning, as do the (857) stars that were praising You even before I came into existence. They are all stars possessing as much obedience as stability. They are in jubilation wherever You ordain them to go. *Lætatæ sunt, et dixerunt: Adsumus, et*

JEANNE'S ORIGINAL DRAFT

luxerunt ei cum jucunditate, qui fecit illas. (The stars) rejoiced, and they said: Here we are. And with cheerfulness they have shined forth to him that made them. (Bar 3:34b-35)

Most August Trinity, accomplish everything You wish in your servant; gratify her, gratify her! In your Name, the Prophet forbids her to give her glory to others. He tells her: *Ne tradas alteri gloriam tuam, et dignitatem tuam genti alienæ. Give not thy honor to another, nor thy dignity to a strange nation.* (Bar 4:3) Unable to converse with creatures after having seen the Creator, I replied a number of times: *Videnti Creatorem angusta est omnis creatura. It is the anguish of every creature that sees the Creator.*

Your wisdom, that governs all things, chose to lead me to the altar on the your feast day, Divine Word made Flesh. You then shared your goodness with me and were my total consolation all during the Octave of this Sacrament of Love. You said to me: "My daughter, I have placed the word of reconciliation within you, and, since almost the entire earth seems to be at war, pray to Me for all sinners." "O God of mercy, I will pray for myself, for I think that I am the greatest sinner on earth. (858) If all other sinners were to receive the graces You give me, they would accomplish the good that I do not do and would not do the evil I do. For this, I most humbly ask your pardon."

As I reflected upon all graces You give me, I conceived a deep desire to have them acknowledged by all in heaven and on earth. With the Prince of the Apostles, I said to You: *Exi a me, quia homo peccator sum, Domine. Depart from me, for I am a sinful man, O Lord.* (Lk 5:8) I would say this, Divine Love, did I not know that your goodness is self-giving and that I would offend the inclination it displays for me if I did not accept all the graces and favors You give me. Redoubling your caresses with great sweetness, You told me: "My daughter, when I was mortal, I declared upon admiring the Centurion's faith: *Non inveni tantam fidem in Israel. I have not found so great faith in Israel.* (Matt 8:10) Today I am telling you that I have not found any confidence to equal yours that urges Me to give you even all that you have

JEANNE'S ORIGINAL DRAFT

not thought to request of Me. You entrust yourself entirely to Me for time and for eternity. Lovingly, I tell you: *Confide filia; Be of good heart, daughter.* (Matt 9:22) From Me, I send a benevolence that is incomprehensible to you: *Qui confidunt in Domino, sicut mons Sion: non commovebitur in æternum. They that trust in the Lord shall be as mount Sion: he shall not be moved for ever.* (Ps 124:1)

On the Feast of Saint John the Baptist, You gave me a thousand blessings during the Mass offered in our chapel by the Bishop of Condon. (859) Afterward, I told him about them, as I have done with all those You have imparted to me since the beginning of June when your wise Providence sent him to me to assist me by his protection against all those who had assembled in council as was recounted above.

This Prelate, who is very devout and zealous for your glory, undertook to do for me what Saint Germain, Bishop of Auxerre, did for Saint Genevieve, after learning that the envy and questionable zeal of a number of people had lead them to treat me uncharitably, even though they thought they would accomplish something great by so doing. He took the trouble to visit me often and to write me almost daily so as to know the graces your goodness had deigned to give me so profusely. Having asked to see what followed the *Inventory of Graces* in my *Autobiography* that the Most Eminent Cardinal of Lyons had ordered me to write, he seemed even more convinced that it is You who guides me. He inquired of the Jesuit Fathers here in Paris who had seen letters from my past directors who are now stationed in other provinces. He also planned to see Father Jean-Baptiste Carré, Dominican, who had guided me for a number of years. From this encounter, he was also convinced that it is You, my Divine Love, who grants me all these ineffable liberalities, for Father Carré assured him that he had never known anyone more enlightened with such abundant illuminations as those You deigned to communicate to me ever since I was a child. (860) In the conversation with the said priest, he felt such satisfaction that he tried to see him as often as possible. He loudly proclaimed his esteem for the virtues of this priest. A number of people whom he had helped tried to besmirch his name by calumnies that turned against the

JEANNE'S ORIGINAL DRAFT

very ones who uttered them.

My true Oracle, You will fulfill what You told me about the matter when Father Rudolph was in this city. You commanded me to assure him that You wanted a general novitiate established and that You had chosen him to be its prior. He was to be the ox to work hard. Frankly, I did so. Some time later, You also told me that, after he had worked hard on this novitiate, he would be sanctified by his own sons and a number of others who thought they would be pleasing You, but they did not consult You. Your arms are certainly long, my Lord, to assist whoever is made to suffer without reason. I do not want to speak about how long they are in punishing those who, because they do not know You, afflict those whom You wish to protect.

Delighted with your favors to me, Bishop Condon urged me to pray for him. With a filial heart, I did so, since You have given him to me as a father. His devotion to your Blessed Mother was redoubled for me by my conversation with him. (861) You told me on the Feast of Saints John and Paul, martyrs, that at the holy feet of this Mother of Fair Love, I would find all graces and favors, that her eyes were pools of grace and glory, that she was the miraculous pool wherein all the sick were healed ever since the Angel Gabriel descended to greet her, telling her that she was full of grace and that You were with her. These words troubled her: *Quæ cum audisset, turbata est in sermone eius, et cogitabat qualis esset ista salutatio. Who, having heard, was troubled at his saying and thought with herself what manner of salutation this should be.* (Lk 1:29)

The one who had troubled her had to assure her that You had chosen her to be your Blessed Mother. She was the pool You wished to enter so as to heal the pain that Moses perceived in You at the time that You sent the deluge because of the sins of mankind: *Videns autem Deus quod multa malitia hominum esset in terra, et cuncta cogitatio cordis intenta esset ad malum omni tempore, poenituit eum quod hominem fuisset in terra. Et tactus dolore cordis intrinsecus: poenitet enim me fuisse eos. And God seeing that the wickedness of men was great on the earth, and that all the*

JEANNE'S ORIGINAL DRAFT

thought of their heart was bent upon evil at all times, It repented him that he had made man on the earth. And being touched inwardly with sorrow of heart: It repenteth me that I have made them. (Gen 6:5-6;7c)

Dear Love, this regret proceeded from your goodness, which impelled You personally to remedy human misery. You became Man in the womb of this Virgin, assuming all our infirmities. You let me understand that You considered this miraculous pool within your ideas so as to dwell enclosed there for nine months, followed by thirty years at her feet as her subject. (862) You invited me to place myself at these sacred feet, saying that, through them, I would have her heart and affections. She told me as You did: *Ego diligentes me diligo. I love them that love me.* (Prov 8:17) You added that You have placed everything at her feet, as well as at the feet of the Apostles in the Militant Church.

On the Feast of the Visitation, while I was preparing to solemnize this feast with five persons who observed it with great joy in Zachary's house, I was deeply astounded that it should be spent in tears. Through an intellectual view, I saw that the Mother of Fair Love seemed to be leaving Paris, taking with her the Child of Holy Love and Love Itself. I lay flat on the floor in our little chapel, weeping almost inconsolably. I have no words with which to express my desolation, unaware of what was occurring at the gate of Saint Antoine where there was furious fighting and massacring. Mothers lost their children there; children became orphans there; married women who went there became widows, not being more desolate than I was. I exclaimed: "O, my Queen! Oh, my august one, where are you taking my Jesus, who is my God? If you and He leave Paris, we are lost. I have greater strength and constancy than did Micheas to stop you with your Child who is my true God. Do not say to me: *Quid tibi vis? cur clamas? What aileth thee? Why dost thou cry?* (Judg 18:23c) You know that I cannot be nor live without Him. He is your Son, but He is also my Spouse. (863) I see Him as the Unicorn in your virginal breast where You have detained Him, most marvelous *Alma*, incomparable Virgin. Do not be offended if I sit on the floor to call Him and hold Him on mine. He placed Himself on the altar purposely. With my tears, I

JEANNE'S ORIGINAL DRAFT

would detain you together with Him. When He was visible among mortals, He did not ignore them. With their tears the widow of Naim and Lazarus's sister caused Him to make the dead rise again, the former from his coffin, and the latter from the tomb after having been there four days.

You let me understand that He rejects the tabernacles of Joseph and wants nothing to do with Ephraim. So many have multiplied as Joseph did and cry out to Him. So many people, like Ephraim, were nurtured at the royal breast in peace. Will all these be rejected by Him as by you? *Repulit tabernaculum Joseph, et tribum Ephraim non elegit, sed elegit tribum Juda. Monstra te esse matrem, sumat per te preces, qui pro nobis natus tulit esse tuus. And he rejected the tabernacle of Joseph: and chose not the tribe of Ephraim. But he chose the tribe of Juda.* (Ps 77:67-68a) *Show yourself a mother. May He who, born for us, deigned to be your Son, receive our prayers through you.* (Ave Maris Stella) Holy Mary, remember that I am the daughter of Judas whom He delivered from the judges and was not sentenced. He has been my Daniel, the Host of desire. I am the daughter of desire; you and He will answer the desires of my heart for this royal city through goodness. I will not cease praying to both of you until I see our King and his family return to Paris. (864) My tears were dried by your goodness, for You assured me that your Mother and You would not leave Paris and that You would be with me. I was not to fear famine, for You could not see me undergoing the miseries that others dreaded. The Bishop of Condon came to inform me: "My daughter, the Superioress of the Carmelites has asked me if you have sufficient provisions of wheat for your whole Congregation which now numbers seventy-seven persons." I replied that Monsieur de la Piardière had insisted so much that, to satisfy him, I had purchased two measures of wheat at forty pounds the measure, but that I did not think that our Congregation would use all this during the inflation. This surprised him, for he thought that I had no economy nor concern for providing for our needs. Our baker, whom we had employed from the time of the first war, would never allow us to be in need. I commend him to You, my Love and my King, knowing very well that You could not fail her who was extremely confident of your providence.

JEANNE'S ORIGINAL DRAFT

CHAPTER CXXI

The Incarnate Word desired to be my philosopher's stone. His favors to me on the Feasts of Saint Magdalen, Saint Anne, Saint Martha and Saint Ignatius of Loyola.

After Holy Communion, You told me: "My daughter, many people waste their time, their possessions and often their very souls looking for the philosopher's stone. How many have found it or even know about it?" "Lord, I do not know." (865) "My daughter, my goodness has offered it to you, and your confidence has received it within your breast. My dearest, it is I who am this stone. My feet are supported on foundations of gold, and my head is of fine gold that spiritually and corporeally, interiorly and exteriorly enriches you. The angels are your speedy vessels who have charge of obtaining for you what you desire."

You told me a thousand marvels about your providence over me. I reported all this to Monsieur de la Piardière who felt such great admiration that he declared he had never heard such lovely things spoken about your wise and rich providence over me. He was sorry he had not brought paper and ink to be recording them as I spoke. However, just as a torrent cannot be stopped, he told me that he could not speak about what I told him with holy eloquence. You said to me: "My daughter, today I have made you like another Eden, my delightful paradise. I am the tree of life in the center of your heart. I produce this eloquence and river of grace that irrigates my paradise and divides the waters of my wisdom into four rivers.

"As for the first, you are enriched by the merits of my Sacred Humanity which is more precious that any expensive rubies, diamonds and pearls.

JEANNE'S ORIGINAL DRAFT

"The second is the cleansing-place you possess in your confessions that cleanse all the indignities of Ethiopia, sins and imperfections with which your soul is too often stained. My mercies envelop you and follow you everywhere. Within your heart, I am seated upon the throne of my graces. There I am your God and your King:" (866) *Qui adimplet quasi Euphrates sensum, qui multiplicat quasi Jordanes in tempore messis; qui mittit disciplinam sicut lucem, et assistens, quasi Gehon in die vindemiæ. Who maketh understanding to abound as the Euphrates: who multiplied it as the Jordan in the time of the harvest. Who sendeth knowledge as the light and riseth up as Gehon in the time of the vintage.* (Eccli 24:36-37)

These rivers are sovereign and favorable to me, my Divine Love, against any vanity and sensuality. They help me overcome the Assyrians and make me victorious over the most powerful enemies, like another Judith over Holofernes. By your strong assistance, I can often say that the Angel of the Great Council never leaves me. The fruits You produce for me show me that You are this Euphrates for me by replenishing me with your divine knowledge that makes You marvelous in a simple young woman. Often she exclaims: *Mirabilis facta est scientia tua ex me: confortata est, et non potero ad eam. Thy knowledge is become wonderful to me: it is high, and I cannot reach to it.* (Ps 138:6)

On the Feast of Saint Magdalen, You told me: "My daughter, the man who desired to reach a point outside the limits of earth, so as to lift its entire mass, did not obtain his wish. The thoughts of men are often vain: *Dominus scit cogitationes hominum, quoniam vanæ sunt. The Lord knoweth the thoughts of men, that they are vain.* (Ps 93:11)

"More fortunate than he, Magdalen had both feet outside the earth, having attached herself to mine which are heavenly. Supported by the hypostasis of the Word, My Humanity is outside the earth by its subsistence. Hers was the better part, for she was taken by her love who made her like the desert, elevating her seven times daily by heavenly spirits that have no body. They borrow one when they appear in human form, even preparing one from the air

JEANNE'S ORIGINAL DRAFT

in accordance with my will which they carry out faithfully. (867)

"My daughter, withdraw your affections from anything that is of earth, and you will make them heavenly. It is an elevation that all my saints love and admire, because it pleases Me. Mine are in the love of my Father, which prompted me to say to the Jews: 'How long will I be with you, disbelieving generation that does not love my Father on whom depends all paternity, for you despised the Son who came personally to save you? Your affections are earthly. Isaias certainly prophesied well about Me, when he told you in the person of my Father: 'This people declares with their lips that they love me, but their heart is far from Me.' And elsewhere: *Quis credidit auditui nostro? et brachium Domini cui revelatum est? Who hath believed our report? And to whom is the arm of the Lord revealed?'* (Is 53:1)

"With confidence, Magdalen knelt at my feet. I defended her from all her enemies. Later, I raised her up to heaven near Me, her Friend. I am the Chosen One from among a thousand, white with purity and red with charity as the bride declares: *Dilectus meus mihi, et ego illi. My beloved to me, and I to him."* (Cant 2:16)

Continuing to praise your loved ones, You entertained me for several hours, commanding me to write a part of what You told me about them. After dinner, I did so. When Father Carré arrived, he asked me for this. I sent him a copy. It may be seen among my writings, for I could not include it here.

On the Feast of your grandmother, Saint Anne, I humbled myself before your Majesty, desiring to praise You with all the angels and saints. (868) You commanded me, a simple young woman, to proclaim the inexhaustible riches destined for Saint Anne that had been concealed for ages in your divinity. You told me that, with justice, all the saints render ineffable veneration to this wonderful mother of your Blessed Mother, her daughter. She believed that You would give her daughter back to her when she entered the Empyrean.

Divine Love, You told me about the marvels of the merits and glory of your

JEANNE'S ORIGINAL DRAFT

grandmother, Saint Anne, which I recorded the very same day. So as not to be too wordy, I am not adding them here. In the morning, when I received Communion in our little chapel, You told me that from your bounty I received the graces that You would have given the Queen had she been in this small chapel, that You were not displeased by the recommendation I made for this simple princess. She was very acceptable to You. You said that this devout Queen had offered You the royal palace wherein to place your adorable Sacrament with all your daughters. In exchange, I was to pray that You would give her lodging with her two princes in your royal, Divine Heart.

In the afternoon, when I went to the Theatine Fathers to adore You there on your Throne of love and receive the blessing of the mother of the one who had borne You, Son of the blessed God, You received me with as much courtesy as goodness. Your providence allowed someone to give me a chair right in front of You exposed there, for I was too weak to remain kneeling. (869) You said to me: "My daughter, your are between two of my servants, your spiritual children who are kneeling and you seated. The three of you comprise the fleur-de-lys. Offer it to Me with the praises that the Queen and her two sons would give Me were they present in this church." I did so to the best of my ability. I offered them to You, my Lord and my God, not only in this church, but everywhere that I do pray and will pray to You. Bless the mother, bless the children, these two wonderful princes whom You had entrusted to me even before they were born in the years 1628 and 1634. You placed them upon my shoulders like two sprays of lilies so that I might offer them to You and be responsible for them. Your principality is upon my shoulders, according to the declaration of your Evangelical Prophet: *Et factus est principatus super humerum eius. And the government is upon his shoulder.* (Is 9:6c) My Love, make the care You have entrusted to me of these two princes be blessed with your holy, loving benedictions. May they share in your marvelous gifts as a strong Councillor, the Father of future ages and Prince of peace. *Da pacem, Domine, in diebus nostris. Lord, grant peace in our day.*

On the Feast of Saint Martha, You conversed with me about your esteem

JEANNE'S ORIGINAL DRAFT

for the two sisters who were your two spouses. You had great confidence in them (just as Lamech had in his two wives), and they in You. They were sure that your presence would have prevented death from taking away the soul of their brother Lazarus, your friend, whom your Father had ordained to die so as to show forth your glory and your powerful confidence in Him. You offered to die to restore life to the adolescent Lazarus, whose death caused You deep sorrow. When You saw Mary weeping, You sighed and were troubled; You trembled and wept. You obliged Yourself to descend person- ally to Limbo for him. Yet your soul was not thereby divided from your divine support. It was the composite that became separated. O, what a wound! The Man-God died and remained wounded for all mankind! The death of Lazarus was the death of an adolescent whom the God-Man restored to life after having been moved to loving compassion. (871)

The death of Lazarus was avenged seven times, but in a marvelous way. Jesus was the death of his death and the sting of his hell and, together with this new life, endowed him with the seven gifts of his Holy Spirit. That of Jesus Christ was *Septuagies septies; Seventy times seven times* (Matt 18:22b) for him, avenged with a terrible vengeance. Those who scorned the blood of the Testament experienced this, for they stamped upon the blood of the Testament and despised the Son of God who died for them. They have fallen and will fall into the hands of the Living God. The destruction of Jerusalem pales beside such contempt and such a precious death. The offence is infinite. Under- standably, the punishment connected with this should be infinite: *Justus es, Domine, et rectum judicium tuum. Thou art just, O Lord: and thy judgment is right.* (Ps 118:137)

Jesus, my Love, the death of your friend Lazarus caused You to tremble. Ours fills us with dread. Adam had caused the death of his prosperity. Lazarus was mortal, included in his father's covenant. You, New Adam, died only because You chose to do so. You are a Son of Adam without being a sinner, for You are impeccable by nature, but it is love that made You become mortal, subjected You to death and reduced You to the level of those who are subject to death. Because You are free, it is charity that impelled You to taste

JEANNE'S ORIGINAL DRAFT

death so as to impart to us the life of grace and glory. (872)

On the Feast of Saint Ignatius of Loyola, the Institutor and Founder of your Society, You gave me a thousand favors and told me about the marvels You had accomplished in this saint for your greater glory and the salvation of souls, as well as for his sanctification. During our times, he taught all people meditation and offered the Spiritual Exercises. Most applicable to him are the words of the Introit of the Mass: *Os justi meditabitur sapientiam. The mouth of the just shall meditate wisdom* (Ps 36:30). The following also apply to him: *Gaudeamus in Domino; Let us rejoice in the Lord.*

You showed me that he was your faithful servant and father of a family. He was so vigilant that, at all times, he examined his words and actions so as to be ready to give You an account of the goods and talents You had entrusted to him. He had come into the world to set it ablaze in imitation of You. When he was at Monserrat whose chapel shook, he was afire like a Cherubim at the gate of Paradise which is your Blessed Mother. He was a cannon that breached the Empyrean heaven and made your Eternal Father emerge, who recommended him to You on the way to Rome as a generous captain who would conquer the world and all its children. All this would be for the greater glory of the Most Holy Trinity, who elevated him to make him its councillor of war. He belonged to the Great Council. You showed him the blessings of your goodness, for which he thanked You at the beginning of all his examens. You told me so many marvelous things about him that I cannot go into more detail about them here. Monsieur de la Piardière knows some of them, for I shared them with him when I came from Holy Communion. (873) Above all, You assured me that You had given him true knowledge, as well as to those who belong to him. Whoever would be against them would be conquered and confounded. You told me that their teaching is true, that our father Saint Augustine and Saint Thomas were closely united to him. Everyone would be happier on receiving God's graces instead of contradicting the veritable bounties of your loving dilection. You have died for all; I was to dispose myself to receive them all, while a number of doctors would lose them in disputes. They are not motivated by true charity. These doctors ought to be choirs of armies

JEANNE'S ORIGINAL DRAFT

ranged against the chariots of Aminadab, against those outside the Church and there to receive and gather those who wander off on devious ways. They consider these too narrow, unable to attain the university of your ways which are mercy and truth. The Royal Prophet, who knew this by his own personal experience, has well addressed the issue. He also often requested You to show them to him and to illuminate them by your face.

The brevity I wish to maintain does not allow me to express everything here. Whenever Monsieur de La Piardière returns from Touraine, where he urgently had to go to attend to his children and personal affairs, we can see what he wrote about this, if, my Divine Savior, You give me the grace to see him again.

JEANNE'S ORIGINAL DRAFT

CHAPTER CXXII

The illuminations and favors that the divine goodness granted me on the Feasts of the Transfiguration, Saint Lawrence and the triumphant Assumption of Our Lady

On the Feast of the Transfiguration, You chose to give me signs of your universal and singular love, taking me up with You to the mount of purity where You allowed Yourself to be seen, adorable Savior, as the beauty that enraptures hearts. You also displayed how You are the good and the beautiful by essence and par excellence. You satisfied the spouse that desires nothing but your glory. You showed her Tabor where You appeared in your glory, conversing with her from the excess of your charity.

On the Feast of this wonderful Levite [Saint Lawrence], who is all laurel, You let me experience ardent and brilliant illuminations. After I had enjoyed your divine delights, You told me: *"Surge velociter; Go quickly* to carry off the spoils of your enemies; the weapons and field remain for Me." With indescribable advantages, You made me triumphant over my visible and invisible enemies. Yours be the glory for all this triumph and the others You deigned to give me.

On the eve of the glorious Assumption of your admirable Mother, O loving Mary, You let me understand that You descended into her garden and that the next day You took her up to yours. (875) On the eve of her death, You allowed her to gather myrrh and spices, mingled with joy and pain with which to prepare a bouquet. Love reminded her of her sufferings and merits that had brought about a price of infinite glory. They were presented to the Most August Trinity, weighed in the sanctuary and found to have inestimable worth and price in the eyes of angels and men. Your love was its weight. You

JEANNE'S ORIGINAL DRAFT

summoned Moses by death, having shown him the Promised Land, but telling him that he would not enter therein. You expressed the displeasure You had felt at the waters of contradiction.

You could find no fault with your all-holy and Immaculate One. With love and reverence, You accepted her spirit, for You were her subject, as well as her God. In a most divine way, You united her to Yourself: *Et possidebit Dominus Judam partem suam in terra sanctificata, et eliget adhuc Jerusalem. Sileat omnis caro a facie Domini, quia consurrexit de habitaculo sancto suo. And the Lord shall possess Juda his portion in the sanctified land: and he shall yet choose Jerusalem. Let all flesh be silent at the presence of the Lord: for he is risen up out of his holy habitation.* (Zach 2:12-13)

Divine Sun, the day You made when You personally radiated the triumph of your august Mother, was so brilliant that heaven had not seen nor could see another like it except the one of your marvelous Ascension, the day of glory of a God-Man who displayed that He had possessed this glory before the world was created. From the first instant of its creation, your blessed soul enjoyed it in its superior part, for, simultaneously, You were supported by your divine hypostasis. (876) Such rejoicing appeared to me to be novel. Your inferior part and your Sacred Body, to which this glory is due because of the divine support, would be deprived thereof by the divine economy to show your love for mankind. You are their Pontiff who assumed a share in their weakness, choosing to be their companion in their misery, although exempt from ignorance and sin.

Dear Love, You were pleased that I should contemplate You, elevating your miraculous ark, sanctified by You personally, above angels and men. What a marvel You showed me: a globe brilliant with light held by three fingers by your Three Divine Persons who ineffably give this glorious globe the weight of power, wisdom and goodness. You told me that this globe is filled with God and that the Virgin is the sublime land, replete with your Majesty's glory. She is your elevated throne, before whom the Seraphim fold their wings

JEANNE'S ORIGINAL DRAFT

as they say: "Holy is the Virgin Land, Daughter of the Almighty Father. Holy is the Virgin Land, Mother of the most wise Son. Holy is the Virgin Land, Spouse of the most ardent Holy Spirit who is all-love. (877) She bore the Incarnate Word on life's journey and is borne aloft by Him at life's end, a marvelous spectacle of glory for all the saints."

I heard your Divine Father say: "Land of purity, listen to the Word of God. Blessed Land, enter into the Word of God who entered you, as soon as you said: *Fiat mihi secundum verbum tuum; Be it done to me according to your word.* Priestly Land, enter the glory of the Word because You resemble Him. Enter the heavens adorned personally by the Holy Spirit and affirmed by the Word: *Verbo Domini cæli firmati sunt; et spiritu oris eius omnis virtus eorum. By the word of the Lord the heavens were established; and all the power of them by the spirit of his mouth.* (Ps 32:6)

My soul became engrossed in the delights of contemplating the Virgin seated on the throne of light, and I noted that neither angels nor men invested with glory could behold the brilliance of this glory without being protected by the power of your right hand. It modified or tempered these rays to allow them not to be blinded by her splendors that were like those of the Sun of Justice with which she was invested. This was You, my Divine Orient, re-turned to the bosom of your Father from whom You had come to become incarnate in this Virgin. But, am I now free to speak, engulfed by your all-blazing light that heaven admires like the flaming bush that was not consumed? Do I not consider this a miracle, filled with the thorns of my sins, of the miseries of this life? (878) Through your goodness, I enjoy your delightful ardors without losing my being therein, in possession of a loving life through divine dispensation. I speak, and everything remains in silence, unaware of your divine features. I entered your great powers, and You invited me to advance further, urging me to be seated at the banquet of glory. You allowed me to repose with You in the virginal heart where You wanted me join the virgins in singing the hymn due to your Majesty. The holy peace given this Virgin and, by her, to the whole heavenly Court in peace, has become her place. She is in You, my God, and You are in her. You display and conceal

JEANNE'S ORIGINAL DRAFT

her in your hidden light which simultaneously is both darkness and light.

Divine Majesty, I am unable to recount your marvels, being lost in the abyss of your greatness. Blessed Virgin, you are above all that is not God, except for your Son, the Man-God, who is the right hand of the Father to whom He is equal and who made Himself the supreme heaven. During this entire Octave, my soul was gratified with the favors of your most august Mother and magnificent Queen of God made Man. (879)

CHAPTER CXXII

The desire given me by the Incarnate Word to be perfectly detached from anything that is not God. His goodness in lodging me within his Heart. The many graces He gave me through his Blessed Mother, as I entrusted our Order to Saint Michael and his angels.

On the Feast of the Apostle Saint Bartholomew, I felt a deep desire to pray unceasingly and to be detached from anything that is not You, my God. I adored You, the greatest and the least: the greatest, through your immensity; the least, from the simplicity of your being without any addition. You are your center which is everywhere, whose circumference is in no single place. You are sovereignly abstract, dwelling in a light that is inaccessible to all pure creatures. You are sufficient unto Yourself, pure act, more appropriately praised by negation than by affirmation.

Great Apostle, you were flayed, stripped of your skin which had been

JEANNE'S ORIGINAL DRAFT

spread out like the heavens. Like a glorious, holy vestment, this flaying invested you with light.

On the Feast of Saint Louis, King of France, my soul dwelt in the hospital of the poor, your sacred side. O, how it wanted to tell You: *Tibi derelictus est pauper; orphano tu eris adjutor.* (880) *To thee is the poor man left: thou wilt be a helper to the orphan.* (Ps 9:14c) You were this, my God, when You fulfilled my desires and accepted the preparation of my heart. I experienced what the Prophet-King said: *Desiderium pauperum exaudivit Dominus; præparationem cordis eorum audivit auris tua. The Lord hath heard the desire of the poor: thy ear hath heard the preparation of their heart.* (Ps 9:17) Many prepare bows and arrows so as in the darkness to wound the one who was willing to do everything possible for You and for them and endure with an upright heart, seeking only your glory and the salvation of everyone: *Quoniam quæ perfecisti destruxerunt: justus autem quid fecit? For they have destroyed the things which thou hast made: but what has the just man done?* (Ps10:4)

Monsieur de la Piardière left Paris on this royal day to go to Touraine. He left me with my daughters in his home, asking me not to leave until he had returned so as to take us back to our monastery. O, God! How his request caused me pain, but You rewarded this generously. How right Saint Teresa was when she declared: "To suffer or to die," since You know how to console those who belong entirely to You.

Loving Savior, on August 27th, when I knelt to adore and offer You my affliction due to the ingratitude of those whom I loved for love of You, You invited me to rest under your Cross. Since You gave me the fruit of your work that was so sweet, I could say: *Sub umbra illius quam desideraverum sedi, et fructus eius dulcis gutturi meo. I sat down under his shadow, whom I desired: and his fruit was sweet to my palate.* (Cant 2:3c)

Dear Love, you well know how to charm afflicted hearts, delighting to help them forget their burdens and to think only of your love. (881) Because I was

JEANNE'S ORIGINAL DRAFT

abandoned by all who could divert me from my sorrow, but not remove them, You decided to assume them Yourself, and, like a good nurse, take the bitter medicine to give me milk from your own breast, telling me that this was better than the wine of any consolation from pure creatures. You took me into your cellar where your charity commanded me to love all those who afflicted me. I was to pray for them, marveling at your goodness that set up the banner of your pure love in my heart. You induce the soul to reside more in the One it loves than in what it animates, for charity does not strive for what is agreeable but for whatever belongs to You, my All and my greatest glory, so that the bride may belong entirely to her Spouse.

One morning as I prayed before an *Ecce Homo*, I was thinking of You, my Divine Love. While I was filled with shame, You caused me to hear these words of the Prophet Isaias: *Non est species ei, neque decor; There is no beauty in him, nor comeliness*; (Is 53:2b) and what follows in the chapter up to: *Et nos putavimus eum quasi leprosum, et percussum a Deo, et humiliatum; And we have thought him as it were a leper, and as one struck by God and afflicted.* (Is 53:4b)

"My daughter, some people do not believe that I speak through you nor that I display the power of my arm through your weakness. They consider you through their own eyes that cannot perceive what I do in you. They scorn you, saying that you are neither a lay person nor a religious. They do not understand my direction of you, which you view in the sentiments you have of your nothingness, adoring Me in spirit and in truth. They think that you are blind, making religious of young women, conferring the habit but not taking it. They state that you do not want to submit to the Order you have founded, as though you did not observe my will in the state you are living. (882)

"Be consoled, dear daughter, by contemplating Me in my ignominy. When I was nailed to the Cross, it was said: "He saves others, but He cannot come down from the Cross!" I endured everything, because I had willingly offered to suffer every contempt. It was as though I thirsted for the opprobrium that my loved ones would undergo. I made an offering of this to my Eternal

JEANNE'S ORIGINAL DRAFT

Father, thus sanctifying their sufferings by an oblation. I sanctified them all. Have patience and you will possess your soul united to my all-holy One."

On the Birthday of your wonderful Mother, my soul wanted to join all creatures in receiving the joy that her birth caused those who possess life. Only the demons and the condemned were excluded from this jubilation. At your command, I wrote the Bishop of Condon about the illuminations You had communicated to me, my Divine Sun. I am not adding them here, because they are recorded on special pages, as well as a number of others which your goodness had given me to understand.

On the Feast of the Exaltation of your victorious Cross, You chose to offer me the Precious Blood of this adorable Cross by which You had removed all bitterness caused me from persecution by a number of persons. You told me that your Precious Blood pacified heaven and earth in me, that Jacob's fountain which You had given me as pure gift was in this cross, just as formerly Jacob had given his son Joseph the price and the fountain. Your gifts are unreservedly made; You delight in teaching me; You are the true Messias; You are my love and my all, just as You are my salvation. My treasure and my heart are in your chalice. I was to pray fervently for peace for Paris, as You had promised me a few days earlier. (883) Continuing these charming conversations, You told me: "My daughter, accept the word of the Cross so that it may not perish. Raise your eyes to the One from whom all good things come and will come, who was raised up upon this wood. I am the Lord who created heaven and earth. Climb the palm tree and gather its fruit. Trust in my Blessed Mother. Do not doubt the promises she made you before you left your father's house. I have accomplished and later will continue to accomplish great marvels all alone. *Confide, filia, fides tua te salvam fecit. Be of good heart, daughter, thy faith had made thee whole.* (Mt 9:22)

"You have touched the fringe of my robe and will continue to do so. You do well to place yourself at my feet where a gentle power constantly emanates to give you consolation, since you are the first one in my Order. In accordance with my advice, you chose the last place. You are despised by the

JEANNE'S ORIGINAL DRAFT

world. Hold it in contempt and, with the Apostle, declare that the world is crucified to you and you to the world. I came for what was mine, and those who belonged to Me did not accept Me. The Jews have rejected Me. On Good Friday, the Church prays for them. Pray to Me for whoever has been unfaithful to you. Whoever welcomes you, welcomes the One who sent you. You are not the one, my daughter, that is despised; it is I who consider it done to Myself."

While I prayed to your goodness for those who were unfaithful to their duties, You showed me a field of withered grass upon the ground, telling me as You did the Prophet Isaias: "Cry out, my daughter!" "O! what shall I cry out?" "That all flesh is grass." At the same time, You told me that You preserved a flower in which your Holy Spirit dwelt, who strengthened it and endowed it with his graces. (884)

In the church of the discalced Augustinian Fathers on the eve of the Feast of St. Michael, as I attended Holy Mass and received Holy Communion, You were pleased to elevate me near this Prince and all his angels. You told me that these Morning Stars joined in jubilantly praising You for the conversion of our loving Father Saint Augustine. Because of it, they engage upon a great and solemn feast. All this is unutterable.

It pleased You, Divine Love, to entrust our Order to this magnificent Prince and all these spiritual beings. You commanded me anew to take care of all your daughters, a number of whom You showed me were going astray like lost sheep led or kept by persons who were severe or mercenary, not to say cruel. The ground to which they had been led was a narrow path between two thorny hedges. The dust seemed to choke them. Grass was placed upon their backs and not in their mouths. At sight of this, my heart was filled with pity and compassion, for they were being treated so harshly that they seemed to be taken to slaughter.

JEANNE'S ORIGINAL DRAFT

CHAPTER CXXIV

The gracious reception that Saint Genevieve gave me in the crypt where her tomb is located. The peace that God promised me for Paris. The marvels of Saint Francis. My sufferings on the Feast of Saint Denis and a number of other days.

On October 2, 1652, the Bishop of Condon sent me a message that, as I had requested, he would offer Mass upon the altar of Saint Genevieve, near the tomb of this virgin in thanksgiving for the healing of Mademoiselle Angelique de Beauvais. (885) As soon as I entered, this Virgin, the Patroness of Paris, received me with inexpressible sweetness and signs of friendship. She told me that our common Spouse would grant me my request for peace in Paris, and that, in a few days, I would see proof of this. She entertained me with the words of Saint Agatha and Saint Lucy when she had prayed at their tombs. Enraptured with delight, my soul was engulfed and considered only heaven in this holy crypt. Had love not commanded charity, my soul would have left my body to dwell in the One it loved. However, Bishop de Condon had arranged for me to be taken in his carriage to Monsieur de la Piardiere's home where our community was accommodated with me because of the war. All that day and the next, through You, my Divine Spouse, I enjoyed the delights of your peace that surpasses all understanding.

In the evening on the eve of the Feast of St. Francis, my spirit was elevated by splendor, embraced by the ardor that the Cherubim and Seraphim had communicated to this saint who seemed to be a replica of You. With Saint Paul, he could truly say that he lived, but not he himself: it was You who lived in him. You showed him to me as a censor that burns incense before You, by praying unceasingly, as a holy temple, as a marvelous tabernacle where You, your Eternal Father and the Holy Spirit were adored in spirit and in truth.

JEANNE'S ORIGINAL DRAFT

(886) You told me: "Pray to me now for peace for Paris so that the King may come there. Join my seraphic Francis, who is all love, in asking me for this."

The next day, You conversed with me about the marvels of this saint. You told me: "My daughter, listen to a great mystery. The Incarnate Word, your love, like the supreme heaven above all the heavens, on this day appeared to the glorified saint with shining wounds like a spectacle of glory, and Francis proportionately did the same. With his bleeding wounds, Saint Francis hid in a cave, remaining standing to delight whoever could descend there. This is a copy of the holy original that is mine. I wanted to show mortal men the features by an ineffable marvel. Moses prepared the tent he had been shown upon the mountain. Francis became like the original that he saw on the mountain of Alvernia as was declared: 'Whatever God joins together, let men not separate.' I say to you that the mark of my stigmata on St. Francis cannot be effaced or removed, even by death that destroys everything. And if I want this holy body to symbolize Me when I was crucified until I come again, who can prevent Me from doing so?" You enlightened me about the marvels of my seraphic father, telling me that You had given me many favors through this saint to whom I had been dedicated even before I was born. It would take me too long to describe them here.

On the Feast of the Apostle of France, the great Saint Denis, I received a letter, informing me of the cruelty and inhumanity with which my poor sheep were being treated. The vision had upset me, but this letter distressed and wounded me so much that I was outraged with pain and wept bitterly. (887) My sufferings were inexplicable and still are, because, like Rachel, I weep and cry inconsolably to You over the daughters who are dead and those who languish in a distant place. I could not go see and assist them because of obstacles that were as cruel and upsetting to me as were their deaths. Since they go up to heaven to enjoy your glory, our Community knows that they always come to bid me farewell by some signal, either in my room or elsewhere, if I do not have the suffrages offered for them as is proper in all the monasteries. This occurs when there is a delay in informing me of their deaths, with the excuse that, for various reasons, the Sisters fear to give me such sad

JEANNE'S ORIGINAL DRAFT

news. This they had to acknowledge when I informed them that I believed certain Sisters had died. What still perturbs me is that, during all this time, they deprived Purgatory of the suffrages, prayers, Masses and Communions which the Constitutions oblige our monasteries to offer for them.

On the Feast of St. Luke, St. Simon and St. Jude, I said to You: "How is it, dear Love, that You communicate Yourself to me, the most unworthy one, and not to so many others who are virtuous while I am not?" You told me: "I desire mercy for you, and for the others I expect the sacrifices they have promised Me in view of their temporal and eternal benefits, as I did of Jephte who vowed to offer Me in sacrifice the first living thing he met that belonged to him after he had won his victory. I wanted the fulfillment of this, not exempting him as I did Abraham from the real death of his Isaac whom he would have willingly sacrificed. I stopped the effect, suspended his arm and sword when he raised it to kill his son, thus prohibiting him from sacrificing him, but placing a ram there to symbolize my death which would be a reality." (888) Dear Love, I offer You to your Divine Father, for all You have allowed and granted me. Through your kind clemency, You have given me grace for grace, telling me that my confidence caused it to be given to me in advance. This is how good and merciful You are toward me.

On the Feast of All Saints, You deigned to provide a great feast for me. Your Blessed Mother gave me splendid gifts to which You agreed with inexpressible goodness. I understood that all your saints are with her near the altars where You repose in the adorable Eucharist, which You had instituted to make up for the omissions of mankind, even for their contempt toward this adorable sacrament, their impiety and terrible crimes. Also, vengeance is required for trampling underfoot the Blood of the Testament. Dear Love, You know my reactions to these just demands. I wept so profusely that it seemed that I would lose my sight. These tears did not extinguish the fire of your wrath, which increased to the extent that I offered myself as a sacrifice to be entirely consumed. Seeing that I was enduring these unbearable ardors without your assistance, You lovingly said to me: "Tell Me that you are languishing for love." Obeying You, I prayed to all your saints to tell You what You did

JEANNE'S ORIGINAL DRAFT

not ignore, since You commanded me to express my languishing to You through them. My loving martyrdom became intensified when they explained to me how great my flame was, by the recital I gave them, that enraptured me also so that I became happily engulfed in your adorable splendors. Without being the secretary of your Majesty, I was marvelously crushed by your glory. (889)

CHAPTER CXXV

My vision about the entrance of the saints into our little chapel and the marvels that the Incarnate Word and his Blessed Mother taught me there. He was the ram that was sacrificed and the one who offered the sacrifice. The multiple graces I received.

On December 5, 1642, the Bishop of Condon came to visit me as he graciously did as often as possible. He told me that he had offered Mass at the Sorbonne where a number of bishops had assisted the day before for a service in honor of the late Cardinal Richelieu. I told him: "I have a deep desire to attend a pontifical Mass." He laughed at my desire, telling me that the chapel where I attended Mass was only a small room, for we had not yet returned to our monastery in the Saint Germain suburb. We were still staying at Monsieur de la Piardière's home that was located near the Richelieu entrance on Vivienne Street.

In the evening, I entered this little room as I usually did, for it was here that Holy Mass was offered daily for us. My Divine Pontiff, You were pleased to tell me that You wanted to fulfil my desire, sympathizing with my needs, but

JEANNE'S ORIGINAL DRAFT

also ready to grant my inclinations and fulfill my desire. At the same time, in a most sublime vision, in spirit I saw all your saints carrying a well, that I could see was very deep, which they placed in this chapel. They told me: "This is the well of wisdom." They peered into it with profound attention. They drew these waters in such a wonderful way without my noting that they used the cord that was there that was well-placed and had a pulley to descend, but I did not see any receptacle. (890)

In spirit, all your saints drew forth knowledge and wisdom that still remained immense and did not diminish when they shared in them. They let me understand that, even though I was but a young woman, You had placed this well within my soul. You delighted for them to come see this marvel of knowledge that You had placed in me, informing me about their compliance with your desire. Even though they abide in heaven, they come down to earth to admire your goodness here and learn your secrets from a young woman whom You thus favor. You told them that in me could be found their apocalypse, and they could be enraptured by your ineffable favors to me. You told me: "Come see the sacrifice of love, sorrow and power upon Mount Moriah. First view the symbol, and then I will show you the reality and let you enjoy it. Consider Abraham offering up his Isaac with his arm raised ready to sacrifice him and see my loving providence that substituted for him by producing a ram caught by the horns among the thorns that Adam's sin had produced.

"This ram, my daughter, symbolized Me, offering Myself to my Eternal Father under this figure that changed Abraham's extreme pain into ecstatic joy. He had submitted his paternal feelings to the divine command, his understanding gripped in the service of the faith. Without losing any of its justice, the divinity was satisfied with him. It disposed that I, with my Mother, should pay for all the debts of mankind by rigors that you could not understand. I granted Abraham the joy that was unparalleled on earth before my Resurrection. As I did with Isaac, I provided him with seed. I granted him all blessings and joys. (891) As for Me, I assumed every cross, sustaining the weight of sin and the culpability before divine justice. Thus, by my voluntary submission and although impassible, I fell into the hands of the Living God so as to be and seem

JEANNE'S ORIGINAL DRAFT

to be the dead God in his presence and in that of all reasoning creatures, not only upon Calvary, but on the Last Day, when the sign of the Son of Man will appear upon the seat of Majesty.

"My daughter, the ram was I. It was I, my daughter; it was I, my favorite one." When for the third time, I heard: "It was I, my daughter and my chosen one," my soul nearly left my body to enter into You, for I was beside myself. You stopped me by telling me: "Stand firm to see the Virgin of virgins, my Blessed Mother, who offers the sacrifice, who offers and sacrifices the Eternal Pontiff, her flesh and blood. He, in turn, offers and presents Himself as an adorable and real oblation for a thousand, thousand worlds, showing that love is greater than death.

"This marvelous sacrificer remained standing between the temple and the altar. Since the sacrifice was part of her substance that she offered for everyone, the sun hid in mourning, the earth trembled, the rocks split asunder, the tombs opened, the veil of the temple was rent. All nature seemed to have reached the point of destruction. The Virgin Mother remained steadfast beside the altar where she offered and sacrificed her Victim. She offered Him to my Eternal Father as a perfect holocaust, thus able to declare: *Introibo in domum tuam in holocaustis; reddam tibi vota mea quæ distinxerunt labia mea. Et locutum est os meum in tribulatione mea. I will go into thy house with burnt offerings: I will pay thee my vows, which my lips have uttered. And my mouth hath spoken, when I was in trouble."* (Ps 65:13-14a) (892)

"I offer you all the sacrifices and holocausts by offering You my Son in my sorrow. You will not suffer, holy Father. The essence He received from You is unchangeable. It is the nature He received from me that suffers. He has consummated everything. If You are not satisfied, here I am to accept the lance-thrust that your Holy Spirit predicted for me by the lips of Simeon, who was his representative. This Spirit, who assured him that he would see his salvation and supernatural life before natural death closed his eyes, found me steadfast at the foot of the Cross. It was the altar of my sorrow where my

JEANNE'S ORIGINAL DRAFT

Son was nailed so as courageously to receive the lance thrust that would be the pitiless sword to pierce my soul. It brought about daylight for many whose thoughts in their hearts were in darkness, whose sighs could neither produce nor explain them."

This wonderful and real Amazon was victorious over the Lord of Hosts who had ordered unleashed the most terrible assault ever seen in heaven, earth or hell. The angels wept bitterly; the demons of war were there despoiled of all their powers. The guilty saw the One whom they had pierced with their lances that were more cruel than the one that opened his side. Victorious over all, the Virgin Mother remained standing and saw the consummation of the mystery of God concealed in the tomb, being the true Savior. Victorious over a man, Judith was acclaimed by all her people, but Mary is the admiration of God Himself, the jubilation of heaven, earth and Limbo.

Suspended at the sight of these spectacles of love, my spirit had left its body in such great cold that it took a long time for it to become warm. This caused such a great secretion in one knee that the bone seemed to have been infected. It did not heal until after Easter. Although a number of remedies were made there, the nerve remained weak or shrunken. I said to You: "Angel of the Great Council, when You called me to Calvary's sorrow, You sprained one of my nerves as You did the wrestler from whom You withdrew vanquished." (893)

On another day, as I attended Holy Mass in this little chapel, at my right side I saw the Pope's tiara. You let me hear: "My daughter, those who find fault with the fact that devout men take council from a young woman do not know that my Spirit, who governs the Church, uses you whereby to declare his plans to them. You are a daughter of the Church. Take care to commend to Me its visible Head that he may make my will known about questions that trouble souls, who discuss grace while resisting grace. My daughter, receive grace for grace and correspond with it with your liberty. Saint Paul exhorts Christians not to receive it in vain."

JEANNE'S ORIGINAL DRAFT

In Paris and elsewhere, a number of clergy strove to turn away the one You had called to the dignity of the priesthood and sent me to teach and guide him to the perfection You asked of him according to the lights your goodness imparted to me. In a derisive manner, one of them told him that your Church had not yet fallen to the spindle (meaning: into the hands of women). Your goodness, who chooses weak things with which to confound those who presume upon their wisdom, allowed this cleric to fall victim to an illness that did not allow him one moment of reason with which to receive the sacraments. He had to be bound during the four or five days remaining him of life, and he expired in this condition.

A number of others who sought to destroy your Order and to cause embarrassment to the one whom your goodness protects have already demonstrated by their own fall that there is no council that can successfully stand against You, my Lord and my God. Three have died during the present year who were expected to live a long time. The others have been forced to resign from their charges or dignities because of the powerlessness to which You had reduced them. (894)

JEANNE'S ORIGINAL DRAFT

CHAPTER CXXVI

With a diamond, the Incarnate Word and Saint John, your favorite, had me admire the Immaculate Conception of Our Lady, who appeared to me holding the Blessed Sacrament in one hand and a Crown of Thorns in the other; the many favors I received on the Feasts of Saint Lucy, Saint Thomas, Christmas night and the Feast of the Holy Innocents.

On the night of the Eve of the Conception of your all-pure Mother in 1652, I saw a river or a sea, with ships. Approaching one that was apart from the others, I saw a fisherman aboard, dressed in a white and red robe and holding a diamond between his thumb and finger, that had never been worked on by the hands of men. Instead of angles or points, there were flames which did not burn exteriorly. This diamond enclosed all the light of the sun, the moon, the stars and fire. The fisherman who held and contemplated the diamond was Saint John the Evangelist. On the bank, he had received it from a very gracious Man, also dressed in a long white and red robe. It was You, my Love, who commanded your favorite disciple to give me this diamond to show that it should be esteemed.

I was astonished that people near me did not marvel at this diamond given me by your favorite disciple, whom I saw as another You. I was delighted to see that You and Saint John were but one. You let me understand that, being the Son of the Virgin, You wanted Saint John to be that also. (895) Your infinite love had made him what You are—for love tends to unity—that each of you had given me this diamond. By a divine favor, You had shown me the purity of your holy Mother and her most pure Conception. You told me that this Immaculate Mother was all-beautiful, totally resplendent and filled with light, but that she retained her illuminations without allowing them to be visible

JEANNE'S ORIGINAL DRAFT

except to those whom your wise goodness gratified with the privilege of seeing and touching this marvel, like Saint John who saw and touched the Word of Life whom this Virgin enclosed within her womb wherein He was invested with her most pure substance. It is You, Divine Love, who bears your Divine Father's entire word. You are the figure of his substance, the image of his goodness, the stainless mirror of his Majesty, the splendor of his glory. Lost in your illuminations, together with your three Apostles, I fell down at the sight of your splendor: *Pulchritudinem candoris eius admirabatur oculus, et super imbrem eius expavescet cor. The eye admireth at the beauty of the whiteness thereof: and the heart is astonished at the shower thereof.* (Eccl 43:20) The Sacred Body that You assumed within the virginal womb is whiter than snow. The sunshine of your face, as brilliant as possible, dazzles the eyes and makes the heart faint away: blessed languishing. Had You been willing, I would have wished to die as a result of this.

Confined to bed because of my knee problem, I gently excused myself. Seeing that I was unable to remain kneeling, You let me understand that I was not to be embarrassed by my posture, that your Blessed Mother had been seated when the Archangel Gabriel announced your Incarnation to her and your Spirit came upon her. (896) Troubled at his words, she was overwhelmed by the brilliance of light with which this glorious Spirit appeared, announcing the coming within her of the Sun of Justice, the Orient from on high. It is You, my God, Light of light, that came to become incarnate within her. So as to remove my every anxiety, You also had me understand, Divine Love, that your disciples were seated in the Cenacle when You sent them your Spirit of fire, that the great wind might have overthrown them and that it was better for them to be seated when You sent them this Spirit by which they were to judge men. The Virgin of Virgins is the seat of your Majesty who can, under the palm of victory that she bears, judge Israel with greater power and knowledge than did Deborah.

My knee problem confined me to bed longer than my fervor preferred. Your Blessed Mother appeared to me, in one hand bearing the Sacred Host over a chalice and, in the other, a Crown of Thorns that she presented to me

JEANNE'S ORIGINAL DRAFT

as being grace itself. Who would not have accepted this wonderful grace, the Holy Eucharist presented by the one who is full of grace? It would have to be a demon who hated his goodness. Dear Love, let me love her as much as I should and that she could be loved in heaven and on earth. Let me love You through your own love. Let me live and die in it. Let love be stronger in me than death, and its jealousy harder than hell. (897)

My Divine Love, on the Feast of Saint Lucy, virgin and martyr, You deigned to show me your spouse all-brilliant, like her name, adorned with her Bridegroom. She was marvelously beautiful and of wonderful grace, in my opinion. This vision consoled me during my troubles. For a number of years, she has favored me on her feastday.

On the Feast of the expectation of the Birth of your Virgin Mother, having favored me for many years on these days, You were pleased to continue your blessings. Unwilling to possess by myself the joy You communicated to me, I felt impelled by your Spirit to tell the Abbé de St. Just that I was announcing a great joy to him, knowing that Monsieur de Nay would soon be the Archbishop of Lyons and that he would be his Vicar General. He replied that I would always be the wonderful one, as the cherished spouse of the One who is so by essence and par excellence. It is of You, my Divine Love, that he speaks in this delightul letter of January 10, 1652, in which he told me that I would always triumph over the contradictions made me by my enemies.

On the night of the Feast of St. Thomas the Apostle, toward whom You had given me a strong devotion—loving him because he wanted to die with You, by exhorting his fellow disciples to satisfy yours when You went to console Martha and Mary by bringing back to life their brother and your friend, Lazarus—You showed me a violet flower with which I played, although it was enclosed in a frame. (898) It was also present there as in a flower plot. Without my breaking the glass when I touched it with a ring, it flew to my lips.

Since the next day, the Feast of Saint Thomas, was a Sunday, I observed a

JEANNE'S ORIGINAL DRAFT

day of joy and rejoicing. It pleased You, my Divine Healer, to tell me that I would rejoice immediately, that You agreed with your saints and that You delight in the music chanted in heaven. Your goodness allowed me to participate with them. St. Michael said: *Quis ut Deus; Who is like to God;* the Royal Chanter: *Rex meus et Deus meus; My king and my God* (Ps 83:4); St. Thomas: *Dominus meus et Deus; My Lord and my God*; and the most unworthy one: *Jesus, amor meus; Jesus, my Love.* I have no words with which to express the grace You gave me. May all your saints thank you for this, Jesus, my Love.

On Christmas night, I had to hear Matins while in bed because my knee hurt me more than it had a few days before. I was consoled a little, because there was only a limited separation between my daughters who sang them and myself. (899) The chapel where Holy Mass was offered was level, as was the parlor and the room I inhabited that faced both places. You consoled me even more by the thought that many sick persons cannot attend Matins nor even Holy Mass, because I was helped by one of my daughters to be able to attend.

Your ordinary generosity tending toward me, (if I may so speak), You let me understand that my afflictions moved You to pity and that I was like the apple of your loving eyes. Whoever resisted me, resisted You, because their resistance was motivated by injustice. You said to them: *Discedite a me omnes qui operamini iniquitatem; Depart from me, all ye workers of iniquity,* (Ps 6:9a) that you wanted to hear the voice of my cries and that my tears would be present before You.

Dear Love, You know for whom my tears were offered to You. I am obligated to all your angels and saints. With marvelous grace, one said: *Dixit Dominus Domino meo; Sede a dextris meis, donec ponam inimicos tuos scabellum pedum tuorum. The Lord said to my Lord: Sit thou at my right hand: Until I make thy enemies thy footstool.* (Ps 109:1) When I finished this entire Psalm, You let me know what You wanted to do to my enemies who, You told me, were yours also. You would strike down a

JEANNE'S ORIGINAL DRAFT

number of them and elevate me near You, who are my Head, after I had imbibed from the torrent of contradictions that You allowed for your glory and my well-being.

On the Feast of the Holy Innocents, You favored me with your loving caresses that are not effeminate. You let me understand that the cruel death of these little innocent ones made them like towers, citadels and boulevards. They had saved your life. Through them, You had vanquished Herod who thought He had killed You among their number. Although he assuaged his rage with this carnage along life's journey, he reserved his punishment for the next life. Through power and patience, You endured his cruelty and treachery when he told the Wise Men that he wanted to go adore You, although he had resolved to have You killed: *Inimici Domini mentiti sunt ei, et erit tempus eorum in sæcula. The enemies of the Lord have lied to him; and their time shall be forever.* (Ps 80:16)

CHAPTER CXXVII

The New Year's gifts that the Incarnate Word gave me. The marvels He let me understand on the Octave of the Feasts of St. John and the Holy Innocents, the Royal Prophet David and the Epiphany.

On the Feast of the Circumcision in 1653, You let me understand: "My daughter, as a New Year's gift, I am giving you Holy Scripture. (901) I am called Jesus the Nazarean, and today I am giving you a new Jerusalem. The first letter of my holy Name is the same as yours, and the last one, like the first one in the Bible, begins with the same one. Genesis begins with "I": *In*

JEANNE'S ORIGINAL DRAFT

principio, *In the beginning* and the last one ends the Apocalypse. *Veni Domine Jesus Amen, Come, Lord Jesus, Amen* said my favorite, St. John, who commenced his Gospel *In principio* and ended his Apocalypse with *Jesus, Amen.* What belongs to your Bridegroom belongs to you; He is your ornament. This is what delights the heavenly citizens."

On the Feast of the Octave of St. John, your favorite disciple invited me to approach You to show me this special disciple resting upon your breast. You said to me: "Contemplate this child of love reposing in such a way upon the source of grace that possesses all the treasures of heaven and earth. The two feet of his affections are in Me. He is in ecstasy, elevated by the One who is supreme heaven. There is no point in him ouside earth, which was the desire of the one who vainly boasted that he could raise its entire mass if he were to have a foothold outside this massive element. (902) This beloved is at peace during the trouble of all the disciples, and mine also, that he referred to in his rapture and records in his Gospel, having heard that whoever receives Me receives my Father: *Qui autem me accipit, accipit eum qui me misit. Cum hæc dixisset Jesus, turbatus est spiritu. He that receiveth me receiveth him that sent me. When Jesus had said these things, he was troubled in spirit.* (Jn 13:20c-21a)

"My daughter, if this favorite one had been alone on earth, I would have come to wash his feet and prepare him as my love. Through my sacrament, I wanted to remain in him and him in Me, making him my Mother's son through my loving and all-powerful word."

Dear Love, allow this young woman to ask You how she could understand your declaration that, from among those born of women, no one is greater than John the Baptist. "My daughter, understand this secret. It was during John the Baptist's time that I uttered these words due to his holiness and penance. But, on the day of my Supper, the day that I made, sacramentally reproducing my Body, my Blood and my Soul through concomitance with my indivisible divinity, John the Evangelist was another I, receiving a divine birth upon my breast. (902-2) He is a phoenix that is reborn, not from my ashes,

JEANNE'S ORIGINAL DRAFT

but from my flames. He possessed the grace to subsist in eternal ardor amid the splendor of holiness before the Feast of the Resurrection of my physical and natural Body. My Apostle applied these words of the Prophet King to my Resurrection: *Dominus dixit a me: Filius meus es tu, Ego hodie genui te. The Lord hath said to me: Thou art my son; this day have I begotten thee.* (Ps 2:7)

"He was speaking to Me in the person of my Father, and I applied them to John, my heart's favorite. I gave birth to him before my death and Resurrection. I made him a priest, serving as his miter and vestment. I made him holy and consecrated him upon my breast, the adorable and adored altar. Just as I am, I was my Eternal Father's ointment, unction and oil of rejoicing. Aaron's consecration prefigured mine and the one I would give, by consecrating John, who was to assist at my exterior death. He possessed the interior one within himself through the Eucharistic sacrament that I placed in this marvelous ark to the admiration of all the angels. I showed them that my wisdom possessed as much and even more care of preserving this divine manna than the one they had kneaded and given the Israelites in the desert which was but the symbol. Since my love was stronger than death, I remained in John after my death. (902-3) My love kept him standing upon Calvary with our Blessed Mother. I say "our Mother", because we are her two sons. She had told the Archangel Gabriel: *Fiat mihi secundum verbum tuum; Be it done to me according to thy word.* (Lk 1:38) The Word became flesh in her. The Word became Man within her womb through this all-powerful word. In the Cenacle, John became the son of God and of the Virgin and was declared such upon Calvary, when He said: *Mulier ecce filius tuus; Woman, behold thy son;* and to John: *Ecce mater tua; Behold thy Mother.* This is what upheld them at the foot of the Cross while all nature was moved, rocks split, and tombs opened, allowing the dead to emerge, for they were called to this unheard of spectacle."

My Divine Master, could I express and produce in ink upon this paper the illuminations You gave my understanding, calling me by name to see this favorite upon your adorable breast? Did I not tell you: "I will go see this great vision that contains all good"? In accordance with this favorite, You let me

JEANNE'S ORIGINAL DRAFT

understand your eternal generation, and, after a thousand, thousand favors, You told me that You wanted me to know the loving excess of your death. (903) Can I express and live it after these loving words? 'Farewell, my daughter, I am leaving this hemisphere, and I am going to Limbo.' I would lose both life and being were You not to be each of them for me. I cannot express the marvels I understood. If I could do so, they would not be ineffable to me.

On the Feast of the Octave of the Holy Innocents, who had accepted me as their sister in 1619, they wanted immediately to treat me as such. Agreeing to this, your Majesty let me know that, through weakness, You wanted to demonstrate the power of grace, elevating these Holy Innocents near your throne, rewarding them for the death they endured, which served You as a shield, a tower, a dungeon and citadel. They were struck down to deprive them of life, but You were not among them as Herod erroneously thought .

You allowed me to admire them like suns, moons and stars, chanting the hymn of your glory. Their lips and hands are unstained, for they never sullied either body or soul. (904) By their innocent simplicity, they outwitted Herod's astuteness, when he determined to murder a King by massacring the little Innocents. By doing so, he made them all kings, as well as victims, who follow the slain Lamb wherever He goes, singing a canticle that only virgins may sing as they do.

You let me know that there was great joy in heaven due to the glory of these innocent infants. Dear Love, what an antithesis! The Militant Church shows us Rachel, weeping and refusing to be consoled, and the Triumphant Church chants with jubilation. You told me: "My daughter, however much heaven's music differs from that of earth, it does correspond by order of the Holy Spirit who directs the measure of each of them. The Militant one is wailing and weeping along life's journey, and the Triumphant one in the next life is jubilant and joyful. This Holy Spirit prays and groans in the hearts of the pilgrims: *Gemitibus inenarrabilibus; Unspeakable groanings* (Rom 8:26) at the same time that He fills the heavenly citizens with rejoicing, while they are

JEANNE'S ORIGINAL DRAFT

engulfed in the way of their glorious Lord.

On the Eve of Epiphany, I reflected on David's good fortune in his city, the One whom the Kings came to adore as the Son of God and King of the Jews and his Son according to the flesh as Saint Paul declares: *Qui prædestinatus est Filius Dei in virtute secundum spiritum sanctificationis. Who was predestinated the Son of God in power, according to the spirit of sanctification.* (Rom 1:4) (905) My daughter, admire the goodness of my Eternal Father who has given you this same Son, making you his mother and the mother of his Order. Every day pray that He may give you a kiss. He has done so for thirty-three years through daily Communion. Through your lips, open your heart, and there receive the Word grafted in goodness who can save your soul. As mother and spouse of the Word, speak about the glory of the most beautiful among the children of men. Do not fear if people on earth blame you. I will defend your cause in the presence of my Eternal Father and his angels. Remember what Peter and my other Apostles said to those who forbade them to speak about Me, to teach in my Name: *Obedire oportet Deo magis quam hominibus. We ought to obey God rather than men.* (Acts 5:29b)

If you are filled with the Holy Spirit who gives testimony to you and prompts you to speak, can men impose silence upon you? The princes, Scribes and Pharisees urged Me to impose it upon little children. Had Eve spoken about the marvels of God who created her in the earthly garden, resisting the serpent as did Michael in the heavenly one when he said: "Who is like to God to exceed his commandments?", she would not have taken the forbidden fruit and given it to Adam. Neither one of them would have eaten it. They would not have pricked Me with the thorns that this fruit produced.

On the Feast of the Epiphany, in the stable, I wordlessly adored You, seeing You as the mute Word while the Kings marveled in silence. (906) You showed me a sphere and let me understand: "My daughter, I am the sphere. On observing my abasement in the stable, these Kings were unspeakably dumbfounded as they contemplated Me. They saw my horoscope, sufferings,

AUTOBIOGRAPHY

JEANNE'S ORIGINAL DRAFT

and voluntary death. They saw the sun, the orient from on high abased. They saw this wonderful moon, my Blessed Mother and the star of Jacob—Joseph, the son of Jacob. The star that led them was only the symbol. It disappeared after having shown them the place where lay the Child, the Son of God and of the Virgin.

"These Kings were delighted, as were my Blessed Mother and her chaste spouse, with the report of my Evangelist: *Erat pater eius et mater mirantes. His father and mother were wondering.* (Lk 2:33a) After adoring Me and offering their gifts, they left the stable and, at the command of the angel, took a different route. They pondered over the marvels they had seen and adored until the day that my Apostle Thomas declared to them the marvels of my life, the cruel death inflicted upon me by the Jews. He assured them of my resurrection and glory, telling them that they had been irreproachable witnesses, for they had seen Me and my glorious Wounds. After instructing them, he baptized them and allowed them to assist in preaching the Gospel."

While I was in the chapel to attend Holy Mass and Communion, my spirit became engulfed in an inexpressible confusion. (907) After having received You in your sacrament, I rose from your holy table to withdraw to a corner behind the chapel door. All our religious daughters were there with a lighted candle, renewing their vows in the presence of the Sacred Host which the priest gave them after their renovation. At sight and sound of their sacrifices, I became even more confused, saying: "Lord, I have chosen to be the last, the servant, the cook and the domestic in your house. In imitation of You, I prefer these lowly offices and humiliations to any empire or crown. In spirit, I kiss the feet of your spouses." On noticing that one of them had hers at the entrance and thinking that she was concentrated on what she was doing, concealed behind this door, bowing and bending forward I lifted the back of her cloak without her noticing and kissed them with great respect and humiliation. I considered the acts that your merciful greatness had produced in me with sentiments of my nothingness. I did so, seeing that I could not take the solemn vows of poverty and obedience. (908) I resigned myself to your good pleasure in this for as long as your Holy Spirit deemed it appropriate for me to

175

JEANNE'S ORIGINAL DRAFT

do so. I knew that He inspires what He wants in those whom he chooses and that He allows his voice to be heard in many ways: *Spiritus ubi vult spirat, et vocem eius audis, sed nescis unde veniat, aut quo vadat: sic est omnis qui natus est ex Spiritu. The Spirit breatheth where he will and thou hearest his voice: but thou knowest not whence he cometh and whither he goeth. So is every one that is born of the Spirit.* (Jn 3:8)

He knows from whence He comes from and where He is going. No mortal knows this unless the same Spirit, together with the Word and the Father, reveals it to him, as his only principle and He the immense expression of their production. O Divine Spirit, your secret belongs to You. *Cum regnaverit Dominus exercituum in monte Sion et in Jerusalem et in conspectu senium suorum fuerit glorificatus. The Lord of Hosts had reigned on Mount Sion and had been glorified in Jerusalem and in the presence of the elders.* (Non biblical)

Humbled before You, my soul would wait as long as it pleased You. The grace You have given our daughters is great. They are as elevated as I am humbled. "My daughter, listen to my Royal Prophet, who told you that I look upon my humble ones and listen attentively and lovingly to their prayer and that I do not reject their prayers: *Respexit in orationem humilium et non sprevit preces eorum. Scribantur hæc in generatione altera, et populus qui creabitur laudabit Dominum. He hath regard to the prayer of the humble: and he hath not despised their petition. Let these things be written unto another generation: and the people that shall be created shall praise the Lord.* (Ps 101:18)

"My goodness will make your humiliations produce my glory in you; they will be recorded for generations to come. (909) Some Congregations that are similar to mine will profit from them, and the peoples I will create shall praise me because of them." You explained the other verses for my benefit and told me: *Quia prospexit de excelso sancto suo. Dominus de cælo in terram aspexit; ut audiret gemitus compeditorum, ut solveret filios interemptorum; ut annuntient in Sion nomen Domini, et laudem eius in Jerusalem. Be-*

JEANNE'S ORIGINAL DRAFT

cause he hath looked forth from his high sanctuary: from heaven the Lord hath looked upon the earth. That he might hear the groans of them that are in fetters: that he might release the children of the slain. That they may declare the name of the Lord in Sion; and his praise in Jerusalem. (Ps 101:20-22)

CHAPTER CXXVIII

Admiration of St. Joachim and St. Anne, with allusion to that of the Virgin and St. Joseph. St. John the Baptist's humility at the Savior's baptism and the sorrow of the Virgin Mother and St. Joseph. The favors I received on the Feasts of Saint Paul, the first hermit, and Saint Anthony, abbot.

On January 7th, I was reflecting upon the happiness of St. Joseph on living with his Virgin Spouse and her Child-God. I recalled the joy of St. Joachim and St. Anne upon contemplating their daughter during the three years they kept her at home. I understood that they were two Cherubim who protected this propitiatory who was of their substance, the daughter who could claim to be the mercy of these two merciful persons who had produced this marvelous olive, the beautiful one par excellence, chosen to be the Mother of God. (910) The silence of both of them imposed a similar one upon me until the Word would prompt me to speak. On January 8th, as I was wondering why the Circumcision had no Octave, You let me understand that there is no end of delays and sufferings in this life and that You were giving me yours as a New Year's gift. I was to consider You in them, my magnificent Savior, and in You I would find all well-being. You are the glory of your chosen ones, and You are all things to them. You give Yourself to me, and I abandon myself to You,

JEANNE'S ORIGINAL DRAFT

giving myself entirely to my All.

On the day of the Octave of the Kings in the Gospel, the Church presents your marvelous baptism that made your Precursor marvel, who was sanctified by You personally, the fountain of purity. He said to You: *Ego a te debeo baptizari, et tu venis ad me? I ought to be baptized by thee, and comest thou to me?* (Mt 3:14) You let me understand that St. John's humility was very profound when he ingenuously said that he did not know who You were except through the Spirit who sent him to the Jordan. The sign He was given whereby to recognize You was the coming of a dove. Thus, he showed that he did not consider himself a prophet, although his father had called him a prophet of the Most High and You personally called him a prophet. (911) He realized that prophecy is an act and not a habit, that it is a light that You give whenever it pleases You to do so, that You are a free oracle as well as a voluntary mirror. If he called himself the Voice, it was so as to prepare a perfect people for You. He was like the trumpet sent by the king when he enters the field: his eyes are blindfolded. John was sent by You when You sanctified him in his mother's womb and made You known as soon as he was born. You withdrew to Nazareth, remaining thirty years without showing Yourself to him. He could not endure being considered a prophet—yet he recognized You as the Word of God, who is all light, all purity and all holiness. He told You that this perception of your attributes led him to You to be baptized, if so You desired, just as You were the Christ, Son of the Living God, begotten in eternity and not made in time, just as You had created him to be your simple servant, for the most insignificant one in heaven was greater than he.

You had me understand, Divine Love, that his feelings of unworthiness at your baptism were incomparably deeper than what is admired, when he acknowledged that he was not the Christ. He could not accept this quality that was and is due to You as the true Messias. As for being a prophet, he could accept that. (912) As I marveled at the humble sentiments of my patron, You let me understand: "Admire what I told him, that he and I should accept and accomplish all justice, obeying him on being baptized, pouring the river water

JEANNE'S ORIGINAL DRAFT

upon my head and I, by taking a basin of water with which to wash the feet of my Apostles and of Judas, the most unfortunate among men, as I was the most blessed since I am the Beloved Son of my Divine Father and the beatitude of all the saints. My birth gave glory in heaven to God the Most High and peace on earth to men of good will. It is said of Judas that it would have been better had he never been born. Judas opened hell when he went down there, and I the heavens by ascending there as belonging to Me.

John heard the nuptial chant of the Spouse and rejoiced because of it. When Judas saw the beloved pour oil upon the feet of the sacred Bridegroom, he was filled with indignation. John wanted all glory and sweetness given the Incarnate Word, that heaven and earth should honor Him and bow down before Him. He humbled himself and bowed his head. He wanted Jesus to increase and be known as God of God. Judas begrudged Him the ointment and anointing that Mary gave Him in preparation for his burial, for He was to endure the death that this traitor procured for him by selling and delivering Him up to his enemies. It sufficed that he dwelt on this envy that hell encloses in its dungeons. (913) Love, allow your little disciple to admire You while your Father declares aloud that You are his delight and the Spirit come down from heaven, that is open, inflames the angels with an ardent desire to contemplate You: *Spiritu sancto misso de cælo, in quem desiderant angeli prospicere. The Holy Ghost being sent down from heaven, on whom the angels desire to look.* (1 P 1:12)

But who would have thought that the Holy Spirit wished to bid on your ignominy, when together with sinners, You were submitted to the river of penitence. Did it not suffice that You humbled Yourself without being chased and sent by Him into the desert with the beasts, as St. Mark declares: *Et statim Spiritus expulit eum in desertum. Et erat in deserto quadraginta diebus, et quadraginta noctibus: et tentabatur a Satana: eratque cum bestiis. And immediately the Spirit drove him out into the desert. And he was in the desert forty days and forty nights, and was tempted by Satan. And he was with beasts.* (Mk 1:12-13)

On the Sunday when the Church uses the Gospel that your Mother searched

JEANNE'S ORIGINAL DRAFT

for You for three days, I offered to accompany her and share in her anguish. She let me understand that her sorrow was as excessive as her loss was great. Because her Son had not yet brought about the redemption of mankind, and since good souls fear where there is no reason to fear, she thought that she had not taken enough care of her Divine Child, that the sword predicted by Simeon could possibly be this deprivation of her Savior as well as that of all mankind. (914) When she found Him, love induced her to tell Him about the sorrow that Saint Joseph and she had felt: *Fili, quid fecisti nobis sic? ecce pater tuus et ego dolentes quærebamus te? Son, why hast thou done so to us? Behold thy father and I have sought thee sorrowing.* (Lk 2:48b)

Although her Son gave a response that should have assured her that, as the Son of the Eternal Father, He was not abandoning her at all when He occupied Himself with the works of his glory and the salvation of mankind, the Evangelist said that she and Saint Joseph did not understand what He said. Their souls were filled with sadness that obscured their understanding and overwhelmed their hearts. *Et ipsi non intellexerunt verbum, quod locutus est et ad eos. And they understood not the word that he spoke unto them.* (Lk 2:49c) To console them, He went down to Nazareth with them and was subject to them: *Et descendit cum eis, et venit Nazareth: et erat subditus illis. Et mater eius conservabat omnia verba hæc in corde suo. And he went down with them and came to Nazareth and was subject to them. And his mother kept all these words in her heart.* (Lk 2:51)

Dear wonderful one, keep these divine words in your heart as the balm that will heal your wound. Engulf your spirit in this strong, living fountain after having searched for it, not at a loss of breath, but rather almost at a loss of life. You feel worse than David did. Jesus Christ is your life more than he was for Saint Paul. You live in Him more than in yourself. By possessing Him, You have your prize, your treasure, your life and your God. Dear Mother of my Spouse, may He be all these things to me through your care. (915)

On the Feast of St. Paul, the first hermit, as I reflected on the life of this saint in the desert to which he had retired, fleeing the persecution of the

JEANNE'S ORIGINAL DRAFT

emperors, I marveled at your wisdom that works miracles which men do not consider. As a youngster at the age of fifteen, Saint Paul did not possess the courage necessary for the martyr's palm nor for enduring the persecution by his brother-in-law in the cities or his home. The desert received him and became his city of refuge. A palm tree is his source of food and clothing. With it, near it, he triumphed over the world, the flesh and the devil. He became an angel without ceasing to be a man. Fleeing the cruelty of the emperors of earth and of his relatives, he was accepted by You, my heavenly Emperor. He became a citizen of heaven and a servant of God. His name, as was that of Saint Anthony, was written in the Book of Life. By your divine revelation, they became acquainted with one another. Miraculously did your providence nurture them and lead them to confer together about a marvelous life unknown to the world. It would inspire so many friends to love the desert and withdraw there. This simple St. Paul, great in your eyes and those of the angels, would not die until marvelous Anthony, father of so many monks—like another Abraham, the father of multitudes—had learned the secret that heaven concealed in him. (916)

Incarnate Word, my love whom I adore, did You not tell your saints: *Num celare potero; Can I hide* (Gen 18:17) from Anthony what I have done and will do for Paul. My tendency is to display the graces I have done by my nature which is good. Being God, I am good in and of Myself. I cannot conceal my marvels from Anthony. I want him to know them and to declare them for my glory and the salvation of many. I want him to inform mankind that the providence of my Eternal Father divinely governs heaven and earth, that life hidden in God is manifested at the time He ordains. He who fled persecution by the emperors, because he felt too weak, is the admiration of the one who, impressed by reading his wonderful life, withdrew courtesans from the imperial delights that they realized were tortures because of the pain and anxiety they experienced in their search for perishable and imaginary favors. Anthony's life, which Paul read and admired, reveals that solitude is preferred by the heavenly courtesans to living in cities and conversing with the princes of earth. (917)

JEANNE'S ORIGINAL DRAFT

Reflecting upon the happiness possessed by these two anchorites, my soul loved nothing in the world any more, regretting that I could not leave it to give myself entirely to You, my Savior, as have done my daughters to whom I accorded the habit and religious profession. Charity required me to deprive myself of this consolation, for I wanted nothing for myself but for Jesus Christ. What is your greatest glory, my Divine Love? You told me: "Do not be upset, my dearest. You are invested with my Blood, as I told you before. You are interiorly invested with your Crucified Jesus. I wore the white robe only during the time I was sent from Herod to Pilate, and the purple and scarlet mantle only to appear as the Man of Sorrows, who offered Himself to his Eternal Father for the salvation of mankind. At sight of Him, all the people cried out: 'Crucify Him, Crucify Him!' When I was made to carry my Cross, my mantle was removed, but my clothes were returned to Me so that I might thereby be recognized by all while I carried my Cross. My daughter, then, do not be upset if you will have the red and white habit for only a little while, to show that you are the one who has, at my command, shown it to the world and given it to my daughters who are also yours. They have worn it, are wearing it now and will wear it in the future. (918)

"When, at the tabernacle door, Moses entered the cloud, he was enveloped by it, and it was there that I spoke to him. Only on his head did he have the horns of light that dazzled the eyes of the children of Israel. With his veil, he had to cover his face that shone with my splendors, because the Israelites could not endure these lights. Could there be any doubt about his priesthood or the vestments he received on the mountain, where I spoke to him face to face as to my friend. I covered him with light, as with a heavenly vestment, consecrating and ornamenting him in a marvelous way. Do not be afflicted, my daughter, that externally you are not dressed in my liveries. And do not trouble yourself because others declare that you confer the habit but do not wear it yourself, that you make religious, but you yourself are not one. Believe in God the Father and in Me, his Son, coequal and consubstantial with Him together with the Holy Spirit.

"There are many mansions and different vestments in my Father's house.

JEANNE'S ORIGINAL DRAFT

Be my new Jerusalem, invested with your Spouse. I am your God, your life and your interior vestment. All the beauty of the royal daughter is within. Your daughters are the embroidery on your robe. (919) You are an enigma to many. It is the prerogative of the One who knows and considers the heart to know you perfectly. Placing my mantle upon you, I am your neighbor, I am your Spouse and your Shepherd and all things. So much did Saint Anthony honor the robe that Saint Paul gave him that he wore it on the outstanding feasts of Easter and Pentecost. While you will not have the holy habit exteriorly until the passage from this life to the other, the Holy Spirit, by his flames, can consume the holocaust you offer Me by desire until the day when you will be consummated in the One you love and who loved you first. By his goodness and mercy, He will prepare and guide you."

These charming consolations restored my courage amidst my persecutors, assisting me to turn the winepress of their hatred without rancor. As much as possible, I withdrew in solitude, confined to bed, because of my knee problem. I offered You my heart that expressed its pain to You. Covered with tears, I turned my face toward the burning rays of yours, a sun that can dry them. I wanted to serve those who did not like me. You let me understand that You were pleased that I felt no gall toward them and that You had drunk vinegar before You died. (920) Yet You wanted to taste the gall, having nothing against your enemies, because You were going to offer your sacrifice of goodness to your Divine Father, asking Him to pardon them for the evil they unknowingly committed.

JEANNE'S ORIGINAL DRAFT

CHAPTER CXXIX

The favors You gave me on the Sunday of the Wedding Feast; the marvels of St. Vincent; the feast You gave me, and, during the following days, joys and sadness, relieving my spirit by a strong dilection.

In 1653, on the Sunday when the Church presents the wedding in Cana during which You changed the water into wine, dissatisfied with someone's refusal to provide me with some wine for Holy Mass that day, I said to You: "Dear Spouse, show forth your power." You demonstrated it for the consolation of those who hope in You, humiliating those who had upset me so much and refused this small quantity of wine. You did not satisfy the spirit of those who had caused this, thereby showing that whoever does not gather with You disperses. You arranged for us to be provided with it by someone who is all liberality for You and for your poor.[1]

---

[1]Note pasted on this page by Mother de Bely:

"Having been a witness of the refusal concerning the wine for our convent Mass, at this part, I want to add what our devout Foundress says very moderately that, when the container of wine was going to be opened for the celebration of the Feast of the Kings, for which the lady had kept it, there was not a single drop a few days after her refusal. This occurred during the second war in Paris when our Foundress, the venerable Mother de Matel, lived with our community in the first apartment of the home of Monsieur de la Piardière, abbé of P_laine,* Seine, then in Touraine. In faith of which I sign this detail:

Sister Jeanne de Jesus de Bely, unworthy religious of the monastery of the Incarnate Word in Paris and presently in that of Lyons on this September 28, 1705."

*Illegible

JEANNE'S ORIGINAL DRAFT

On the Feast of the great deacon, Saint Vincent, You let me understand that this victor had been crowned by roses and lilies by his very enemies who were also yours. (921) You did not allow him to die upon the iron bed. I remembered the words of St. Zachary: *Salutem ex inimicis nostris, et de manu omnium qui oderunt nos. Salvation from our enemies and from the hand of all who hate us.* (Lk 1:71)

You wanted him placed upon a soft bed so as to be a sweet fragrance for You. Exposed to the beasts, his holy body was not approached except to preserve him. The raven, bird of prey, well understood that he was not to be its food, but stood guard and chased away any other animals that drew near him. His glorious soul appeared to a woman, requesting her to place him in her field like a lily that should bloom again for all eternity. This victorious just man will sprout and flourish in your sight as long as your eternity endures after the General Resurrection.

My joy over the glory of this victor elevated my superior part, but the affliction caused by my enemies made me feel two contraries within myself, affecting me almost equally as I wept bitterly. Inclining toward me, You told me that You had accepted the tears of Saint Magdalen and of St. Peter and would not reject mine. With them, I provided a wash basin for your holy feet, drying them with the thoughts You had given me. (922) These were my hair from which St. Joseph had made a necklace. My tears were the pearls attached to this necklace, most delightfully prepared in order to entertain your childhood in the stable and the manger. As a recompense for your gifts, (for loving tears are regarded or esteemed to be a gift of your charity) You offered me milk from your Virgin Mother's breasts. She presented to me the milk and honey of your delights, preparing a way of kindness for me, a path of milk and honey, even though my promptitude made me seem like lightning when I zealously spoke to those who opposed your glory. Since I felt embarrassed at these words, You told me not to be troubled. I approached the throne of your merciful goodness where I found the rainbow of peace that surpasses all understanding. You wanted me to speak firmly to animate those weakened in your service by laxity. Their mediocrity would provoke You to vomit them up

JEANNE'S ORIGINAL DRAFT

again if they did not become animated by the ardent words You produced after they had received You, as declared Saint John Chrysostom. Inviting me to the feast You were preparing, You told me: "Saint Vincent is wine; Saint Ignatius, bread; and Saint Lawrence, meat." (923)

On the Feast of Saint Emerentiana, Saint Agnes' nursling sister, You gave me to understand: "You are my Blessed Mother's nursling sister, for you had been dedicated to Saint Anne, my grandmother who nurtured you with the milk of kindness. You are also my sister, for my Blessed Mother presented and gave you the milk with which she had nurtured Me." What delight, my Love! Ah! what should I think? Should I not fear being mistaken? But could I fast at the feast of the Bridegroom and be fearful in your arms, reposing upon your heart, since it is your benignity that invites me to be there. You reproduce graces to draw me there very gently. You let me experience that your Name is an oil spread out, but it is an oil of gladness in which You are not only the ointment, but the anointing also. When your goodness redoubled its favors to the one who considered herself unworthy of them, You told me: "My daughter, my spouse, you are my Christ-bearer in the stable, Mount Tabor, Mount Calvary and the Mount of Olives. Receive me as the grafted Word who can, through indulgence, save your soul." (924)

Dear Love, You know well what I had to endure on the twenty-fifth of the month when, unknown to me, You summoned Rev. Father John Baptist Carré to Yourself. At about one o'clock in the afternoon on this day, I heard a knock at the door to my room. My secretary Gravier went to see who it was, for she recognized that it was a sign of farewell. Thinking that it would be one of my daughters in Avignon who was giving me a sign of her death as others had done, she tried to get me to read a letter I was writing, for she feared that I would be upset, as she knew I would be at the death of my daughters.

The next morning, the Bishop of Condon came to inform me about the death of this good Father (at that hour) whose virtue he highly regarded as well might be, for he had had special dealings with him. He knew what many ignored; that is, the goodness of a heart that loved its most cruel enemies and

JEANNE'S ORIGINAL DRAFT

who cordially did good to everyone. Seeing that I was overwhelmed by this death, he left me after having heard my confession for Communion at the common Mass that was offered as soon as he left me. He said to me: "My daughter, you have lost a great deal by the death of this fine priest whom you tenderly loved in Our Lord." (925)

When I was near the altar where I was to receive Communion, You wanted to console me, my Divine Spouse, approving my love for this good priest who had returned it just as strongly. Showing me his soul stripped of its body, You told me: "*Ecce quomodo amabat eum; Behold how he loved him.* (Jn 11:36) My daughter, you feared not having enough affection for this priest. You had as much as I permitted. You are not ungrateful; he is satisfied with you. I accept your offer of annual Masses for the repose of his soul. Because of your generous heart, you weep. Be consoled and come back up to Me; I was yesterday, and I am today and I will never die. I am and will be your entire consolation."

On January thirtieth, as I reflected on the great Saint Martine who had been suspended by her hair, it pleased You, my Divine Spouse, to let me know that this virgin had wounded You with her hair that served as darts and arrows flung straight to heaven. You wanted me to take them by a loving affection and lance them anew with the bow of my desires stretched by your goodness which is favorable to me. (926) You showed me how to use these weapons with which to wound You through your own love, kneeling on only one knee because the other one was so bad that I could not even bend it. It was the posture of an archer. Considering this, I told You: "Is it in this way that You want to be wounded by me? My eyes and heart are on the point of these arrows, flying toward You like a feather in the wind. Please come to me even faster so that I may declare together with the Royal Prophet: *Sagittæ tuæ infixæ sunt mihi, et confirmasti super me manum tuam. Thy arrows are fastened in me: and thy hand hath been strong upon me.* (Ps 37:3)

JEANNE'S ORIGINAL DRAFT

CHAPTER CXXX

The flames and lights with which Saint Ignatius was afire and illuminated; his desire to suffer; the purification of Our Lady; the sword of sorrow and the favors I received on the Feast of Saint Blaise and the following day.

The first of February 1643. This great martyr or a Seraphim would have to take a burning coal from the sacred altar and purify my lips so that I might properly speak of the marvels You let me understand about this man of fire who was called Christ-Bearer and God's Portal. (927) He yearned to be torn apart, dismembered and subjected to every torment invented, not only by men but also by demons. His love for You outweighed death, and his emulation was harder than hell. Could the spirits firmly planted in their rage and hatred for their Creator bring about the antithesis with the persevering love of Ignatius for his Creator and his Redeemer? His love, who was his weight, was crucified. It is You Yourself, my Jesus and my love. He possessed the fortunate and blessed union of love which You had requested at the Supper. As a disciple of your favorite one, he had imbibed water from this strong, living source that, by its impetuous flames, carried him away to his weight, love and center. He was the disciple and child of thunder, St. John, who could not die by either fire or poison. St. Ignatius feared being spared by the elements. He resolved to irritate the cruelest animals, begging the Christians not to hinder this action. (928) He was certain that he would gloriously triumph if the belly of these animals would be the triumphant chariot of his body, just as he hoped that your flames would take his spirit up to the Empyrean near the Seraphim, your closest neighbors. He wanted to chant with them: *Holy, Holy, Holy* and to be engulfed in You who are at the right hand and in the bosom of your Father. You absorb death within the ocean of life, but an unfading life. You were everything possible to him: vision and blessed breaking of bread. Near

JEANNE'S ORIGINAL DRAFT

You, he saw the heavenly prodigy, your most august Mother who gave him ineffable splendors. She used neither ink nor paper to write to him. You are the Word who expresses all that You want him to know about your Father, You and the Holy Spirit. With all the saints, he adores and loves your unity of essence and distinctions of support. His glory is so wonderful that the Church can declare of him that no one else has kept your law so well. (929) This is a marvel to your saints who view You as wonderful and omnipotent. You do everything You wish in heaven and on earth. You wanted to prove the words You had declared that your disciples would perform the things You had done and, through the power which You gave them, even greater ones. By assuming their infirmities, You shared your strength with them.

Saint Ignatius defied everything, prepared himself against everything. Nothing visible could stop him in his fervent desire to see You, You who are called the image of the invisible God. He is armed against all. The evening before your death, You were overcome by terror, by fright, beset by problems, brought down by sadness. Blood and water trickled from your pores, your spirit trembled. You were troubled and looked for consolation in your sleeping Apostles who abandoned You, except for John whom You had called the "Son of Thunder". Upon your own breast, he had received your strength, like a child who weakens his mother by drinking her milk and, thereby, her blood and life. (930) Saint Paul stated that You became poor in order to enrich us. You chose to die so as to make us live. You died so that I might live. I want to die so that You may reign for all eternity.

When he was a child, Saint Ignatius received forestalling grace from You. He was blessed to be in your arms when You declared that, if those near You do not become like this little child, they will not enter into the kingdom of heaven. From that moment, You lit the fire that brought You down upon earth that continually burns all the way to its original fire that is more ardent than any fires to be feared. He was afire with a heavenly, supercelestial fire. His center was God Himself. The all-blazing Empyrean was to be his abode. Could this holy fire remain on earth in a human heart without exploding like lightning? The statements made by Ignatius were about brilliant, blazing corruscations.

JEANNE'S ORIGINAL DRAFT

From the abundance of his heart did his mouth speak.

In the evening, filled with understandings and afire with the echoes of the splendors and ardors of this all-zealous saint, as though he were entirely of light, I felt I could not live any longer should these ardors intensify. I wished for the fountain which is on high, but I still had to wait on earth to live here in languor.(931) I could say with David: *Heu mihi, quia incolatus meus prolongatus est! Habitavi cum habitantibus Cedar; multum incola fuit anima mea. Woe is me, that my sojourning is prolonged! I have dwelt with the inhabitants of Cedar: my soul hath been long a sojourner.* (Ps 119:5-6)

I could not yet return to our monastery, for I had promised Monsieur de la Piardière to wait until Lent, since he had commanded me to be in Paris. I considered myself to be like *the inhabitants of Cedar*; who were the people I served and respected for love of You, my Savior. I expected nothing from their good will, experiencing their rudeness and peacefully submitting to a number of signs of their hatred. *Cum his qui oderunt me pacificus; cum loquebar illis, impugnabant me gratis. With them that hated peace I was peaceable: when I spoke to them they fought against me without cause.* (Ps 119:7) I looked up to You who always help me. You let me see the pontifical tiara covered by a pavilion like the cover over the tabernacle where You remain in the adorable Eucharist. You told me that You protect me as a daughter of the Church against those who oppose me. You cover me like your tabernacle. Later I would understand the meaning of this vision, and I was to have a little more patience. (932)

The next day, the Feast of the Purification of your most pure Blessed Mother, You told me so many marvels that it would take too long to record them here. There I saw the glory of Israel; the light and revelation of the Gentiles; your glory, my Savior; that of your Blessed Mother; St. Joseph; St. Simeon and St. Anne, the prophetess; but this glory stemmed from humiliations and suffering. Death was the refuge of the one whom You saw as the object of all contradictions. Your Blessed Mother, the Mother of Sorrows,

JEANNE'S ORIGINAL DRAFT

who had been pierced by a pitiless, not to say cruel, sword was the figure of the lance that could be termed cruel. Dear Love, who would have thought that this sign was to chant your glory while peacefully dying. It would proclaim your ignominy and the bloody tragedy that occurred in Jerusalem and upon Calvary.

"My daughter, although joy was offered Me, I chose the Cross. (933) Filled with my Spirit who led him to the temple, Simeon expressed what had been determined in the Council on high. This is an explosion of fire that burns within my heart. Thunder will be heard when the Gentiles will be introduced by Philip shortly before my Passion, when he was told: *Domine, volumus Jesum videre; Sir, we would see Jesus.* (Jn 12:21) I replied: *Venit hora, ut clarificatur Filius hominis; The hour is come that the Son of Man should be glorified.* (Jn 12:23) Also, the following: *Nunc anima mea turbata est. Et quid dicam? Pater, salvifica me ex hac hora, sed propterea veni in horam hanc. Pater, clarifica nomen tuum. Venit ergo vox de cælo: et clarificavi, et iterum clarificabo. Turba ergo, quæ stabat, et audierat, dicebat tonitruum esse factum. Now is my soul troubled. And what shall I say? Father, save me from this hour. But for this cause I came unto this hour. Father, glorify thy name. A voice therefore came from heaven: I have both glorified and will glorify it again. The multitude therefore that stood and heard, said that it thundered.* (Jn 12:27-29)

"My daughter, everything is present to the Spirit who spoke through Saint Simeon. I knew what I had to endure, and I freely offered to do so." Dear Love, did You not tremble upon the breast of your Blessed Mother when You considered the sword that would pierce her soul and all that would happen during your bloody Passion? (934) Simeon acted wisely in requesting to be dismissed and go into retirement if he perceived the malice of the princes of the priests: the Scribes and the Pharisees. If, through prophecy, he had known and seen the rain of blood and water that would flow in the Garden, as well as that which fell in Pilate's house and upon Calvary, this holy old man would have died in greater innocence than Elias upon seeing the Author of Life die upon the Cross and the lance of a blind person pierce the soul of the

JEANNE'S ORIGINAL DRAFT

Mother of fair love, allowing by this thrust the thoughts of many distressed hearts to be seen.

On the thirteenth of February, as I waited for Holy Mass, I was honoring Saint Blaise for your glory and his sufferings, to which I am indebted as well as to the rest of the saints, especially for having been delivered from the possibility others had suggested to me, not only of being deprived of corporal nourishment but also the spiritual, that is to say, the Blessed Sacrament. (935) After I had invoked this saint, I was thereby marvelously assisted. I asked him not to allow the deprivation of passing things prevent us from receiving the food that nourished You, my loving Savior, that is, the will of your Divine Father: *Meus cibus est ut faciam voluntatem qui misit me, ut perficiam opus eius. My meat is to do the will of him that sent me, that I may perfect his work.* (Jn 4:34)

In the evening, as I made my prayer, while many of those living in the Richelieu district where we still remained departed to see Cardinal Mazarin enter Paris, your goodness, always favorable toward me, told me: "My daughter, I am your Cardinal. Rejoice that you daily receive Me in my sacrament. (936) My Blessed Mother, all my angels and saints rejoice when they see my graces, as a deposit of my goodness, mark the mansion where you will enter and dwell through loving dilection."

At the same time, You appeared to me, my sovereign Pontiff. You were crowned with a diadem of thorns like a tiara, wearing a robe that was adorable, since it was of your Precious Blood, a robe that covered You down to your heels. Incomparable Pontiff, enter your sanctuary, adorned with your Precious Blood. O, how beautiful You are, my Love and my All! The other Pontiffs, Cardinals and Prelates need someone to pray for them before the people. (937) They are mortals, but You, dear Love, are the eternal Pontiff of whom Saint Paul declared: *Hic autem eo quod maneat in æternum, sempiternum habet sacerdotium. Unde et salvare in perpetuum potest accedentes par semetipsum ad Deum: semper vivens ad interpellandum pro nobis. Talis enim decebat ut nobis esset pontifex, sanctus, innocens,*

JEANNE'S ORIGINAL DRAFT

impollutus, segregatus a peccatoribus, et excelsior cælis factus. But this, for that he continueth for ever, hath an everlasting priesthood: Whereby he is able also to save for ever them that come to God by him; always living to make intercession for us. For it was fitting that we should have such a high priest, holy, innocent, undefiled, separated from sinners, and made higher than the heavens. (Heb 7:24-26)

The next day at my Communion, preparing a great feast for me, You elevated my spirit, since your Magnificence wanted it near You and a number of Cardinals. (938) There I considered Cardinal Berulle who had instituted a Congregation of priests that took only the vows that priests make when they receive sacred Orders. You said to me: "My daughter, do not be embarrassed. Daily when you receive Me, I invest you with Myself."

Dear Love, I know well that I am unworthy of your divine favors or of the habit of your Order, but so much is said because I do not receive it. Make it understood that I give it to our daughters on the premise that I am deprived of this visible consolation because of my sins.

"My daughter, to whom must you give an account if not to Me who have said that you are not to become committed until I tell you to do so? Your directors hold no opinion contrary to mine. (939) Thus, do not worry; you are like Melchisedech: without father, mother or any relative to help you establish my Order which is also yours. This is what astonishes many upon seeing a young woman unaided by anyone, by holy union, found and establish so many houses. I am the one who provides you with both spiritual and corporal means. Although he was not a priest, Saint Francis commanded the priests. Rest content, my dearest. I am doing and will do everything in you. I will bring my project to completion. I will bring down the hills of the world along the route of my eternity."

Lord, my God, can I not offer the prayer of the Prophet? *Domine, audivi auditionem tuam, et timui. Domine, opus tuum, in medio annorum vivificat illud. O Lord, I have heard thy hearing and was afraid. O Lord, thy*

JEANNE'S ORIGINAL DRAFT

work, in the midst of the years bring it to life. (Hab 3:2)

And the rest which would take too long to add here. *Ego autem in Domino gaudebo. Et exultabo in Deo Jesu meo. But I will rejoice in the Lord: and I will joy in God my Jesus.* (Hab 3:18) (940)

CHAPTER CXXXI

God is the power and sustenance of his loved ones, whom He elevates by a fatherly care and delivers them from persecution by their enemies. Visions I had. How this Divine Love consoled his beloved at the sight of his sorrows and by accepting her own sufferings. He overcame her enemies and raised her up by his caresses.

On the Feast of Saint Agatha 1653, my Divine Spouse, You let me understand that your love was a lamp of fire and flame for me, that none of the waters or torrents of persecutions and contradictions could extinguish or diminish their ardors nor darken their light. In the presence of your elect, You, who are the Angel of the Great Council, had written that a simple, willing soul had honored You by promoting your glory in establishing your Order. I pray for Roanne as Saint Agatha had prayed for Catania and Saint Genevieve for Paris. You told me that many had slandered Saint Genevieve and that the tyrant had ordered that Saint Agatha have her breasts wrenched and cut off, but your Apostle Saint Peter replaced them. Saint Germain, Bishop of Auxerre, proclaimed the innocence of Saint Genevieve. (941) The Bishop of Condon had imitated this saint by correcting those who maliciously strove to judge my

JEANNE'S ORIGINAL DRAFT

naiveté. Efforts were made to twist the breast of your blessings, but You replaced them when they had been cut off for me. You would always provide me with a heavenly milk of wisdom and knowledge for nurturing the daughters and children You would give me. You had entrusted the care of my needs to the angels. You told me: "My daughter, I will nourish and elevate you upon the waters of my wisdom, converting you to Me even while your enemies, in their malice, cause you to be in the darkness of an almost mortal sadness (which I permitted). I am with you, your life and your light, that the world neither accepts nor knows. My rod and staff will be your consolation. I am your ordinary nourishment, *Parasti in conspectu*, etc. *Thou hast prepared a table*, etc. (Ps 22:5) "It is a table that strengthens you against your enemies. I abundantly pour out the anointing of my sweetness upon you. My chalice delights and embellishes you. O, how lovely and delightful, *calix meus inebrians; my chalice which inebriated me!* (Ps 22:5d) Like a cortege, my mercy will follow you all the days of your life.

On February seventh, I was lovingly complaining to You, my Divine Spouse, because I had learned that, for her fidelity to me in filial affection, an innocent person was suffering, due to those who were more obligated to me than she was. (942) You said to me: "My daughter, imitate Me. Pray for those who afflict you. I suffered when Barabbas was preferred to Me. Proportionately, put up with the fact that others are preferred to you who lack your natural sympathy. Prepare to endure mortal sufferings. You can do so by my grace. My Blessed Mother was still on earth when my witnesses were put to death, especially Saint Stephen who was the first to seal his faith with his blood."

In the evening, dear Love, You showed me a leopard at the foot of my bed. I prayed to You, my Conquering Lion, Lion of the tribe of Juda, to disperse and vanquish all my enemies. Entrusting myself to You, I went to sleep, leaving the care of everything to your providence.

On the eighth, when I awoke, You told me: "My daughter, today is the Octave of my beloved Ignatius who aspired to be my wheat ground by the teeth of beasts and declared that the ten soldiers who took him to Rome were

JEANNE'S ORIGINAL DRAFT

ten leopards. He instructed them about their duties toward Me, but, through malice they redoubled the sufferings they inflicted upon him and became worse than beasts. Through goodness, Christians even offered them gifts so that they would spare him. (943) Those to whom You gave your charitable liberalities intensified their cruelty, which they did not consider to be such, because they did not take into consideration your maternal afflictions. These helped you advance and rejoice in Me after your sufferings which you cannot express.

"Remember, my daughter, that I was the Man of Sorrows, interiorly and exteriorly suffering in all my members. My head was crowned with thorns, my face covered with spittle, my cheeks stung due to blows. This brilliant face which the angels want to contemplate continually, was veiled so that its charms would not attract love. Since the time of hatred and darkness was running its course while truth was hidden and justice violated, then what good could be accomplished?

On February 14th, when the Church observes the Feast of Saint Valentine, priest and martyr, You gave me many favors through your goodness. You assured me of your benevolence while my enemies prepared evil things against me, being assembled so as to slander me, thinking that thereby they were offering You a wonderful service, not to say a great sacrifice. They considered themselves to be zealous for your glory, judging what they could not know through earthly prudence which You often destroy just when they think they have succeeded by their subtleties. (944) These they employ for their bows and arrows against your loved ones who, like innocent sheep and doves, proceed in all innocence. The former aim to seduce the latter and captivate their hearts. But, like David, they maintain theirs according to yours. You are their protector, just as God preserves your graces in these vessels of love. You let me understand that your saints in glory arm themselves against such persons, begging your justice to discern between the cause of your faithful ones and that of the wicked. You temporarily allow the latter to test the others by persecution, separating them from the sentiments of flesh and blood, thereby showing that these faithful souls are born of and from your Spirit. Their faith will make them victorious over the world, the devil and the

AUTOBIOGRAPHY

JEANNE'S ORIGINAL DRAFT

flesh. Through You, they will triumph over everything. Since your kindness invited me to trust in You and to take refuge in your arms, could I fear any evil that my enemies undertake against me?

On Sunday, February sixteenth, I was inexpressibly caressed by your loving goodness. You invited me to rejoice in You like a bride with her Divine Spouse. Through your divine mercy, I had found grace in your eyes.

On Monday, the seventeenth, I saw a mother seated among a number of children who did not carry out their duties. She made every effort to turn them to You, as is said of St. John the Baptist who prepared a perfect people for You. (945)

When night came on Tuesday, February 18th, You allowed war to be unleashed against me by anxiety, pain and repugnance—I do not dare say hell—and to reduce me to an inexplicable anguish. I recalled that it was the Feast of St. Simeon, Bishop of Jerusalem, who had been crucified for You, my Jesus, Son of God and Son of David. I fervently requested him to pray and obtain the strength for me to suffer even to the death on the cross. I opened my arms as someone desiring to be nailed to the cross, for I felt an indescribable abandonment without telling You why I felt that way. My visible enemies did not know this condition, but the invisible ones could because of the excess of sadness that made me feel at the point of death. Also, they could know by my eyes, overtaxed from being raised to heaven and almost bloody from all the sorrowful tears I shed as though my head had become a fountain of boiling water. I thought: And so, my God, is it to this that You reduce me? You have deprived me of spiritual fathers who consoled me. Father Carré, whom you took from this world about three weeks ago, would have consoled me had You left him here. (946) He opposed those who wanted to afflict me unfairly with sufferings that You do not consider appropriate for your glory to record here. If these sufferings are meant to glorify You, let them come with all their torment. Your grace can support me. I would pray to St. Simeon, the second Bishop of Jersualem, begging this anointed one not to reject me.

JEANNE'S ORIGINAL DRAFT

As though jealous, your love told me: "My daughter, say the third bishop of Jerusalem, for I was the first and James the second. As he rent his robe, Caiphas declared that I deserved death and that I should die for all the people. From that day on, by my Blood, I went up to the sanctuary and performed the office of high priest upon the Cross. At the Last Supper, I offered the sacrifice of Melchisedech; on Calvary, I offered Aaron's which was I Myself as the victim and perfect sacrifice.

By considering your deep sorrows, how could I not accept my own that were small but oppressive, because of my weakness and the limited degree of love I possessed in comparison with yours. I was almost overwhelmed by my tears, worn out by my work. Straight ahead of me and near my bed, I saw a religious of St. Dominic's Order. This vision was sensible as well as imaginary, because I could see the serge of his habit as though I wanted to examine the cloth and see its texture. (947) I did not raise my eyes to see his face, rather I considered his posture without addressing a single word to him nor did he to me. This vision is still so vividly impressed upon my memory that it seems to be present to me.

In the morning, I told Monseigneur de Langlade, the Prior of Molesson, who heard my confession and gave me Communion, that I had seen a religious of St. Dominic stop without being able to go where he wanted. A few days later, when he came to say Mass as he ordinarily did, he told me that the Archbishop of Avignon would soon come to Paris in the name of His Holiness to ask the king for Cardinal de Retz.

As I reflected upon this, in your presence I thought that this prelate, coming on business matters, had plans that he considered just. I would be exposed by my enemies to his stern examination, while he would have been given information by persons unknown to him but whom You know, my God and my All, who penetrate hearts and sound their depths. I told the Bishop of Condon that Monsieur de Langlade had informed me that this prelate was coming. He declared: "My daughter, the late Father Carré had received a letter written by his command at the behest of those who totally bind you. I

JEANNE'S ORIGINAL DRAFT

did not want the said priest to send you that letter. I told him that he should answer it. (948) Knowing your dove-like innocence, he did so and thereby shamed those who had offended the Incarnate Word by prompting this prelate, who had never seen nor heard you, to oppose you. If he does come to Paris, I will see him, together with four other prelates who know you better than he does: The Archbishop of Toulouse, the Bishop of Lodève, the Bishop of Amiens, the Bishop of Dol and a number of others, if necessary. The priest who wanted to denigrate you has already been very humiliated. I believe and I see that anyone who goes against you will find himself against God Himself without knowing it. Since God loves and favors you as He does, who can possibly harm you! With the proofs of his goodness toward you, what should you fear?"

Dear Love, You prompted this devout priest to tell me this and made known to him your love for me. On Wednesday, the 19th, your loving Majesty told me while caressing me: "My daughter, I will be glorified in you; you will overcome your enemies. My saints offer your prayers, tears and sufferings to my Eternal Father who graciously accepts them so as to reward you for them."

God of my heart, how powerful are your consolations! They destroy the power of our enemies and confound them. Together with the Prophet-King I declare: If an army is ready to attack me, my heart will not fear. With the Lord aiding me, what can man do? If God is for me, who will be powerful against me? (949)

JEANNE'S ORIGINAL DRAFT

CHAPTER CXXXII

Our Lord's prayer on behalf of Saint Peter. The twelve foundations of the Holy City. St. Thomas appeared to me like an angel elevated by the power of grace and by the spirit of wisdom even to the rising of the sun when he writes about the Incarnation; In the year one thousand six hundred and nineteen (1619), I was commanded to write about and proclaim the Immaculate Conception of the Blessed Virgin.

On the 22nd, when the Church prays the Office in honor of Saint Peter's Chair, You let me understand the great things that You had done for this Prince of the Apostles, when You told him: *Tu es Petrus, et super hanc petram ædificabo ecclesiam meam. Thou art Peter, and upon this rock I will build my Church.* (Mt 16:18) The gates of hell will not prevail against it. Satan wanted to overpower it, but You had prayed that her faith would not falter, that I was to have confidence in Him, that He loved me. Just as when the women showed Him the robes Dorcas had made for them, when they presented her to him deceased, He prayed and, after calling her by name, brought her back to life, because of her charitable acts and the knowledge these poor women had of that. You also considered the daughters I had invested and those who were already in glory, showing You the habits I had given them, which are your liveries, that became for them robes of glory and immortality. (950)

On the Feast of St. Matthias, I understood that the twelve precious stones were the twelve Apostles and the foundation stones of the Holy City. Saint Matthias was represented by the amethyst. I was wondering which stone would represent Saint Paul, the thirteenth one, and understood that, governed and instructed only by the Holy Spirit, the Church compared him to jasper, as

JEANNE'S ORIGINAL DRAFT

brilliant as crystal: *Et lumen eius simile lapidi pretioso tanquam lapidi jaspidis, sicut cristallum. And the light thereof was like to a precious stone, even as crystal.* (Ap 21:11)

This Apostle is symbolized by jasper, just as was St. Peter, the first foundation stone. It was a proof of the greatness of St. Paul whom the Church names together with St. Peter. This favor of the Holy Spirit does not lessen Saint Peter's authority. To avert any subject of jealousy for the Gentiles, this Spirit of love wanted Saint Paul to be akin to Saint Peter and the Church to have the feast of one be the commemoration of the other. Desiring his apostolate to be known, Saint Paul declared: *Qui enim operatus est Petro in apostolatum circumcisionis, operatus est et mihi inter gentes et cum cognovissent gratiam, quæ data est mihi, Jacobus, et Cephas, et Joannes, qui videbantur columnæ esse, dextras dederunt mihi, et Barnabæ societatis; ut nos in gente,* etc. *For he who wrought in Peter to the apostleship of the circumcision wrought in me also among the Gentiles. And when they had known the grace that was given to me, James and Cephas and John, who seemed to be pillars, gave to me and Barnabas the right hand of fellowship: that we should go unto the Gentiles,* (Gal 2:8-9)

Also, at the beginning of the Epistle to the Galatians, he said: *Paulus Apostolus, non ab hominibus, neque per hominem, sed per Jesus Christum, et Deum Patrem,* and further down: *Notum enim vobis facio, fratres Evangelium, quod evangelizatum est a me, quia non est secundum hominem: neque enim ego ab* (951) *homine accepi illud, neque didici, sed per revelationem Jesu Christi. Paul, an apostle, not of men, neither by man, but by Jesus Christ and God the Father [...]. For I give you to understand, brethren, that the gospel which was preached by me is not according to man.. For neither did I receive it of man: nor did I learn it but by the revelation of Jesus Christ.* (Gal 1:1; 11-12)

He then related how he had persecuted God's Church, prompted by zeal to have the tradition of his fathers observed: *Cum autem placuit ei, qui me segregavit ex utero matris meæ, et vocavit per gratiam suam, ut revelaret*

AUTOBIOGRAPHY

JEANNE'S ORIGINAL DRAFT

filium suum in me, ut evangelizarem illum in gentibus: continuo non acquievi carni et sanguini. But when it pleased him who separated me from my mother's womb and called me by his grace, to reveal his Son in me, that I might preach him among the Gentiles: immediately I conde-scended not to flesh and blood. (Gal 1:15-16)

Included also is the following that shows how You were glorified by him. My God, You had separated and called him to be an Apostle even from his mother's womb to show forth your marvels to the Gentiles through him. He taught them that faith justifies through You, my gentle Jesus Christ, when he declared: *Scientes autem quod non justificatur homo ex operibus legis, nisi per fidem Jesu Christi: et nos in Christo Jesu credimus, ut justificetur ex fide Christi,*—saying—*in fide vivo Filii Dei, qui dilexit me, et tradidit semetipsum pro me. Non abjicio gratiam Dei. But knowing that man is not justified by the works of the law, but by the faith of Jesus Christ, we also believe in Christ Jesus, that we may be justified by the faith of Christ. I live in the faith of the Son of God, who loved me and delivered himself for me.* (Gal 2:16; 20c-21)

Great Apostle, pray, pray to the One who gave Himself for you that I may be grateful for what He has done for me. Since He has loved me, may I love Him through his pure love; and you, Saint Peter, the summit of theology, ask Him that I may love Him with the love He required of you, more than anything else and above all things. (952) According to the statement of your partner, I can acquire the emulation of the finest charity, the eminent knowledge that does not make one proud, but that builds up. It is the condition of the saints in light, the same state that fell to Matthias whom I beg to pray to your Holy Spirit for me to be numbered among your faithful and dearest spouses, since, being a simple, young woman, I cannot be among the Apostles. You are able to appear great within me, Jesus, love of my heart, which can find rest only in You since it was made for You.

On the first Sunday of Lent, You offered me your victories through your loving Passion and intense dilection.

JEANNE'S ORIGINAL DRAFT

On Monday, You chose to invite me to possess your kingdom as the blessed one of your Eternal Father.

On the Feast of St. Thomas Aquinas, You told me: "Come see a different angel from those that are spiritual beings, that is to say, that have no body but are all spirit. It is Thomas who, by the power of my grace and the spirit of wisdom, was elevated to the sunrise, by writing marvels about my incarnation, and he was enabled to see my dawn in her most pure conception, a mystery concealed from many (in former ages) in God who created all things. My Blessed Mother's holiness is a great sacrament that contains the inexhaustible riches of my humanity, in which corporeally dwells all the fullness of my divinity. (953) Formed by that of my purest Mother, this Sacred Body could not stem from a creature, contaminated by original sin, that is the poverty and corruption of all Adam's children who are sinners. By nature, I was exempt from this; so was my Blessed Mother, through grace and propriety. This fault could have no place in her; she is always all-beautiful and immaculate. Neither her spirit nor her body have ever been submitted to the corruption of sin.

"My daughter, proclaim my incomprehensible riches and the divine dispensation of this sacrament concealed in God, who, when He created all things, chose to exempt a daughter of grace from any disgrace, one only Virgin from any fault so as to be the bodily source of her innocent Son, unstained and separated from sinners.

"The Church, which I illuminate like a sun, transforms my ministers from light to light, as St. Paul declares, until they become the light of my Spirit who will raise and remove any veil when I will be seen as I am. I will no longer be viewed only partially nor by mystery. The saints in glory possess this blessed view. In heaven, Thomas knows the reasons my wisdom had for concealing during one age what it made manifest in another. He is so humble that he rejoices that I make known this purity in time through a young woman to whom today, in the presence of all the saints, I say that she is the Tabor whereupon the Incarnate Word manifests his glory. (954) My daughter, you can declare as Deborah did to Barac: 'The victory will be attributed to a

JEANNE'S ORIGINAL DRAFT

woman of Lapedoth (They were pelted with flashes of lightning). This young woman had no fear of lightning, thunder or flashes. She firmly announced: *In principio erat verbum; In the beginning was the word.* (Jn 1:1) Following the example of your patron, the Son of Thunder, valiantly ascend Mount Tabor and listen to the voice of my Eternal Father without falling down. Do not be dazzled by the brilliant cloud that conceals Me from my Apostles. Through goodness, the Angel of the Great Council submits to you; He has no fear of the coming of dawn. He is your Sun and the Orient from on high that visits you through the eternal mercy of his Divine Father's bosom and that of my wonderful Mother. Thomas, the angel of theology, makes way for you at sight of the graces I have imparted to you.

Great doctor, I will not leave you unless you give me your humble and most abundant blessing. You look at me without speaking; your eyes smile and, bending your head toward me, you commission me to tell the people of this age that Mary, worthy Virgin Mother of the Incarnate Word, was conceived without sin. I was not to fear declaring this before anyone to whom this mystery is still unknown. Even if they are like Esau, an Israelite by divine favor, strong against God, I should have no fear.

Great Saint Thomas, you know how you appeared to me and that I saw you just as I said I did. (955) In the Eucharist, Jesus Christ taught me about the mystery of the Most Immaculate Conception in the year one thousand six hundred and nineteen (1619). This occurred during a rapture which I could not resist and from which I was unable to withdraw until I had promised to write about what I had understood. I have complied, for I did not learn it from men.

JEANNE'S ORIGINAL DRAFT

CHAPTER CXXXIII

The Incarnate Word's eyes are the Blessed Virgin's altars and mirrors; they are also the prodigies and altars for his beloved to whom He grants the dwelling wherein to see that of the Divine Father of sacrifices. The Blessed Virgin. The happiness of the faithful soul and the contrary for those who allow themselves to be blinded by sin.

On the third Sunday of Lent, when I lifted my eyes to You, my Divine Love, You let yours be my altars. You told me that they were your Blessed Mother's and the mirrors where she gazed at herself when she contemplated You. She received your loveliness, marvelously imprinting your divine face upon hers, and reflecting rays, flashes and flames that, without consuming your sacred breast, holily burn there. In your divinely adorable eyes, she makes constant, indescribable sacrifices of love, praise, peace and glory. (956)

I felt that your eyes were my prodigies as well as my altars where, to the extent that your grace allowed me, I should make my dwelling. It was the house of sunshine. There I would see that of your Divine Father whose divine delight You unceasingly provide. Through a marvelous circumincession, He is in You, and You are in Him.

With so much grace and glory did your heavenly Mother make a sacrifice that the saints admire these perfect holocausts. With singular piety, she offers You her ineffable respects. When your favorite disciple was on earth, he delighted to look at her when she raised her eyes to the God of her heart, for they were holily expressive. Since your love was their weight, I saw them suspended by rays of light produced by and emanating from the eyes of your Blessed Mother together with yours. You raised her up to You with greater

AUTOBIOGRAPHY

JEANNE'S ORIGINAL DRAFT

power than the angel who carried the Prophet Habacuc by his hair to the Prophet Daniel. When I witnessed this marvel, it was impossible to describe the state it produced in my spirit except the unity You requested at the Supper. Just as You were pleased to let me know the blessedness and happiness of the soul united to You in spirit, You let me perceive the unhappiness of those divided by mortal sin and the horrible desolation of souls that are the dwelling place of your enemy. (957) He exercises a more cruel dominion when one who has been baptized and becomes your bride violates her duties toward You. You told me that, even after such a one has been illuminated and united to You by the sacrament of regeneration and enlightenment, the demons therein make their fortress which they reinforce with greater rage against You. They gloat over having their snare in the Aquilon and, by the sins of this unfaithful soul, of possessing a seat similar to yours, as king of that empire. You explained these words to me: *Qui non est mecum, contra me est: et qui non colligit mecum, dispergit. He that is not with me is against me; and he that gathereth not with me scattereth.* (Lk 11:23)

Whoever is blinded by sin does not understand such loss and division in this life. His condition provides a new entrance to unclean spirits that cause the one adhering to them to become guiltier, committing one sin after another. As predicted by Daniel, he becomes the abomination of desolation, for, having been sanctified by baptism, he had become the temple of God who has been adored in the state of grace. By sin, it has become the horror of all who deem it to be the dwelling-place of the enemy of all purity. This soul has become soiled by so much filth that it appears to be filth itself, abusing his free will. Being unfaithful to grace, he voluntarily becomes a slave to sin, for the demons cannot force him to do so. (958)

206

JEANNE'S ORIGINAL DRAFT

CHAPTER CXXXIV

Our return to our monastery after the war (2nd peace). The Feasts of Saint Joseph, Saint Joachim, Saint Benedict were the joy and blessing of victory that, through his providence over me, God gave me over my enemies. My feelings over the death of the Cardinal of Lyons. St. Gabriel and the spiritual beings visited me. Simultaneously, my spirit was filled with joy and sadness.

Having stopped to take care of the King's business in Loche in Touraine, Monsieur de la Piardière sent me a message that he could not return for a long time. I then requested permission of him to leave his home to return to our monastery in the Saint Germain suburb.

You made me understand: "My daughter, exclaim joyously: *In exitu Israel de Ægypto, Domus Jacob de populo barbaro; When Israel went out of Egypt, the house of Jacob from a barbarous people.*" (Ps 113:1) We departed in 1653, on the eve of the Feast of your foster-father, Saint Joseph, whom I could call your savior and liberator, for he delivered You from Herod's cruelties. Our joy was inexpressible. We seemed to enter the desert where the next day we saw the heavenly manna enter our tabernacle at the hand of the priest who, as your minister, produced it by your word. This manna did not melt or fade away—not to say, disappear because of the sun. (959) Its rays formed your tabernacle which, as Divine Spouse, You came into my breast, your nuptial chamber, not with giant strides, but with the speed of flashes that light up earth and sky. As your heavens, your angels bow before it, adoring the high mountains of your Three August Persons who, by concomitance and necessary follow-up, are present in this sacrament of love, for One is within the Other. These divine attachments cause coruscations, not

JEANNE'S ORIGINAL DRAFT

of smoke, but more the vapors of divine power and the true emanation of your all-powerful light that penetrates the soul, converting it into light and flame, making it divine through participation, dwelling in it so as to transform it into You. What joy to dwell in your tabernacles, to abide in your wisdom! Conversation with it is never tiring. It extends from one end to the other, disposing the exterior and interior parts with as much power as gentleness.

The Feast of St. Joachim was no less happy and delightful for us. We were filled with joy on considering it. We honored You, divine Savior of his substance, for in his daughter You had assumed a Body which is supported by your divine substance. This sacred Body formed from Mary's is the substance from Joachim and Anne.

On the Feast of St. Benedict, You immersed my soul with his multiple blessings of charity, delightful sweetness and favor. (960) Through this saint, You allowed me to see those that your goodness had given the Patriarch Joseph, but with an inexpressible abundance. You let me perceive those of the Ancients as shadows and figures of the ancient law and, in St. Benedict, veritable and eternal happiness because of the eternal blessings that St. Paul alludes to in Hebrews in this better Testament. You became poor so as to enrich him and those belonging to him. They are saints and will be because, by contemplating You in your immense greatness, he had regarded all creatures to be too small and really nothingness. I received great favors from this saint, for he attested to me that he had accepted my appeal at the time of the visit required by my enemies who thereby wanted to confound me. I do not know if they offended against heaven, but the evils they prepared for me fell back upon themselves. Their anger seemed to have produced a Red Sea that extended to provinces that I shall not name. They were places where the said overzealous persons became known by procuring laurels for me by the sufferings they made me endure (and that lasted a long time). By anticipation, they opposed your plan of being glorified in the places which belong to You as your own.

I beg You, Divine Love, to take possession of them and show them that all

JEANNE'S ORIGINAL DRAFT

power is given You in heaven and on earth. (961) You give me faith that can move the mountains of opposition, changing them into places of adoration of your divine greatness, where your Divine Father may be adored in spirit and in truth. Through You, my Divine Messias, who give grace upon grace, I hope for this grace. You let me understand that, ever since a few months ago, You had enabled His Eminence of Lyons to repent. He had resisted You, but his time had run out. My sorrow for his approaching end was indescribable. You allowed it, dear Love, so as to give my Prelate this act of gratitude. Were I able to go to Lyons, I would kneel at his feet and plead for your foundation. By my absence, I verified what You had said about your own: *Quæritis me, et non invenietis; You shall seek me, and shall not find me.* (Jn 7:34a)

My soul felt pity; his body had to remain at the place where he had fallen ill; he was unable to go any further. Through human respect, he did not care to retract the words he had uttered aloud. Those who visited him when he was ill could make this holy project known to him, and I have learned that he would then have granted what he had refused before. *Spiritus ubi vult spirat, et vocem eius audis, sed nescis unde veniat, aut quo vadat. The Spirit breatheth where he will and thou hearest his voice: but thou knowest not whence he cometh and whither he goeth.* (Jn 3:8)

Had he believed the words of the oracle, and had he not become hardened by resisting it, he would not have died of dropsy, due to water and loss of blood. He would have had a gentle death in the bed of the Cardinal of Lyons rather than in that of Dom Alphonse. (962) Had he not been warned about everything that would happen to him, he would have had no regrets at death. He would have been consoled by the Word of Life, meaning You, my Love and my God. Who can resist You and possess peace in his soul? No political or apparent peace can equal true peace. There is no stable council against You, Lord. Whoever strives to falsify true revelations or cast aspersions upon your illuminations will certainly repent at the end of his life, and, ordinarily, this is too late. You know, dear Love, the sadness that I have had since this death that, enlightened by your illuminations, I had warned him about in writing. When he asked me if the oracle had anything to say, You told me to tell him

JEANNE'S ORIGINAL DRAFT

that You are not bound, saying: "Tell him that *Verbum Dei non est alligatum; The Word of God is not tied down.*" When he received this letter in Paris at his Lyons hotel, he sent me word to let him know what he did not want to believe, increasingly hardening his spirit until he realized the truth of all that I had written him and that I had kept secret for a number of years. I had told only two or three persons, first among whom was Father Carré, Dominican, who was my confessor. He is now dead; the others are living. (963)

On March 24, 1653, preparing as best I could for the Feast of your loving Incarnation, I confidently and respectfully invoked the great Saint Gabriel, your marvelous paranymph. It was the day that the Oratorian fathers celebrated their feast. I joined their solemnity to honor this archangel, the messenger of your goodness. His name means "power of God." I asked him to come to our chapel together with all the zealous spirits who do your will, to assist and serve them; in a word, with the entire celestial militia to whom I am inexpressibly indebted.

I was not disdained by these heavenly citizens and courtiers. Joining them, I blessed your Holy Name by saying: *Benedic, anima mea, Domino, et omnia quæ intra me sunt nomini sancto eius, et noli oblivisci omnes retributiones eius. Bless the Lord, O my soul: and let all that is within me bless his holy name, and never forget all he hath done for thee.* (Ps 102:1; 2b)

I was astounded to experience a feast of joy and sadness; joy in sharing that of these happiest of beings, sadness over the death of the Cardinal of Lyons who died tonight while silence enveloped many spirits. I had not yet met the Bishop of Condon until during the war in Paris at our retreat in Monsieur de la Piardière's home. Thus, he had not yet been in our monastery. (964) He arrived here after dinner and, upon noticing my sadness in this wonderful desert I had so yearned for, he inquired about the reason. I told him: "Monseigneur, my pastor died tonight, and that is what has caused me to be so sorrowful." This devout prelate was not at all surprised, knowing how much I loved him, but, to console me, he told me that the Cardinal would no

JEANNE'S ORIGINAL DRAFT

longer obstruct the establishment of the Order of the Incarnate Word in Lyons and that its daughters could be sanctified by the vows of religion in this desert. He left me in this understandable sadness. O, how painful was the misfortune of my pastor for the one who loved him most among his sheep! I dare say these words are true, because, while he was still Archbishop of Aix, Bishop Nesme offered him my respects as though to the Archbishop of Lyons. Jephte's daughter was the first of those belonging to him who came to meet him to share in her father's joy that was changed into sadness. Obeying God and her father and pastor, this daughter did not request to be exempt from the sacrifice when she asked for a delay to go weep with her companions for what she might have laughed at had she not perceived that she would be deprived of any hope in contributing to the planning of all the marriages whose objective was the coming of the Messias, but without knowing from which one He would come. (965) Our divine Emmanuel, Isaias had still not predicted that it would be from a Virgin of David's race and line that You would be virginally conceived, carried and born, while she always remained a virgin.

The next day your loving goodness chose to console me. Spirit and God of truth, You chose to pass the great Sabbath within the virginal womb that was purer than any of the spirits assisting before your throne. Your Holy Spirit had selected her, superabundantly filled her with profusions of his goodness that are inexpressible to me or anyone else, thus retracting the following words, if I may so speak: *Non permanebit spiritus meus in homine in æternum, quia caro est. My spirit shall not remain in man for ever, because he is flesh.* (Gen 6:3)

The Word, who is You, Spirit and living God, became flesh in this Virgin through the ineffable operation of your most Holy Spirit. In the shadow of your highest and most holy power, your Mother conceived You, becoming a Mother while remaining a Virgin, but Mother of God while being his Daughter. My pen cannot express what You gave me to understand about this virginal maternity and maternal virginity. With the Church, I exclaim to myself: *Mirabile mysterium declaratur hodie: Innovantur naturæ, Deus homo factus est: id quod fuit permansit, et quod non erat assumpsit: non commixtionem*

JEANNE'S ORIGINAL DRAFT

passus, neque divisionem. A wondrous mystery is revealed this day: natures show a new aspect, God has become man. He remained what He was, and took on what He was not, undergoing neither confusion nor division. (Antiphon, Office of the BVM, after Christmas)

Dear Love, You know that, for a number of years, I have adored You during the nine months You were enclosed in the virginal cloister of your Blessed Mother and the favor You gave my spirit of being welcome near You. (966) You filled it with marvelous, loving blessings, being the blessed Son of God, blessed fruit of this sublime land. Could my soul possibly tire in such sacred company? The new Adam and the new Eve abide in the paradise of the Divine Father's will, the food of this adorable Son and virginal Mother. Dear Love, nourish me at this table that makes me one with You. By this grace, your Blessed Mother anticipated the Supper.

CHAPTER CXXXV

The Jubilee that I wanted to gain a number of times. My directors ordered me to continue recording and giving an account as the late Cardinal of Lyons had commanded me to do. The Apostle of glory had given me his right hand to proclaim the Sacred Name of the Incarnate Word before great and small, and the motto which would make his daughters known: *Jesus Amor Meus*. The raptures of my spirit on the Feasts of the Visitation and of Saint Magdalen, 1653.

The Father Prior, Vicar General of Bishop de Metz, abbot of St. Germain-des-Pres Abbey, as superior of our monastery of Paris, wrote me on Palm

JEANNE'S ORIGINAL DRAFT

Sunday to tell me to prepare my daughters for the Jubilee. He offered to send confessors to the houses and convents that had not participated in the request for the visit mentioned several times in this narrative. This shows your providence over the one who trusts in You, my Love and my All. (967)

You conferred many graces upon me during the two months of the Jubilee. I tried to gain it twice, despite what it cost me to say the vocal prayers required for gaining it. This problem in oral prayer let me experience the great difficulty, not to say impossibility, I had to contend with in saying an Office when I was obligated to do so, even that of your exemplary Mother.

Holy Week required that I meditate upon your great love for mankind. You had undergone such bitter torments and such a cruel, ignominious death. I recalled the words of the Apostle: *Hoc enim sentite in vobis; For let this mind be in you.* (Phil 2:5a) I strove to feel your sufferings and to empathize with You. Since You did not take delight in Yourself, I wanted to hate myself and to imitate You in your love for humiliations which You preferred, patiently enduring contradiction from sinners. I adore You in your suffering love. I wanted to die to everything that is not your pure love. Through it, You have loved me, giving Yourself to be my salvation and to become all things to me. Be my God and my All forever, Divine Love.

The Jubilee could be gained twice in two months. That is why I strove to gain it at Pentecost as I did at Easter. (968) Because the Apostle exhorts us to rejoice right away, I wanted to do so during this time of jubilation that the Church calls joyful and repeats the *Alleluias.*

During these two months, the solemnity of your Resurrection, your Ascension and the Descent of the Holy Spirit took place during which You gave me a feast with your royal, divine magnificence. Each day it cost me quite an effort to do even a limited amount of manual work. I have alluded to this in other writings. I will not repeat that here nor linger over the marvels your August Trinity gave me to understand. I have written about them a number of times in various notebooks. Your goodness and the poor condition of my eyes, as well as the death of the Cardinal of Lyons, dispensed me from this. It

JEANNE'S ORIGINAL DRAFT

was at his command that I have written this account in different notebooks, having given and sent them to him as he wished. At his death, my confessors and directors—presently at St. Louis, Fathers de Lingendes, Discret and de Condé of your Society—did not allow me to stop. Also, Father Gibalin of the same Society, joined them in commanding me to continue to bring to light the graces You liberally give me. Thus, I will not dispense myself from doing so, since they, together with the Bishop of Condon, represent your will for me. I am offering You a continual sacrifice of my will with acknowledgment and gratitude for your infinite, merciful liberalities toward me, your most unworthy spouse. Lord, let all creatures say and chant in heaven and the holy land: "*Holy, Holy is the strong and powerful Lord.*" (969)

After the feast of your Most August Trinity, adorable mystery that is so kind and favorable toward my soul, I was invited to the banquet of your loving Eucharist. I humbled myself before your Majesty, aware of my unworthiness as was the Canaanite woman. Like Lazarus, I felt my wounds and my need and requested the crumbs that fall from your table. You are infinitely rich, owning all the treasures of your Divine Father which You conceal in this loving Eucharist, the Sacred Body that possesses the fullness of the Godhead.

Dear Love, could You allow this poor, languishing person to starve who has as many mouths to ask You for this favor as she has open wounds caused by the arrows of your love? Is she indifferent to You because of her weaknesses? Does not her languor cause You to pity her, You who are the throne of mercy? Unwilling to restrain You by your wisdom, your goodness made me understand that You are filled with humanity and are the only God and true Man. You aimed to make the banquet of this adorable Supper with your friends to satisfy them with the wheat of the elect and to inebriate them with the wine that engenders virgins, You who are their crown. You are the Lamb that receives them in this park, nurtures them personally, being their very narrow path, certain truth and unfading life. (970) You enter their breasts through Communion to lodge them in your own by a divine transformation.

If the angel told Zachary that many shared in his joy at the birth of his son,

JEANNE'S ORIGINAL DRAFT

your great Precursor—whose name means nothing other than grace—although unworthy, could my soul, so long fortified by it, be deprived of its jubilation? Your love wants this for me. Preserve it within me as long as You wish, but, through charity, permanently give me that of your principal Spirit so that I may display that your ways and your paths are straight. Let those who try to turn away be converted to You, enlightened by those who belong to You and in You. Let them be a perfect people for You.

Could the one to whom You have so often given David's key, which is trust in your goodness that opens your heart to her without its ever being closed against her, be rejected by the One to whom You have given the key to heaven? No, because He shared part of the illuminations he had had with her, not only upon Mount Tabor at your right hand, obtaining this grace from your loving heart. Delightfully and strongly, she has experienced the blessing of participating in your divine nature. (971)

The Apostle of glory had been a pilgrim along life's way and wanted to be anathema to his brothers and sisters. Then, at its end, could he possess less fervor for this little sister who is also his daughter, without comparing her to Saint Thecla? No, he has been so generous to me that I cannot describe his wonderful charity. Did I not hear heaven and earth proclaim that he has given me his right hand to join him in bearing your Sacred Name before great and small. It is the insignia that makes your daughters known, Divine Word made Flesh, not upon their countenance, but upon their hearts with these words: *Jesus Amor Meus.*

Daughter of the Father, Mother of the Son, Spouse of the Holy Spirit and the magnificence of these Three August Persons elevated above all the heavens, who could express the ineffable favors you gave me on the Feast of your Visitation? This visit raised my spirit up to heaven, and, by a marvelous power, preserved it in the earth of its body. Two contrary situations equally assisted and operated in one same subject: the desire to die so as soon to be in the other life and the patience to keep on breathing, remaining along life's journey with the words: "Possess your life in patience and death by desire."

JEANNE'S ORIGINAL DRAFT

Because I want to be brief, I will not go into detail about the favors I received during the entire summer. But how could I not mention the ardors of your loved one whom the Church maintains excels above the other saints! She deserved to be the first one to see You on the day of your glorious Resurrection. (972) You told her not to detain You at the tomb, for You had not yet ascended to your Father. You made her the Evangelist of the Apostles, entrusting her with the beneficial mission and most glorious commission of informing them that You had triumphed over death, that You were going to ascend to your Father and ours, to your God and ours, that the glory of your Sacred Body had not been lessened because of your intimacy with them. Appearing to her as a gardener, You showed her that You wanted to make her your Eden and your disciple. Since the Apostles had to throw their lines into the sea, You did not disdain teaching them their work as fishermen. You ate with them; You were, I would say, their cook, for there were no angels to roast the fish that You showed them on the coals, nor any baker to prepare the bread for them that accompanied the fish. You extended an invitation to Thomas to place his fingers in the wounds made by the nails in your hands and feet and with his hand fearlessly to touch the opening in your sacred side. Certainly, the Resurrection had not changed your lovability nor removed humility from your Divine Heart that yearned to be forever an asylum for sinners. By these visible things, You wanted to elevate them to the invisible ones, being their royal, divine Physician. You spoke to them about the kingdom of God in which You were going to prepare seats and thrones for them to make them judges and kings. (973) You would breathe your Holy Spirit into them and upon them, making them gods, giving them power to remit sins. If You corrected them by rebuking and reproaching them for their difficulty in believing after so many obvious apparitions and visible, sensible signs of your Resurrection, it was because You wanted them to become informed doctors by this serious test. Then, ascending to your right hand, You imparted your holy blessing to them, thus fulfilling the request of the Royal Prophet: *Benedicat nos Deus, Deus noster! Benedicat nos Deus, et metuant eum omnes fines terræ. May God, our God bless us. May God bless us: and all the ends of the earth fear him.* (Ps 66:7b-8)

To show your correction, test and efficacious blessing in ten days, You sent

JEANNE'S ORIGINAL DRAFT

them your Holy Paraclete. He made them doctors of all knowledge, enabling their voices to be heard throughout the earth: *In omnem terram exivit sonus eorum, et in fines orbis terræ verba eorum. Their sound hath gone forth into all the earth: and their words unto the ends of the world.* (Ps 18:5)

CHAPTER CXXXVI

The day of Fire that envelops the infernal powers. Graces I received on the Feast of Saint Anne. Our Father, Saint Augustine, preferred preparation for grace to disputing about it. What occurred for the purchase of my house located in the Orangerie. God's providence and favorable guidance. Favors I received on the birthday of Our Lady and about my infirmities. (974)

I wanted to prepare a brief inventory of your goodness toward me, thinking that I ought not speak about the flames of the Day of fire, Day of wind, Day of great noise that astounded the infernal powers, subjecting them to fishermen who, after your Ascension, had been locked in a room through fear of the Jews. As their Master, You had commanded them to remain there until the day You promised to visit them, invested and armed with power from on high. With these weapons of fire, You would forewarn the enemies and destroy them by your Cross, which was a scandal to the Jews and foolishness to the Gentiles. Yet this did not prevent it from being set even over imperial crowns, for it has always been the terror of the wicked and of the demons.

I received many graces, my divine Word made Man, on the Feast of your grandmother. Her name is grace itself and, not to contradict this, she imparted important communications to me. Please let me use them well and not receive them uselessly. Among those who cooperate fully with their free will, the

JEANNE'S ORIGINAL DRAFT

victorious are triumphant; ordinary people are effective. This willing cooperation concurs with your goodness, for You grant grace for grace. (975) Lord, although You created us without our free will, You do not want to save us without our free consent. I will stop at this idea of my Father, Saint Augustine, who, one day in the year 1644 in the company of St. Thomas of Aquinas, witnessed to me that they would be filled with profound joy—which I could term accidental glory—if those who trouble themselves and upset many others by their disputes would instead prepare themselves to receive the graces they had lost by their arguments. They do so unaware of their passion, considering it to be great zeal. Grace is like charity, if not its replica. It is not ambitious, it does not seek its own glory but yours, my Jesus. Fill my heart with it and spread it on my lips. May my thoughts, words, and actions all be in grace, from grace, for grace and through grace so that I may say in truth with the great Apostle: "I am what your grace has made me to be."

On the Feast of Our Lady of the Angels, I was inspired to go to the church of the Recollect Sisters. At sight of the bench where I would receive the benediction of your Blessed Sacrament and gain the indulgence You personally granted to your faithful imitator, St. Francis, You showed me the care You took of your daughters as well as of me. I would not have received this intimation had I not gone there. Your angels, my heavenly protectors, guided me there. It is not the first time that I recognize the good deeds they do for me. (976)

On the Eve of the Assumption of your august Mother, You urged me to go out for your glory. You wanted me to purchase, not a chateau, but houses and gardens in which to accommodate You in your own home. I recalled what I had often told You during the ten years that I was in Paris: Dear Love, the foxes and many people finer and more dexterous than I am and birds, that are more skillful in providing for themselves than I am, have their nests with great, sumptuous designs. But You, Incarnate Word, to whom everything belongs, do not possess in Paris a foot of ground on which to lay your Sacred Head. Stop this complaint, dearly Beloved. From what You have given me through the care the angels take of me, I want to purchase one for You. Since

JEANNE'S ORIGINAL DRAFT

You commanded them to care for me, they have inspired those who sell these houses to offer them to others at a price they did not want to offer me, exacting 45 thousand pounds, whereas before the wars in Paris they wanted 50 thousand pounds for them.

Heavenly treasurers, what can I do to show my gratitude for your charitable care? I offer you what both the elder and the younger Tobias gave great Saint Raphael. My obligations to you and to all in general do not prevent me from acknowledging those I owe the holy physician and prudent guide who defended me against my enemies. He provided me with friends, curing a number of them whom I confidently recommended to him in his wise benignity. I know that he does everything according to your will to which I submit according to your good pleasure. (977) Were I to desire or request something that is not conformable, You would give me the grace to refuse it. May this toothache, which I have had for several days due to the evening humidity, abate my satisfaction. I want to endure it as long as You wish.

On the Feast of the Beheading of my great patron, your holy Precursor, You allowed the contract of the purchase of the house in the Orangerie to be settled and for me to pay twenty-five thousand pounds in cash. When I was unable to settle the payment of one of the mortgages belonging to minors, I would wait until it was mature, confident that your knowing wisdom disposes everything strongly and gently. This toothache tempered my satisfaction in this acquisition which was more than seventeen thousand pounds minus what I had to deposit five or six years before, in addition to which the lots would have been larger. Monsieur Lalive, the owner, refused two promises of seventeen thousand pounds from Monsieur Cantarini, because he feared bankruptcy on the part of the latter, which I did not fear at all. I knew the latter to be a man of honor, a good banker and my friend. Monsieur Lalive told those who were of his opinion that I ought not entrust my money to this banker. I was confident of your protection and that Monsieur Cantarini, as a man of honor, could not perform a cowardly act toward me; or, as a man of affairs, any injustice. Since he was my friend, I did not want to upset him.

JEANNE'S ORIGINAL DRAFT

Dear Love, shortly thereafter, he paid me and did not cause anyone to lose, for he did not become bankrupt. He fears and loves You and wants his children to do likewise. (978) Before the wars, he entrusted two of his daughters to me for upbringing. I prayed for your glory and their salvation, because his two daughters were taught in our Congregation, for he entrusted them to me and to no one else.

As I considered that these three houses and gardens now belonged to me, I was satisfied with all the transactions. You reminded me of a vision I had had in Lyons before I departed to establish the monasteries in Grenoble and Paris. I saw myself seated in a lovely place with trees whose fruit I could not see, yet I was amid many daughters. While I was there, someone brought me a parasol. I would have omitted this detail except that, while I was here, one of my little boarders brought me a parasol in reality. Thus, You showed me that You are faithful in all the figures or prophecies that You have shown me. I had the *Veni Creator* prayed in choir for the following days, since this acquisition was made through your Spirit.

The Feast of the Nativity of your Blessed Mother brought me many favors, although my toothache prevented me from sleeping for a number of nights. Being infirm, I was strong in this Virgin who held all my enemies chained up, walking upon the asp and basilisk, and treading upon the dragon. Admiring this marvel, all the angels exclaimed: *Quæ est ista quæ progreditur quasi aurora, etc. Who is she that cometh forth as the morning rising,* etc. (Cant 6:9)

David declared: "The Lord is my help, what can man do against me?" (979) Mary has come to my aid; what, then, can my enemies do? She is as terrible as an army arrayed in battle. Mary, joy of heaven and earth, Joachim's rejoicing, Anne's delight! Mary, benevolent grace of travelers, and the brilliant glory of those in heaven after the God-Man who is substantial grace and the beatific vision! Holy Church loudly proclaims that her birth is universal joy. With Isaias, St. Paul declared: "O, most immense Increated Word, You became the abbreviated Word through the Incarnation in Mary's womb. Your

JEANNE'S ORIGINAL DRAFT

joy is that You endured the Cross, submitting to the contradiction of sinners." On seeing Mary, who would be the Coadjutrix of the Redemption and would be steadfast beneath your Cross where You made reparation for all sin, your Divine Father was more than satisfied. He gave You a Name above any other name before which every knee should bend.

CHAPTER CXXXVII

St. Matthew is the good publican. True confession of our faults and the reparation God requires of us. He is the immaculate Lamb and the Blessed Virgin Mother, the holy Shepherdess.

On the Feast of St. Matthew, I learned great marvels about the graces You had given him. (980) You told me: "Do not think that he was the publican who entered the temple, striking his breast, not daring to raise his eyes while the proud Pharisee praised himself with vain thoughts, blaming this penitent whom God justified while he humbled himself."

Dear Love, I reply with the words St. John gave the old man who was being questioned: *Domine mi, tu scis; Lord, you know.* I know that the publican whose feast we solemnly observe followed You and died for You. Also, he attained your glory through great trials. He is the victim of virginity. With desire, I want to make a perfect confession so as to be pleasing to You and to follow You at the moment You call me.

My divine Pastor and most loving Director, You chose to tell me: "Offer my Divine Father the contrition I had in the Garden of Olives where both love and sorrow caused Me agony. Water and blood trickled from my sacred

JEANNE'S ORIGINAL DRAFT

pores to cleanse the earth. Offer Me the confession I made before Pilate, *bonam confessionem; a good confession* after which I bore all the sins of mankind upon Calvary, freely offering Myself for death in remission for them. To satisfy love, offer the Holy Spirit the blood and water that flowed from my side. (981) With this blood and water, I made satisfaction and a gift to my most worthy Mother and my beloved Magdalen. I gave my holy Mother the pure Blood she had given me at my conception. I had lovingly kept this blood in my breast with which to make my treasure there where my heart is situated. Likewise, I gave Magdalen this holy water in return for her tears for Me. By the ardor of my love, from it I had made a wonderful marvel, just as the sun draws forth the vapors by its heat and converts them into rain.

After all these marvelous favors, I thanked You for your inexpressible goodness. I got up from my place to go do the cooking, but had not even left the choir when You appeared to me as a snow-white Lamb. You were borne up by white clouds upon which You galloped happily, turning to call me to follow You and acting as my Precursor.

On the Feast of St. Thecla at the end of my prayer, your Blessed Mother appeared to me, standing at my right side. I was filled with joy at sight of her eyes that were lovelier than the sun and her color more delightful than the dawn. She said to me: "I am my Lamb's Shepherdess. I am going to follow Him to Lyons where He and I call you."

My charming Shepherdess, You seemed to me to be about seventeen or eighteen years of age. You were like grace itself. If we have received the law from Moses, should I refuse the grace that the Son and his Mother offer me? (982) I said to You: "My august One, with my heart's love and delight, I follow You and no longer belong in Paris. I am leaving this royal palace to follow your Son to the holy mountain. Dispose of everything for this voyage and of all hearts that must consent so that I may undertake it." My Divine Love, You did so marvelously, saying to me: "Go, Deborah, to Mount Tabor where the Incarnate Word will show forth his glory, and fear nothing. Take Barac with you and conquer Sisara. Rest assured that you will be victorious

JEANNE'S ORIGINAL DRAFT

and that this will be attributed to a young woman seated under the palm tree. You will judge Israel upon the holy mountain where my martyrs shall cover you with their palms and crown you with their laurels because of the suffering you will there endure for Me."

A few days later, accompanied by Monsieur de la Piardière, I went to the abbey to request the Prior, Vicar General for the Bishop of Metz, to give me four Sisters from our monastery to take to Lyons with me. You did what You had told me by consenting finally to allow me to leave Paris and satisfy myself, provided that I promise to return should it be necessary to do so, God willing.

When venerable Father Yvan came to see me, he brought a letter that recounted marvels to me about persons who to all appearances yielded to all my wishes. (983) I did not believe this, unable to accept whatever was not an article of faith and which I could prove to the contrary. The prudence of this time could have been my glory in the sight of this good priest. On that day, because of my tears, I seemed to be a mother overwhelmed by suffering, an innocent young woman considered to be guilty while not being so.

Father Yvan returned on another day after obtaining better knowledge of my true feelings. He satisfied me by not finding fault with my compassion as mother and told me that God Himself inspires founders and foundresses with the guidance of the Orders He has prompted them to establish. As I considered this good priest, I had a premonition that he would live only a few days more and told him so when he left the parlor.

On the eve of the Feast of St. Denis, Apostle of France, I was brought a note at about nine o'clock in the morning informing me that he had suddenly died that very morning. Since he had lived many years as a faithful servant of your Majesty, You wanted to withdraw his body and soul to avoid allowing the demons a long period of time to trouble him during the passage from death to life. May he forever be in your eternal rest, and may your Spirit prompt him to pray to You for me that I may be faithful to You. (984)

JEANNE'S ORIGINAL DRAFT

CHAPTER CXXXVIII

Our journey to Lyons, the divine protection, his favors toward his unworthy servant. Our arrival in Roanne and entrance into Lyons.

After I had made all the arrangements for departure, as well as Monsieur de la Piardière whom You told me was also Barac, we departed on Friday, October the seventeenth, eve of the Feast of St. Luke, St. Paul's companion on his pilgrimages. I prayed to him to accompany us and You, my loving Sun, to be favorable to us. By your ardent and luminous rays, You led us to Lyons. This was the sign I had asked You for without insisting too much, but to stop the rumors that maintained that the Abbé de la Piardière's daughter, four years and several months old, could not endure the cold or bad weather that this season in the previous years had brought.

You gave me confidence, dear Love, that You would be along on our journey and that we would have good weather on the way to Lyons. The sun would be our star and would not fade. Everyone could testify to this in Paris, Lyons and in a hundred places in the surrounding area. (985) The confessor of our monastery in Paris, Mr. de L[anglade] wrote me at the beginning of November, saying that the Countess of Rochefort recounted to him that in Paris this weather was being called Mother de Matel's summer. They could express it even better by calling it the Incarnate Word's summer.

We arrived early in Briarre. Father de la Piardière told me that he wanted to go see the canal, and I replied that I would go to church to adore You there, You who are the source of the waters of life. In your sacrosanct Humanity, You wanted me to experience the profusions of your Sacred Wounds, which are channels of grace for souls who seek only your love. He changed his mind and came to church with me. If I recall correctly, it is dedicated to

JEANNE'S ORIGINAL DRAFT

the holy levite and first martyr, St. Stephen. President Chausse accompanied us there. I had not knelt very long when You showed me that I was welcome, gratifying me with many favors, reminding me that I had received the first grace in Roanne, that is, by my baptism in St. Stephen's parish church. I became enraptured and heard these delightful words: *Orietur stella Jacob Virgo peperit salvatorem. A star shall rise up out of Jacob.* (Num 24:17c)

With ineffable sentiments, I adored You, born of your Blessed Mother. You were pleased to tell me: "My beloved, you will produce me through my Institute, remaining a virgin in imitation of my incomparable Mother. (986) I have chosen you to be my star, by which I will burst forth, and you will give Me another birth." O my divine Savior, with joy and satisfaction, I receive this good news from your goodness.

On Sunday morning, I felt an indescribable abandonment and dreaded the praise of my compatriots, becoming sadder than I can say. The priest, our guide, who was observing me, asked me the reason for this sadness that was apparent by my expression. Since he was my confessor, the one to whom I had an obligation and in whom I trusted, I told him that divine wisdom had ordained or permitted this condition that I cherished, since it detached me from anything that might attract me according to flesh and blood, that I would deprive myself of visiting my only sister whom I had not seen except for two or three hours in twenty-five years, if You preferred that to my joy in seeing her. You were satisfied with my disposition in which You interiorly retained me during the four days that we stayed at her home. What a visit! What joy, because all the people joined her and my brother-in-law, de Grimaud, her husband, showing me by their generosity what cordiality there is in being related. United to You, my soul could not enjoy all this applause. I felt two contraries to be in one same subject: an apparent, voluntary satisfaction not to bother anyone and entertaining myself with everyone as though Roanne were my earthly paradise and all the people my natural inclinations. During their acclamations, my soul felt like a stranger among relatives. You divided the waters from the waters, making a firmament of confidence with You in my spirit and in my exterior, the waters of distrust in myself. (987) Yet I made all

JEANNE'S ORIGINAL DRAFT

those around me happy, not wanting to diminish their hope that I would return whenever your providence so ordained.

On Thursday, October thirtieth, we left Roanne quite late to arrive in Lyons on All Saints Day. Caressing me through goodness, your Majesty had me understand the following and all the rest: *Ego ante te ibo, et gloriosos terræ humilitabo; portas aereas conteram, et vectes ferreos confringam. Et dabo tibi thesauros absconditos, et arcana secretorum, ut scias quia ego Dominus, qui voco nomen tuum Deus Israel. I will go before thee and will humble the great ones of the earth. I will break in pieces the gates of brass and will burst the bars of iron. And I will give thee hidden treasures and the concealed riches of secret places: that thou mayest know that I am the Lord who call thee by thy name, the God of Israel.* (Is 45:2-3)

As we entered the Saint Just gate in Lyons, I reached out of the carriage, calling to those who guarded the entrance. I announced our arrival to them, that we were fourteen persons, namely, the Abbé de la Piardière, two small girls, four Sisters of the Incarnate Word, and Mother de Matel. Surprised that they said nothing to me nor to my companion, I said to You: "Lord, it is You who have entered as absolute Lord, without anyone to question You nor to inquire who You are."

When we arrived, we met many people accompanying the body of the late Monsieur Parisot for burial. A number of them recognized me and came to testify to their joy on having me return. This embarrassed me deeply. All glory be to You who know the violence I did myself by leaving our monastery in Paris sooner than I wished, but in obedience to the Abbé, our guide. He thought my presence necessary to my daughters whom I had left afflicted by our departure. (988)

JEANNE'S ORIGINAL DRAFT

CHAPTER CXXXIX

Our entrance into our Congregation. What occurred regarding myself with those from whom I should have expected complete joy and consolation and the trial in which God placed me.

When we entered our small chapel, I requested that we four religious chant the *Veni Creator Spiritus*, because I wanted to enter our Congregation in your Spirit as did Saint Simeon in the temple. In your small tabernacle, I adored You as my great God. Dear Love, You told me: *Ascende tu qui evangelizas Sion; exalta in fortitudine vocem tuam. Noli timere. Get thee up upon a high mountain, thou that bringest good tidings to Sion. Lift up thy voice with strength, thou that bringest good tidings to Sion. Fear not.* (Is 40:9b)

At your command, I entered the Congregation. When I met those who were at the entrance to welcome me, sadness overcame me, because I perceived that You were not loved as much as I desired. The world and its vanities were installed there. Addressing everyone, and some members in particular, I spoke as You ordered me to do so: *Quis credidit auditui nostro? et brachium Domini cui revelatum est? Who hath believed our report? And to whom is the arm of the Lord revealed?* (Is 53:1)

There were no true feelings for your glory; your words were scorned, as St. Paul had predicted when he wrote to St. Timothy: (989) *Erit enim tempus, cum sanam doctrinam non sustinebunt, sed ad sua desideria coacervabunt sibi magistros, prurientes auribus, et a veritate quidem auditum avertent, ad fabulas autem convertentur. For there shall be a time when they will not endure sound doctrine, but, according to their own desires, they will heap to themselves teachers, having itching ears.*

JEANNE'S ORIGINAL DRAFT

And will indeed turn away their hearing from the truth, but will be turned unto fables. (2 Tm 4:3-4)

When unseen by me, they did not really fulfill their duties. Yet I loved and cherished them all, especially the one who was obligated by vow to stability in your Congregation. I was upset by those who had departed during the winter. You told me that in zeal You once expelled the buyers and sellers from the Temple, for You could not endure having your house desecrated—not to say profaned. You said that the doves and the sheep were sold, and they freed themselves. The full weight of work was left to a poor young woman who was as overworked as an ox. Their departure caused me to tell You in full heart and cry: *Zelus domus tuæ comedit me; The zeal of thy house hath eaten me up.* (Jn 2:17b) You want your house to be a house of prayer. I beg You that all your saints, whose feast we observe, may make reparation for everyone's defects and also mine. (990) You did not reject me, for the heavenly courtiers inclined toward me like heavens, granting me inexplicable blessings. What illuminations and delight did this night bring me, for I marveled at You with your holy martyrs, You who came upon the white cloud!

Since the next day was meant to assist the Souls in Purgatory, after Holy Communion I prayed to You to visit them, so that they all said: "Behold our Redeemer who comes!" I asked You to let them share in the banquet of glory; You did not reject my prayer. You reminded me of this sorrowful compassion that I might go up with You and your saints who fly like white clouds, saying to me: "I have led captivity captive. I will grant gifts to people who will be favorable toward you."

After Holy Mass, Abbé de la Piardière informed me that he was going to visit the Abbé of Saint Just according to our wishes and plan. Upon greeting him at Ainay, he was welcomed graciously, but when he alluded to me, he noted that the Abbé became distant. Astounded, he told him: "Monsieur, how indifferent you are while I am greeting you in the name of someone who, for so many years has cherished you, esteeming and honoring your friendship!" Unaware of the reason for this coldness, he learned that it was because I had

JEANNE'S ORIGINAL DRAFT

omitted writing to him about my leaving Paris or my entrance with religious into Lyons. (991) Monsieur de la Piardière replied that he was the one who had insisted upon the journey, that the obedience of the four religious had been granted by the letter of Monsieur de Ville, Vicar General while the See was vacant, that I was happy to come to Lyons close to the Archbishop who was favorable toward our establishment, that in Paris I had been assured of his graciousness toward me. I learned this fact from those who had told him about my joy that he would be my dear prelate when he was given my regards and greetings. They might have added that for a number of years I had prayed to your Majesty that he might succeed to the See after the death of His Eminence, although I did not desire this death, because I loved and honored him as my pastor.

When Abbé de la Piardière returned, I asked him how the Archbishop was and what his reception had been by the Abbé of Saint Just. He was too polite and charitable to tell me anything except that he had been welcomed with great honor and warmth. While he was thus speaking to me, I said to him: "Everything is fine for you, but there is coldness for me. This idea is uppermost in my mind. (992) Surely, you underwent humiliation. You are too sincere to conceal this cross from me following the *Benedictus* of the palms in Roanne. I am prepared to hear myself called insane by great and small, by my angels as well as my enemies in Lyons. If the Lord is doing this or allowing it, I will keep silent and adapt to all his desires or permissions. I will imitate Abraham. I will hope against hope, without daring to trust that my confidence will be reputed unto justice."

Dear Love, all this confidence at the point of my spirit left my inferior part astounded and sad. The waters were separated from the waters. I felt that two contrary situations existed in one same subject. I noted a solid firmament of confidence in You and the waters of distrust within myself. In a state of astonishment, I declared: "I have fallen from the clouds. O Lord, I flow forth like water!"

Dear Love, may your will be done. Were I to dare disobey and be

JEANNE'S ORIGINAL DRAFT

prompted to write for permission from my pastor and Archbishop to come have my soul converted, I would have done so. The sinful woman of the city did not ask You if she might enter the banquet hall to be at your feet and weep with heart and soul. She is not blamed for having come to her Savior, but her Redeemer's goodness is unfairly accused for befriending her. (993) I entrust mine to You, dear Love, which is your own. I am sad and somewhat troubled for having unknowingly displeased my prelate. In great compassion, cherished and divine Love, your goodness let me understand: *Et quid dicam? And what shall I say?* (Jn 12:27) Wondering about the meaning of these words, and not having my little Latin Bible with me, for I had left it in the Abbé de la Piardière's bag, I consulted the Concordance and found the twelfth chapter of St. John who recorded that You had uttered these words. (994)

CHAPTER CXL

Old and new fruit that I offered the Incarnate Word. Graces that the saints obtained for me on their solemn feasts while I was busy with the delays in the foundation. They continued their favors to me to provide me with strength to participate daily in my divine Food.

Plantaverat autem Dominus Deus paradisum voluptatis a principio, in quo posuit hominem quem formaverat. And the Lord God had planted a paradise of pleasure from the beginning: wherein he placed man whom he had formed. (Gen 2:8) Had Moses not said that You had created the Garden of Eden and had personally planted the trees and grass, filling it with flowers and fruit, I would not dare declare that, at the beginning of Advent, You invited me to enter your garden. There I was to see and gather flowers

JEANNE'S ORIGINAL DRAFT

and fruit, both old and new, to present them to You as yours. I offered them to You and do so again, my divine Gardener and loving Spouse. I offer You the fruit on the tree of the Cross, the great St. Andrew, as the first one You received, for he was sent to You by your Precursor. St. John the Baptist's fidelity would soon reach the end of its career, and Andrew would be at the beginning of his. John yearned to diminish, knowing that You must increase. (995) He wanted to conceal himself in Limbo, and You, my Savior, to appear upon Tabor and Calvary at the midday of your great love for the redemption of mankind. Habacuc asked You, in the midst of the course of time, to vivify your work. As for me, I beg You to make it perfect at midday, that I may find my table and bed and may not go astray: *Post greges sodalium tuorum. After the steps of your flocks.* (Cant 1:7b)

On the Feast of St. Xavier, my soul was so filled with your goodness that I said to You: "Dear Love, enough of enjoying delights. I want to endure torments for You. I yearn for the crucifix that the crayfish took the Apostle of the Indies. It is glorious for You when a soul that has fallen away advances and that, while others think it possesses great imperfections and the demons feel certain that, because of these faults, it draws near their abysses, that You address the words of the Royal Prophet to it: *Dextera Domini exaltavit me; Dextera Domini fecit virtutem. Non moriar, sed vivam; et narrabo opera Domini. The right hand of the Lord hath exalted me: the right hand of the Lord hath wrought strength. I shall not die, but live: and shall declare the works of the Lord.* (Ps 117:16b-17) (996)

By correcting me, You show that I am your child, not allowing me to be in danger from my enemies. In a fatherly way, You urge me to ask to enter your heart that is grieved for love of me. This distress is my justice as well as my healing: *Aperite mihi portas justitiæ: Ingressus in eas, confitebor Domino. Hæc porta Domini, justi intrabunt in eam. Open ye to me the gates of justice: I will go in to them, and give praise to the Lord. This is the gate of the Lord: the just shall enter into it.* (Ps 117:19-20)

I want to praise You, my Lord, for your mercies which forestalled me.

JEANNE'S ORIGINAL DRAFT

When I offered You my misery and prayers, You heard me, because You want to redeem me. Since You are good and just toward me, it is fitting that those who represent You should scorn me like the stone rejected by the builders: *Hic factus est in caput anguli; The same is become the head of the corner.* (Ps 117:22b) Your goodness performs marvels, which astounds those who ignore their beginning or end, unaware of the place from which your forestalling Spirit emanates. It is the day You made by your loving presence within Israelite souls, as they saw and feared God. Through your illuminations, they rejoice, while those who swoop upon them because of their authority enjoy temporal happiness. Dear Love, may they attain eternal joys through the fulfillment of all your desires.

You were light, charity and graciousness toward me on the Feasts of Saint Barbara, Saint Nicolas and Saint Ambrose: light and lamp through the prayers of Saint Barbara, charity through those of Saint Nicolas. (997) I asked You in Communion to renew our sacred marriage, and also for lovability and ambrosia through this doctor who is ambrosia itself. Could we not say to You: *Crastina die delebitur iniquitas terræ. Et regnabit super nos Salvator mundi. Tomorrow the iniquity of the earth shall be blotted out. And the Savior of the world shall rule over us.* (Antiphon: Vigil of Christmas)

When he saw the Immaculate Conception of the one who crushed him under her feet, beginning at the very moment she was conceived, the ancient serpent—the iniquity of earth—found his hope to deceive all mankind wrested from him. She heard the Sovereign King say to her: *Veni electa mea; Come, my chosen one.* You are all-beautiful, and in you there is no stain and there never will be any. Worthy Mother of God, who could express the favors you let me experience during Holy Communion and those that your Son, upon the altar in his loving Eucharist, poured into my soul. To make the sacrifice I offered Him burn even better, He induced me to weep abundantly, by recalling Elias' sacrifice. True and Living God, be blessed and adored by everyone.

On the Feast of St. Damasus, my soul was busy praising your August

JEANNE'S ORIGINAL DRAFT

Trinity, thanking You for the inspiration You granted this great Pope to love St. Jerome. They both contributed to having the West sing the *Gloria Patri* that is chanted in the East. (998) I rejoiced even more that the angels, who are morning stars, praised You all together in the Empyrean before the creation of mankind. I asked You to let him teach it to us after our creation, while we are on this lowly earth, hoping that one day we will praise You forever with them in the sublime earth, the land of the living, declaring to You with David: *Beati qui habitant in domo tua, Domine; in sæcula sæculorum laudabunt te. Blessed are they that dwell in thy house, O Lord: they shall praise thee for ever and ever.* (Ps 83:5)

On the Feast of St. Lucy, to whom I have obligations that are old and new, she let me share in the constancy of her love. I trusted in divine Love, meaning You, vivifying Spirit of life, who inflamed her heart. You elevated her soul by your flames and made her body heavy, that holy temple that belonged to You which the wicked wanted to violate by exposing it to sinners. This holy temple became immovable. Love placed its weight therein, causing confusion for all the insane spirits, entering her virginal breast in the Eucharist, which she received into her most pure lips where You showered your graces, becoming her principal Assistant. With her, You received the sword-thrust that cut her throat. Having partaken of a meal with the Prince—in fact, that consisted of the Prince Himself—she felt no fear. Love cast it aside; she considered herself your couch in the midst of her heart. You were charity itself for the joy of all the daughters of Jerusalem. (999) Your place and its abode in Sion were at peace. You entered into her to have her enter and dwell within You, letting her experience your promise.

On December 18th, I did not feel a bold presumption while waiting for your Blessed Mother to give birth, because I was prepared by your goodness with delight, and I did not experience the pain that many others do. It occurred before dawn whose sun would be weak during the day. For me, your Name was an abundant oil—not to say spilled over—ardently burning my heart and enlightening my mind so that, because of your presence, my Divine Spouse, night was as bright as day to me: *Quia tenebræ non*

JEANNE'S ORIGINAL DRAFT

obscurabuntur a te, et nox sicut dies illuminabitur. But darkness shall not be dark to thee, and night shall be light as the day. (Ps 138:12)

On the 21st, the Feast of St. Thomas, leaving many others to meditate upon his unbelief, my spirit was elevated to contemplate his loving zeal that made him encourage the disciples to exert courage by accompanying You to the places You wanted to go, impelled by your love. He even offered to die there with You. He said to them: *Eamus et nos, ut moriamur cum eo. Let us also go, that we may die with him.* (Jn 11:16b) As I marveled at this fervor before your Passion, I passed over the Red Sea. (1000) Being transported to the Cenacle with this saint, I adored You as my Lord and my God. By repeating these loving words a number of times, I acknowledged with my heart rather than with my lips that You are everything to me. With these loving thoughts that filled my heart with so much joy, I entered your house where I heard your holy cantors who welcomed me into their choirs, inviting me to participate in their music (as they did before). I was delighted to hear the great St. Michael proclaim You as God; David as his king and the same God that St. Thomas acknowledged to be his Lord. I ended by saying: "Jesus, my Love, who are our King, our Lord and our God."

On Christmas day, a bad case of influenza and the heavy fog confined me to bed after I had attended the three Masses during the night and receiving Communion after the midnight one. You made me experience the peace that was unbroken by the silence or the darkness. You were born of the bosom of your Divine Father and that of your virginal Mother. You came to occupy a royal place in mine, after, as You instructed me to do, I had made acts of adoration, thanksgiving, contrition, offering, conformity and abandonment into the hands of your adorable Father and those of your miraculous Mother, who wrapped You in linen cloths and placed You in the manger. (1001)

Dear Love, within my breast You were an adorable cloud. You could consecrate your temple by filling it with your marvels. Since I was unable to accomplish my ordinary functions, should I not, like the ministers in the temple, yield to this cloud that filled your house? *Nebula implevit domum Domini,*

JEANNE'S ORIGINAL DRAFT

et non poterant sacerdotes stare et ministrare propter nebulum. A cloud filled the house of the Lord. And the priests could not stand to minister because of the cloud. (3 K 8:10c-11a)

My case of influenza lasted more than forty days. Very thick fog remained almost as long as that of Lyons. Although I kept to my room, I did not become bored there. Your goodness kept my spirit busy by charming my bodily pains. I slept very little, fearing that the congestion and cough would deprive me of receiving You. You arranged to have me receive You every day at the community Mass, becoming my divine food and my true element. (1002)

CHAPTER CXLI

The Blessed Virgin prepared a holy banquet for us to which she invited us. My ordinary mortifications. How divine goodness accepts our thoughts and tears. The two tablets that Moses showed me. The Incarnate Word is my first and last Hermit, my beginning and my end. He is both Shepherd and Lamb.

On the Feast of your Circumcision in 1654, as I considered the knife that cut your innocent Flesh upon your entrance into the world, could I not say that You were the grape plucked from the vines of Engaddi, while your Blessed Mother declared as she pressed You to her bosom: *Fasciculus myrrhœ dilectus meus mihi: inter ubera mea commorabitur. A bundle of myrrh is my beloved to me: he shall abide between my breasts.* (Cant 1:12) Combining her tears and milk with yours and your Blood, she prepared a feast for me and invited me to eat and drink until I would become inebriated by this virginal, divine wine that does not make the senses dull. Instead, it elevates

JEANNE'S ORIGINAL DRAFT

them to feel your goodness and search for You by finding You with simplicity of heart in accordance with the counsel of the Prophet: *Quærite Dominum, et confirmamini; Quærite faciem eius semper.* *Seek ye the Lord, and be strengthened: seek his face evermore.* (Ps 104:4)

On the Feast of the Kings, as I listened to our Sisters renewing their vows, my soul renewed its mortifications by its ordinary thoughts for those days, being deprived by your command of what is prescribed for the Order. You told me, O King of my heart: "Offer me your thoughts while your daughters are offering me their vows, and have no doubt that He who receives the lambs of my ewe also lovingly accepts the hair or thoughts of the one who ascends the mountain of Galaad like a herd of goats. *Oculi tui columbarum, absque eo quod intrinsecus latet.* *Capilli tui sicut greges caprarum quæ ascenderunt de monte Galaad.* *Thy eyes are doves' eyes besides what is hid within.* *Thy hair is as flocks of goats which come up from mount Galaad.* (Cant 4:1b)

"Goat hair was offered and accepted at the temple for making marvelous things that served in different ways for the sanctuary. It was made into thread and twisted; it was worked into shape, dyed scarlet and employed according to orders from heaven. Your cheeks covered with tears and this intimate love please Me as much as and even more than these vows, these elevated and redoubled thoughts that ascend to my very throne together with my martyrs: *Galaad auricus testimonii; Galaad has heard your testimonies.* They testify that I am their God and their love, *Galaad abjectio; Galaad was spurned.* On seeing them held in contempt, (1004) I brought them up to my glory: *Super te Jerusalem orietur Dominus, et gloria eius in te videbitur.* *The Lord shall arise upon thee Jerusalem and his glory shall be seen upon thee.* " (Is 60:2d) During the marvelous forty days that You were in the stable with your glorious Mother and her virginal spouse, You gave me many graces. Your saints joyfully entertained me as though by ordinary festivities: *Lætentur cæli, et exultet terra; Let the heavens rejoice, and let the earth be glad.* (Ps 95:11)

JEANNE'S ORIGINAL DRAFT

Moses appeared to me bearing blank tablets. Astonished when I looked at them, I understood that this legislator joined the saints in singing about the Law of Grace there and that I was to search in it for the Law of Love. Then I would know what You desired me to do.

On the Feasts of St. Anthony and St. Paul, the first hermit; of St. Sebastian, St. Agnes, St. Vincent, St. Emerentiana, St. Timothy—disciple of St. Paul—Divine Word wrapped in linen cloths, You were generous and free in granting your graces to the one who adored You in this stable. (1005) You were her Sun whom she adored, turning her back upon the other one. You were her first and last hermit, being her beginning and her end. She considered nothing in time except the One who is eternity. She wanted always to be the object and mark for receiving all your arrows, so as to be pierced with them some day. These would then be doors by which your rays would illuminate the whole earth. Your arrows are as resplendent and brilliant as they are volatile and strong. Divine Lamb, she desired the same eternal blessings to be given to You as the true Jacob blessed by the Divine Father. She was the daughter of desire; she aspired to follow You everywhere with St. Agnes and St. Emerentiana, as their nursling sister, since she could not be related by blood. She did not have the grace, as they did, of being a martyr. She reflected upon You who came to conquer so as to be conquered, not only crowned, but conferring the crowns of grace and glory.

This hidden manna possessed a new name known by You and the soul that received it. It is your will, or better still, your delight. (1006) Without going to the earthly Rome, my soul visited the heavenly, divine temple, continually asking You for the same favor of dwelling there all the days of her life, according to your good measure. There she adores You, invisible King of immortal ages. May everything created render you homage there, and may You possess the eternal empire together with the Father and the Holy Spirit, the glory essential to You that no creature may take away.

St. Paul told St. Timothy that You are immortal and invisible, as well as impassible, while remaining God. Yet, he assures us that, as Man, You are

JEANNE'S ORIGINAL DRAFT

the Pontiff who sympathizes with our infirmities. From your own lips, he heard: *"Saule, Saule, quid me persequeris? Saul, Saul, why persecutest thou me?* (Acts 26:14) You were already risen; death no longer had any power over You, for You, the Living God forever, had subjected it to your own, having destroyed the body of sin.

You complained about Saul's persecution. When he appeared, *lupus rapax, like a ravenous wolf,* You became his prey, and he became yours. Your light blinded him, and your voice struck him down. You nullified the power he had received from the highpriest. (1007) This raiding wolf had to acknowledge that the Lamb, from the beginning of the world represented You; that You, whom he persecuted, were the One he adored, worthy of all honor and glory. He also had to concede that You are the eternal Priest according to the order of Melchisedech and, like Aaron, called by God; that You are God-Man, the judge of the living and the dead; that at your Name every knee must bend in heaven, on earth and in hell. He astounded everyone who saw and heard him in Damascas by saying: *Quoniam hic est Filius Dei; That he is the Son of God.* (Acts 9:20b) He confounded the Jews who lived in Damascas when he affirmed: *Quoniam hic est Christus; This is the Christ.* (Acts 9:22) He was alluding to You, my Lamb, who had conquered this wolf and made him shepherd of the sheep that he wanted to persecute by wresting them from your fold, for You are the great Shepherd of souls, as well as the Lamb that takes away the sins of the world. With confidence in your goodness, I pray You to take mine away. Please anoint the *Sancta Sanctorum, Holy of Holies* by shortening the weeks. Take away the sins that must be endured; offer your death through love to your divine Father, You who are the God-Christ, for everyone as well as for me.

One would need the golden lips of St. Chrysostom to speak appropriately about the perfections of this Apostle of glory and praise him. (1008) On his feast-day, I kept a respectful silence: from the abundance of your heart which is the altar of gold, speak, great Prelate. Your lips enrich us by distributing to us the marvels of this Apostle. His charity deserves our emulation; it is the perfect knowledge that he advised us to learn from him through You.

JEANNE'S ORIGINAL DRAFT

On the Feast of St. Ignatius, he treated me with great magnificence. Since I spoke at length about him last year, I will not repeat what I then said. Annually he grants me great favors. His love is all fire, flame and light; he is also the donor of the heavenly prodigy that appears in the temple on the second day of February. The Christ-like Virgin who bore Christ anointed him deeply so as to present him to the Divine Father, the First-born from among the dead, the glory of the tribe of Levi, the sceptre and crown of that of Juda, whose sacrifice and praise honors his eternal Father with infinite honor. (1009)

CHAPTER CXLII

The graces and favors that God gave me from Septuagesima until Easter, and how He was the object of my reflections according to the ideas presented in the Gospel of the day. He is very generous to those who run to Him without idleness.

On Septuagesima Sunday, You were good to me although I appeared to be idle, remaining until the final hour in your vineyard without working except through desire. You granted me your favors without being unfair to those whose work You justly recompensed.

Dear Love, I find it excessive that your mercy pardons my idleness, and your goodness prompts and sends me to work in your vineyard at the last hour. This is an indescribable favor for me. Humbled, my soul remains enraptured when it realizes that You fill it with your loving blessings. It exclaims: God of my heart, how good and merciful You are! You are merciful because You want to be merciful. (1010) Many run and search for You. Your love grants the price to whomever You please, not depriving those

JEANNE'S ORIGINAL DRAFT

of your blessings who cry out so as to please You and not for love of themselves.

The Word of God is a perfect fruit that produces holiness in the soul that loves Him.[1]

On Sexagesima Sunday, You let me experience that You are the Divine Sower come to sow the Word of life in our hearts and souls. When it is received and kept in our hearts with patience, it produces perfect fruit which You accept with pleasure.

The soul should divest itself of everything so as to hear the secret of your Passion.

On Quinquagesima Sunday, yearning to ascend near You in Jerusalem, my soul left everything, divesting itself of everything to be able to hear the secret of your bitter Passion, of your bloody flagellation. It begged You for a share in this and that it would view all creatures only in You, my Crucified Jesus, that in truth I might declare with the Apostle: *Christo confixus sum crucis. Vivo autem, jam non ego, vivit vero in me Christus. With Christ I am nailed to the cross. And I live, now not I: but Christ liveth in me.* (Gal 2:19b-20a)

You let me see an emissary goat. I said to You: "Lord, You became the curse for all, and for me in particular. (1011) I do not refuse contempt and sufferings, begging You not to abandon me during them. With You, Divine Love, I can do all things if You console me and consent to be my contempt, my sorrow and my poverty. I would be very happy in this condition with You. Whoever possesses God possesses everything. How miserly is the one for whom God does not suffice. My sufficiency will always be in You and through You, my Love and my All."

---

[1]This chapter contains titles or resumés in the margin.

JEANNE'S ORIGINAL DRAFT

Led into the desert by the Holy Spirit, Jesus Christ allowed the demon to tempt Him. He teaches us how to overcome temptation.

On Brandon Sunday [the First Sunday in Lent], the desert appealed to me, for I found You there, not only chased there by the high-priest, but by your Holy Spirit as St. Mark says, as soon as your Divine Father told You: *Tu es filius meus dilectus, in te complacui. Et statim Spiritus expulit eum in desertum. Thou art my beloved Son; in thee I am well pleased. And immediately the Spirit drove him out into the desert.* (Mk 1:11b-12)

There You remained forty days and forty nights, as You know, considering all the sins of mankind for which You have answered all alone and for all. Unaware of the honor You have given them, men become like animals. (1012) St. Mark then says: *Et tentabatur a Satana: eratque cum bestiis. And was tempted by Satan. And he was with beasts.* (Mk 1:13b) What a battle, my Lord, did the demon unleash against You! It was what he employs in the world through the three temptations which You chose to experience, You who are not of the world, having overcome it. Your ministers, the angels, came to serve You. Dear Love, through goodness, transport me from the world in You so that I may converse with the angels. Let me share in your victories. Be my faith that overcomes the world.

St. Matthias filled the vacancy left by Judas and entered the Divine Heart.

On the Feast of St. Matthias, your charitable, loving goodness gave me many graces. He received from your Spirit the condition of the apostolate, the light and fidelity that Judas had refused to accept. Unwilling to divest himself of avarice and personal interest, he did not receive charity that is the lot of the saints in light. Divine Sun, You shone in this darkness, yet he, hating the light, became a slave of the demon and of a devil similar to what he loved.

Matthias became divinized. Like the other Apostles, he carried the light. He filled the vacancy left by Judas who went to his place, which is hell.

JEANNE'S ORIGINAL DRAFT

Matthias entered your Heart, which is Paradise. Great St. Matthias, remember me now that you are in your kingdom. (1013) On this day, may I be in the Paradise of charity, loving our good Master.

How upon Mount Tabor, the Incarnate Word spread out nets up to heaven and upon earth.

On the second Sunday of Lent, You took me with You upon Mount Tabor, where I contemplated You as You spread nets and ropes up to heaven and on earth. Your Father and the Holy Spirit were there, bound and drawn through love, if I may express it in such a way. Moses and Elias and three of your Apostles there fell to the earth. What charm, what fascination enraptured heaven and earth! Only obstinate hell had no part in this light.

Dear Love, my status is in your hands. My spirit is before your eyes. My treasure is in your bosom. You are good to me wherever You may be. Since St. Peter did not know what he was saying, I want to learn from You what You want me to do. You want me to remain; your divine Father commands me to listen to You. Speak, Lord, for your servant is keeping still to listen to you in peace and tranquillity. She wants to see only Jesus of Nazareth, her flourishing Spouse. It is the end of your Transfiguration. (1014) Be united to me; bind me with your bonds. I wish to be your captive. If I am as mute as a fish, entwine me in your net. In You, I will find my element and nourishment, for You are the immense ocean where my spirit may spread out and therein become lost. You are my life. My gain is in You alone.

The soul that possesses peace is the Lord's reign.

On the third Sunday, I asked You to keep your empire in peace, that You would be a strong army within me, that I might not become divided, because, as You had said, every divided kingdom becomes desolate. Infallible Truth, grant me the grace to belong entirely to You, and be my Love and my All. Bless the one who carried You, gave birth to You and nurtured You.

JEANNE'S ORIGINAL DRAFT

My desires and requests on the day of the canonization of the holy saints.

On the Feast of the great Pope St. Gregory, my soul received great favors, requesting a share in his merits and the joy of the saints canonized on that day so that You would be glorified, Lord, You who are admirable in your saints. (1015) With St. Ignatius, I wanted to do everything for your glory. With St. Xavier, I wanted to convert everyone who did not possess the light of the Gospel, to proclaim to all that You are their salvation. With St. Philip Neri, I wanted to glorify you by your teaching, which You said belongs to your Father whose will I want to do. I offered all my works with St. Isidore's, detaching myself from everything created with St. Teresa. In all truth, I wanted to be able to declare that whatever is not You, my God, my Love, is nothing to me. To suffer or to die, to suffer for You and to die to myself so as to live in You, of You, through You and for You. Grant me these graces, my Divine Savior.

I was a sharer in the banquet that the Lord prepared for those who followed Him in the desert.

On the fourth Sunday of Lent, You might have omitted me from your great banquet for those who had followed You by passing through the sea. My soul dwelt in Lyons as in a desert, by my desires passing beyond all the tempests incited by the world, which is a sea. I wanted only You who are *my Love and my Weight, Amor meus, pondus meum.* I will be satisfied when your glory appears to me, when I see that You are loved as the Sovereign Good, sovereignly loving. (1016)

Again entering the heart of his beloved, the Incarnate Word made it his sanctuary and invited her to imitate his loved Magdalen.

On the fifth Sunday, since the Jews expelled You from their temple, I prayed that You would come into my heart which You could renew by making it your sanctuary. Entering therein by your Blood, like an eternal Pontiff, You prepared a new way for entering into You through your very own Precious

JEANNE'S ORIGINAL DRAFT

Blood. I obtained new confidence when I listened to the words of the Apostle: *Habentes itaque fratres fiduciam in introitu Sanctorum in sanguine Christi, quam initiavit nobis viam novam, et viventem per velamen, id est, carnem suam. Having therefore, brethren, a confidence in the entering into the holies by the blood of Christ: A new and living way which he hath dedicated for us through the veil, that is to say, his flesh.* (Heb 10:19-20)

I adore You, High-Priest, God and Man, Master of your temple, which is your holy and sacred home. By the help of your grace, I tried to go up with grateful heart, filled with faith and confidence in your goodness, cleansed by the water and Blood You had shed for me as You did for all mankind.

On Thursday of this Passion Week, as I viewed the holy penitent woman at your feet, washing them with her tears and drying them with her hair, You invited me to approach, to kiss them lovingly and reverently. (1017) Imitating this loved one, I said to You: "Lord, since I have many sins that I acknowledge at your feet, grant me great love, and pardon them through your charity."

Filled with compassion, I shattered my heart at the feet of Jesus Christ.

On Palm Sunday, I begged You to come to me, for I am in You. I prepared a supper for You in imitation of St. Martha, while in spirit I was at your feet with Mary. I poured out all my desires upon them and upon your head, shattering my heart, that was filled with repentance, as she did the vessel, so as not to retain there any affection or thought. I offered You everything that I am.

The Testament wherein occurs the miracle of love and the sign that heaven had never before seen.

On Thursday, I prepared to assist at your Supper. There You wanted to show your Apostles the power of your love. You gave them your Sacred

JEANNE'S ORIGINAL DRAFT

Body as food and your Precious Blood as drink. You entered into them so as to change and convert them into You. Your angel had given only water to the Prophet Elias. King David, as prophet, did not dare hope for wine so as to be converted to You who guided him. He said: *Super aquam refectionis educavit me, anima meam convertit. He hath brought me up on the water of refreshment: he hath converted my soul.* (Ps 22:2b-3a) Why? Because the vine prophetically seen by Jacob had not yet produced the blood of the grape with which to cleanse the mantle of his son Judas, who would provide the prey that he would personally trap. (1018) The eyes of all these lion cubs were as lovely as wine and their teeth as white as milk. As the red and white Spouse, nurturing and clothing your bride, You wanted to treat me royally and divinely to show that You are my magnificent, peaceful King. In the meantime, hell and the powers of darkness unleashed against You the fiercest war ever seen. Certain of your death that was more loving than painful, You made your wonderful Testament, a great miracle of love unheard of in past ages until this night.

It is the great sacrament concealed in God that corporeally contains all your inexhaustible riches and the fullness of your divinity. And I, the most insignificant of all your creatures, receive this fullness and its riches within me in order to proclaim them to all your saints in glory. I also receive the multiple gifts of your unique Holy Spirit who is all love. He gives the greatest sign ever seen by heaven and earth: an extension of your loving Incarnation that occurred in the shadow of the most high and divine power within the virginal womb. The Species of bread and wine serve as shadow and veil. I will repose beneath the shadow of Him whom my soul loves. (1019)

The largess granted by the Incarnate Word upon the wood of the Cross where He was acknowledged to be the Head of angels and mankind and the true Son of the Living God. He invites us to abide within his Sacred Wounds.

On Good Friday, the gifts You had given at the Supper had not in the least diminished the treasures of your bounty when You gave Yourself totally during

AUTOBIOGRAPHY

JEANNE'S ORIGINAL DRAFT

it. You extended the largess of your graces, as well as of your Blood, to all mankind by climbing Calvary burdened with your Cross, carrying it so as to be borne aloft by it. Elevated by this wood, You drew all things to Yourself. If the heavens opened at your baptism of water to marvel at your innocent humility in the River Jordan, there would be no door to conceal the excess of your charity from the heavenly spirits.

In this baptism of your own Blood: *Spiritu sancto misso de cælo, in quem desiderant angeli prospicere. The Holy Ghost being sent down from heaven, on whom the angels desire to look.* (1 P 1:12c) Dear Love, upon this wood You were acknowledged to be the Messias; You were proclaimed to be the Head of mankind and angels, the true Son of the Living God, given to the world to save it personally. You were the Sovereign Pontiff ascending the sanctuary, cleansing sin, pardoning sin that You washed away in your own Blood.

Attracting me with ineffable sweetness, your benign clemency said to me: "Come, my daughter, receive the papal absolution. Come, kiss my slippers embroidered with my Precious Blood, my sacred Feet nailed upon this wood; they are adorable. (1020) My Sacred Wounds are roses that will for all eternity preserve their color and fragrance."

Divine Savior, am I not guilty of your death through my sins? *Cor meum conturbatum est in me, et formido mortis cecidit super me. Quis dabit mihi pennas sicut columbæ, et volabo, et requiescam? My heart is troubled within me: and the fear of death is fallen upon me. Who will give me wings like a dove, and I will fly and be at rest?* (Ps 54:5, 7) It is You, my Love and my God: *Ecce elongavi fugiens; et mansi in solitudine; Lo, I have gone far off, flying away: and I abode in the wilderness.* (Ps 54:8) I choose your most holy Wounds, since, through your mercy, You give me the choice. *Qui salvum me fecit a pusillanimitate spiritus, et tempestate; I waited for him that hath saved me from pusillanimity of spirit and a storm.* (Ps 54:9b) In the niches of the rock, I will be your dove. I will make my dwelling in the cavern of your sacred side.

JEANNE'S ORIGINAL DRAFT

CHAPTER CXLIII

The Incarnate Word delights in extending great largess, and He wants the soul to request important things; the vision of a Lamb upon a Cross and the reason for this.

On Easter Sunday in 1654, when I saw You glorious and victorious over sin, death and hell, creating a day of light, joy and delight, the beauty of the immense fields of your divinity and of the most wonderful village of your Humanity, my soul went out of itself and of everything that was an excess. (1021) It recreated in your ravishing steps, followed by the captives of your love whom You had delivered from the prison of your justice, which was dark Limbo. I declared: *Hæc est dies quam fecit Dominus; exultemus, et lætemur in ea. O Domine, salvum me fac; O Domine, bene prosperare. Benedictus qui venit in nomine Domini. Benediximus vobis de domo Domini. Deus Dominus, et illuxit nobis. This is the day which the Lord hath made: let us be glad and rejoice therein. O Lord, save me: O Lord, give good success. Blessed be he that cometh in the name of the Lord. We have blessed you out of the house of the Lord. The Lord is God, and he hath shone upon us.* (Ps 117:24-27) Divine Love, You allowed me to address these words to You as a joyful canticle on seeing You triumphant after your Passion. You had generously passed through the Red Sea of your Precious Blood wherein You saved the true Israelites and extirpated sin and the demons as You did the Egyptians.

Enraptured with delight, your Blessed Mother said to You: "Rise up, my glory; listen to my harp and psaltery in heaven and on earth. With everything rejoicing, could I be sad? Risen Jesus, whoever does not love You becomes anathema, but whoever loves You rejoices in jubilation. Adorable Sower, even if the doors were closed, You could enter hearts, like that of St. Thomas

JEANNE'S ORIGINAL DRAFT

that stubbornly adhered only to what can be experienced by their eyes, ears and hands. (1022) Through charity, You could then convince them of whatever their faith could not accept, for it was apparently dead and buried in your tomb. Their hearts were as hard as the rocks which You gloriously penetrated, inviting them to approach You. They could find themselves in You, and You in them, as they exclaimed in admiration: *Dominus meus et Deus meus; My Lord and my God.* (Jn 20:28)

Animated by charity, faith causes the soul to be profusely gratified by divine gifts and has the Holy Spirit make his dwelling in it. Divine Beloved, it is this Spirit that You wanted your disciples to request of your Father so that their joy might be full. They were to consider as insignificant anything they had asked for until the day that (impelled by this love) You urged them to pray for his magnificent goodness which is self-communicative: *Usque modo non petistis quidquam in nomine meo. Petite, et accipietis, ut gaudiam vestrum sit plenum. Hitherto, you have not asked anything in my name. Ask, and you shall receive; that your joy may be full.* (Jn 16:24)

How often You have graciously invited me to ask you for great things, making me understand that You enjoy giving largess to souls who trust in your goodness, hoping for complete pardon and every gift from your mercy of which the earth is full. Heaven is filled with your justice, because, by your Precious Blood that has infinite merit, You have acquired the kingdom where You accommodate the just. You have more than satisfied the full extent of justice, for You became poor to enrich us; You died to give us your life.

On the Feast of the Finding of your Holy Cross, You appeared to me as a Lamb walking in a thick woods where I could detect no grass. Your wool covered You down to the earth. You had me understand: "It is my seamless robe with which I have wanted to invest mankind. In this woods, my food is the will of my Father who loved the world so much as to give them his own Son to save them by the wood. My daughter, my love is my weight. I love the Cross, because through it I am and will be the King of lovers and love itself." As I adored and contemplated You walking all alone in this woods,

JEANNE'S ORIGINAL DRAFT

You approached me. I said to You: "Dearest and gentlest Lamb, do You want me to be your shepherdess? (1024) Even as a child I wanted to follow You wherever You choose to go."

As a favor, tell me: Are You the one, my Lamb, who gallops among the clouds, dressed in the very clouds that your Mother wanted me to follow all the way to Lyons? Have You come down to this woods to be subsequently sacrificed as a humble, gentle victim? O dearest Love, I heed the mystery: You became everything so as to win me over completely. When You had me come from Paris with a great following (which mortified me quite a bit), You flew like the clouds. Now that I am humiliated by those who resist You more than they do me, You sympathize with me in this woods where I find myself alone with You. Dearest Love, my Isaac and my Lord, with joy I go down to this woods, lowering my eyes that You had raised up to the clouds to walk with You. How happy I am to have my Bridegroom here. Please lead me to the tent of Sara, your Blessed Mother, and You will cause all your elect to rejoice. I am your Rebecca. (1025) Aided by your grace, I will valiantly endure the combats or resistance of two peoples that You want me to carry in my breast. I know, my Savior, that I must suffer contradictions as You did. In light of those that sinners caused You, You who are innocence itself, why should I be exempt, I who am a very great sinner? I can do everything in You who comfort me, no matter what contradiction is made against your plans.

Dear Love, I recall that Moses appeared to me a few months ago, carrying two tablets whereon I saw nothing written. They were like tablets of expectation. I understood that I should not give up hope about the plans of your powerful goodness to me when I was abandoned by those who owe everything to You, not having received your commands. You would rewrite them, and You had placed me among your holy patriarchs, prophets, apostles, martyrs, confessors and virgins. I was to endure everything for your Name, witnessing to your truths, whether those You have accomplished, are accomplishing or will accomplish. (1026) You personally witness to Yourself, giving me a knowledge which my enemies, who are also yours, cannot resist. I was to practice patience, and in it I would possess my soul.

JEANNE'S ORIGINAL DRAFT

CHAPTER CXLIV

The ardent desire of my soul to follow the Incarnate Word in his glory. My solitude during which God gave me an abundance of tears. The state in which I found myself until Pentecost and the Feast of the Trinity. I was divinely treated, being maintained in a glorious state.

On the Feast of your Ascension, my soul yearned to follow You. It was only with great effort and inexplicable violence that I remained in this valley of tears and miseries. It resolved to endure its miserable life for love of You who caused it to say amid frequent sighs: O, let me endure martyrdom, deprived of everything that attracts me! Adoring You in your delights, I consent to having You ascend to your Louvre of glory, but I languish from remaining on earth amid prolonged tortures. (1027) You reproached your Apostles for their hardness of heart and disbelief after so many signs of your Resurrection. They were enraptured by your Ascension. Their gaze fixed upon You, they were unable to turn away until two angels intervened, to whom You had given orders and appeared to them in human form. They would have preferred to remain upon the Mount of Olives, like St. Peter upon Tabor. The cloud and the angels deprived them of their preferences. I must experience the same deprivation and live in a languishing condition, for You command me to remain in this exile. You told me that You ascended in order to be my Advocate with your Father, personally speaking, You Yourself, after having spoken in many ways through your prophets and angels. Hasten, my Beloved, and let me hear your voice. Dear Love, I hear it tell me that You are the Eternal Word, that You speak for me in heaven and that You leave me my pen with which to record the marvels of your love for your glory on earth. (1028)

The ten days I spent in prayer and tears caused me such a loss of sight that

JEANNE'S ORIGINAL DRAFT

the doctor informed me that I apparently had a cataract. He ordered repeated purgations to remedy the situation on time. You blessed them, my Love. I will not express my mortification in restraining my tears through obedience so as not to lose my sight as was feared for me. Had I not refrained, being unable to read or write, I would hardly have been able to pray with fervor, because I often experience that the flames set afire by the ardor of your Holy Spirit cause the soul to shed abundant tears. *Flabit Spiritus eius, et fluent aquæ; his wind shall blow, and the waters shall run.* (Ps 147:18)

It was necessary for me in spirit to feel useless to myself. As for the body, I did what I did not care to do, and I endured visits that often importuned me. I preferred to remain alone with You. I did offer vocal prayers, as You know my ways of doing them, and prayed my rosary a number of times (day and night), walking through the rooms, since I could not endure the open air. I often visited You in your dwelling of love, your holy and most loving Eucharist. I remained either standing or sitting, for, having a problem in one knee, I could not kneel very long. (1029)

Whenever allowed by your charitable goodness to take a walk, I did so in church, when it was closed, or in the choir. My intention is to walk in procession as others do, praying to all the saints and angels to assist by offering my prayers to your adorable Majesty, as I united my intentions to yours and theirs. Sometimes, I would ask You to elevate my spirit, as Enoch was elevated in body when he was favored by walking with You. If I prayed standing, I considered how You looked at St. Stephen; if seated, as though I were seated at the right hand of your Divine Father or at the Supper. If I were prostrate, I thought of You at the feet of your Apostles or in the Garden of Olives, begging You to pray for me and allow me to help You by wiping your brow. I prayed that You would give me your Precious Blood which flowed to the ground. I told You that this divine dew could enrich, decorate and justify me in the eyes of your Father and your holy angels. I prayed to the one who comforted You to help me offer a prayer that would be acceptable to You. I wanted to be this earth, opening my breast for these divine drops so as there to beget the Savior, who is You, my Love and my God.

JEANNE'S ORIGINAL DRAFT

On the Feast of Pentecost, and during the entire Octave, You did not deprive me of the gift that your Father and You sent to the Cenacle. (1030) I could well declare that your law was in the midst of my heart and that my enemies could not overcome me as long as this fort, armed with the weapons of love, protected me and that its charity was spread about there. It is goodness that is self-communicative.

On the Feast of your Most Holy and Most August Trinity, you treated me divinely. You showed me a very strong arm with the hand full of unction to fortify me and temper all the contradictions made against me and against your Order. In the evening, after having taken corporal remedies, since I wanted to repose, your loving and most August Society welcomed me with extreme graciousness and made me experience an ineffable grace. It put me in a glorious, peaceful state, suspending all the vexations that gave way before this divine favor. This suspension elevated my spirit, without causing me any headache, because very often such suspensions resemble violent elevations or raptures. It was very delightful for the spirit and an alleviation for the body. Since it was May 31st, when the Church observes the Feast of St. Petronilla, a virgin of ravishing beauty appeared to me and remained a long while with me without speaking, but she delighted me by her visit. (1031) Thinking that I was asleep, the Sister who was my infirmarian did not disturb my repose. However, seeing that it was time to give me something to eat, she told me that it was late and almost midnight. Complying with her, I forced myself to withdraw from these divine caresses and rapturous elevations.

JEANNE'S ORIGINAL DRAFT

CHAPTER CXLV

Royal and divine profusions and a holy anointing by Jesus Christ, St. Peter and St. Paul. Graces given me by a number of saints, and the tranquillity which God granted my soul.

On your Feast and during its entire Octave, my Divine Sacrament, You granted me magnificent graces, as your loving goodness prompted You to do with royal, divine profusion. I invited the heavenly Sion to praise You with the prose expressed daily during the Octave in the presence of this adorable marvel that is visible when it is concealed and is concealed when it is visible upon our altars. (1032) It is You, divine Eucharist, who are the wonderful grace of earth, that enraptures the heavenly citizens who adore while admiring it and admire while adoring these formidable and most wonderful mysteries, You are exposed at the door of our tabernacles, in the fervor of midday, to provide a dwelling and enrapture souls journeying along life's way. You are their Viaticum during mysterious deaths—I dare not say mystical ones—for the soul that receives this marvelous ambrosia becomes ecstatic, languishes and exclaims to itself: *Mihi enim vivere Christus est, et mori lucrum; For to me, to live in Christ: and to die is gain.* (Phil 1:21) With greater advantage than David, the soul declares: *In pace in idipsum dormiam, et requiescam; In peace in the selfsame I will sleep, and I will rest.* (Ps 4:9)

St. Claude, St. Anthony of Padua and St. Basil the Great have obtained many favors for me on their feastdays. Glad to gratify me, they extended great charity to me. Right now I cannot express what they did for me. My customary request is for heavenly gifts and divine graces that all the saints have received and those from which the condemned never profited. I begged the Holy Spirit to accept the glory for this, communicating it to his saints in thanksgiving for me.

JEANNE'S ORIGINAL DRAFT

Divine Savior, You know that your Precursor, my great patron, brings universal joy to the soul that wants to love You. Also, she who bears this gracious name asks You grace for grace through his intercession, for You filled him with graces even in his mother's womb. (1033) You visited her when You were within your Blessed Mother's womb. Could the Acme of Theology and the Vessel of Election and Dilection, St. Peter and St. Paul, forget me on the days of their splendor when I had only to take a place in the shadow of the former by considering him near You, my Sun, as I returned from Communion. Likewise, in tears, I prayed to the latter to lend me his handkerchief with which to dry them and to deliver me from my sadness of spirit, if You so wished, as a relief. I did receive these consolations from both of them.

On June thirtieth, after Communion, You filled my soul with superabundant rejoicing. As You poured upon it your sacred anointing, O my Divine Pontiff, You had me understand: "My daughter, yesterday was the feast of the Arch-bishop of Lyons; today is yours. Yesterday he was consecrated by three bishops of the Militant Church. Today, my Apostles Peter and Paul of the Triumphant Church have come with Me to consecrate you entirely to Me and for Me. The arm and hand that you have seen inexplicably pouring out the anointing of a grace showed you my goodness that was pleased to pour profusions of love over and within you. I have fulfilled what you predicted in December 1652, around the Feast of St. Thomas, to the Abbé of St. Just, announcing a great joy to him. (1034) Yesterday he saw the realities of what I commanded you to predict to him. He believed them."

Dear Love, at the present time, he seems to spurn the illuminations that formerly he had esteemed. It is either because he no longer sees his little directee or that his office as Vicar General has caused him to change his mind. "My daughter, my Church was established as a consequence of the one my Divine Father gave Peter when He revealed my divinity to him. After this revelation, I told him that he was blessed: *Beatus es, Simon Bar Jona: quia caro et sanguis non revelavit tibi, sed Pater meus, qui in cælis est. Et ego dico tibi, quia tu es Petrus et super hanc petram ædificabo ecclesiam meam. Blessed art thou, Simon Bar-Jona: because flesh and blood hath*

JEANNE'S ORIGINAL DRAFT

not revealed it to thee, but my Father who is in heaven. And I say to thee: That thou art Peter, and upon this rock I will build my church." (Mt 16:17b-18)

Dear Love, Word of the Father, You have always accepted whatever was pleasing to your Father, for You are one God together with the Holy Spirit, the Spirit of Truth. I adore You in unity of essence and trinity of Persons. You are Three who witness in heaven, and your Three Persons are but one God, and three who witness on earth: water, blood and spirit, and these three form but one Jesus Christ. As for me, I say to You with David: *Testimonia tua credibilia facta sunt nimis; Thy testimonies are become exceedingly credible.* (Ps 92:5a) Your loving goodness graciously accepted my confession to it.

On this same morning, I reported in writing to the Abbé of St. Just the graces You had given me, but received no reply about them. (1035) Monsieur de Gresole insisted that I see him, unaware of what I had already written the former. Prompted by zeal, he told him about the establishment of your Order, but this was not well received, for your hour had not yet come.

The next day, Monsieur de Gresole came to visit me. He was satisfied, my adorable Lord, when he saw that I was resigned to your will. Because he saw the constancy that You provided your little daughter, he told me to remain in this state of hope and silence until he would return to Lyons to receive your orders there. This would be during the fourth part of Lent. (1036)

JEANNE'S ORIGINAL DRAFT

CHAPTER CXLVI

Zeal for the salvation of the Souls in Purgatory prompted me to pray with tears for their salvation. The Blessed Virgin let me participate in the triumph of her Assumption. Ingratitude caused me sadness that let me know my weakness, and I saw the Holy Father's tiara.

In the month of July 1654, You were my Lion of the Tribe of Juda, and like that of Samson, your strength and gentleness comprised the subject of my colloquy. I could instead use the term "enigma" that no one would know about if You did not explain it to me at the proper time, for I entrusted my heart to You alone, who have faithfully loved me. You did not allow me to be exposed to the power of my enemies, who were more cruel than the Philistines toward Samson after they had blinded him. They had allowed him to live that he might serve and entertain them. They would not have been opposed to him had they not considered him to be their enemy. They were totally unaware that he was resolved to destroy them, because he considered them to be your enemies, my Lord and my God. Through your Spirit, who made him stronger when he began to fight against them, he overcame them. This is stated several times in the Book of Judges: *Irruit autem Spiritus Domini in Samson; And the spirit of the Lord came upon Samson.* (Jgs 14:6a)

Dear Love, You well know that persons uncircumcised in heart who do not love You hate me and turn far away from your plans. (1037) Filled with zeal by your Spirit, mine acquired spiritual strength and reason: to overcome them, not with the jaw of an ass, but by the lips of your simple daughter upon whom You beneficently shower your graces and blessings that confounded them for your glory. My adorable Conqueror, these victories belong to You. Be victorious as the strongest and most powerful in battle and the Lord of Hosts

JEANNE'S ORIGINAL DRAFT

and King of glory. Enter the hearts that have resisted You so that they may cooperate with the graces of their vocation, especially for my daughter who has not persevered as she had commenced.

During this month of August, when so many people dreaded the solar eclipse and what ensues, fearing lest they die because of it, my spirit trusted in your ardent, enlightening illuminations. It had no fear of this obscurity that was almost imperceptible nor of the bodily ills that were considered to be inevitable. My fear consists in offending You and of causing others to do so. (1038) Sometimes I concealed the faults that others committed, not seeing in them any tendency to do penance, as I waited for them to repent through your mercy. Weeping with confidence before your Majesty, I begged You that they might do penance in this world. With gentle, merciful eyes, You considered the tears that your Spirit produced in me. I begged Him to intercede within me, for me and for those whom I presented to Him with unspeakable groaning.

On the eve of the triumphant Assumption of the holy Spouse, as the most beloved Daughter of the Father and the most august Mother of the Son—who are You, my Divine Love—I was filled with divine consolations. I shared in her delights so that my heart and body rejoiced in the glory of this Blessed Mother, holy Daughter and holy Spouse of the Three Divine Persons. They led me to marvel at her, teaching me that she is their perfect contentment. I could call her the fulfillment of this August Trinity. (1038-2) I have no words with which to express what I understood and felt on the day of perfect happiness in a pure creature who is the immaculate Daughter, the Virgin-Spouse, and the fruitful but most perfectly virgin Mother of her Creator.

On August thirtieth, You allowed hell to show me its rage and afflict me through persons who were obligated to me and did not yet want to be known as the authoresses of these crimes and black ingratitude. Although successful in convincing them of this, I remained satisfied with the protests these persons made that they were unaware of what I was telling them. I felt delivered from this trial that You allowed my weakness. At the time, I did not consider such,

JEANNE'S ORIGINAL DRAFT

because I could see no strength of spirit but rather an inexplicable dejection, encountering nothing that might fortify me. The sacraments and prayer provided me with such little consolation that, unless You had suspended my spirit so as not to allow me to fall into the abysses of these dark desolations, I do not know if I would have continued my daily Communions and ordinary confessions. But You are faithful.

During this time of trial, the tiara of our Holy Father appeared to me. It was suspended, and, over it was the earth, as though it had emerged from the tomb. (1038-3) You said that it would persist for several months. I shared it with Father Gibalin and the confidants who were leaving for Turin. They are still living and certainly recall this prediction.

CHAPTER CXLVII

A trial from which God delivered me. I was invited to consider a wonderful sacrifice; its meaning. The vision I had of an elevated Pontiff, wearing his tiara and having his breast open.

On the Feast of St. Luke, I prayed to You to have me advance in class. As my Divine Master, You could easily deliver me from the ignorance that not only ranked me with animals but placed me lower than they. I was reduced to nothingness, not seeing in myself any power nor tendency to do good. Often I remained near the altar so that You might look at me with your merciful eyes, but my blindness could not see them. (1039) I was blind, deaf and mute in your presence. O God, what a condition!

JEANNE'S ORIGINAL DRAFT

This holy Evangelist, painter and physician was charitable toward me. I have experienced this a number of times on his feastdays. Even though I was not possessed by the demon whom You expelled, as this saint records for us, I perceived that interiorly I had inexplicable frailties, despite the fact that my bodily eyes, tongue and ears functioned as You meant them to do. I could not hear You speak your efficacious, charming words, for I did not experience your brilliant illuminations. I did not know if, hoping against hope, I should speak to your Majesty as before or if I should remain mute, deaf and blind.

On the Feast of the holy Apostles St. Simon and St. Jude, I asked them to pray to You for me and to mark out for me in my soul the dwelling of your Majesty, followed by all your saints. It is characteristic of your goodness to produce light from darkness, as is assured by the Apostle whom You illuminated by blinding him: *Quoniam Deus, qui dixit de tenebris lucem splendescere, ipse illuxit in cordibus nostris ad illuminationem scientiæ claritatis Dei.* (1040) *For God, who commanded the light to shine out of darkness, hath shined in our hearts, to give the light of the knowledge of the glory of God.* (2 Cor 4:6) O delight of all nations, You let me experience your delight on listening to the earth as it prays to heaven and at how magnificent and admirable You are in your sacraments. From that day on, my darkness and troubles were dispelled.

In the evening on the eve of All Saints, as I entered our little church to make my prayer, I understood: "You are invited to the sacrifice. *Veni ad Victimam; Come as a victim.*" No sooner did I kneel than You elevated my spirit in a marvelous way and let me see a multitude of saints over the altar, among whom I detected St. Peter. All these saints appeared to me with their bodies, as agile as spirits. They were busy carrying a Lamb that was weightless. This Lamb was the Victim that offered itself and whom they unanimously joined in sacrificing. It was not a bloody sacrifice; its death was mystical. It remained entire, being communicated in a wonderful, ineffable manner that cannot be expressed. (1041)

The marvels that I learned and understood and the state of my soul during

JEANNE'S ORIGINAL DRAFT

the time that I contemplated these mysterious visions are totally inexpressible. With the Prophet, I said to You: *A, a, a, Domine Deus, ecce nescio loqui; Ah, ah, ah, Lord God, behold, I cannot speak.* (Jer 1:6) By this invitation, I well understood that I must suffer. That very evening, Monsieur de la Piardière's little daughter became ill with a malignant fever from which the doctors had no hope of recovery. Soon this six-year-old child broke out with small pox, *purpura, senepon* and innumerable other kinds of ills that for three whole months kept her in pitiful straits. During this time, I wept so much that my head resembled a source of water, for I knew that her relatives on the side of her late mother would not be appeased without a miracle. Also, they would unceasingly blame the father for having left me his only daughter a hundred leagues away from him. If at times I was consoled by your goodness, I could not accept your consolations deep within me. Instead, I said to You with Agar: (1042) "I cannot see the child of your faithful Abraham die." Agar was speaking these words about her own, and as for me, I begged You to heed the voice of this little orphan whom I had received into my arms and lodged in my heart, when at the age of two she had lost her mother and was released from the care of three nurses. May your Blessed Mother take care of her. I am not worthy to be answered. Addressing all the saints, I begged them always to have pity on me by praying to You to allow the little one I loved to recover. I love her more than I can say.

Father Gibalin said to me: "Mother, you should not fear her death. The Lamb you saw carried and offered for all the saints did not die. He was offered as a victim, but remained alive. This vision is compelling. It comprises a number of mysteries and promises you great graces, both interior and exterior. God always deals with you as his favorite. I know no other person who has a similar protection of his. He fulfilled all the predictions that He gave you for his glory and your benefit. If He is testing you, He intends to make you advance more in his sight and in that of the angels and saints. One must always acknowledge his goodness and divine guidance. (1043) You should faithfully take note of this providence over you, that never abandons you, and all this for his glory and the increase of his Order. I am most confident that his Holy Spirit is in you."

JEANNE'S ORIGINAL DRAFT

Dearest Love, I ask pardon for my delays in describing your favors during which time a number of them might have been forgotten unless You had personally marked or reproduced them in my memory. This You do by your repeated reproductions through the Spirit You sent your Apostles who was to remind them of what You had said to them.

While I was at prayer on the Feast of the Dedication of St. Peter and St. Paul, You let me see an elevated Pontiff wearing his tiara, whose breast was open. Therein was a multitude of victims who offered themselves in his breast together with him. They were consumed in a holocaust, losing their human and natural life there, and there they received the divine, supernatural one. This consummation of themselves divinized them. I saw a white dove that was newly accepted, which attached itself to this sacred breast to be consumed together with the other victims that no longer possessed their own life or feelings. (1044) This dove suffered from still remaining in a condition of being returned to earth and being able to fly through the air. Could it have possibly spoken, it would have declared: "Why am I still in this mortal life? Love has impelled me to die with the rest and to be consumed in this breast which has changed the natural, human life of these fortunate victims into a divine life. I see them happily lost to everything that is not You, O my God and my All."

How fortunate and blessed are these souls to experience the divine words You have declared, divine Savior. Whoever loses his soul in this world will find and preserve it in the other. What happiness can compare to an entire eternity in your sacred breast! By possessing You, they are possessed by You. They enjoy an inestimable treasure that You allowed me to see. O, if I could only possess it and die right now, how happy I would be! But I realize that I must still live life's course, that I am the dove that sees itself burning and being consumed within the breast that burns brighter than any furnace, a breast that is all fire. It is the altar of marvelous holocausts. (1045) These marvels are both incomprehensible and ineffable to me. What I have said only poorly expresses this mystery that is elevated higher than the wings of the Seraphim. One must empty oneself completely in order to enter there and to become completely lost therein. One can only chant: *Holy, Holy, Holy.* Silence is

JEANNE'S ORIGINAL DRAFT

more appropriate than any word to make known the height, depth, width and length of this charity and to be engulfed in it in all God's plenitude.

Divine Savior, is it this plenitude of joy that You command me to request of your Divine Father? Father—holy, loving Father, grant it to me, since your Son wants me to request You for it. He merited it by always fulfilling what was pleasing to You.

After I had witnessed this marvel, You let me understand, dear Love, that You gave the Sovereign Pontiff all the treasures of your merits and of all the saints. Faithful souls are united in the Pontiff's breast there to receive the divine operations and different forms from the Unique Spirit of your Father and your own. (1046) He is the Holy Spirit that governs the Church in the person of the Roman Pontiff. What a joy to my soul to be a daughter of the Church! Your goodness has granted me this grace that I esteem so highly.

These divine favors alleviated the worries that the illness of our little Parisian caused me. I prayed to You for her without stopping. My Divine Love, I hoped for your charitable compassion on my tears and that, when You saw them, You would take pity upon me. Trusting in her benignity, I conjure your august Mother to show her power in everything pertaining to your glory. I told her, as I did You, all that came to my mind about the sorrow and compassion I had for the sufferings of this little one.

JEANNE'S ORIGINAL DRAFT

CHAPTER CXLVIII

Two abysses. The holy fruit offered me by St. Stephen and St. John and their visits with me. The repose that the Incarnate Word gave me upon his breast. Holy energumens and a delicate Sabbath. The Holy Innocents are the Lord's children. Their hands are full of hyacinths.

These vexations were like ongoing night to me until the first Sunday of Advent when the Church tells us: *Nox præcessit, dies autem appropinquavit; The night is passed, and the day is at hand.* (Rom 13:12) (1047) Thus, dawn is announced, the holy Precursor who, by his miraculous life, draws down heavenly angels upon earth. They considered this great man (whom you have honored, divine Word Incarnate, by your first visit) to be worthy of commanding them in their Louvre of glory, the Empyrean heaven. He beseiged and struck it with such violence that You assured was powerful enough to have carried it away unless You had suspended his influence to give him Yourself through your human-divine graciousness after your Ascension.

The waiting period for your Blessed Mother to give birth rejoiced the daughter of Sion and filled the daughter of Jerusalem with joy, foretelling the coming of her peaceful King: *Dicite Filiæ Sion: Ecce rex tuus venit tibi iustus, et salvator. Shout for joy, O daughter of Sion: BEHOLD THY KING will come to thee, the just and saviour.* (Zach 9:9b) (1048)

The Apostle, an abyss of disbelief enlightened by the bright rays of your human divinity that made him an abyss of fidelity, declared: *Dominus meus et Deus meus; My Lord and my God.* (Jn 20:28) It submerged my spirit in divine exultation, making me say and repeat: *Benedictus Domine qui intueris abyssos; Blessed be the Lord that beholdest the depths.* (Dan 3:55a)

JEANNE'S ORIGINAL DRAFT

On Christmas night when it pleased You, divine Orient from on high, to be born of the humblest of all pure creatures, my soul was engulfed in the lower parts of earth where your divine rays deigned to illuminate it by penetrations that it could perceive and feel, yet not reproduce nor express. You are the only one, eternal and temporal Holy Child, to make these holy reproductions.

On the Feast of St. Stephen, your first martyr, while I was in the church where I received the first grace through the sacrament of illumination, I prayed to him with new confidence to obtain from You new blessings for me. (1049) Appearing with an angelic face while being stoned, this levite was as prompt as flames of fire to present my prayer to You. He obtained grace upon grace for me. United by You in an ineffable union to this favorite whose name You had given me, I fleetingly experienced a happiness that represented all created things to me. It was an earthly Paradise because I was still on earth, representing to me such a diversity of beautiful fruit that was wonderfully delightful and good that your omnipotent goodness produced to have me enjoy here. Like the Hebrews, I could say: "Manna! What is it?" This manna was offered to me together with divine flavors. Since my spirit and heart, which were made for You, were meant to have the consolation of highest things, your saints entertained me with your divine attributes. My desire to possess You perfectly and enter into your divine joy impelled me to ascend higher and to become blissfully lost in my Center. (1050) Did I not have reason to be satisfied, for You let me repose upon your bosom, together with the cherished disciple of your heart! He was the delight of the loved one who possessed Him, since she belonged to God.

What a holy energumen, who is silent and impelled by the Holy Spirit—the expression of the fruitful will of your Father and You, who unceasingly produce Him as the most unique principle! In Him, You possess your delicate Sabbath, celebrating the goodness that this love divinely regards, for it delights in spreading about with divine profusion.

What a maze I would have been in had the little Innocents not withdrawn me by Adam's net to listen to the cries due to the blows of the executioners.

JEANNE'S ORIGINAL DRAFT

The earth that produced them was reddened by their innocent blood. Bethlehem was the field of Damascus where they were spread out in the plaza to be elevated up to the throne of the Lamb by the bond of charity. He accepted and received this as New Year's gifts in payment for what You did all by Yourself. (1051)

Dear Love, on Calvary your Divine Father offered them and called them his children. He used them as a mortgage for all the possessions of his legitimate Son and Heir, meaning You, my Divine Savior. On the day of the Supper, You told Him that You wanted those who belong to You to have the same beatitude that is yours and for them to be one as your Father and You are one, possessing the same charity.

On the Feast of the Circumcision 1655, your hands that held me did not withdraw, being filled with hyacinths which pleased the Father and the Holy Spirit as well as You, my Love, when they imparted something like light and goodness to me. Opening them, You filled body and spirit with heavenly blessings. I knelt at your feet, O Just One by essence and par excellence, who assumed the stigma of the sinner. (1052)

JEANNE'S ORIGINAL DRAFT

CHAPTER CXLIX

Three miracles of sanctified rivers: the river of love and grace. The martyrdom of the Blessed Virgin. The fountain that created a river and became light and sun. The torrent that gives us life and holy, new fruit.

On the day adorned by three miracles, the Trinity in heaven and the trinity on earth let me share in their magnificence because of the little gifts I had offered them with the Magi. On the day of the royal Octave, I wanted to be baptized anew in this river sanctified by You. Divine Lamb that takes away the sins of the world, I begged You to deliver me from those I have committed and do commit. Preferring mercy to sacrifice in a contrite and humble heart, your benignity welcomed me with gentleness. (1053) You reminded me that You had appeared to me in this figure of a Lamb that allowed itself to be shorn, and I understood that You are pleased by the stripping away of everything that is not for your glory. I said to You: I will enter your house as a holocaust there to offer You my vows, even though externally I do not appear to be invested as are my daughters: *Introibo in domum tuam in holocaustis: Reddam tibi vota mea quæ distinxerunt labia mea. I will go into thy house with burnt offerings: I will pay thee my vows, which my lips have uttered.* (Ps 65:13)

I offer them to You, my God and my Spouse, through a mysterious silence that my lips lovingly utter. Recalling that my daughters had renewed theirs on the Feast of the Kings, I wanted to celebrate this Octave, even if I could not do so as heaven and earth celebrate it. I said with the great Baptist: *Ecce Agnus Dei. Ecce qui tollit peccata mundi; Behold the Lamb of God. Behold him who takes away the sins of the world.* (Jn 1:29) With delight, I heard God your Father say: *Hic est Filius meus dilectus, in quo mihi bene*

AUTOBIOGRAPHY

JEANNE'S ORIGINAL DRAFT

complacui. This is my beloved Son, in whom I am well pleased. (2 P 1:17) As I was deciding to stay with these delightful caresses, I understood that the Spirit, holily jealous, expelled and pushed You into the desert with the savage beasts: *Et statim Spiritus expulit eum in desertum; And immediately the Spirit drove him out into the desert.* (Mk 1:12) (1054) What a severe measure it was to send the innocent Lamb into exile for the sins of guilty he-goats! O, the height and depth of the wisdom and knowledge of God: *Quis enim cognovit sensum Domini? Aut quis consiliarius eius fuit? For who hath known the mind of the Lord? Or who hath been his counsellor?* (Rom 11:34)

It is the same Spirit who prompted Simeon, the holy old man, to enter the temple, amid delight, to announce to your holy, innocent Mother the most cruel torments ever announced even to the most criminal persons, because their sufferings end with death. But this death, prophesied thirty-three years before the fact, is the beginning of the one to be endured by the incomparable Virgin Mother, by every right, the Queen of martyrs, your heart and soul are pierced by the pitiless sword that brings to light so many others, expressing their thoughts: *Et tuam ipsius animam pertransibit gladius ut revelentur ex multis cordibus cogitationes. And thy own soul a sword shall pierce, that, out of many hearts thoughts may be revealed.* (Lk 2:35)

Blessed Virgin, could I remain in delight while your Son and you endure continual suffering? His Circumcision and your Purification have no Octave to show us that one must unceasingly subtract and purify whatever is not most pure. (1055) For all eternity, angels and mankind marvel at the fact that the God-Man was circumcised and the Virgin Mother presented herself for the Purification: *Qui sanctus est, sanctificatur adhuc; He that is holy, let him be sanctified still.* (Ap 22:11c) Let all Christians humble themselves and all the just unceasingly become justified in order to please the Just One by essence and par excellence.

Sufferings justify faithful souls whom God tests as gold in the furnace to make them worthy of Him. All the saints were subjected to trials. Were your

267

JEANNE'S ORIGINAL DRAFT

favorite one still on the Isle of Patmos, on seeing them all brilliant and luminous, he would ask (if he dared) the Ancient of Days who they were and where they came from. *Hi sunt, qui venerunt de tribulatione magna; These are they who are come out of great tribulation.* (Ap 7:14) They have cleansed and whitened their robes in the Blood of the Lamb. Through love and for love, they have endured great tribulations and have merited the robes that the Lamb has made precious by his Blood which He began to shed at his Circumcision until after his death when, at the opening of his side, there was a river of Blood mingled with water that flowed forth: *Et deducet eos ad vitæ fontes aquarum; And shall lead them to the fountains of the waters of life.* (Ap 7:17) (1056) To enter this divine Heart, the spouse must be cleansed and whitened by this sacred river which the lance of a soldier opened and prompted: *Unus militum lancea latus eius aperuit, et continuo exivit sanguis et aqua; One of the soldiers with a spear opened his side: and immediately there came out blood and water.* (Jn 19:34) It is the river of grace; it is the river of love that makes the bride resemble the Spouse, a bride of Blood, for He is the Spouse of Blood. *Sponsus sanguinis tu mihi est; You are a spouse of blood to me* is what she can say to Him as she admires, adores and loves Him through Love Himself.

Virgin Mother, at the opening of this Sacred Heart, your own was grieved. This lance pierced your own. Your spirit, that could subsist in your virginal body after your Son had yielded his to his Eternal Father, seemed to be strength personified. It remained firm at the sight, sound and feeling of this lance-thrust that was ten thousand times mortal. (1057) Ten thousand mothers would have died had they been present at similar cruelties carried out upon the bodies of their children who died innocent. Lady, you are the only strong Woman. You remain standing so as to appear to angels, mankind and demons as the miracle of miracles and the spectacle for angels, mankind and God Himself.

My Blessed Princess, Mardochai was astounded at the little fountain that grew into a river and became light and sun. Esther declared: *Parvus fons, qui crevit in fluvium, et in lucem, solemque conversus est, et in aqua*

JEANNE'S ORIGINAL DRAFT

plurimas redundavit; The little fountain which grew into a river, and was turned into a light, and into the sun, and abounded into many waters. (Esth 10:6) I am certainly more astounded at the fountain that stems from your Son's side. It is the water and blood from your breast that makes a river, a sun, a sea and an ocean.

Humble Virgin, little fountain that produced this river and has given rise to this light: *Quia ex te ortus est sol justitiæ Christus Deus noster; Because of you was born the Sun of Justice, Christ our Lord.* He came forth from you, sea from the sea, being born of his Divine Father, Light of light and God of God. (1058) From your Son, who died on Calvary for all mankind, emanated a little fountain of Blood and Water that will inundate the entire earth. It will ascend to the very throne of God where the Church is produced. All redeemed souls can be cleansed there in the crystalline water and adorned with this very crimson Blood. Through the river, that is also the Blood of the Cross, heaven and earth have been pacified. After the death of your Son, the fountain gushed forth from insufficient life up to eternal life. If the Humanity died, the Divinity still abides in the Body; it is invulnerable as well as immortal.

Wonderful Mother of God, through you I was enabled to plunge into this river that has become an ocean where I feel engulfed, simultaneously living and dying. There I am in a torrent where the waters excel those of the torrent into which the Prophet Ezechiel was led and guided by a man from the orient: *Qui habebat funiculum in manu sua; That had the line in his hand* (Ez 47:3b) to measure it several times. (1059) It increased in the sight of the prophet who was in it and exclaimed that the waters were so deep that he could not cross over: *Torrentem quem non potui pertransire, quoniam intumuerunt aquæ profundis torrentis, qui non potes transvadare; It was a torrent which I could not pass over: for the waters were risen so as to make a deep torrent which could not be passed over.* (Ez 47:5c)

This torrent provided life, an abundance of life through new fruit which did not fail, because the waters from the sanctuary drenched them: *Quia aquæ eius de sanctuario egredientur: et erunt fructus eius in cibum, et folia*

269

JEANNE'S ORIGINAL DRAFT

eius ad medecinam. Because the waters thereof shall issue out of the sanctuary: and the fruits thereof shall be for food, and the leaves thereof for medicine. (Ez 47:12d)

My august goddess, if it is allowed for me to call you that (why not?), since I acknowledge you to be the Mother of the Sovereign God of the God-Man who has produced this torrent and has come to measure it. He led me there and will withdraw me from it when He deems it fitting. (1060) What marvels have I seen! I cannot express them. I understood that I may not say anything about them and that men and angels should be profoundly astonished about the mysteries hidden in God for ages unless the Holy Spirit teaches them about them, as He did St. Paul, when He imparted the grace and privilege to him to teach them: *Mihi omnium sanctorum minimo data est gratia hæc, in gentibus evangelizare investigabiles divitias Christi, et illuminar omnes, quæ sit dispensatio sacramenti absconditi a sæculis in Deo, qui omnia creavit: ut innotescat principatibus et potestatibus in cælestibus per Ecclesiam, multiformis sapientia Dei, secundum præfinitionem sæculorum, quam fecit in Christo Jesu Domino nostro. To me, the least of all the saints, is given this grace, to preach among the Gentiles the unsearchable riches of Christ: And to enlighten all men, that they may see what is the dispensation of the mystery which hath been hidden from eternity in God who created all things: That the manifold wisdom of God may be known to the principalities and powers in heavenly places through the church, According to the eternal purpose which he made in Christ Jesus our Lord.* (Eph 3:8-11)

Great Apostle, you accepted all the sufferings determined by the Lord to make you a worthy Vessel of Election and Dilection. I beg you to pray to Him that I may correspond with all his designs for me and that I may courageously endure everything that may contribute to his glory. May I promote his glory in every way for the salvation of my neighbor as well as for my own. (1061) May I not lose courage during the persecutions waged against me by those who show a signal ingratitude in his divine presence and that of his angels and some persons. I beg not to evidence to this, because the latter

JEANNE'S ORIGINAL DRAFT

would be thrown into a strange confusion and could be punished according to their faults. I pray your goodness to pardon their fault and lessen the pain for them. I await the Great Jubilee for such persons and for myself that your divine mercy may completely absolve us and that we may all walk in newness of life.

The sufferings that I do not want to mention here are of such a nature that they would have caused me to die a thousand times, Divine Love, had You not given me a thousand lives by continually preserving me in the one You had given me once. You have told me that my kingdom pertains to the sufferings that David endured from his children and that I would suffer from mine. (1062) Speaking on your behalf, Isaias told heaven and earth to listen to your word: *Dominus locutus est. Filios enutrivi, et exaltavi; ipsi autem spreverunt me. For the Lord hath spoken. I have brought up children and exalted them: but they have despised me.* (Is 1:2b)

I began Lent and continued observing it with sadness and sufferings known to You, divine Searcher of hearts. You considered mine and the palpitations that I could not alleviate. I lived and died at the same time, because of the constant dread caused me by those who do not love You and who ignore the goodness You have placed in this heart that is afflicted for them. I said to You: *Exaudi, Deus, orationem meam cum deprecor; a timore inimici eripe animam meam. Protexisti me a conventu malignantium, a multitudine operantium iniquitatem, etc. Hear, O God, my prayer, when I make supplication to thee: deliver my soul from the fear of the enemy. Thou hast protected me from the assembly of the malignant: from the multitudes of the workers of iniquity.* etc. (Ps 63:2-3)

My hope is in You, Lord, where permanent joy is to be found. Make us upright of heart so that we may be glorified in You alone who are eternal happiness. (1063)

JEANNE'S ORIGINAL DRAFT

CHAPTER CL

I begged the Incarnate Word to send the sixty strong ones, his assistants, to Rome; the good odor of his sacrifice upon Calvary; the mental suffering which I experienced.

A few days before Easter, the official, Monsieur de Ville, came to see me and expressed his concern that the Cardinals had not yet come to an agreement for the election of a Sovereign Pontiff. I asked him to describe to me the ceremonies for electing a Pope. He did not refuse me this consolation, telling me everything he had experienced (when Innocent X was elected), when he was in Rome with his Eminence from Lyons. These marvelous ceremonies fascinated me and prompted me to pray to You, my God and my All, to give us one according to your Heart. I said to him: "Monseigneur, I trust in our Divine Solomon, the Incarnate Word, whom I beg with confidence to send to Rome the sixty strong ones who assist near his divine couch to frighten and expel the nocturnal spirits. (1064) May his Spirit, who intercedes for all the saints, pray within us to give us one who will fulfill his will entirely." On Wednesday, someone relayed the message to me to go the next day to visit the Archbishop and ask for his holy blessing after he had consecrated the holy oils. Someone else sent me word that I would be refused there, that he had declared he would have nothing to do with Mother de Matel.

On Holy Thursday, I said to You, my Divine Love: "Give me the papal benediction. You are the eternal Pontiff, living always *ad interpellandum pro nobis; interceding for us.* You are holy, innocent, indefectible, separated from sinners. You are the supreme heaven. You can personally do all things. I hope for all favors and graces from your omnipotent goodness.

The next day, Good Friday, when I arose to go adore You in your divine

JEANNE'S ORIGINAL DRAFT

sacrament, I saw my bed covered with lavender. I understood these loving words: *Dum esset rex in accubitu suo, nardus tua. While the king was at his repose, my spikenard [sent forth the odor thereof].* (Cant 1:11) (1065) When the King of Love lay upon his bed of honor, your lavender and spikenard exuded their perfume. Divine King of lovers, the pestilence of my sins and those of all mankind caused You to die upon Calvary, but the perfume You have left there by your most holy sacrifice has surmounted these bad odors. Your Eternal Father told You in the presence of all your angels: "Behold the odor of my Son which is like a field that I have blessed with every blessing."

On Easter Sunday and during the entire Octave, You were Resurrection and life to me. With David, I could say to You: "Rise up, my glory, rise up harp and psalterion!" You did rise, my Love, but very early in the morning, forewarning me by your delightful visits that the eyes of owls could not sustain, because they caused the day which is all of light.

Certain persons who considered my crosses and did not see your anointings felt very sorry for me. They said to me: "The Archbishop is wonderful toward everyone else. He is not so toward you. (1066) On Easter Tuesday, he promised the Visitation Sisters to establish a third monastery in Lyons. The Abbé of Saint Just is close to and has high esteem for the Sisters of Saint Elizabeth who will soon be your neighbors near the Minime Fathers, and the Sisters from Holland (*Béguines*) have permission to be established, but he does not take your foundation into consideration!" These words were repeated to me at the grill of the Blessed Sacrament by the priest who was preparing to give Benediction on Easter Monday, to which day the Feast of your Incarnation had been postponed.

What did I say to You, dear Love, on seeing You in the hands of this priest who held You up and blessed us with You Yourself? Everything that You know I cannot include here nor my feelings when he offered the prayer for our Archbishop. At the word "Camille", what fervor for this dearest prelate and for our Sovereign Pontiff for whose election I had begged You to send the

JEANNE'S ORIGINAL DRAFT

sixty strong ones who assist at your divine couch. (1067) The next day and during the entire second week after Easter, a number of persons came to visit me. They informed me that the Sisters of Saint Mary of the Antiquaille should certainly have invited me to be present on Easter Tuesday, when the Archbishop had gone there with Monsieur de Fléchère to see their monastery and the house and vineyard they had bought from Monsieur Le Roux and also to consider what the Sisters of Saint Elizabeth had purchased and acquired from Monsieur de Sirode.

Divine Oracle, You let me understand that your hour had not yet come, that I was not to be upset. I shed tears in your presence, my loving Spouse. With greater gentleness and tenderness than Elcana toward Anne, You said to me: *Joanna, cur fles? nunquid non ego melior tibi sum, quam decem filiæ? Jeanne, why weepest thou? Am not I better to thee than ten daughters?* (I S 1:8) Jeanne, my daughter and my spouse, why is your soul troubled? Am I not more attentive in your solitude than ten daughters, indeed than ten monasteries? Am I not the Chosen One among a thousand? I am and will be your Samuel sent by God, and God Himself. Do not be upset when you see those that are fruitful and popular. Listen, my daughter, to the words of the Prophet Jeremias addressed to the persons who adhere to human sentiments: *Qui dereliquerunt me*, etc. *Who have forsaken me*, etc. (Jer 1:16b) You will see these words verified to the letter. Just wait a while: *Adhuc unum modicwwum est*, etc. *Yet one little while*, etc. (Hag 2:7b) (1068)

JEANNE'S ORIGINAL DRAFT

CHAPTER CLI

The Apostles' fervor during the ten days after the Ascension. The unheard of miracle and divine profusions of the Blessed Sacrament. How I had these sentiments by God's order during the different events and remained therein.

On the Feast of your supreme, triumphant Ascension, unceasingly I wanted to see my captivity captive, hoping that your human benignity would grant me gifts through compassion for the sorrows I endured on still being numbered among the inhabitants of Cedar: *Heu mihi, quia incolatus! Woe is me, that my sojourning,* etc. (Ps 119:5) I raised my eyes to heaven and the heavenly mountains from which my help could come; to You, my Lord and my God, the Creator of heaven and earth. (1069) By merit as well as essence, all power in each of these belongs to You. I beg all your saints to intercede for me, as I follow You in thought during the ten days that your Apostles fervently pray for your Spirit Consoler, their marvelous consolation that made them all fire and flame to set hearts ablaze with your sacred love. You do not refuse those who ask You for this Spirit of goodness. He is good and a Giver as are You and your Father. He wants our sanctification.

With what desire are You prompted to baptize us with the baptism of fire? To give it to us, You have shed all your Precious Blood. (1070) You gave Yourself as food, drink, grace and glory. By your divine dilection in your sacred Flesh, You have opened a new way for us. O miracle that suspends all understanding! Unheard of miracle until the time that You showed forth the inventions of your love that placed You in a continual ecstasy, offering Yourself for our sanctification. *Una enim oblatione, consummavit in sempternum sanctificatos. Quam initiavit nobis viam novam, et viventem per velamen, id est, carnem suam. Habentes itaque fiduciam in introitu sanctorum*

JEANNE'S ORIGINAL DRAFT

in sanguine Christi. For by one oblation he hath perfected for ever them that are sanctified. A new and living way which he hath dedicated for us through the veil, that is to say, his flesh: Having therefore, brethren, a confidence in the entering into the holies by the blood of Christ. (Heb 10:14, 20, 19)

It resulted from the sacrament that You made a memorial, an abridgement of your marvels. You enter into us to change us into You; You remain with us until the end of time. During this Octave, although concealed, You were at the door of our tabernacles to welcome pilgrims who have the angelic gift of ever living and adoring this Sacred Bread that possesses all good and all beauty. (1071) It is the wheat of the elect and the Bread that begets virgins: *Quid enim bonum eius est, et quid pulchrum eius, nisi frumentum electorum, et vinum germinans virgines? For what is the good thing of him and what is his beautiful thing, but the corn of the elect and wine springing forth virgins?* (Zach 9:17)

By this sacred Bread of the strong, by this table, I could live on the sea. Despite my weaknesses, I can subsist and resist all my enemies and say to You with David: *Nam, et si ambulavero in medio umbræ mortis, non timebo mala, quoniam tu mecum es. Parasti in conspectu meo mensam, adversus eos qui tribulant me; Impinguasti in oleo caput meum; et calix meus inebrians quam præclarus es! For though I should walk in the midst of the shadow of death, I will fear no evils, for thou art with me. Thou has prepared a table before me, against them that afflict me. Thou hast anointed my head with oil; and my chalice which inebriated me, how goodly is it!* (Ps 22:4a, b-5)

Through the strength provided by the bread that an angel brought him, Elias went up Mount of Horeb to You, my God. This bread that was but the figure produced great strength in him and gave him such courage when he had lost it and had fallen asleep from sadness. (1072) He actually thought that he could endure no more persecution which led him to wish for death: *Petivit animæ suæ ut moreretur, et ait: Sufficit mihi Domine, tolle animam meam. He*

JEANNE'S ORIGINAL DRAFT

requested for his soul that he might die, and said: it is enough for me. Lord, take away my soul. (1 K 19:4c) You delighted in pouring your sacred ointment upon my head, enlightening my mind, strengthening my will by this chalice that adorns but neither stupefies nor lowers the senses, but instead elevates them.

On the 24th, we celebrated the feast of the great Baptist, who came to do violence to heaven, but was subjected to violence from the time he was born. Your goodness assured us of the greatness of his person and his magnanimous, steadfast courage in practicing virtue. Also, the spiritual beings by their resolutions caused me to hope for victory against my enemies, as I chanted with the Royal Psalmist: *Mihi autem nimis honorificati sunt amici tui, Deus; nimis confortabus est principatus eorum. But to me thy friends, O God, are made exceedingly honorable: their principality is exceedingly strengthened.* (Ps 138:17) (1073)

On the 29th, I found myself being assisted by the one You had named Prince and Head of the Apostles, who was to defy the gates of hell. He was followed by his colleague, the Apostle of the Gentiles, who, assured of your power, feared no one. What could make me fear all those who prepared to work against me? With these two princes at my side, together with You, my Divine Monarch, I dared utter the following words: *Quis me separabit; Who will separate me [...].*

On July 2nd, when your Blessed Mother carried You in her womb, she fortified me by her visits. This caused me to thrill with joy, despite the fact that others planned to overwhelm me by sadness. Acknowledging that these favors came to me from your benevolence, I exclaimed: *Confitebor.*

On July 8th, I commended myself to St. Raphael, the holy angel who preserved me from the discomforts that overwhelm the weak during this month. May he guide all my projects that are meant to promote your glory. (1074) The physician, who is totally ardent, embraced me with his holy flames. He let me know that my situation was even more beneficial. I heard these sacred

JEANNE'S ORIGINAL DRAFT

words: *Et dormiatis inter madios cleros pennæ columbæ deargentatæ et posteriora dorsi eius in pallore auri. If you sleep in the midst of fortune, the dove's feathers will be of silver and its back part will shine as gold.* (non-biblical)

I recognized You, my Beloved, in the gentle breeze, as Elias did. If the chariot transports me, I will say to You with Saint Margaret: You are my pearl of great price. I can find nothing comparable. When I give my heart so as to possess You, I find myself rich and opulent. Then my heart wants to return all these good things to You that I have received from You through the blessing of your grace. (1075) With my heart as broken as alabaster and my eyes converted into two rivulets, I represented Magdalen, ceasing to speak in order to weep. My Love and my All, when your kind eyes saw these two fountains, regarding your features therein, You loved them as Yourself. You forgot my sins; You admired your graces in me, and did not allow the Pharisees to find me guilty. You acknowledged Yourself to be the debtor for her who is insolvent.

When I met the supplantor, one of Zebedee's children, he perceived from the flame in my heart that I was your beloved. The grace speaking through me made known great marvels. Anne, your grandmother, O my King, gave birth to the unparalleled one, the wonderful Mother whom all the angels proclaim to be incomparable and the purest of all pure creatures. She is the Immaculate, the all-beautiful one. (1076) The day that the humble St. Francis named her their Lady, as well as of created things, was one on which You granted him an unheard of Jubilee in her presence and that of all the blessed spirits. They all rejoiced intensely for this favor granted to mankind from which they obtain salvation that is ineffable to me, together witth the favors that You and she, my God, have granted me.

On August 5th, You had me admire this Virgin in the edifice she had requested to be built upon Mount Esquilinus. It stood for her purity because of the snow that designates the place, which bears her name as well as her excellent greatness (St. Mary Major). (1077) It was there that You chose to

JEANNE'S ORIGINAL DRAFT

grant the first Bull for your Order, divine Incarnate Word, my Love, through the lips of your oracle, Pope Urban VIII, of happy memory. You had prolonged his life by fifteen years, thus granting the very humble request I made You in the year one thousand six hundred twenty-nine [1629], when I sent our petition to Rome (recommended by Queen Marie de Medicis, the late King's mother) to his Holiness. You have blessed him and his nephews with many benedictions for having favored your project. I beg You, my Divine Love, to bless them with your eternal benedictions at the hour of their death after a length of days.

Unintentionally, I went off on a tangent. (1078) You know what glory You ought to receive for it. Thereby I want nothing else for myself than the grace to adhere always and in everything to your orders and to follow your will. Knowing that You do not spurn the prayer of humble hearts, I wanted to go to the Visitation Church, according to the vow I had made, to obtain from the heart of Blessed Francis de Sales the health of our little Piardière boarder. How fortunate I was that the Abbé of St. Just offered Holy Mass there after which he gave us this most gentle heart, that had been all-loving, to kiss. After kissing it in his hands, I said to him: "Monsieur, may God grant you the gentleness and goodness toward me that this holy heart had for Mother de Chantal." He told me that he did not possess the charity of this holy heart. I replied: "Monsieur, your modesty prompts you to speak that way. (1079) My desire neither takes from nor diminishes in any way this worthy heart of the blessed one."

From here, I went to the parlor to greet the Reverend Mother Superioress, in whom I saw nothing of the gentleness of this blessed heart. On the contrary, I found her to be harsh. Her words were arrows to me. At this, I said to her: "My Mother, has the Holy Spirit inspired another St. Simeon to address such harsh words to me through you that my soul might be pierced? The Incarnate Word, whom I have received in Holy Communion, diverted the sting and moderated the pain. I hear what you are telling me that is quite stinging, but, for the sake of the Incarnate Word, I desire even more." (1080)

AUTOBIOGRAPHY

JEANNE'S ORIGINAL DRAFT

CHAPTER CLII

The strength that the Incarnate Word provides in sufferings. St. Lawrence, by his death, vivified the children of the Church. A number of victims of love in the Blessed Trinity, the Blessed Virgin, the angels and saints; desires to praise and imitate the Blessed Virgin Mother, St. Bartholomew, and my patron, St. John the Baptist.

Jesus, splendor of the glory of the Father, figure of his substance, You appeared all glorious upon your Tabor. By your goodness, You consoled me, alleviating by your anointing the harsh words addressed to me on the preceding day. You made me understand that You will manifest your glory in me. A number of times, You told me that your goodness made me the Tabor where You wanted to appear glorious, that courageous souls do not become frightened when they are told about struggles. (1081) Assured of your help, with love they endure all the blows provided them by heaven, earth and hell. Fortified by love, with joy they endure everything that timid souls fear: *Omnia vincit amor; Love conquers all.*

On the Feast of this invincible Levite, who is completely of laurel reclining upon his bed of blazing fire, he offered himself as a holocaust to be wholly consumed. I compared him to a Seraphim. His ardent heart unceasingly declared that he was motivated by two desires, as was the great Apostle: to be with You in the Empyrean and still remain on earth for the salvation of all the world which he wanted to satisfy with his own person. His blood flowing upon the grill and coals reminded me of the pelican that pierces its own heart to shed its blood for its young that were stung by the serpent, lovingly giving up its life for them. By giving his life to You, Lawrence vivified many children of the Church who belong to You, my Divine Savior. (1082)

JEANNE'S ORIGINAL DRAFT

When he wanted to place the miraculous Ark in the temple that You desired on earth, in imitation of his father David, Solomon offered You so many sacrifices and victims that the ways along which they were brought could have been called altars consecrated thereby. I mean, by these fortunate and blessed victims.

Yet all the ancient sacrifices and victims were but figures and shadows of the mysterious, marvelous, divine and solemn one You would prepare at the time of your Blessed Mother. She is the true Ark of the Covenant of the eternal and the temporal aspect; of your divinity and our humanity that occurred within her chaste womb. This adorable Humanity was supported by your divine hypostasis. It is inseparable, although distinct from that of the Father and of the Holy Spirit. It is a support that will never be removed, a hypostatic vision that will last as long as You are God. The entire Blessed Trinity, all the angels and saints, like holy victims and heavenly, divine and blazing cantors, offer themselves and rejoice in a divine festivity and in a most eminent elevation that only the Three August Persons could encompass. They enhance the holy assumption of the Daughter of the Father, the Mother of the Son and the Spouse of the Holy Spirit. (1083) You elevate her, Divine Pontiff, up to your sovereign grandeur. Since You became the supreme heaven, You placed her at your right hand of glory, crowned with You Yourself. She is adorned with all the loveliness that your wisdom chose to produce through the constant excess of your divine love that is as ardent as it is brilliant or blazing. She made admirable and indescribable entries in You who are the house of delights in heaven, as she was yours on earth.

On the seventeenth, which is the Octave of the holy deacon who entered the Empyrean by means of a bed of fire that blazed brighter than the flaming chariot that elevated Elias up to the earthly Paradise, I was taken up by all my ardent sighs that tended lovingly toward You, my Love and my All. I prayed that You would remember your poor one to whom so often You had given your charitable treasures to enrich her by your gifts. These were so multiple that she frequently acknowledged that You are the infinitely liberal Giver, giving Yourself with your divine plenitude that is so full of love. I said to You:

JEANNE'S ORIGINAL DRAFT

Omnia excelsa tua, et fluctus tui super me transierunt. All thy heights and thy billows have passed over me. (Ps 41:8b) (1084)

On August 22nd of this year 1655, I recalled that in 1620 your august and holy Mother had obtained from your Divine Father for me the blessing that may be called all-good. You became my portion and my heritage even in the land of the dying and wanted to be my Viaticum. In thanksgiving, I offered You all that You had given me: You Yourself with all the loving reproductions You make upon our altars. With the Apostle all covered with blood, for he had been completely flayed, I wanted to be a perpetual sacrifice, praising and adoring You unceasingly. Seeing heaven and earth filled with your glory and the Seraphim whom the Prophet Isaias saw, I wanted to say unceasingly : *Holy, Holy, Holy.*

On the day of the beheading of your great Precursor, my wonderful patron, who aspired to fulfill all justice, as You had said, having been cleansed in the blood flowing from his holy body after the dancer had removed his precious head from the horrible prison which was more honored than the altar of holocausts in the temple that was the marvel of the world, You let me know and experience that those in power can well make the body of your chosen ones die, but that they have no power over their souls: *Justorum animæ; The souls of the just.* (1085)

On the Birth of your wonderful, incomparable Mother, I cannot say the number of times that I invited all people in general, but Christians in particular, with these Christian verses: "Adore the lovely dawn, that your misfortune may change into happiness." On the Feast of the Exaltation of your victorious Cross, I marveled at You, full of glory, the joy of heaven and earth, telling all nations that You, the new Adam, through the wood upon Calvary together with the new Eve, had conquered the one who had given death to the old Adam in the earthly Paradise by seducing the ancient Eve.

JEANNE'S ORIGINAL DRAFT

CHAPTER CLIII

The grace God gave me to deliver a prisoner. The truly poor St. Francis arrested the Sun of Justice; his days are continual light and his body an expression of that of the Incarnate Word upon Calvary; about the Feast of St. Denis.

On the Eve of the Feast of the Prince of Angels, the great St. Michael, You wanted me to go down to the prison called Roanne and pay five thousand six hundred sixty-five pounds for the release of a prisoner. (1086) Then the decree against all his goods would be lifted. All his relatives had abandoned him: father, mother and brother, who might have been able to assist him. I felt that You were prompting me to deliver him, Divine Love, and this gave me ineffable joy. In the evening and the next day, the feast of this great Saint whose name means *Quis sicut Deus; Who is like God*, You caressed me divinely. Several times, You summoned me: "Little liberatrix, come with St. Michael and his angels to listen to my praises for the generosity I have placed in your heart."

Completely embarrassed by your goodness, I divested myself of everything that is not You, rendering You your divine glory. Now I could proportionately understand what the Apostle had said of You: *Cum autem subjecta fuerint illi omnia: tunc et ipse filius subiectus erit ei, qui subiecit sibi omnia, ut sit Deus omnia in omnibus. And when all things shall be subdued unto him, then the Son also himself shall be subject to him that put all things under him, that God may be all in all.* (1 Cor 15:28)

The overwhelming shame that I noted in this man who was saved from the threats and power of his creditors aroused different ideas in me, as I humbled myself in your presence. In the light of my own infinite obligations toward your

JEANNE'S ORIGINAL DRAFT

divine charity and loving kindness, with the Apostle, I said: *In fide vivo Filii Dei, qui dilexit me, et tradidit semetipsum pro me. I live in the faith of the Son of God, who loved me and delivered himself for me.* (Gal 2:20b) (1087)

When night came on the Feast of St. Francis, You let me understand that this saint had been a miraculous Joshua through whom You had performed marvels I cannot describe. He had conducted and guided innumerable people to the Promised Land. He had kept You, Sun of Justice, from punishing your enemies, praying that instead You would convert and pardon them. Thus, the Feast of Francis is a continual light with no intermission in the Church Triumphant. His soul shines there in marvelous splendor. His body is a copy compared with the original that is yours, with which the Militant Church is honored. He is the ongoing miracle that is not allowed to mortal men to view without dying. Could not those who desire to see it be told what was said to Moses long ago: "During mortal life, man cannot see the immortal God without dying, nor the body of Francis except at the risk of his life?" Experience has proven this to be true.

This holy body, stigmatized with your own Wounds through seraphic love—meaning deified love—is an expression of your own upon Calvary. His pierced hands, his feet with holes in them and his open side let us see that You have left us the portrait of Yourself. (1088) You emerged gloriously from the tomb to ascend above all the heavens, becoming the supreme heaven. It is the glorious proof of your divine love. You wanted the body of St. Francis to remain upright in a cave as a sorrowful sign of your own love, marked by the signs of our Redemption. It is a mystery that You conceal. Ah, who would dare ask You how long it would take or whether it would be until the perpetual sacrifice would be removed! I will not be so bold as to do that, bearing in mind what You replied to your Apostles and disciples when they asked You when You would re-establish the kingdom of Israel: *Non est vestrum nosse tempora vel momenta quæ Pater posuit in sua potestate. It is not for you to know the times or moments which the Father hath put in his own power.* (Acts 1:7)

JEANNE'S ORIGINAL DRAFT

I beg You to let me remain with yours which I receive daily through your great mercy until the end of my mortal life. May it be my Viaticum when, in your great mercy, You call me to the immortal one. May I live the life of grace through the reception of this Sacred Body. May it be my New Year's gift in the life of glory. I ask You for a double favor. If I so dare, I will ask You for the third one, that I may see You elevated, and these three will be but one beatitude begun, continued and consummated, since grace in this life is glory begun, and glory in the other is grace consummated. (1089) Through your magnificent mercy, I ask You for this grace, and I beg You not to consider me too bold if, like your Eliseus, I ask You to give it to me as did Elias. Why did You tell me so many marvels on this feast of your miraculous Francis through the openness of your goodness which is self-communicative? If I presume upon this goodness, it is that it has been excessive toward me, although I am the most insignificant and unworthy of all your creatures. Seeing that I am abased to the uttermost parts of the earth, I see You elevated above all the heavens. My memory does not assist me now to recall the favors You gave me on the eve of the Feast of the great St. Denis, since his name is a holy distillation. I will simply record here that my soul was overwhelmed when You visited me both on the eve of his feast and on that day. You spoke to my heart and listened to me gently. Give me the form and figure that please You. I belong to You, my God and my All. (1090)

JEANNE'S ORIGINAL DRAFT

CHAPTER CLIV

Our Most Illustrious Archbishop honored me by repeated visits to become acquainted with my Congregation and leadership; how he approved everything, graciously according its perfect establishment. God assured me that it was this gracious Archbishop whom He had shown me a number of years previously.

On October 20, 1655, You inspired Monseigneur Camille de Neuville, our most worthy Archbishop, to accord me his blessing by coming up the holy mountain to visit me and tell me personally that he had offered Holy Mass three times to know your will. Because of these three Masses, You had inspired him to establish your monastery in Lyons and to ask if I would provide the foundation, and, if so, the amount. Very grateful for your divine favors and his pastoral ones, I replied that I would give six thousand ecus for the foundation. He was satisfied. I was, too, on seeing your persevering truth and promises verified by the inspiration You had given our beloved pastor whom I had seen only in a vision in 1627. That was when You predicted to me the death of Monseigneur Miron, when You told me in Latin: "I will strike down the shepherd and the sheep will be dispersed." (1091)

The next day was dedicated to the solemnity of Saint Ursula and her holy companions, the eleven thousand virgins. Crowned in red and white and accompanied by all her holy virgins and martyrs, this saint showed me that she was very pleased with the visit I made to her churches, that is, the one at Saint Just. She told me that I was strong and courageous, hoping for all benefits from your providence, which was gracious toward those whom it had destined for great enterprises. By order of your divine wisdom, she was not only directress of her companions—the eleven thousand virgins—but also their mother, for, through her zeal, she had given birth to them. Although they died in tears, they were reborn in possession of palms. Their virginal blood had

JEANNE'S ORIGINAL DRAFT

given birth to virgins, of whom she was truly called the mother. She treated them as her daughters, although she had not taken the habit of cloistered religious life before her martyrdom. (1092) I was her sister through the vow of virginity and because of the many sufferings required for the establishment of the Order entrusted to me by your wisdom. You had made me its Mother and its Mistress: *Os enim Domini locutum est: Benedictus Dominus Deus Israel.* etc. *For the mouth of the Lord hath spoken it. Blessed be the Lord God of Israel,* etc.(Is 58:14; Lk 1:68)

On the Feast of All Saints, our Archbishop honored me by his visit on the holy mountain a second time. Entering your home and his, my Divine Word made Flesh, he gave me his holy blessing and told me that, for the fourth time, he had offered Holy Mass to know your Divine Will better. He said that You had inspired him to make this foundation. He had come in order to comply with your will and to see how I wanted to arrange the foundation. I showed him the contracts for more than fifty thousand pounds in rents, houses and land. On seeing that the foundation I gave His Grandeur for this monastery was securely established, he told Monsieur de Saint Just who was present: "This house is established. I approve everything done by Monseigneurs Miron and de Marquemont." He did not allude to the late Cardinal of Lyons. (1093)

Prompted by pastoral zeal, he exhorted me to confer the veil upon young women and empowered me to do so. He said that we should settle the contract as soon as possible. He was motivated by zeal for your glory and was so gracious toward me that I was filled with confusion and joy. Modesty prevents me from expressing it here (but I do want to praise your divine wisdom so that You may fill him with your graces and heroic goodness to undertake and succeed in great things for God's glory and the public benefit.)

I said to him: "Monseigneur, of all the sufferings caused me by a deferred hope, the coldness of the Abbé of St. Just has been the worst." The very virtuous Abbé told me that, doubting that the Archbishop would make the foundation after such a long refusal by the late Cardinal, he had feared that I would insist that he do something impossible for him to do. That is why he

JEANNE'S ORIGINAL DRAFT

had acted so coldly toward me.

Because of the inexplicable goodness in the support and discourse of my kind Prelate, I was extremely astounded. To think that this most amiable Pastor totally favored the one who possessed more happiness than merit! I could say with David: (1094) *Thabor et Hermon in nomine tuo exultabunt; tuum brachium cum potentis. Thabor and Hermon shall rejoice in thy name: thy arm is with might.* (Ps 88:13b-14a)

CHAPTER CLV

The second visit with which the Archbishop honored me and the foundation contract for this Monastery in Lyons.

The Archbishop was satisfied with everything I had reported to him about the origins of our Congregation. When he was about to leave, after he had visited a section of our house and blessed all my daughters and me, he said that the contract would be drawn up as I wished and that he would sign it. The one who zealously undertook the responsibility for this and to whom I was very grateful had made me hasten my return from Paris. His ideas did not accord with mine, for I found them to be harsh and without unction. In my simplicity, I could not conceal my reaction.

I asked the president, Monsieur Chausse, whom the Archbishop liked very much, to take the letter that your goodness inspired me to write him to Vimy. Together with the respects of his most humble daughter, You would tell him through Baruch: *Ne tradas alteri gloriam tuam, et dignitatem tuam genti*

JEANNE'S ORIGINAL DRAFT

alienæ. Give not thy honor to another, nor thy dignity to a strange nation. (Bar 4:3)

I begged him not to sign the contract that had been sent him until I had had the opportunity of being at his feet to express my opinion. (1095) This kind pastor told the one who had taken my letter that he would not sign until he had heard me personally. I was to be the mistress, and he would come to Lyons on Christmas Eve. He wanted to satisfy me in everything concerning the foundation. At this reply, I was filled with embarrassment and gratitude, marveling at your attention toward me, as so often before, for I bore in mind what he had said the day after he had received the King's decree. He had told those in Paris who offered him my obedience: "I want this new posiition of Archbishop to provide me with occasions to serve her; she will be the directress." At this, I said to You: "Lord, is this just courtly politeness?" "No, my daughter, it is my Spirit who speaks through him. He is your Archbishop and pastor: *Os enim Domini locutum est; For the mouth of the Lord hath spoken it.* (Is 58:14)

Who would not have thought that I was the happiest of women, since I had been given a promise of so many favors from my worthy Prelate who was always favorable toward his unworthy daughter. Added to this, I ought to enjoy all the blessings of heaven and earth as I awaited the joy of being at his blessed feet, anticipating every attention from his kindness. (1096) All-knowing God, who let me enjoy a delightful transfiguration, You knew that after twice six winters, what a Calvary and death of spirit would be mine. You knew it, my Love. Those who learned it later on have said to me: *Cui comparabo te, vel cui assimilabo te? To what shall I compare thee, or to what shall I liken thee?* (Lam 2:13)

The curtain must be drawn. Nothing can express my sadness or pain upon seeing that God was so undeservedly offended in full knowledge by those who closed their eyes to his lights and refused to listen to his divine remonstrances. It is a piercing sword that caused a more sorrowful division than that of the soul and spirit. I do not compare it to the one your Apostle mentioned, but,

JEANNE'S ORIGINAL DRAFT

for my consolation, I must borrow his words: *Habentes ergo pontificem 1magnum, qui penetravit cœlos, Jesum Filium Dei, teneamus confessionem. Non enim habemus pontificem, qui non possit compati infirmitatibus nostris:* (1097) *Adeamus ergo cum fiducia ad thronum gratiæ: ut misericordiam consequamur, et gratiam inveniamus. Having therefore a great high priest that hath passed into the heavens, Jesus the Son of God: let us hold fast our confession. For we have not a high priest who cannot have compassion on our infirmities: Let us go therefore with confidence to the throne of grace, that we may obtain mercy and find grace.* (Heb 4:14-16)

I spent several days in anguish and solitude, entreating You to relieve me from these bitter waters and that they might not drown me. It was like one abyss calling to another. Great Saint Thomas, who suffered an abyss of sadness because of your death, was my consolation. On the eve and the day of his feast, I felt some relief. I thank You, my Abyss of love, my Lord and my God. Be my All at all times and everywhere.

On the eve of your loving birth on which your wonderful Humanity appeared to us, the pastor who represents You arrived. (1098) My secretary, Sister Gravier, who is always graciously welcomed by him, went to his hotel where she learned that he was in the cathedral, assisting at First Vespers that begin with the words: *Rex pacificus magnificatus est, cujus vultum desidera universa terra. The King of peace is exalted, and the whole world desires to see his face.* (1st Vespers; Christmas)

After she had delivered my most humble, respectful regards to him, she was told: "I am ready to sign the contract as I promised. Tell that to your Mother." He kept urging his Vicar General, for he felt that the days were like years, telling him to bring me the original document of the contract so that together we might review it. The Vicar General did so, and I spoke to him at the grill of our church. I also took the opportunity to express my filial protests to him about his coldness during the time that I was deprived of the honor of seeing my pastor. He maintained that he had wanted to prepare me by these

JEANNE'S ORIGINAL DRAFT

mortifications for your blessings of delight and those of our Archbishop. (1099) My secretary, to whom he showed every kindness, took the liberty to tell him in all confidence: "Monsieur, who would ever have thought that you were trying to conceal your charitable and fervent benevolence for our dear Mother with apparent coldness. Also, by your absence, you gave us reason to believe that she would no longer enjoy the affection you had shown her for more than twenty consecutive years. What cautious behavior you showed to mortify the one you honor with your friendship and benevolence!"

He left the original document with me, telling me that the Archbishop was waiting for the notary to present him the contract for his signature. After that, he would return it to me so that I might add my signature after his. When the Prior of Denicé went to the archbishopric, he saw persons there who did not favor me as kindly as my Prelate did. Therefore, he thought it better for me to go personally to the archbishopric. He did not report to me that Monseigneur had told him that I should not trouble to descend our mountain, but, on the contrary, told me that it would be preferable to go to his hotel. (1100) When Monseigneur saw me, he said that he had not wanted me to take this trouble and had so informed the said Prior de Denicé who quietly slipped out of the room to avoid any kindly reproof. As for me, I mentioned that he had not wanted to deprive me of the honor of going to the Archbishop's hotel to present my most humble regards and receive his holy blessing. Prevented from talking very much with me, because of the great number of people waiting to speak to him, he sent someone to summon two persons who he thought were very close to me. I did not think so, and I was not mistaken. Since I could not dissimulate this, I immediately informed these persons that I was not satisfied with their ideas.

Since he constantly wanted to oblige me, Monseigneur told me that he was the Archbishop and father of my daughters and that I would be their directress in everything. He wanted to satisfy me, and he declared that these persons whom I considered contrary to me had spoken advantageously to him about me and on my behalf. Thus, won over by these signs of benevolence, I willingly signed after His Grandeur had done so. (1101) He showed that he

JEANNE'S ORIGINAL DRAFT

was content, repeating several times that all he wanted was my satisfaction, that he had no doubt at all that I would benefit my daughters more than I had promised, that I was their true Mother. I said to him: "Monseigneur, you well know my natural disposition that is won over by goodness by which you obligate me." The Abbé of St. Just said: "Your daughters are blessed to have such a wonderful Father and such a good Mother." I then knelt to receive the blessing of my dearest pastor. He passed to the third door, that is, from his office to the parlor where I again knelt for this wonderful blessing. It did not remove my displeasure for the severity of the two persons that I nevertheless pardoned, convinced that men abound in their opinions. One has died since. I beg You, my God, allow him to dwell in your glory and to multiply your graces toward the other.

In the evening, I went to our chapel to thank and adore You in your Blessed Sacrament, my divine Incarnate Word. (1102) By your loving kindness, You inclined toward me and said: "Why are you sad, my spouse, after seeing my veritable promises and predictions fulfilled? Rejoice that I have made your dear Prelate so kind and generous toward you. Consider the good, and realize that he is the pastor I showed you in a vision in the year 1627, while he was offering Mass and, by a divine favor, elevated together with the altar. I then assured you that he was the one who would establish the Monastery in Lyons during his time. I forewarned you, announcing the death of the pastor whom you cherished and esteemed, saying to you: *Percutiam pastorem, et dispergentur oves gregis; I will strike the shepherd: and the sheep of the flock shall be dispersed.* (Mt 26:31b) You told me that in advance you already felt this dispersion, lest the precious flock of our sheepfold be entirely destroyed. I assured you of my pastoral care. You could say with the crowned Shepherd: *Dominus regit me, et nihil mihi deerit: in loco pascuæ ibi me colocavit; super aquam refectionis,* etc. *The Lord ruleth me: and I shall want nothing. He hath set me in a place of pasture. He hath brought me up on the water of refreshment.* (Ps 22:1-2)

"What graces did you not experience, by entrusting yourself and being converted to Me! With sure step, you proceeded among the shadows of so

JEANNE'S ORIGINAL DRAFT

much death without fearing any horror, because I accompanied you everywhere. The sufferings that overwhelmed entire peoples, the rods of my indignation, plague, war and famine are occasions when you experience my protection. (1103) I guide you according to my will which you do not always understand. I nurture you Myself, from my divine table, which overthrew those who strove to trouble you. It abundantly poured out upon you the delightful unction of my divine blessings, inebriating you with my own chalice. This caused the bride, thus supported by her Divine Spouse, to be filled with delight. Thus, often astonished, my angels would say to one another: *Quæ est ista, quæ ascendit de deserto, deliciis affluens, innixa super dilectum suum? Pone me ut signaculum super cor tuum. Ut signaculum super brachium tuum. Quia fortis est ut mors dilectio, dura sicut infernus æmulatio. Who is this that cometh up from the desert, flowing with delights, leaning upon her beloved? Put me as a seal upon thy heart, as a seal upon thy arm: for love is strong as death, jealousy as hard as hell."* (Cant 8:5a-6a)

With such a charming repetition of your divine favors, how could any melancholy not change into ineffable jubilation? Besides, I cannot express it. These marvelous graces occurred in the year one thousand six hundred fifty-five [1655]. (1104)

JEANNE'S ORIGINAL DRAFT

CHAPTER CLVI

Prayers, aspirations and transports of love during the divine, loving solemnities of the Incarnate Word and the saints until Pentecost; what occurred in my soul during these solemn times.

When the year 1656 began, I adored You, marveling at You in the stable as on a throne of love and mercy. Marked by my miseries, You had become like the flesh of sin, although You had not committed any, and could see the resplendent Seraphim with six wings: two covering their feet, two their head and flying with the two extended ones. They invite one another to sing the Trisagion, proclaiming You three times: *Holy, Holy, Holy is the God of Hosts lying upon the hay.* With the Evangelical Prophet, I exclaimed privately: *Omnis caro foenum, et omnis gloria eius quasi flos agri. Verbum autem Domini nostri manet in æternum. All flesh is grass, and all the glory thereof as the flower of the field. The word of our Lord endureth for ever.* (Is 40:6c; 8b) (1105)

My enraptured spirit understood the marvels proclaimed in all the rest of this chapter which is the 40th one of this Prophet of the royal race of kings, thrice holy in the city where You chose to be born. There You received the Circumcision and the Name of the Savior. You cleansed us in your Precious Blood which You made to be a cleansing place and an open fountain for us as prophesied by Zacharias: *In die illa erit fons potens Domui David, in ablutionem peccatoris. In that day there shall be a fountain open to the house of David, for the washing of the sinner.* (Zach 13:1)

On the Feast of the Kings, I adored You with them and offered You everything that has been, is and will be in time and in eternity. Attracting me lovingly, You let me understand: *Surge et illuminare, Jerusalem; Arise, be*

JEANNE'S ORIGINAL DRAFT

enlightened, O Jerusalem. (Is 60:1) I am your light that provides light before, over, within, around and after you. Kings and peoples will follow the light you leave in your writings, a light that proceeds from Me. I accept your gifts; I give you Myself, I who am Paradise." (1106) Indeed, King of ineffable love, these few tears I have shed are too richly rewarded by one look from your loving, adorable eyes, Monarch of men and angels!

After the wonderful forty days had passed, You were taken to the temple like a holy fire concealed amid blessed linen. Under the form of a slave, You were presented as were the other first-born infants. Simeon recognized You to be God blazing with light, presented by the white virginal cloud of purity and red of charity, upon whose breast You shone as the Sun of Justice. You made known your wonderful Mother, that beloved, loving nurse whose heart was pierced by the pitiless sword that brought to light the thoughts of many other hearts. Mine was not closed nor insensible to this loving pain that caused the division of soul from spirit, a pain that makes the soul happy to suffer for love and because of Love itself: *Vivus est enim sermo Dei, et efficax et penetrabilior omni gladio ancipiti: et pertingens usque ad divisionem animœ ac spiritus: compagnum quoque ac medullarum, et discretor cogitationum et intentionum cordis. For the word of God is livng and effectual and more piercing than any two edged sword and reaching unto the division of the soul and the spirit, of the joints also and the marrow: and is a discerner of the thoughts and intents of the heart.* Heb 4(:12) (1107)

The virgins adorned in white and red, Saint Agatha and Saint Dorothy, seemed to me to be very gracious, drawing me after them to praise You with their canticle and following You everywhere, You who are their path of milk after the Virgin, your Mother. I wanted to be among them, giving my blood for You as they did, since You are the red and white Spouse.

On the nineteenth, I considered Saint Appolonia who, burning with divine flame, cast herself into the fire herself. Grace impelled her to consume her holocaust in order to enter your house of glory.

JEANNE'S ORIGINAL DRAFT

The next day, I asked Saint Scholastica to pray to You for me, You who are blessed by men, angels and your Divine Father, to remain with me every night of my life so that I might be with You during eternity, the infinite day of the next life. She did not reject my prayer. (1108)

I marveled at the grace received by St. William who was converted by St. Bernard. He proclaimed your extraordinary mystery. You cast him down to earth to raise him up to heaven by his conversion and ascetic penance, giving to the Church what he had wrested from it: *Crescens mirabiliter in consommatione; He grew admirably in his consummation.* His spirit grew in your sight, my Divine Love, consuming his body through fasting.

On the Feast of St. Peter's Chair in Antioch, I wanted to be truly Christian. This title had been given the faithful who were the first to be honored with this glorious title.

On the Feast of St. Matthias, as I ordinarily did, I requested You for the condition of the saints in light and that, with fidelity, I might receive the grace of the one who is your faithful witness. You are the One, my Divine Love, who regarded the heart of St. Matthias to make him your Apostle, replacing the perfidious Judas. On noticing that several persons were hypocritical, I suffered for all and through all, because they betrayed You and were guilty of your Precious Blood. (1109)

On the first day of the month dedicated to our faithful Guardians, who take marvelous care to make us worthy to bear laurel and palms for all eternity, for their great jubilation, I yearned for the conversion of sinful souls and the increase of grace for justified souls still on life's course. *Qui justus est, justificetur adhuc; He that is just, let him be justified still.* (Ap 22:11c) They possess perfect charity, wanting us to be holy as God is holy. By what means could we ever acknowledge these heavenly favors, unless your love itself were their eternal, joyous recompense?

You wanted to reward your angelic doctor, because he had written so

JEANNE'S ORIGINAL DRAFT

profusely about You. When urged to state what he desired as a reward, he said: "Nothing other than You Yourself." You are an abyss. Request another abyss: *Abyssus abyssum invocat; Deep calleth on deep.* (Ps 41:8a) (1110) He asked in accordance with his name, and You told him: *Fiat ut petitur; Granted as petitioned.* I beg You, my Divine Savior, through goodness, to give me grace for grace according to my request: *Gratiam pro gratia.*

All favors and graces come to us from your plenitude and through her who is the Treasurer ever since You assumed a body within her virginal womb. This occurred by the overshadowing of your Holy Spirit while the power of the Most High protected her by his shadow to have her remain alive and bear a God of light and fire who had told Moses: *"Man living the natural life cannot see Me".* You also spoke to him in the shadow that toned down your brilliance.

What is this, Lord of the abysses? I am in the abyss. Behold me in the ocean with You who are an abyss of grace, an abyss that made its voice heard by saying: *Secundum verbum tuum; According to thy word.* (Lk 1:38c) (1111) But, marvel upon marvel, upon the bosom of your Virgin Mother, I see the adorable manna: *Manhu, What is this?* The Hebrews were astounded when they saw the manna in the desert that was to nurture them for only forty years. I have greater reason for astonishment and delight beyond myself as I marvel at the manna in the virginal womb that is an adorable desert. I adore You there, Increated and Incarnate Word, and receive You there, for it is your delight for me to be united to You there. Whatever gives delight sustains, and whatever provides delight nourishes. Invest me with purple and linen. You nourish me Yourself, providing me with a perpetual banquet. Take me to the Supper; allow me to repose upon your breast. Willingly would I enter this paradise with your favorite disciple to be a balm for your dying, palpitating Heart upon noting the devil going with You into the heart of the traitor who sold and delivered You to the perfidious Jews. (1112) I would not leave You: *Mihi enim vivere Christus est, et mori lucrum; For to me, to live in Christ: and to die is gain.* (Phil 1:21) I prefer this garden sprinkled by the torrent from your wounds to the Empyrean with its wonderful river. There is

JEANNE'S ORIGINAL DRAFT

no comparison between the drops that fall in clots and the twelve pearls that form the twelve gates to the marvelous city: *Civitas in quadro posita est; The city lieth in a four-square.* (Ap 21:16a)

None of these brilliant precious stones in the walls and foundation of the Empyrean compares with these priceless graces of the night, for they come from a God-Man, on whose face they had been focused and from which they radiated. What is this *manhu*? The first myrrh that freely flows by the ardor of love and envelops the beloved and me, together with You, most loving Lord. You live and die through love, which caused two contraries in one same subject, simultaneously operating and suffering to the same degree. (1113)

Arise, my adorable Heart, and draw me to You by the odor of your anointing, perfuming all the streets You pass and the places You enter and pause for a while. Let me carry your Cross and die with You, since You carry my sins attached to it. You satisfy for me, redeeming me personally, giving everything to deliver me from my enemies and yours, as the Apostle told the Colossians: *Et vos cum mortui essetis in delictis, convivificavit cum illo, donans vobis omnia delicta: delens quod adversus nos erat chirographum decreti, quod erat contrarium nobis, et ipsum tulit de medio, affigens illud cruci: et expolians principatus, et potestates traduxit confidenter, palam triumphans illos in semetipso. And you, when you were dead in your sins and the uncircumcision of your flesh, he hath quickened together with him, forgiving you all your offences: Blotting out the handwriting of the decree that was contrary to us. And he hath taken the same out of the way, fastening it to the cross. And despoiling the principalities and powers, he hath exposed them confidently in open show.* (Col 2:13-15)

Gloriously risen from the dead, your Body was endowed with the four marvelous attributes of light, subtility, agility and impassibility and could say: (1114) *Ero mors tua, o mors! Morsus tuo ero, inferne!; O death, I will be thy death; O hell, I will be thy bite.* (Os 13:14c)

AUTOBIOGRAPHY

JEANNE'S ORIGINAL DRAFT

Dear Love, You certainly were the death of death, and the sting of my hell, because those who had contended that I would die of the trouble brought about by all hell are still fuming and continuing their malicious deeds. By your powerful goodness, You made me victorious over all their artifices and treacheries and will continue to do so, please, my victorious Monarch. You declared that all power is given You in heaven and on earth, showing that You are the delight of souls who remain faithful during the trials You send. To each of them, Isaias said: *Ego Dominus Deus tuus, docens te utilia, gubernans te in via qua ambulas. Utinam attendisses mandata mea: facta fuisset sicut flumen pax tua, et iustitia tua sunt gurgites maris. I am the Lord thy God that teach thee profitable things, that govern thee in the way that thou walkest. O that thou hadst hearkened to my commandments: thy peace had been as a river, and thy justice as the waves of the sea.* (Is 48:17b-18)

On the Feast of the Ascension, You chose to fortify me to endure this absence that caused me to die and die again. (1115) You left me on earth where I felt a stranger even in my own home with the daughters of my heart. Like the pelican, I pierced it to pour out blood for them, since tears are called the heart's blood. Freely would I renounce my own temporal life to obtain for them the eternal one, delivering them from the serpent's poison. I thought of the mother who, transported by love for her son, agreed that he should open her side and see the womb wherein he had been conceived and carried with more than a maternal love. She loved this cruelty to facilitate royalty for him. I want to endure whatever You tell me so that they may possess the crown and the Empyrean. (1116)

JEANNE'S ORIGINAL DRAFT

CHAPTER CLVII

The furnace of divine charity abides in the Blessed Sacrament. A vision of a Lamb. God tests souls through suffering. He sustained mine during the repeated anguish of the journey of two Sisters whom I sent to Paris.

On the Feast of the Descent of your Spirit of fire, who is the Consoler par excellence, I begged Him to vivify your promises, remaining with me to console me in all my sufferings, that are certainly not just a few. I have no words with which to describe or express them. You know them, my God, and have foreseen them: *Intellexisti cogitationes meas de longe; Semitam meam et funiculum meum investigasti; et omnes vias meas prævidisti, quia non est sermo in lingua mea. Thou hast understood my thoughts afar off: my path and my line thou has searched out. And thou hast foreseen all my ways: for there is no speech in my tongue.* (Ps 138:3-4)

On your holy Feast, the ardor of your love had You exposed upon our altars at the door of our tabernacles for pilgrim souls. (1117) You urged them to accept the relief that your goodness has offered them, the all-holy Bread that was prepared, not upon ashes but in the rich furnace of your charity. The butter, milk and fattened calf represent nothing other than You, my Beloved, our element and our Food, our Beloved and the One who loves us. I pray all the saints to descend from their seat of glory to adore You on earth, true prodigy of the miracle of love, and to supply all the praise that I cannot give You nor know how to do so.

The birth of the great Baptist, announced by an angel to his father Zacharias while he was offering incense, astonished everyone then in the temple when they saw the one who had heard the oracle without words. I do not know if

JEANNE'S ORIGINAL DRAFT

mine was similar, when I saw You, my Divine Savior, in the form of a lamb that You hid and withdrew under a little straw chair on the Feast of the Octave of this joyful solemnity. (1118) I do know very well that I felt extremely pained to see You in such a lowly, restricted place. You let me understand that I was to protect You and oppose the evil things planned against You. I could not endure having You there without being extremely pained. I did not know how to withdraw from there. I did not dare get up, being seated on the chair under which You seemed to hide. Your enemies did not clearly appear to me. You could see them Yourself, and You did not express the offences they gave You. I was to protect You from their malignant plans and connivances. Had such persons been as flexible as St. Paul in doing your will, You would have been as good toward them as toward him. However, seeing them intent on their path of willful ignorance, You would have said to them: "Why do You persecute your Savior? You are as cruel as abducting wolves, and I am gentleness itself. Are you not afraid that I will punish you and cast you to the roaring lions that stalk you to devour you?"

Most holy Empress, on the Feast of St. Thecla, You told me that You were your Lamb's shepherdess. Where did You leave Him now? When He gamboled and leaped among the clouds, You came to follow Him to Lyons. I entrust his glory to You. I told You that in spirit and will I was already in Lyons and only corporeally was I in Paris. It was a great honor to follow You there and everywhere You chose to indicate to me, despite the sufferings prepared for me there. (1119) I considered them to be great and very numerous, but I did not know what they would be. I was unaware of their quality and quantity.

On the Feast of All Saints in 1656, while the Church was chanting their victory, I was weeping over my struggles. This filled me with confusion. I thought I was not displeasing You, my kind Savior, because I was unable to overcome the resistance or antipathy that were obvious to the very ones who did not love me. I resolved to tell my problems to the Prior of Denicé, my faithful director and charitable confessor, whom I have completely trusted for many years. I saw that he was astounded, but, since he is resigned to

JEANNE'S ORIGINAL DRAFT

everything You allow, he alludes very little to whatever he perceives and did not completely let me know his compassion for my desolation. He judged it better for me to drink this chalice patiently for as long as You allowed, my Lord and my God.

You allowed Satan to test Job whom You deemed to be the simplest and most faithful of his day. Satan did not overlook anything possible to make Job lose patience of which he is the mirror and miracle. He kept his soul reserved steadfastly for You, no matter what opinion his friends had of him. (1120)

Your Holy Spirit assures us by the following words in Holy Scripture that Job, the patient one par excellence, did not sin: *In omnibus his non peccavit Job labiis suis; In all these things Job sinned not by his lips.* (Job 1:22) Lamb of God, do not allow me to sin any more, either interiorly or exteriorly. Help me by your grace, for without it I can do nothing. Afflicted by persons who externally please me in everything for your glory and the perfection of my Order, I place my spirit in your hands. Pardon the ignorance of the one who guides her and causes me distress that I cannot declare. Your wise providence will arrange those matters.

The one who seemed closer to me than to herself acted as though she would withdraw from me. Then, to please me, she changed her tactics. She approached me, convinced that she was loved by everyone who saw her. Great Savior, You know our hearts and that I want to consecrate them to You completely. It is impossible to conceal the fact that they do not love You perfectly. I have always had great antipathy for dissimulation. I want to please You in everything, my beloved Savior, for your glory. My situation is always in your hands; in your eyes, my resilience; in your bosom, my treasures: *Da mihi sedium tuarum assistricem sapientiam. Et noli me reprobare a pueris tuis. Give me wisdom that sitteth by thy throne, and cast me not off from among thy children.* (Wis 9:4)

Great Saint Clement, Pope, who sent St. Denis to France, pray for me that I may send persons where this great saint went and that it may be for the glory

JEANNE'S ORIGINAL DRAFT

of my God. (1121) In all confidence, I can say that You heard my prayer, for on the Feast of St. Catherine, Virgin and Martyr, a virtuous clergyman from Provence came to visit me. He offered to assist and accompany my daughters to Paris where he was going, so as to offer Holy Mass for them and administer the sacraments to them. I was happy over this offer and readily accepted, although he had little time because of his special companions, who were priests and religious scheduled to make the journey with him. Thus, I had only from five o'clock in the evening until five o'clock in the morning to prepare my daughters for this journey, that is to say, two Sisters and my secretary Gravier to accompany them. The latter went promptly at six o'clock to our Archbishop to obtain permission and to receive the honor of his holy blessing.

The next day was the Feast of St. Peter, Patriarch of Alexandria, to whom I entrusted my daughters, who departed to join the group. Because of this, I did not consider the extreme cold, trusting in your divine goodness and in the one who had been faithful to You by fighting for your divine equality and consubstantiality with your Divine Father.

On the Feast of your Apostle Saint Andrew, 1656, I learned from the man who had driven the carriage with my two Sisters that my secretary had fallen from her horse into a half-frozen river. With her clothes dripping wet, she climbed back on the horse to follow the coach, but was hampered by being wet and the extreme cold that had frozen her clothes like diamonds all about her. (1122) Besides this, it was impossible to make the horse proceed, as she desired, for she had neither spurs nor whip with which to control it. The muleteer did not take into consideration that this daughter was unfamiliar with the route and, therefore, could not follow the coach. He did stop her once to feed her horse some grain as he had done the others. He left her there, telling her to get to the main road. Everything was covered with ice and rocks, delaying her more than she wished. Because of this, she was at least a quarter of a league behind the coach that the muleteer kept moving along, unconcerned about the one behind him. Meanwhile, this daughter was alone on a main road in the country, truly in trouble. She assured me that her fright was intense and that she remembered that I had entrusted them to St. Raphael, to

JEANNE'S ORIGINAL DRAFT

whom she commended herself in this extreme need. She then saw a rider approaching who was greatly astounded on seeing her alone. After several conversations, he believed her and delivered her from sorrow and affliction by assisting her to gallop across the fields. He led her to the other carriages, and, when there, soundly reprimanded the muleteer. He charitably but firmly insisted that he look after her. All this had a good effect and filled my daughter with joy. It was as though she had been delivered by an angel from heaven. She believed that it was Saint Raphael, since he resembled the gentleman who helped us during our voyage in 1653.

On his return, the muleteer reported to me these disastrous experiences of my secretary. I was so filled with apprehension, that I felt a pain in my side that persisted a long time, during which I did not record anything that occurred during the months of December, January, February and March in 1657, even though your goodness granted me favors as You usually did through pure charity. (1123) I begged You, not only to cover the multitude of my sins, but to destroy them completely and always to guide me by your grace that is unceasingly necessary for me. I certainly experienced its power during the great sufferings You allowed me to have, finding myself persecuted even by important persons who too readily accept reports or accusations from those who must acknowledge that they are obligated to me for the benefits your goodness allowed me to do for them. So much ingratitude and arrogance to which I have been subjected led me to think that what a crime it is not to love You and be perfectly grateful for your goodness and divine mercies. I beg You grant them to me always by giving me the strength and constancy to endure whatever may come to the very end.

On the Feast of St. Benedict 1657, some persons of religious profession uttered things against me to please the hosts that had invited them. I beg You to pardon them for the liberal slander reported to their superior in order to belittle me. (1124)

JEANNE'S ORIGINAL DRAFT

CHAPTER CLVII (bis)

The marvels that the Prophet Ezechiel saw are divinely expressed for us in the donation and thanksgiving that Our Lord made at the Supper.

On Holy Thursday, in a helpless condition to love what is good, I wept a great deal, but my tears seemed useless in obtaining your love and through it the love of my neighbor. Such helplessness on this day was most upsetting to me, because this holy day is the one on which You showed your infinite love for those who belong to You. Having everything in your hands, You give everything by giving Yourself. Knowing all things, that You would leave this world to return to your Divine Father, You wanted to give us the greatest sign of your excessive love.

When I was engulfed in an abyss of pain and sorrow, You had me recall that, when the Prophet Ezechiel had been with the prisoners near the Chobar River he had visions of God and the chariot of his glory. Elevating my thought, I said to You: "Ah, Lord, your lovely eyes that You lift up today are more wonderful than all the glory seen by the holy Prophet! They merit admiration, for they are God's eyes; their visions are divine. You are their divinely human elevations and humanly divine ones, for they are theandric. The Sacred Body that You give at this Supper is the chariot of the glory of your divinity. You are everything symbolized by these visions; You are the reality of these figures and forms. You are Man, You are a lion, You are an ox, You are an eagle. You are like God, in both East and West, North and South. In this adorable reproduction, You are where You choose to be. Everywhere that your love bears You, You reproduce. Your desires will be fulfilled. You take Yourself; You receive Yourself; You reunite with Yourself (if I may so speak). (1125)

JEANNE'S ORIGINAL DRAFT

Inseparable from your Divine Person, Increated Word and Incarnate Word, by concomitance your Father and your Holy Spirit are present in this reproduction. I perceive the divine circumincession there, by an inexplicable penetration. Their distinction of support in no manner divides the unity of essence nor the simplicity of nature. The Body and Precious Blood You have assumed from your Virgin Mother is holily supported by your divine hypostasis and is as adorable as that of the Father and the Holy Spirit. Your brilliant, blazing eyes enrapture angels and throw Saint John into ecstasy. They are suns that transport, blind and enlighten him as his corporal eyes sleep upon your breast. He sees You with the spiritual ones upon the bosom of your Divine Father where he steadfastly perceives and contemplates your ineffable generation. He will speak and write holily about this when he proclaims to mankind what has been unknown up to this time.

Divine Beloved, what rapture for this holy prisoner, reposing upon your sacred breast. Your bowels are the bonds; he is the child of love reposing upon the breast of flame that is the furnace of charity. (1126) If I do not state that his feet are straight, I ascertain that they were clean. They were cleansed by the holy water that You placed in the basin to sanctify them and all the others. They were all washed by your sacred, holy hands, which You bent over those of all of them, even of Judas who did not profit thereby.

In a holy way, I can apply all the marvels of this Prophet's visions to this gift of your Divine Body in the institution of your Holy Eucharist, this divine synaxis, holy celebration, abridgement of your marvels; I dare say, your miracles, and the miracle of love is Love itself. I see the fire. I see the wheels one within the other, with the Spirit of Life being immensely present everywhere, filling heaven and earth. One of these wheels appeared to all mankind, your gracious humanity, grace and goodness.

On Good Friday, I could say: *Mihi vivere Christus est, et mori lucrum; For to me, to live is Christ and to die is gain.* (Phil 1:21) Whatever is not You had no power to satisfy me. If You visited me after your Resurrection, it was as a flash, for You saw that I was sad on Holy Saturday. (1127) I

JEANNE'S ORIGINAL DRAFT

strove to draw strength from my weakness, reflecting that St. Peter and St. John ran to ascertain what Magdalen had told them: that You had been removed from the tomb. I followed them with the love and palpitation of my heart. You favored me by inviting me to enter with them, saying to me: "My beloved, be consoled. Experience what the Prophet Isaias said: that my tomb is glorious. Enjoy the delights of my Resurrection together with my beloved companion." On this day and the next, which was Sunday, and during the entire Octave, after having given me your peace, You disappeared. I could well say that You had gone beyond the limits. I could no longer see You; my joy faded away with You. (1128)

CHAPTER CLVIII

We must love our enemies and do good to them, together with Jesus Christ so that we may ascend to the Divine Father with Him. My sadness because of an unfaithful person. With tears and prayer, I begged the angels and saints to ask the Incarnate Word to maintain his Order, pouring out his gifts upon it.

On the Feast of St. James and St. Philip in 1657, I adored You in your Divine Father. I begged You to place me in the dwellings that are meant to accommodate pilgrim souls who follow You, along the paths You mark out for them, granting them the confidence to dare strive to arrive someday where You had ascended. You are the supreme heaven, elevating us in spirit even though our earthly bodies are infirm: *Audientes igitur semper, scientes quoniam dum sumus in corpore, peregrinamus a Domino: (per fidem enim ambulamus, et non per speciem) audemus autem, et bonam voluntatem habemus, magis peregrinari a corpore, et præsentes ad*

JEANNE'S ORIGINAL DRAFT

Dominum. Et ideo contendimus sive absentes, sive præsentes placere illi. Therefore having always confidence, knowing that while we are in the body we are absent from the Lord. (For we walk by faith and not by sight.) But we are confident and have a good will to be absent from the body and to be present with the Lord. And therefore we labor, whether absent or present, to please Him. (2 Cor 5:6-9) (1129)

The next day, the Feast of St. Athanasius, a person of high station together with a priest came to the grill of our church to speak to me. I was told everything that had occurred in Grenoble where a little council had been conducted which You did not confirm, my Eternal Pontiff. You took up for the one that others wanted to banish from the place, Increated and Incarnate Word. I prayed St. Athanasius to represent to You your choice that was being opposed.

On the Feast of the Holy Cross, in order to deceive me, those persons pretended to desire everything they dreaded, and You granted me the grace to act toward them with graciousness and simplicity rather than with severity that I should have used. Through charity, I continued what I should have refused them through justice. Grant me the grace to imitate You by rendering good for evil. Through your infinite mercy, pardon me and them our faults.

Your elevation above the heavens raised up my spirit. I prayed your loving heart that, when You would be in your kingdom, to remember her who had been on the Cross next to You. (1130) The difference was that, in the eyes of your Father, You were always innocent while I was unceasingly guilty, engulfed by death: *Ut vitæ æternæ hæredes efficeremur; That we might be made heirs of life everlasting.* (1 Pet 3:22)

At the end of October, as I was preparing for the Feast of your holy Apostles Simon and Jude, your Majesty's reapers, to help me dwell with all your saints, I learned that some persons, who possibly did not mean to displease You, had laid claim to the benefices of a priest and a canon. I recognized the good will of the canon who was being attacked for what he

JEANNE'S ORIGINAL DRAFT

had done through charity and excessive compassion. Besides this, we had an obligation toward his devotion and zeal, for he often offered Holy Mass for us. Deeply and justly moved, I resolved to pray and have others pray to your Majesty until he would be justified in every way. I assured him and his mother that heaven was on their side and that your goodness denied me nothing that I requested of You in constant trust. Since St. James declared that constant prayer joined to perseverance would obtain from your goodness what I could not deserve, I said with the Prophet-King: *Qui confidunt in Domino, sicut mons Sion: non commovebitur in æternum. They that trust in the Lord shall be as mount Sion: he shall not be moved for ever.* (Ps 124:1) (1131)

I presented to You the mother of this only son, Mademoiselle Mabire, who is as generous as she is devout. I noted in her the Christian and moral virtues to perfection, good common sense and a strong, fine spirit adapted to your will in everything. I thought about the confidence of the Prophet Eliseus, especially when his disciple was frightened by a great number of persecutors. Eliseus told him to think about the great multitude of holy angels or friends who came to assure him and confound his enemies.

JEANNE'S ORIGINAL DRAFT

CHAPTER CLIX

I prayed to all the saints with confidence, desiring to love and suffer to make reparation for my offenses and earn lilies, roses and laurels. How I was elevated to consider the greatness of St. Joachim. In Jesus Christ, he is the prince of all the saints. He and St. Anne were participants of the Lord's kiss, the dawn that gave birth to the Sun on Christmas night.

On November the first, I reflected on all your saints, on the Saint of saints by essence and par excellence, who came to our aid. With all devotion possible, I said: *Exultabunt sancti in gloria, et lætabuntur in cubilibus suis. The saints shall rejoice in glory: they shall be joyful in their beds.* (Ps 149:5) It is their glory to love You in heaven and to protect us on earth for love of You, obtaining graces and virtues for us to resemble them. (1132)

It was the Feast of St. Martin, the blessed Pontiff who loved You with all his heart and soul, as the Church chants. He had clothed You with half of his mantle that he gave the poor man. In the presence of your holy angels, You were glorious in it, praising this saint who was but a catechumen. Through him, his profound ardor and the resplendent halo over his head, I offered the Sacrifice of love for your glory and my perfection.

On the Presentation of your Virgin Mother, I prayed to St. Joachim and St. Anne with her that her incomparable merits and her fidelity to your inspirations would make up for my failures. I dwelt on this text: *Sacrificate sacrificium iustitiæ, et sperate in Domino. Offer up the sacrifice of justice, and trust in the Lord.* (Ps 46a) Could I spend these days without addressing the virgins adorned in white and red, St. Cecilia and St. Catherine; without begging them to tell You my sorrows and present my distress (to the One they

JEANNE'S ORIGINAL DRAFT

love and whom I wish to love as much as they do)? My soul languished with love as a daughter of Jerusalem. Could they refuse me flowers and fruit to comfort me in my loving yearnings for my adorable Spouse? (1133)

I did not forget great St. Clement nor the lamb that showed him the fountain. What veneration I owe the great Patriarch of Alexandria to whom You revealed the wrong that Arius was doing You by denying your equality and consubstantiality with your Divine Father. The whole Catholic Church believes it and adores You as one God in Three distinct Persons. With St. John, I declare: *Tres sunt, qui testimonium dant in cælo: Pater, Verbum, et Spiritus Sanctus: et hi tres unum sunt. There are Three who give testimony in heaven, the Father, the Word, and the Holy Ghost. And these three are one.* (1 Jn 5:7) I say to You: Increated Word and Incarnate Word, grant that this young woman, through whom You chose to establish an Order in your Church, who adores You, bearing your title, Incarnate Word and Blessed Sacrament, may be faithful in everything for your glory and service. May she seek your glory in everything, O my Love.

On the Feast of the powerful St. Andrew, I needed strength and love to address the Cross and greet it as good, because through it divine goodness had showered us with its profusions, pouring out every drop of his Precious Blood. (1134) Even after his death, He there opened a fountain wherein to cleanse us and tinge us. His death caused all nature to turn pale, apparently on the point of extinction. Because its Creator was dying upon a gibbet, what could it not fear! His angels of peace wept bitterly; the demons in hell trembled with fright!

On the Feast of the great Saint Francis Xavier, my limited courage caused me embarrassment, overwhelming me under the cross. I almost dared to say: "My Love, that is enough suffering!" However, I realized that such laxity ought to make me blush with shame and confusion. I drew strength from my weakness, or better still, from the fountains of your goodness to which I turned for help because they are intelligent as well as obliging. They are powerful and dynamic, proceeding from You, my God who are strong and living. With

JEANNE'S ORIGINAL DRAFT

David, I said to You: *Quemadmodum desiderat cervus ad fontes aquarum, ita desiderat anima mea ad te, Deus. Sitivit anima mea ad Deum fortem, vivum; Quando veniam, et apparebo ante faciem Dei? As the hart panteth after the fountains of water; so my soul panteth after thee, O God. My soul hath thirsted after the strong living God. When shall I come and appear before the face of God?* (Ps 41:2-3) (1135)

On the Feast of St. Barbara, virgin and martyr, whose throat was cut because of the fury of her father, your sworn enemy who was crueler than wild beasts, my self love seemed even worse due to the sins I commit, causing your death, my Father and my Lord. Lamb of God, who takes away the sins of the world, take away mine. Let me follow You everywhere with the holy virgins and allow me to receive You in grace at the end of my mortal life. Be my holy Viaticum, dying for You, since You have died for me so that I may live for You and through You.

Ever since childhood, I have had devotion and a tendency to honor pontiffs and prelates, archbishops and bishops. Thus, I considered St. Nicolas and St. Ambrose to be brilliant in holiness, miracles and love. One of them provided food for the destitute, giving freely with his right hand in such a way that the left would not know, so as to prevent young women from going astray, etc.

Great Prelate, the Ambrosian gentleness that was yours from early childhood attracted everyone. (1136) With admiration, they praised the virgins who possess glory through their courage to earn lilies, roses and laurels. They were victorious over the demons of the world and the flesh, chanting the Canticle that virgins alone may sing. They follow You, Divine Lamb, wherever You go, bearing You and even stealing You away from the bosom of your Divine Father: *Hæc nubes, aëra, Angelos, sideraque transgrediens, Verbum Dei in ipso sinu Patris invenit, et toto hausit pectore. Beyond the clouds she went, beyond the air, the Angels and the stars; and in the very bosom of the Father she found God's Word, and took Him to herself with all her heart.* (Common of Virgins, Lesson V) (1137)

JEANNE'S ORIGINAL DRAFT

CHAPTER CLIX (bis)

The temporal generation of the most Blessed Virgin Mary, most worthy Mother of the Incarnate Word, and the graces I received through their excessive goodness toward me, their simple daughter and unworthy servant.

On the Feast of the Immaculate Conception of your Blessed and most pure Virgin (1657), I considered your temporal generation from the time of Abraham until St. Joseph, the spouse of this Virgin Mother of whom You were born, Divine Savior, called the Christ. (1137) You were pleased to elevate my spirit with admiration for St. Joachim's greatness, telling me in Latin: *Princeps sanctorum omnium*, that I was to call him the *Prince* or *the first among all the saints*. You told me not to be astonished that, just as You had chosen St. Teresa to make the glory of St. Joseph admired during these recent times, that You were calling me, who am nothing, to proclaim the greatness of St. Joachim, the father of your wonderful Mother, whom he begot by command of the entire Blessed Trinity. At that blessed moment, St. Joachim and St. Anne were sharers in the Lord's kiss, that, through divine dilection, was given this Daughter of the Father, Mother of the Son and Spouse of the Holy Spirit. She was made the holy land, the land of promise, the sublime land, the priestly land, the temple, the dwelling and tabernacle of the Lord. (1138) She had miraculously received the being of nature and grace. She was the elevated throne seen by the Prophet Isaias filled with God's majesty, after which the veiled Seraphim chanted: *Sanctus, Sanctus, Sanctus*, etc.; *Holy, Holy, Holy*.

St. Joachim and St. Anne received as much grace and holiness as was appropriate for the father and mother of the Mother of God and the grandparents of the Incarnate Word. To honor St. Joachim, You were ordinarily called

JEANNE'S ORIGINAL DRAFT

Son of Man. By an inexpressible mystery, these words revealed and concealed Joachim's holiness. You said to me: "My daughter, exclaim with the Prophet Isaias: *Generationem eius quis enarrabit? Who shall declare his generation?* (Is 53:8b)

"None of the angels or men could worthily express this temporal generation nor the holiness of the Immaculate Conception. Joachim is my father and my saint, reserved and withdrawn within Me, I who am the Lord, for whom he has been the preparation before the creation of the world. What I declare of Joachim, I also mean of Anne, my grandmother. Abraham, Isaac and Jacob and the other patriarchs, although their fathers, prefigured them. St. Matthew could write what he recorded up to St. Joseph, the spouse of my Mother, of whom I was born. The Holy Spirit did not command him to record Joachim's generation. With a cloud, the same Holy Spirit also concealed my Mother's Immaculate Conception during the time that I was visible. During these latter times, it had to burst forth, elevating the souls He had chosen from light to light to become transformed into Himself. She is the halo of a Spouse impassioned, to your way of thinking, with his all-beautiful one. He makes her the masterpiece of his delight in his pure creature for the extension of the Incarnation of the Creator and creature of the God-Man who I am.

"To you, little daughter, who acknowledge yourself to be the most unworthy of all creatures, is entrusted the commission to proclaim this mystery concealed in God during the ages. While still in the world, my dear Saint John said that no one had ever seen God. (1140) The Apostle who had been elevated to the third heaven declared that God dwells in inaccessible light that no one has ever seen. I am the only one, the Increated and Incarnate Word, who has seen and sees my Father doing what He does. Through goodness, I have favored you today by instructing you about the excellent qualities of my father, St. Joachim, and commanding you to invoke him with the words: *Principes sanctorum omnium, Prince (first) among all the saints.* My Blessed Mother honors him as her father, even though she is the Queen of men and angels. She is my dear Mother to whom I chose to be subject, and, through her, to Saint Joseph, her husband whom I have called my father.

JEANNE'S ORIGINAL DRAFT

"None of these holy qualities is diminished by honoring St. Joseph. Do you think they would be degraded by rendering respect to St. Joachim, St. Anne's husband? I am their crown. My Mother's flesh is their flesh. She is the substance of their substance, by which they have honored the hidden God and Savior, who paid the ransom for all mankind with the flesh and blood I assumed in my Blessed Mother which is theirs. That flesh and blood has not seen the corruption of sin in my Mother's Conception. (1141) Her innocent soul has always known the paths of life, exempt from all sin by my powerful dilection that is stronger than death and more jealous about her eternal glory than the hardness of hell in its obstinacy against Me. The lamps are of total fire and flame."

I spent Advent in the yearnings of the holy Fathers: *Utinam dirumperes cælos, et descenderes; Rorate, cæli, desuper, et nubes pluant justum; Aperiatur terra, et germinet Salvatorem. O that thou wouldst rend the heavens and wouldst come down; Drop down dew, ye heavens, from above: and let the clouds rain the just. Let the earth be opened and bud forth a saviour.* (Is 64:1a; 45:8)

On the Feast of St. Thomas, as was my custom, I begged him to prepare me to be the dwelling-place of your benevolent Humanity. I prayed to St. Joseph with his Spouse to choose to dwell in the house of David that belonged to the Incarnate Word, our little Emmanuel. He possessed all good things: butter and honey, divinity and humanity united hypostatically within the womb of the virginal spouse who would give birth to Him within three days by a new birth. (1142) I waited to be graciously invited to witness this spiritual birth by a loving faith. My hope was not frustrated, because on this night, that was clearer than day and cold at this season, I saw a sun enveloped in linen cloths. It was ardent and resplendent, and this holy Virgin had borne it for nine entire months without melting away by its heat nor being blinded by its light.

Such a marvelous dawn at the rising of the sun on this morning distilled a dew that never before had been equalled. From her holy eyes flowed heavenly tears upon this Divine Child who relit the flames by a loving antiperistasis

JEANNE'S ORIGINAL DRAFT

of light from which nothing is hidden. By a sublime intelligence, I understood the following three verses: *In sole posuit tabernaculum suum altissimus; et ipse tamquam sponsus procedens de thalamo suo. Exultavit ut gigas ad currendam viam; a summo cælo egressio eius. Et occursus eius usque ad summum eius; nec est qui se abscondat a calore eius.* He hath set his high tabernacle in the sun: and he, as a bridegroom coming out of his bride chamber, hath rejoiced as a giant to run the way. His going out is from the end of heaven. And his circuit even to the end thereof: and there is no one that can hide himself from his heat. (Ps 18:6-7) (1143)

In one same instant, I saw this divine sun shining within the bosom of his Divine Father and quivering as a veritable Infant upon the breast of his virginal Mother. This *comprehenseur* and at the same time traveler enraptured both heaven and earth. In ecstasy, the angels led the shepherds there: *Et pastores erant in regione eadem vigilantes, et custodientes vigilias noctis super gregem suum. Et ecce angelus Domini stetit juxta illos, et claritas Dei circumfulsit illos, et timuerunt timore magno. Et dixit illis angelus: Nolite timere: ecce enim evangelizo vobis gaudium magnum, quod erit omni populo: quia natus est vobis hodie Salvator, qui est Christus Dominus, in civitate David. Et hoc vobis signum: Invenietis infantem. Et subito facta est cum angelo multitudo militiæ cælestis laudantium Deum, et dicentium: Gloria in altissimis Deo, et in terra pax hominibus bonæ voluntatis.* And there were in the same country shepherds watching and keeping the night watches over their flock. And behold an angel of the Lord stood by them and the brightness of God shone round about them: and they feared with a great fear. And the angel said to them: Fear not; for, behold, I bring you good tidings of great joy that shall be to all the people: For, this day is born to you a Saviour, who is Christ the Lord, in the city of David. And this shall be a sign unto you. You shall find the infant. And suddenly there was with the angel a multitude of the heavenly army, praising God and saying: Glory to God in the highest: and on earth peace to men of good will. (Lk 2:8-14) (1144)

JEANNE'S ORIGINAL DRAFT

CHAPTER CLX

In the stable, the Incarnate Word hoisted the banner of love. There his beloved felt distressed, faint and languishing with love. She was admitted to the mystical nuptials. The merciful Humanity was affable toward us and allowed St. Simeon to go console the holy Fathers. Prompted by the Holy Spirit, he thrust the pitiless sword into the heart of the Virgin, who dwells with the spouses faithful to the Cross of Jesus.

On the Feast of your bitter-sweet Circumcision 1658, I felt distressed and almost faint because of your wound. You told me that the sacred unction of your Name lessened the pain and that, by this Name that was an oil spilled over, I would obtain renewed strength: *Oleum effusum nomen tuum; ideo adolescentulæ dilexerunt te. Trahe me, post te curremus in odorem unguentorum tuorum. Introduxit me rex in cellaria sua. Thy name is as oil poured out: therefore young maidens have loved thee. Draw me: we will run after thee to the odour of thy ointments. The king hath brought me into his storerooms.* (Cant 1:2b-4)

On this day as well as on Epiphany, You led me into your storeroom where You let me drink a good, royal, divine wine, that caused me to become holily inebriated after having tasted ineffable delights that cause the soul no longer to belong to itself. (1145) The angels of heaven, with the blessed saints, were invited to these mystical nuptials. They said: *Exultabimus et lætabimur in te, memores uberum tuorum super vinum. Recti diligunt te. We will be glad and rejoice in thee, remembering thy breasts, more than wine. The righteous love thee.* (Cant 1:3d)

After tasting such ineffable delights, the soul no longer belongs to itself. If,

JEANNE'S ORIGINAL DRAFT

transported by love and impelled by the impetuosity of your Spirit, it speaks during its ecstasy of your excellent, supereminent perfections and goodness, few people on earth could understand these marvels. The Divine Spouse needs to explain them Himself and have them understand the excess of his charity: *Introduxit me in cellam vinarium; ordinavit in me charitatem. Fulcite me floribus, stipate me malis, quia amore langueo. He brought me into the cellar of wine: he set in order charity in me. Stay me up with flowers, compass me about with apples: because I languish with love.* (Cant 2:4-5)

Dear Spouse, I well understood that You have wisely and firmly hoisted the banner of your love in my heart by remaining in the stable for forty wonderful days. (1146) Distressed, fainting and languishing with love, I would never have wanted to leave this pleasant dwelling except that your Blessed Mother with St. Joseph departed to take You to the temple. According to the Law of Moses, to which this purest Virgin was not obligated, the days of her purification had been fulfilled. The angels, who are the daughters of Jerusalem, had been forbidden to awake her during this divine, virginal birthing. The Divine Spouse, the Holy Spirit, called and invited her with You: *Vox dilecti mei; the voice of my Beloved.* (Cant 2:8)

In profound adoration, she rose up and left the stable to take You to Jerusalem where the Holy Spirit had prompted Simeon and Anne the Prophetess to be present with love and anticipation. Divine Beloved, You invited me to enter there after them. I heard your voice: *Vox dilecti mei; The voice of my Beloved.* (Cant 2:8) You crossed hills and mountains. (1147) You did not invite the patriarchs, prophets nor the kings who had such a deep desire to see You. Moses, your friend, who desired to see your face as a sign of your love for him, received no other favor during one hundred twenty years (to state it better: six times twenty years) except to see your shoulders as You passed, and yet today St. Simeon holds You in his arms! As a Sovereign, You allowed Moses to die after seeing the Promised Land from the height of a mountain, yet denying him entrance to it. Dear Love, You spoke to Moses as God, while with Simeon You laughed as a Baby. It is that You became

JEANNE'S ORIGINAL DRAFT

incarnate and were like us. Your grace and benevolent Humanity seem very gracious toward us. Saint Simeon requested permission to go console those in the shadows of death to inform them that in a few years they would enjoy the splendor of your face, the Light of the Gentiles and the glory of his nation, of all the people of Israel. (1148)

Holy old man, transported by joy, You bless the Child and his parents who marvel at everything said about Him on this joyful feast. After a blessing, addressing his Mother, You said to her: *Ecce positus est hic in ruinam, et in resurrectionem multorum in Israel, et in signum cui contradicetur: et tuam ipsius animam pertransibit gladius ut revelentur ex multis cordibus cogitationes. Et erat Anna prophetissa, filia Phanuel. Behold this child is set for the fall and for the resurrection of many in Israel and for a sign which shall be contradicted. And thy own soul a sword shall pierce, that, out of many hearts, thoughts may be revealed. And there was one Anna, a prophetess, the daughter of Phanuel.* (Lk 2:34b-36)

After these disturbing words, You had nothing to say to strengthen her. By these severe predictions, You thrust the pitiless sword into her heart and wounded her with dread until her own death. That of her Son did not withdraw it. She would see the ruin of the wicked before the resurrection of the good. (1149) Through You, the Holy Spirit gave her delight and bitterness which remained within her bosom where this beloved Infant reposed and began his struggles. Did He not declare by his silence: "My Father, if it be possible, let this bitter chalice pass without this unstained dove drinking of it."

Holy Spirit, You told her in the stable: *Surge, propera, amica mea, columba mea, formosa mea, et veni. Arise, make haste, my love, my dove, my beautiful one, and come.* (Cant 2:10) Holy Spirit, about twenty years ago, You addressed the same words to me, and I felt their sharp effects. You repeat them to me now. I acknowledge that, because of my offences, I deserve the torments of hell and that I am unworthy of either consolation or grace. In no way at all can I compare with this all-pure, totally-immaculate and all-innocent Virgin Mother.

JEANNE'S ORIGINAL DRAFT

You deign to tell me about the sufferings which you bless and that my new-born Savior, who is in guardianship, will tell You when he is grown that He disposes and destines us to suffer to have a place in his kingdom, just as his Father has destined sufferings for Him, the Innocent One. (1150) I experience them and do so repeatedly, but, as a guilty person, I say to You: *Quoniam die ac nocte gravata est super me manus tua, conversus sum in ærumna mea, dum configitur spina. Delictum meum cognitum tibi feci, et iniustitiam meam non abscondi. Dixi: Confitebor adversum me iniustitiam meam Domino; et tu remisisti impietatem peccati mei. For day and night thy hand was heavy upon me: I am turned in my anguish, whilst the thorn is fastened. I have acknowledged my sin to thee: and my injustice I have not concealed. I said: I will confess against myself my injustice to the Lord. And thou hast forgiven the wickedness of my sin.* (Ps 31:4-5)

At this time, I learned that a young woman from Roanne (to whom I have felt obligated because of her great fidelity for several years in helping your Order) was suffering from an illness that was considered to be terminal. I promptly said that she would not die from it. Regretting this haste as I generally did, I was confirmed in my confidence in You, that You would heal her after I had prayed to You, my sympathethic and merciful Physician. (1151)

I was very sad during Lent, as during other years, unable to abstain or fast completely. This sadness intensified when I heard the Preface of Holy Mass read on the Feasts of St. Matthias, St. Joseph, St. Joachim and St. Benedict, together with that of your Incarnation, my adorable Incarnate Word. You granted me multiple graces. However, I will not include them here, because I recorded the same graces and lights for each of those days elsewhere, and I do not have much time. My Love, be blessed with all benedictions.

JEANNE'S ORIGINAL DRAFT

CHAPTER CLXI

The sign of peace commenced the war against the Almighty. With her mantle, the Mother of mercy hid her Son from my sight and invited me to adore his brilliant Wounds. They reflected their rays upon me. My trip to Roanne. My tenderness toward my compatriots. My devotions. The remedies I took, and my return to Lyons. (1152)

On Wednesday of Holy Week in 1658, I thought about the preparations being made in all the churches to prepare the Paradise, the name commonly used, saying that You were placed in repose from Thursday at noon until Friday at the same time, when the priest would receive You, for he did not consecrate on that day. I wanted heaven and earth to give me the vestments with which to have You dwell within me and to contemplate your mysteries that are lovingly sorrowful and sorrowfully loving. You heard the desires of your poor one and accepted the preparation of my heart. You dispensed me that morning from my kitchen work and all temporal cares. You withdrew my thoughts, arresting my spirit in the consideraton of the treason by Judas and the sale he made at such a base price of the One who is called All-good, containing all the treasures of science, knowledge and divine wisdom. *Quia in ipso inhabitat omnis plenitudo divinitatis corporaliter. For in him dwelleth all the fullness of the Godhead corporeally.* (Col 2:9)

He waged war against You with a sign of peace, by a kiss, delivering You up to your mortal enemies who had arranged a pact with hell. In addition, You told them, Divine Prophet, that this hour was theirs and also of the power of darkness: *Hæc est hora vestra, et potestas tenebrarum; This is your hour and the power of darkness.* (Lk 22:53c) (1153)

AUTOBIOGRAPHY

JEANNE'S ORIGINAL DRAFT

As I was lost amid the terrifying darkness of the sin of Judas, You allowed me to recover myself in You, providing me daylight by your light, showing Yourself to me all covered with wounds. I would not dare declare that I experienced what St. Paul exhorts us to feel, because I do not possess all the love he desires for such an experience. I saw You as the Man of Sorrows, humbled even to emptying Yourself. Without any infringement, You are equal to your Divine Father. Being in the form of God, You assumed that of servant, indeed of a slave—of a slave sold by your traitorous disciple. My soul was confused and distressed with sorrow; and from the eyes of my heart flowed abundant blood, as I underwent the indescribable.

Unable to leave me in this keen anguish, your Blessed Mother, by a wonderful grace, placed a marvelous mantle over You, making me understand that this representation of your sorrows caused me almost to die of compassion (causing me to feel faint and almost without sensation). She gently told me that You would not die again and that I should contemplate You in a glorious state. (1154) All your saints who came after her remained five or six steps from the altar and, with ineffable goodness, she lifted me up and led me to the altar steps. Raising the miraculous mantle with which she had covered You, she invited me to adore your Wounds with her. These Wounds had become as brilliant as suns shining their adorable rays upon me. You seemed to me to be beauty personified. This Virgin Mother looked at You with a loving glance impossible for me to describe or for any artist to depict. She let me understand that You belonged to her by a marvelous possession. No other persons could possess a similar one with their children. Just as the divinity had once assumed humanity within her so as never to leave it, she would always have an infinite possession of everything that You are.

On Holy Thursday, Good Friday and Holy Saturday, I was occupied with the continuation of your goodness that the Church with extraordinary profusions represents to us during these days:

On Thursday, the Sacrament of Love through an infinite love. (1155)

322

JEANNE'S ORIGINAL DRAFT

On Friday, You died for all mankind, shedding all your Precious Blood as You prayed for the plotting Jews.

On Saturday, we prepared for your holy Resurrection, grateful that the Church calls Adam's fault a happy one that has a Redeemer as holy as He is magnificent, who has redeemed us with an abundant redemption.

On Easter Sunday, joyous, victorious and triumphant over all your enemies, You became our Easter or our passage from death to life. But it is a new life, being the death of our death and the sting of hell. On Monday, You intensified our hope; on Tuesday, You gave us your peace in which You abide.

During the week after Easter, I received letters from Roanne urging me to go there on matters referring to your Order and to accommodate my own family members because of the death of my brother-in-law.

Paris insistently urged that I go there. I wanted to consult You, my Divine Oracle, and You had me understand: *Adhuc unum modicum est, et ego commovebo cælum et terram, et movebo omnes gentes et veniet Desideratus cunctis gentibus. Yet one little while, and I will move the heaven and the earth. And I will move all nations:* AND THE DESIRED OF ALL NATIONS SHALL COME. (Hag 2:7b-8b)

I reported this to the Prior of Denicé and others after first having done so to Father Gibalin. (1156) When necessary, I will name those persons. I wrote to the Abbé de Verneuil (Piardière) to allow Gravier, my secretary, to leave Paris to accompany me to Roanne. Since I had not yet arrived when she passed there, she came all the way to Lyons, where my niece, du Mas, sent a carriage to make the trip to Roanne that was so desired and waited for by my relatives and compatriots. I felt very ill in the carriage. On the first day, I was almost faint with weakness, and when I arrived, I had to be carried to the boat. When it stopped near the headquarters for the galleys, I felt recovered and said to You: "Lord, the galley and our home town are incompatible. Nevertheless, at my entrance, I find delight there. What will it be like to see

JEANNE'S ORIGINAL DRAFT

the heavenly one, since on earth one forgets one's ills. O God, how marvelous You are!"

My joy was great when I saw the devotion that had intensified in the place of my birth. I felt inexpressible satisfaction when I adored You in the parish church where I had received the life of grace through the Sacrament of regeneration. (1157) I redoubled my prayers to the fervent, holy Levite, the first of your martyrs, Saint Stephen, who obtained many favors for me. Heaven had been opened to me several times in his church. I recalled the multitude of graces that I had received there during a period of twenty-nine years. You gave me new ones, my Divine Benefactor, on outstanding feasts. I received Communion there almost daily, taking great delight in assisting at a number of Masses at different altars. The High Masses sung there every day elevated my spirit. On solemn feasts, it was only with violence to my spirit that I left church. Seeing all these devout people, I recalled how tenderly St. John Chrysostom dealt with his people in Antioch. He was a good pastor to them, and nothing equalled this dignity.

I possess the love of a shepherdess for your sheep and lambs with whom, in a mystical, holy way, I am in a devout and more than natural society. Everything there charmed me. I did not feel my infirmities so much, and You blessed the remedies prescribed for me by the doctors. The waters of St. Herbam that I took there, without adhering to the rules ordinarily prescribed for me for them, as well as for others who take them at this time, fortified my stomach. (1158) They helped me recover such a fine bodily well-being that it was as though I had received a new constitution and health with which to pursue your Order and your glory. Added to this was the zeal that prompted the pastor and all the clergy of Roanne, as well as the outstanding and ordinary people. All this gave me great satisfaction. I prayed to You, sacred Inspiration of all good counsel, to increase your graces in us and to strengthen them in your plans, blessing them with all temporal and eternal benedictions.

On the Feast of your grandmother, Saint Anne, I was not dispensed from taking my remedies. More than an hour after attending Holy Mass and

JEANNE'S ORIGINAL DRAFT

receiving Communion, I took the medication as I always do. I did not omit Holy Communion. Even though unworthy, I had received Communion daily for thirty-nine years. I was forced to remain in my room.

This charitable princess, the mother of your august Mother, appeared to me with great affability. She assured me that she would assist me in my project for the glory of the the Word made flesh. St. Joachim, as well as she, could tell Him: "You are flesh of my flesh, being the Son of our only daughter." (1159) This delighted me, and in my simplicity I said to her: "Madame, if the pastor comes today, I will see if you want me to tell him about this apparition and what you have said to me. I do not ordinarily request signs. I would fear to be lacking in simplicity and my ordinary confidence that your Grandson would protect me from the evil spirit coming to deceive me by visions which I neither tried nor desired to have. From my youth, I have prayed to Him to lead me to Him through faith which draws souls to Him that are searching only for his glory and not their own." I was convinced, Divine Lover, that You had prompted me to ask for this sign when the pastor came to my room. He had come to visit me the previous day, and it was unusual for him to visit me so often.

I marveled at your divine providence that allowed the younger Monsieur de la Salle, a very devout clergyman, noble by virtue as well as by rank, to come bid me farewell, for he was leaving for Lyons. He went to find a return coach, and it was not until the next day that I learned that he could not depart because the mule-driver did not take him.(1160) My Divine Counselor, in this I saw that You had permitted and considered it preferable so as to show the pastor your will. My secretary took him the notebook with my writings that she had shown Monsieur de la Salle with the permission of and as Father Gibalin wished.

On the Feast of St. Ignatius, Founder of your Society, dear Jesus, total Love, I received Communion in the College church and also prayed to great St. Michael, who has assisted me so much. I was not rejected by this Prince of the Angels. Because I felt very indisposed, I was unable to return for

AUTOBIOGRAPHY

JEANNE'S ORIGINAL DRAFT

Vespers and the sermon. Instead, as I ordinarily did, I went to St. Stephen's Church which was near my sister's home. There I remained for about three months and a few days, asking St. Ignatius to pardon me for not returning to the College church. Excusing me, your goodness told me: *Veni electa mea et ponam in te thronum meum; Come, my chosen one, and I will establish my throne in you.* (Common of Virgins). He loved me as much in this church where I was alone with him and his saints, who were filled with delight in his divine will. He elevated my spirit, and I received favors that I could certainly feel but not express.

On a number of other occasions, I have expressed how assiduous I was in this church, whether on solemn feasts or ferial days during the said three months. This lasted from May twenty-fifth until the birth of your wonderful Mother. (1161)

After receiving Communion in her chapel of the Holy Rosary, I wept with emotion and received the benediction of the priest whom I considered my dear pastor in this place. I took leave of all these wise and devout clergymen, keenly regretting that I had to leave them all. I was extremely upset until I had passed the Loire River. Then You stopped my tears, telling me that You had allowed these tender feelings to show me that I was the spiritual daughter of his holy Society and a dear confrere with all my fellow-citizens. You had blessed them and would bless them more and more until the end by fulfilling your promises to me for your glory and their sanctification. I reflected upon the following words of the Prophet Isaias: *Ecce ego mitam in fundamentis Sion lapidem, probatum angularem, pretiosum, in fundamento fundatum; qui crediderit, non festinet. I will lay a stone in the foundations of Sion, a tried stone, a corner stone, a precious stone, founded in the foundation. He that believeth, let him not hasten.* (Is 28:16c)

The coach in which I traveled was more comfortable than my niece's, which I refused even though it was beautiful with fine, expensive horses. (1162) Yet it lacked the air that this one had that I found to be more convenient for me. Monsieur Dumas, my nephew, wanted me to travel with his

JEANNE'S ORIGINAL DRAFT

nephew, Monsieur Paradis, who was going to Avignon to receive the habit of your Society, my Jesus and my All.

The next day, Monsieur Dumas and his companion returned to Roanne, grateful that I had not become ill. I adored You in your Sacrament of love. I found You to be replete with gentleness upon your holy mountain. You let me know that (although most unworthy of your favors) I was welcome. You said to me: *Transivi per te, et vidi te; et ecce tempus tuum, tempus amantium; Et expandi amictum meum super te. [...] Juravit tibi, et ingressus sum pactum tecum, (ait Dominus Deus) et facta est mihi: Et lavi te aqua, et emundavi sanguinem tuum ex te. I passed by thee and saw thee: and behold thy time was the time of lovers: and I spread my garment over thee. And I swore to thee and I entered into a covenant with thee, saith the Lord God. And thou becamest mine. And I washed thee with water and cleansed away thy blood from thee.* (Ez 16:8-9)

You let me know that You had found acceptable the waters, the bleedings and all the remedies I had taken in Roanne which You had blessed as I already said. I received all the visits from poor persons with greater joy than from the rich, despite the inconvenience I might have from this. This affected the time of my taking the remedies, and I had supper at either 7, 8, 9 or 10 o'clock in the evening. Sometimes, I had none at all. So as not to miss my daily Communion and attend the homily, I did not take the waters until 7, 8 or sometimes 9 o'clock. (1163) Unable to leave church without doing violence to the fascinating attractions of your goodness, sometimes on solemn feast-days I did not drink anything or take a laxative. I would resume them then, and this surprised the physicians that such interruptions did not cause me any problem. Being in a better frame of mind, I resumed my occupations with greater strength, for I needed my health in order to relieve and assist almost all my daughters whom I found ill and infirm upon my return from Roanne even though they had spent a great deal on food and medicine. I continued my work as a cook and directed almost all the charges in the house, which are my enjoyment, without omitting my interior application to your loving mysteries. Amid the andirons and pots, I experienced mystical sleep, obtaining from You

JEANNE'S ORIGINAL DRAFT

the wings of a dove, persevering in my open and sincere simplicity. I corrected the faults that displeased You, that were contrary to your Spirit who cannot dwell in double hearts. (1164) From Ecclesiasticus, I learned: *Væ duplici corde, et labiis scelestis, et manibus malefacientibus, et peccatori terram ingredienti duabus viis! Woe to them that are of a double heart, and to wicked lips, and to the hands that do evil, and to the sinner that goeth on the earth two ways.* (Sir 2:14)

It does not surprise me that St. Peter could not endure the lie of Ananias and Sapphira, because they were lying to the Holy Spirit by whose authority, as well as by yours, Incarnate Word—who are the truth—he deprived them of life and had them removed to be buried by those at the door who witnessed the lie to which they had assented. This caused great dread and fear to everyone who heard that lying to the Holy Spirit is difficult to pardon: *Et factus est timor magnus in universa ecclesia, et in omnes qui audierunt hæc. And there came great fear upon the whole church and upon all that heard these things.* (Acts 5:11)

I could not record here the just punishment by sudden death or accident of ten or twelve persons who invented malicious calumnies against the one You deign to protect by your goodness, not for any merit of her own. She belongs entirely to You, of You, by You and for You. I have prayed that You would pardon their eternal guilt, merciful Savior, as I do for those who continue to offend me. I also pray that You may forgive me my sins. (1165)

Holy Gabriel, pray to the Incarnate Word, our Love, to curtail the weeks of untruths and to put an end to sin. May He apply the merits of his death to us, sanctifying us through the divine anointing of his most Holy Spirit. May the daughter of desire possess peace. May the great Prince St. Michael come to our aid to conquer with us all those who resist the divine will. May all the heavenly princes praise the One whom Daniel saw as a river of charity: *Flavius igneus rapidusque egrediebatur a facie eius; millia millium ministrabant ei, et decies millies centena millia assistebant ei. A swift stream of fire issued forth from before him: thousands of thousands*

JEANNE'S ORIGINAL DRAFT

ministered to him, and ten thousand times a hundred thousand stood before him. (Dan 7:10)

Holy Prophet, be my protector against all the enemies of truth, which, for the glory of the Ancient of Days, will be victorious and will triumph over everything. May we experience the effects of the oracles of the Apostle Saint Paul: *[Sancti] qui per fidem vicerunt regna, operati sunt justitiam, adepti sunt repromissiones. Sancti Dei omnes intercedere dignemini pro nostra omniumque salute. Lætamini in Domino et exultate iusti et g l o r i a m i n i omnes recti corde. Who by faith conquered kingdoms, wrought justice, obtained promises.* (Heb 11:33) *All ye Saints of God, deign to intercede for all of us and for our salvation. (Not biblical) Be glad in the Lord, and rejoice, ye just: and glory, all ye right of heart.* (Ps 31:11) (1166)

CHAPTER CLXII

My devotions, St. Martin, the Presentation of the Blessed Virgin, St. Cecilia, St. Catherine, St. Andrew and St. Xavier, who embraced You as You lay stretched out upon your Cross. A crayfish was his page of honor; like a phoenix, he was reborn upon the couch of your Heart which appeared open to him.

The Feast of All Saints arrived in whom You are admirable: *Exultabunt sancti in gloria, lætabuntur in cubilibus suis. The saints shall rejoice in glory: they shall be joyful in their beds.* (Ps 149:5)

I was thrilled with joy for their glory and rejoiced because of their rest,

JEANNE'S ORIGINAL DRAFT

praying that they would praise your greatness with holy compliments. Let their throats vibrate with exultation as they praise You. May they take up the sword of your absolute power to wreak justice upon those who do not adhere to your plans. I understood the following words to be uttered in justice: *Ut faciant in eis iudicium conscriptum: gloria hæc est omnibus sanctis eius. To execute upon them the judgment that is written. This glory is to all his saints.* (Ps 149:9) (1167)

On the Feast of great St. Martin, I prayed to him to resist the one who told him, during his mortal pilgrimage, that he would always oppose him. I begged him to continue the favors he had done me for a number of consecutive years for the one who has great confidence in his merit. This flaming heart, that appeared bearing a sword of fire upon his head, did not disdain the frailty of a young woman. In charity, he favored her, preparing her for the arrival and departure of the King with ineffable blessings.

Magnificent Benefactor, You granted me great favors on the Feast of the Presentation of your precious Blessed Mother. I understood that the entire Blessed Trinity received more from this offering than whatever heaven and earth might offer You. In all rejoicing, the Holy Spirit wanted to form a body for You from her pure substance that, together with your holy soul, would be united by the hypostatic union to your Divine Person. (1168) One would mutually support the Other. Through Him, this wonderful Mother pronounced or entoned her canticle: *Magnificat anima mea Dominum: et exultavit spiritus meus in Deo salutari meo, etc. My soul doth magnify the Lord. And my spirit hath rejoiced in God my Saviour.* (Lk 1:46-47)

The following day was the Feast of the melodious Virgin, St. Cecilia, who praised You according to the desires of your cantor, the Royal Prophet: *In psalterio et cithara; in ty7mpano et choro; in chordis et organo; in cymbalis benesonantibus; in cymbalis jubilationis. With psaltery and harp; with timbrel and choir; with strings and organ; on high sounding cymbals; on cymbals of joy.* (Ps 150:3-6) The Psalms end thus: *Omnis spiritus laudet Dominum; Let every spirit praise the Lord.* (Ps 150:6)

JEANNE'S ORIGINAL DRAFT

It was very early when You were pleased to elevate my soul to You, granting me inexpressible graces. In accordance with your magnificence, they were magnificently great, for You favored me with an ineffable extension of your loving Incarnation. For a long time, your Holy Spirit, in the form of a dove with extended wings, remained suspended over my head and upon my breast. Your providence prepared me while I was still in bed. (1169) Around three o'clock in the morning, You repeatedly allowed me to hear: *Fundabo te in sapphiris; I will lay thy foundations with sapphires.* (Is 54:11c) To me, his repetition was music that enraptured me. I could not withstand so much delight when not in bed without fainting like an Esther.

The following day, the Feast of St. Clement, Pope, I wanted to focus my conversation in heaven so as there to marvel at the manner of adoring the suavity of your clemency. You let us hope for this wonderful Resurrection, which will make our bodies impassible, communicating to them the qualities of your glorious one in accordance with your goodness.

With the learned and holy Catherine, I wanted to confound earthly wisdom by your teaching that places milk and honey upon our tongue. The mouth You promised to your Apostles would have converted all the philosophers of earth into children desirous of the milk alluded to by St. Peter. (1170) All who are in the darkness of error were favored by seeing this great, marvelous light that You communicated to the holy patriarch of Alexandria, who proclaimed You to be equal to your Divine Father: *Deum de Deo, lumen de lumine, Deum verum de Deo vero. God of God, Light of light, true God of true God.* (Credo) Begotten, not made, born amid the splendor of eternal holiness before all ages. By You, they were made.

On the Feast of St. Andrew whom You strongly and gently love, I recalled how he had heard your holy Precursor who had called You the Lamb of God who takes away the sins of the world. He followed You even to the Cross. There he had the favor of preaching your marvels and of being sacrificed for You after having offered You in Sacrifice upon the altar, giving You to the faithful in this Sacrament of love and death.

JEANNE'S ORIGINAL DRAFT

On the Feast of the zealous St. Francis Xavier, the flames of whose ardent charity could not be extinguished by the entire sea, he could proclaim when he was dying that your lamps are all of fire, embracing You extended upon your Cross. (1171) The crayfish had taken You to him in its claws, serving as his page of honor. It might also be considered a ship that brought him bread from afar with which he was holily satisfied. He could say: *"Satis est Domine, satis est; That is enough, Lord, that it is enough."* His mortal life ended in your holy embraces and divine ardors, and he was reborn like a phoenix upon the loving couch of your divine Heart that was open to him just as he had opened his breast to You when your flames impelled him to expire, gasping for breath and finding the world too small in which to serve such a great God, who returned his voice and speech to him. Thus, it could be declared of him: *In omnem terram exivit sonus eorum, et in fines orbis terræ verba eorum. In sole posuit tabernaculum suum; et ipse tamquam sponsus procedens de thalamo suo. Exultavit ut gigas ad currendam viam; Nec est qui se abscondat a calore eius.* (1172) *Their sound hath gone forth into all the earth: and their words unto the ends of the world. He hath set his tabernacle in the sun: and he, as a bridegroom coming out of his bride chamber, hath rejoiced as a giant to run the way. There is no one that can hide himself from his heat.* (Ps 18:5-6; 7c)

His commissions were prodigious; his apostolic zeal made of him a great Apostle and a very great saint.

JEANNE'S ORIGINAL DRAFT

CHAPTER CLXIII

Saint Anne is the source of the fountain and inspiration of life. Saint Joachim and Saint Anne have been united in Mary, their daughter, and, through her, in Jesus Christ.

On the Feast of the Immaculate Conception of your all-pure Mother, I was treated with great benignity by your most gentle Spirit in the form of a dove. He showed me the inexpressible, marvelous fecundity of your grandmother, Saint Anne. He taught me that she resembled the one she loved and was the delight of the whole adorable Trinity. (1173) The Eternal Father accepted the Daughter par excellence from her. The Son revered her as the person who cared for and nurtured a Mother who was and would be the miracle of miracles. The Holy Spirit illuminated and protected her as the source of the fountain and potentiality of life from whom He wished to form a body for the Increated Word who would be the Incarnate Word, the glory and beatitude of angels and mankind. He then gave me foretastes and New Year's gifts, elevating me in spirit by a sublime, rapturous contemplation. I recalled the following verses that I had composed and recited during my early years while still at my father's house. In a holy rapture and transport of love, I wrote:

Ferme la bouche à la plainte,	Refrain from any complaint,
Mère de la Vierge sainte,	Mother of the Blessed Virgin,
Ah ! c'est assez soupiré	Oh! cease your sighing
De ce que ton flanc stérile	That your sterile womb,
Sans rien produire, infertile,	Remained infertile
A si longtemps demeuré.	For a time so long.
(1174)	

JEANNE'S ORIGINAL DRAFT

Que la tristesse passée
Soit tout à fait effacée,
Et qu'on ne me trouve point
Dans le grand enclos du monde
Une femme si féconde
Qu'elle t'égale en ce point.

Let all past sadness
Be wholly erased,
No one will ever find
In the world's great expanse
Any woman so fertile
Who can equal you in this.

La voix la mieux accordante
N'est de chanter suffisante
Tes privilèges divers,
O du Tout-Puissant l'aïeule
Dont la fille toute seule
Vaut plus que tout l'univers.

The most delightful voice
Can never sufficiently chant
Your varied privileges,
O, grandmother of the Almighty
Whose daughter all alone
Outvalues the entire universe.

Si l'arbre de vie on appelle
Cette divine pucelle,
C'est à bon droit que je dis
Que la terre où prend racine
Une plante si divine
Est un second paradis.

If the term "Tree of Life"
Applies to this holy Virgin
I can rightfully declare
That the earth from which sprang
The rooted plant so divine
Is a second Paradise!

Si, mise au parangon d'elle
La lune semble moins belle
Et Phébus moins rayonnant,
A bon droit je te préfère
A la plus belle sphère
Qui nous aille couronnant.
 (1175)

If, compared to her
The moon is less lovely
And Phoebe less brilliant,
Rightly do I prefer you
To the loveliest orb
That ever encircled us.

At the beginning of Genesis and alluding to Adam and Eve, Sacred Scripture declares: *Erunt duo in carne una; They shall be two in one flesh.* (Gen 2:24c) Thus, St. Joachim, husband of St. Anne, and she are united and one in Mary, their daughter, by anthonomasie, and through her, in You, Divine

JEANNE'S ORIGINAL DRAFT

Word made flesh of her flesh. Yet your flesh is the life of the world, supported by the divine hypostasis. The Holy Spirit reposes upon it and makes his dwelling there. Thus, there was a change in the words uttered against the sinful giants who, by their vices and spirit, had corrupted their body at the time of the deluge. *Non permanebit spiritus meus in homine in æternum, quia caro est. My spirit shall not remain in man for ever, because he is flesh.* (Gen 6:3)

Through Isaias, the holy Prophet of the royal race, He declared that He had in regret changed his justice, coming to us so as, according to the inclinations of his goodness, to assure us that this spirit of purity would repose over the humble Joachim and the faithful Anne whose name is grace.

Through St. Joachim, I beg You, my Divine Savior, to prepare within me a dwelling-place for You and, by the grace of St. Anne, please to adorn it: *Verbo Domini cæli firmati sunt; et spiritu oris eius omnis vertus eorum. By the word of the Lord the heavens were established: and all the power of them by the spirit of his mouth.* (Ps 32:6)   (1176)

JEANNE'S ORIGINAL DRAFT

CHAPTER CLXIV

One must not judge by appearances, but leave the judgment to God who sees the heart and the eyes. He alone can dry the tears of his beloved whom He fortifies during the painful afflictions on the miraculous night. The day that God became Man, He came as our Love.

Just as on earth there are no roses without thorns, while the humble and saintly ones of heaven favored me, the envious ones on earth (thirsting for their own glory) used every means by which to persecute me. Under the guise of zeal for your glory, the demons, who never sleep, incited them to blame and curse what they could not comprehend. By a spirit as precipitate as a whirlwind, they condemned patient perseverance as laxity or coldness. They did not bear in mind, my Savior, that your Spirit is not present in the whirlwind of their natural enterprise and impetuosity, nor in the fire of their presumption. (1177) Also, your ancestor David warned us not to rise before daybreak during the time we eat the bread of sorrow or, full of anguish, drink the waters of tribulation. That is what has been, what is and what will still be the ordinary food of my spirit upheld by my physical prostration. The sufferings that for a number of years I have endured would have caused the death of others, but You have supported me with the Bread of the strong. Also, You declared: *Parasti in conspectu meo mensam, adversus eos qui tribulant me. Thou hast prepared a table before me, against them that afflict me.* (Ps 22:5)

It is your fatherly goodness that allows me to endure so many multiple persecutions, even by my dear daughters among whom I wanted to rest peacefully from the business matters regarding my houses. Grant me the same degree of spirit and blessing that your love allowed the Prophet-King when he lived in this sorrowful life. His son Absalom forced him to leave his throne temporarily and, through ill-prepared and violent measures, made him

JEANNE'S ORIGINAL DRAFT

leave Jerusalem with a small number of faithful friends and pass the torrent of Cedron, taking along the Ark of the Covenant and of your marvels. (1178) He had it carried throughout the city, trusting in your will, for he had renounced his own: *Et dixit rex ad Sadoc: reporta arcam Dei in urbem: Si invenero gratiam in oculis Domini, reducet me, et ostendet mihi eam, et tabernaculum suum. Si autem dixerit mihi: Non places: presto sum, faciat quod bonum est coram se. And the king said to Sadoc: Carry back the ark of God into the city. If I shall find grace in the sight of the Lord, he will bring me again: and he will shew me it, and his tabernacle. But if he shall say to me: Thou pleasest me not: I am ready. Let him do that which is good before him.* (2 Sam 15:25-26)

He told Sadoc the priest: *Videns, revertere in civitatem in pace; Porro David ascendebat clivum Olivarum, scandens et flens, nudis pedibus incedens, et operto capite, sed et omnis populus, qui erat cum eo, operto capite, ascendebat plorans. Seer, return into the city in peace; But David went up by the ascent of Olivet, going up and weeping, walking barefoot, and with his head covered: and all the people that were with them, went up with their heads covered weeping.* (2 Sam 15:27a; 30)

Having learned that Architophel had joined the conspiracy of Absalom, he said to You: *Infatus quæso Domine consilium Architophel; Infatuate, O Lord, I beseech thee, the counsel of Achitophel.* (2 Sam 15:31) My Lord and my God, your providence allowed the advice of Chusai, a friend of David's, to be preferred to his. This prompted Achitophel to hang himself after having left the affairs of his house in order, forgetting the eternal ones and the salvation of his soul. (1179) Trusting in You, David had his prayer answered. Too much had he loved his rebellious son Absalom, who had caused him to leave Jerusalem through his presumptuous pride. He dangled from a tree by his hair, the sign of his vanity, to be pierced through by three lances. Then his body was thrown into a great hole and covered with rocks. His heart had been harder than marble toward David, his loving father, who possessed one of melted wax. This prompted him to say and repeat: *Absalom fili mi, fili mi Absalom: quis mihi tribuat ut ego moriar pro te, Absalom*

JEANNE'S ORIGINAL DRAFT

fili mi, fili mi Absalom. My son Absalom, Absalom my son! Would to God that I might die for thee, Absalom my son, my son Absalom! (2 Sam 18:33b)

Absalom had pretended to present his respects to You and offer You sacrifice in gratitude for the deliverance he had obtained through the goodness of his father David, who told him: *Vade in pace. Et surrexit, et abiit in Hebron. Misit autem Absalom exploratores in universas tribus Israel, dicens: Statim ut audieritis clangorem buccinæ, dicite: Regnavit Absalom in Hebron. Go in peace. And he arose, and went to Hebron. And Absalom sent spies into all the tribes of Israel, saying: As soon as you shall hear the sound of the trumpet, say ye: Absalom reigneth in Hebron.* (2 Sam 15:9-10) (1180)

The two hundred men whom he had selected to go to Jerusalem: *Euntes simplici corde, et causam penitus ignorantes. Accersivit quoque Absalom Achitophel Gilonitem consiliarium David, de civitate sua Gilo. Cumque immolaret victimas, facta est conjuratio valida, populusque concurrens augebatur cum Absalom. Venit igitir nuntius ad David, dicens: Toto corde universus Israel seguitur Absalom. Going with simplicity of heart, and knowing nothing of the design. Absalom also sent for Achitophel the Gilonite, David's counsellor, from his city Gilo. And while he was offering sacrifices, there was a strong conspiracy: and the people running together increased with Absalom. And there came a messenger to David, saying: All Israel with their whole heart followeth Absalom.* (2 Sam 15:11b-13)

To save his life and that of his faithful people, but more especially that of his son Absalom, David left Jerusalem and acted as described above. He commanded Joab and his entire army to preserve his son Absalom for him. His son reigned in David's heart, since the soul of the beloved resides more in the object of its love than in its own body which it animates. Spurned by this perfidious, rebellious son, all these paternal favors, were converted through your just indignation into the type of death that his pride merited. Alas, alas!

JEANNE'S ORIGINAL DRAFT

my Sovereign Judge! I fear that only at the end will we know all the disorder caused by the contrivances of those who aspired after and passionately sought power in this world. This will astound all ages to come. (1181)

Those taken advantage of because of their simplicity contend that people seeking honors and temporal rule who merit being in charge, could very well change their mind about this some day. Let me know your divine will, my Sacred Oracle, either through the code You taught and gave me so as to know it or else through inspiration.

My daughter, you can readily see that those unaware of my plans judge according to appearances. As for Me, I consider the heart and, through my goodness, yours which I form according to my own. I have opened it to view like a Samuel: *Positus a Deo; Placed by God.*

You know, Lord, that I have not received the temporal support from those that I have governed as Mother and tried to enlighten and instruct according to your will. Instead, I am spurned; I, who desire nothing other than your love, my dear Love.

My daughter, I Myself feel the effects of the impertinences and injustices of the persons who oppose my will instead of seeking to comply with it. (1182) I have waited a long time. In my anger, I swear that they shall not enter into my eternal rest. I will not give my glory to anyone else. I am the Omnipotent Lord.

My Lord, You know that, at these words, my heart melted through my eyes as two fountains of tears that I offered You. You did not reject them, telling me that I was like the steadfast Mount Sion; that I was Deborah, Mother of Israel; that I should judge your people under the palm tree of your victories. You told me that I was to erect a temple. With one hand, I should do the work and with the other, I should hold the sword as was done by the two great captains when your Jerusalem was being rebuilt and your temple purified.

JEANNE'S ORIGINAL DRAFT

Great Saint Lucy lengthened the days, although they did not enlighten me completely. As the sun drew closer, I entered into your influence, even though I had not learned the teachings nor maxims of politics. (1183) As I perceived your greatness seated above the Cherubim, who regarded and penetrated the abysses, I was confirmed in my expectations. St. Thomas performed great favors for me. Ever since he said: *Dominus meus, et Deus meus; My Lord and my God* (Jn 20:28), he has served as an abyss of grace and glory. An abyss of confusion invoked him, animated by your compassion for my afflictions which You relieved in a way inexpressible to me.

You saw me weeping over the blindness of someone elevated by your goodness and confirmed in this greatness as a result of the prayers that your unworthy one offered You for that person which You did not reject. Our charitable physician, Monsieur Guillemin, who does not remain indifferent to whatever perturbs me, was deeply moved by my tears, for he is generous. He did not want me to notice his charitable affliction, leaving me to my sufferings in the parlor (because it was somewhat late--about 5 o'clock in the evening.)

I crossed my room to go pour out my heart (1184) through my eyes near your tabernacle. Whenever it pleases You, You make it your great miracle, your antithesis and antiperistasis through this limited amount of water cast out or flowing upon the heart that You set ablaze. You made it completely ardent and our lamps well lit that no river or torrent could ever restrain or interrupt. Were the richest of men to give all his substance to which, as to his glory, he is deeply attached, the soul united to You, my Divine Beloved, esteems all these grandeurs as but a bit of straw, meaning to say, a mere nothing. At the door of your Paradise, You dried my tears; that is, when I entered the chapel to be near your altar. On Christmas night, you let me understand: *Veni in hortum meum, soror mea, sponsa; Messui myrrham meam cum arromatibus meis; Comedi favum cum melle meo; Bibi vinum meum cum lacte meo. I am come into my garden, O my sister, my spouse. I have gathered my myrrh, with my aromatical spices. I have eaten the honeycomb with my honey. I have drunk my wine with my milk.* (Cant 5:1)

JEANNE'S ORIGINAL DRAFT

You were all flower and fruit to me, not only on this night, the miracle of days, but, during the entire Octave of your innocent, miraculous birth. (1185) Also, You said to me: "My daughter, you are criticized for calling me your Love and greeting others in this Name. The important ones on earth find that to be excessive. The Apostle who was raised up to Paradise witnessed the excess of this love. He greeted the Corinthians in the Lord: *Salutant vos in Domino multum; Salutant vos omnes fratres. Salutatio, mea manu Pauli. Si quis non amat Dominum Nostrum Jesum Christum sit anathema, Maran Atha. Salute you much in the Lord. All the brethren salute you. The salutation of me Paul, with my own hand. If any man love not our Lord Jesus Christ, let him be anathema, maran-atha.* (1 Cor 16:19b; 20; 21-22)

Then he added: *Gratia Domini nostri Jesus Christi vobiscum. Charitas mea omnibus vobis in Christo Jesu. Amen. The grace of our Lord Jesus Christ be with you. My charity be with you all in Christ Jesus. Amen.* (1 Cor 16:23-24) (1186)

JEANNE'S ORIGINAL DRAFT

CHAPTER CLXV

1659

New Year's gifts that Divine Love gave his bride. He is the flourishing Spouse and blessed field. The bride resembles the ewes that enter and leave the cleansing-place totally pure, close together and like doves that nest in the niche of the hidden rock where she feeds and rests, contemplating the rivers of grace and the unity of the essence and distinction of the Persons.

On the Feast of your Circumcision in 1659, You were all goodness to me, Divine Child. As a New Year's gift, You gave me your Blood and your hope, having enraptured mine through the excess of your love and the splendor of your beauty. Your anointing caused your all-benign graces to explode in splendor, reproducing You marvellously. I adored the reproductions of You upon our altars. One must become blinded by these lights and say with David: *Dominus illuminatio mea et salus mea. Et nox sicut dies illuminabitur; et nox illuminatio mea in deliciis meis. The Lord is my light and my salvation. And night shall be light as the day; and night shall be my light in my pleasures.* (Ps 26:1a; 138: 12b; 11b)

The Feast of Kings and its entire Octave were days to pray to You for peace, that your prophets might be acknowledged to be true, and that You would deign to confirm in your heavenly Jerusalem what You had allowed to be understood on earth. You could well do so satisfactorily, as indicated by the following words of the Apocalypse: *Nunc facta est salus, et virtus, et regnum Dei nostri, gloriam regni tui dicem. Now is come salvation and strength and the kingdom of our God. Gloriam regni tui dicem; I will speak of the glory of your kingdom.* (Ap 12:10b, 12) (1187)

On the Feast of St. Hilary and St. Paul the first hermit, You gave me many graces that it would take too long to record. In addition, right now I have a

JEANNE'S ORIGINAL DRAFT

bad headache. I will leave them for some other place, having already reported them to Father Gibalin, my director.

On the 17th, I asked this great anchorite Father of so many holy monks to visit us and that heaven might thereby multiply its graces to make us more acceptable to the One who is the flower of the fields and the lily of the valleys and who said: *Pulchritudo agri mecum est; With me is the beauty of the field.* (Ps 49:11b) Flourishing Spouse, You are your Divine Father's blessed field. The bride who leaves herself to enter into You benefits from supreme beauties; leaving nothing, she enters into everything.

On the Feast of St. Peter's Chair, You treated me with magnificence. I saw a crowned procession in which one of my daughters participated. With everyone else, she sang: *Lætatus sum in his quæ dicta sum mihi: in domum Domini ibimus, etc. I rejoiced at the things that were said to me: We shall go into the house of the Lord.* (Ps 121:1) (1188)

The earthly court had departed from Lyons; the heavenly one descended there to give me celestial, divine favors. With royal benevolence, it lodged in the dwelling that belongs entirely to You. You allowed me to understand that it is your mansion and pleasant Sion, reciting the Psalm: *Fundamenta eius in montibus sanctis; diligit Dominus portas Sion super omnia tabernacula Jacob. Gloriosa dicta sunt de te, civitas Dei!* etc. *The foundations thereof are in the holy mountains: The Lord loveth the gates of Sion above all the tabernacles of Jacob. Glorious things are said of thee: O city of God.* etc. (Ps 86:1-3)

You told me that You preferred the very doors of this Sion to all the tabernacles of Jacob. I had pleased You by my retreat, since I had not gone down to see what attracts hearts through the eyes and obligates them through the ears. They become enslaved by the apparent pleasures of the world that is totally set in wickedness, as your beloved disciple declared. He forebade his spiritual children to love the world and whatever belongs to it: *Nolite diligere mundum, neque ea quæ in mundo sunt. Love not the world, nor the*

JEANNE'S ORIGINAL DRAFT

things which are in the world. (1 Jn 2:15) (1189)

The soul that remains in retreat and solitude experiences what the Prophet Jeremias pointed out, in addition to other things: *Sedebit solitarius, et tacebit, quia levavit super se. He shall sit solitary and hold his peace: because he hath taken it up upon himself.* (Lam 3:28)

My strength will be in hope and in silence: *Pars mea Dominus, dixit anima mea; propterea expectabo eum. The Lord is my portion, said my soul: therefore will I wait for him.* (Lam 3:24) If He delays, I must be patient. He will come because He wants to be desired with desire: *Qui crediderit in eum, non confundetur. He that shall believe in him shall not be confounded.* (1 Pet 2:6c)

I yearn for You, my Savior, as the desire of the eternal hills, and, with St. Peter, tell You that I cannot go to anyone else but You who eminently possess the Word of life. Three times You asked St. Peter if he loved You more than anything else You saw present and more than all that You were entrusting to him: the whole Church, all the lambs and sheep You committed to him to feed with spiritual nourishment, the Bread of Life and understanding.

On the 20th, I reflected upon the arrows of the noble and marvelous martyr, St. Sebastian. (1190) They were completely brilliant, enrapturing heaven and earth. I marveled at his steadfast generosity. He could gloriously declare: *Tetendit arcum suum, et posuit me quasi signum ad sagittam; misit in renibus meis filias pharetræ suæ. He hath bent his bow and set me as a mark for his arrows. He hath shot into my reins the daughters of his quiver.* (Lam 3:12-13)

His body was almost completely riddled, and his spirit took flight, flying to your open side, not only because of the lance of Longinus, but more through the love of your heart that was distressed by love itself. You preferred its Wounds to any healing. They are the doors of justice through which the just enter. Also, they are the doors of charity by which loving souls enter, adoring

JEANNE'S ORIGINAL DRAFT

and loving You. When they do leave, it is with the abundance of favors and blessings that they distribute to their neighbors.

The next day, I admired the fine grace of your marvelous Agnes whose cheeks were adorned by the Precious Blood, the source of beauty. I thought that she and her saintly companions were like sheep that enter and leave this sacred cleansing-place all-pure and like doves in the niches of the rock where they find their repose. (1191) There I perceived all good things to greater advantage than Moses did, although he had entreated You for the favor of seeing your face. This was because You had loved him and filled him with blessings even by his name, having had him withdrawn from the waters by Pharaoh's daughter. Because of your love for him, You made a passage for him and all your people through the Red Sea. You went before him, and spoke to him: *Loquebatur autem Dominus ad Moysem facie ad faciem, sicut solet loqui homo ad amicum suum. And the Lord spoke to Moses face to face, as a man is wont to speak to his friend.* (Ex 33:11) Afterward, You gave him so many signs of friendship: *Non poteris videre faciem meam: non enim videbit me homo, et vivet. Thou canst not see my face: for man shall not see me and live.* (Ex 33:20)

All the graces I want to give you are: *Ecce inquit, est locus apud me, et stabis supra petram. Cumque transibit gloria mea, ponam te in foramine petræ, et protegam: dextera mea, donec transeam: tollamque manum meam, et videbis posteriora mea: faciem autem meam videre non poteris.* (1192) *Behold there is a place with me, and thou shalt stand upon the rock. And when my glory shall pass, I will set thee in a hole of the rock, and protect thee with my right hand, till I pass. And I will take away my hand, and thou shalt see my back parts: but my face thou canst not see.* (Ex 33:21-23)

Dear Love, the law set on paper is not the law of grace imprinted in hearts nor spread throughout the heavens by your own Heart to which You lovingly invite your virginal spouses for their delicious meal and delightful repose. They do not live of their human life, but of your divine one. For You, they have

JEANNE'S ORIGINAL DRAFT

endured martyrdom and cruel death, thereby vanquishing tyrants. Neither irons nor hell appalled them, no matter how young they were. Doves found their niches in You and noticed the water and blood. Like St. John, their eyes, cleansed with milk, fixed their gaze upon your rivers of grace: *Super rivulos aquarum, quæ lacte sunt lotæ, et resident juxta fluenta plenissima. (His eyes as doves) upon brooks of waters, which are washed with milk, and sit beside the plentiful streams.* (Cant 5:12)

They contemplate the unity of essence and distinction of supports that are rivers as abundant as their source. (1193) The entire nature belongs to the Son and to the Holy Spirit with the same plenitude as belonging to the Father, who is called the fountain of the whole divine Trinity. My Savior, You granted me great favors on the Feast of the Conversion of your Apostle of glory, since he was called by You, Lord of glory, at the hour of midday. Since he was under your influence, You drew St. Paul by your light. Jericho had been conquered by the sound of trumpets, for the ark carried by the Levites had circled it seven times. Saint Paul had been conquered and vanquished by your splendor and your voice that was more powerful than the sound of trumpets.

O dear Love, if it pleased You to change your enemies who persecuted You into vessels of election and dilection, what joy in heaven to learn that these persecutors became your preachers in imitation of them, submitting to your will in everything! You can do so, Incarnate Word, because You are omnipotent, all-wise and all-good. (1194) Your paranymph Gabriel told your Virgin Mother: *Quia non erit impossibile apud Deum omne Verbum. Because no word shall be impossible with God.* (Lk 1:37)

On the 26th, I contemplated the ardent flame burning in the heart of St. Polycarp. It taught me that grace triumphs although nature may be weakened by old age that is all ice. Totally warlike in adolescence and all afire during manhood, in his old age, David became all ice. The gates of the Empyrean were not opened in the Written Law to prompt one by the desire to enter there at death. One had to descend to Limbo, even were he the brilliant, zealous John the Baptist or Saint Joseph, Saint Joachim or Saint Anne. It was

JEANNE'S ORIGINAL DRAFT

befitting—in fact, expedient and necessary—for Christ to depart, that He die and be buried, that He descend into the inferior parts of the earth to provide strength and courage to the holy souls imprisoned there and raise them up near Him before He ascended above all the heavens to become the supreme heaven. (1195) Through the prophetic spirit, David had declared this: *Christus ascendens in altum captivam duxit captivitatem, dedit dona hominibus. Ascending on high, he led captivity captive: he gave gifts to men.* (Ps 67:19; Eph 4:8)

St. Polycarp received these gifts. He is inflamed by his ardent love for his Sovereign Pontiff who has penetrated the heavens all inflamed after having spread fire upon earth. He desired to make hearts blaze, creating a furnace in them whose flame rises up to Him, the Man-God. He is all fire and flame that the waters of sin could never extinguish. Neither could the jealousy of hell diminish his charity toward mankind. He knows those who belong to Him. Having tested them in these furnaces, He accepts them as holocausts.

On the 27th, I marveled at the eloquence of St. John Chrysostom, which proceeded from the purified love in his heart, whose abundance prompted this Golden Mouth to speak. It is the river of Paradise that is clearer than crystal. It is this river of fire that proceeds from the power of God. (1196) This great saint became one with Him at all times, especially during the celebration of the formidable mysteries during which the superelevated Powers tremble and the heavenly Dominations adore with holy fear. The Seraphim veil their feet and face, unceasingly chanting: *Holy, Holy, Holy.*

On the 28th, I became ecstatic upon seeing a virgin carrying a lamb. She was accompanied by a retinue of resplendent virgins who sang in marvelous harmony. They flew and danced to a wonderful rhythm which could only be imitated or sung by the integrity of the winged clouds admired by the Prophet Isaias, even though he did not know whom they represented. He exclaimed: *Qui sunt isti qui ut nubes volant, et quasi colombæ ad fenestras suas? Who are these who fly as clouds and as doves to their windows?* (Is 60:8)

JEANNE'S ORIGINAL DRAFT

Holy Prophet, they are virgins adorned with white and red in whom the sun is reproduced as in clouds. They are doves that have the right to enter through their windows which are the Sacred Wounds of the greatest Savior wherein they dwell as most pure brides on the feast of his grandeurs. (1197) The great Cardinal Berulle has perceived this very well, arranging for his holy Congregation to solemnize it by a magnificent feast with a lovely Octave. There the eyes of love are marvelous ascensions: *Sublevatis oculis in cælum, dixit: Pater, venit hora. Lifting up his eyes to heaven, he said: Father, the hour is come.* (Jn 17:1b)

On leaving the world to go to his Father, this imperial Eagle shared his own elevations with his eaglet, the virgin St. John, by the contemplation of his adorable lights that were most brilliant rays from the Sun of Justice. He totally satisfied his Father to give us his gentle illuminations that were his own before the creation of the world. He possessed them in his glory as the splendor and figure of his substance, the entire word of his power, the image of his goodness and the stainless mirror of the Majesty. (1198)

I cannot express the graces I joyfully received on February 1, 1659, from this great Saint, the God-Bearer. Although He filled heaven and earth, He did not leave the soul empty that desired only Him. Its crucified love attached it to the Cross where He allowed it to understand that He had satisfied his justice for what it owed due to its sins of body and spirit: *Donans vobis omnia delicta, delens quod adversus nos erat chirographum decreti, quod erat contrarium nobis, et ipsum tulit de medio, affigens illud cruci: et expolians principatus, et potestates traduxit confidenter, palam triumphans illos in semetipso. Forgiving you all offences: blotting out the handwriting of the decree that was against us, which was contrary to us. And he hath taken the same out of the way, fastening it to the cross. And despoiling the principalities and powers, he hath exposed them confidently in open shew, triumphing over them in himself.* (Col 2:13c-15) (1199)

JEANNE'S ORIGINAL DRAFT

CHAPTER CLXVI

By Divine Providence, I was delivered from a dangerous fall. During my prayer, I inquired about the lot of the saints. About night and how I was visited by the Savior's beloved who bent over my face.

It was the Feast of the Purification in 1659 of the one whom, from moment to moment, You have transfigured from light to light, from purity to purity until she became transformed into your Spirit, invested with You, Sun of Justice and the splendor that illuminates heaven and earth. She was your Virgin Mother and You her Divine Child whom she offered to your Divine Father as the Lamb of God who takes away the sins of the world. With no need for sun or moon, by his own power He enlightens the souls in whom, together with this holy Mother, He has his loving sojourn.

On the Feast of St. Blaise, I prayed several times to him to free us completely from someone (a woman) who was an obstacle to your grace for the spiritual welfare of your spouses and caused us to suffer intensely. (1200)

On the Feasts of St. Veronica, St. Agatha, St. Dorothy, St. Appolonia and St. Scholastica, I prayed in particular to each of them during Mass and at other times, for I had confidence in them. I have received signal favors from them which You reward and will increasingly recompense for their glory, my Divine Love.

I was filled with joy on the Feast of St. Simeon, the Bishop of Jerusalem, your cousin according to the flesh and your faithful imitator. (1659) He was blessed to die on the Cross for You at the age of one hundred twenty years, flying from the Militant Church into the Triumphant one.

JEANNE'S ORIGINAL DRAFT

February 20th of the same year was Sexagesima Thursday. In Sunday's Epistle, St. Paul described the perils he had experienced, mentioning that there are different ones in spirit and body caused by various persons in different places. (1201) By your grace, souls that trust in your goodness are delivered from them. In the morning, I went up to St. Joseph's choir where I receive Communion. I had had it enlarged for the recitation of Divine Office and the reception of the holy habit to be conducted there as well. The carpenters had left two slats in the center where one could look down into the courtyard. I saw shavings that could be used for the fire in preparing dinner. Since I was the cook, I gathered them and threw them through this window, thinking that the two slats were attached by nails, as were the others that comprised the choir. As I was looking down so as not to disturb the work on mortar and stones for the wall of Spies, I noticed that two slats were open. This meant that I would have fallen to the paved court below from two stories up breaking everything and causing my death. (1202) I had no time to stop in this evident peril. Through your divine providence or assisting forms, despite my weight and my being bent over, I was pulled back. I did not know the name of these charitable spirits who precipitately stopped me and then withdrew.

Finding myself delivered from this great danger, I was filled with astonishment. Just the idea of this fall has often frightened me and forced me to sit down to marvel and thank your goodness, my Lord. I found myself obligated to thank You again for your divine and angelic protection and to save me from my errors. I pray to all your saints and angels to whom I am obligated, to guide me, to thank You and to pray to You that I may avoid falling into sin or doing whatever is displeasing to You. (1203)

On the Feast of St. Matthias, as I ordinarily did, I asked You through him for the lot of the saints in the light of your blessings. Also, I prayed that my heart might be faithful to You, since You consider the heart, as You told St. Peter and all those assembled to choose and add the one your Holy Spirit would elect to replace the traitor Judas.

At the beginning of Lent (1659), after having prayed to You for two

JEANNE'S ORIGINAL DRAFT

daughters whom You had inspired to take the holy habit, I prayed to your magnificent beloved, St. Magdalen, in whose honor I had nine Masses offered to change the hearts of a number of persons greatly opposed to this. I informed them that I continued to pray to this powerful advocate of all those who trust in your love whose cause He sponsors so as to defend and maintain it. Divine Love, protect these fine daughters and their holy resolve which is for your glory. (1204)

I awoke around three or four o'clock in the morning. Ordinarily, I cannot sleep a long time, and this makes me weak and indisposed, for often midnight or one o'clock arrives and I have not slept at all. I do not always get up to pray, but entrust myself to your loving goodness. I speak or listen to You lying down, just as this beloved is presented in art. I saw her approaching my bed with a majestic manner and bearing. She was dressed in sky-blue, enhanced by embroidery of different colors. Her face was outstanding in beauty; her eyes full of goodness attracted my heart because of their lovely gentleness. Her lovely, golden hair fell gracefully to her shoulders with a part on her cheeks, looking like garden plot: *Sicut areolæ aromatum; Consitæ et pigmentariis. As beds of aromatical spices set by the perfumers,* (Cant 5:13) or flowers that are a delight to see. Her marvelous hair resembled loosened, clear crepe through which beauty shone. (1205) One might add: *Sicut fragmen mali punici, ita genæ tuæ, absque eo quod intrinsecus latet. Sicut turris David collum tuum, quæ ædificata est cum propugnaculis; mille clypei pendent ex ea, omnis armatura fortium. As a scarlet lace: thy cheeks are as a piece of pomegranate, besides that which lieth hid within. Thy neck is as the tower of David, which is built with bulwarks: a thousand bucklers hang upon it, all the armour of valiant men.* (Cant 4:3c-4)

Thus armed and adorned, she was like strength and gentleness, as beautiful and peaceful as Jerusalem. She approached me as a glorious body, neither lifting nor drawing the curtains. Bending over my face, she assured me of her protection. Without speaking, she let me understand marvels which I cannot express but simply admire. (1206)

351

JEANNE'S ORIGINAL DRAFT

CHAPTER CLXVII

The Savior appeared to me in the form of a lion. He let me participate in his joys and sorrows. A vision wherein I was shown unparalleled beauty, accompanied by a multitude of people. The paths by which God draws souls to Himself are unknown to men.

On the first Sunday of Lent, (1659) I prayed to your Divine Father with the prayer of the Evangelical Prophet: *Emitte agnum, Domine, dominatorem terræ, da petra deserti ad montem filiæ Sion. Send forth, O Lord, the Lamb, the ruler of the earth, from Petra of the desert, to the mount of the daughter of Sion.* (Is 16:1)

You appeared to me, not in the figure or form of a lamb, but of a lion. You let me understand that You are the lion of the tribe of Juda, that You keep your eyes open during your sleep to chase away my enemies who are quite numerous. You have more angels to help me than enemies to persecute me. I was alone, persecuted and abandoned, as in a desert, abandoned by those who ought to be protecting me if they loved You in spirit and in truth. (1207) As a Lamb, You would display your goodness and gentleness for me and confound my enemies. You have all eternity, and You would judge justice: *Cum accepero tempus, When I shall take a time.* (Ps 74:3) You were going to lower the hills of the world down to the road of your eternity, meaning those who through presumption vaunt themselves, who take up their dwelling in their own glory. *Et erit: sicut avis fugiens, et pulli de nido avolantes. Audivimus superbiam Moab; superbus est valde; superbia eius, et arrogantia eius, Moab et indignatio eius plus quam fortitudo eius. Et præparabitur in misericordia solium, et sedebit super illud in veritate in tabernaculo David, judicans et quærens judicium, et velociter reddens quod justum est. And it shall come to pass that, as a bird fleeing away,*

JEANNE'S ORIGINAL DRAFT

and as young ones flying out of the nest. We have heard of the pride of Moab: he is exceeding proud. His pride and his arrogancy and his indignation is more than his strength. And a throne shall be prepared in mercy: and one shall sit upon it in truth in the tabernacle of David, judging and seeking judgment, and quickly rendering that which is just. (Is 16:2a, 6, 5)

All during the month of March, You granted me many favors on the feasts of the saints as I have elsewhere indicated. You continued your charity toward me on the Sundays of Lent, despite every effort against my happiness of having You always as my Benefactor and Remunerator of your own graces that You crown with your kindness. (1208) Through an excess of love, You told me what You said to those who came to you in the name of your Precursor: *Beatus est qui non fuerit scandalizatus in me: cæci vident, claudi ambulant, leprosi mundantur, surdi audiunt, mortui resurgunt, pauperes evangelisantur. Blessed is he whosoever shall not be scandalized in me. The blind see, the lame walk, the lepers are made clean, the deaf hear, the dead rise again, to the poor the gospel is preached.* (Lk 7:23; 22c)

On Palm Sunday, You let me share in your joys and sorrows. Your joys came to the daughter of Sion with unutterable graciousness. Your sadness was due to the ingratitude of many who resisted your glory through political prudence. They were annoyed that innocent simplicity praised You as the One who came to save us through goodness. They blamed actions, because they did not understand the reasons of your providence for them. (1209)

On Monday of Holy Week, I thought about the Gospel of the day to contemplate the magnificence of your wonderful beloved. I have already recorded this in other notebooks. I will not repeat it here, for I have such an intense headache that You allowed me to relieve, for You are so good, so that I might attend all the services each day that represent your sufferings to us. We are very honored to be able to share in them, to follow and imitate You lovingly, according to the declaration of Saint Peter: *Sed si bene facientes*

JEANNE'S ORIGINAL DRAFT

patienter sustinetis, hæc est gratia apud Deum. In hoc enim vocati estis: quia et Christus passus est pro nobis, vobis relinquens exemplum ut sequamini vestigia eius, etc. But if doing well you suffer patiently: this is thankworthy before God. For unto this are you called: because Christ also suffered for us, leaving you an example that you should follow his steps. (1 Pet 2:20-21)

Saint Paul, who empathized with your sorrows, told us that momentary sufferings obtain a prize of eternal glory. Your loving, sorrowful Passion has acquired both grace and glory for us in You, Divine Savior. (1210) In advance, we are resuscitated, if we are faithful observers of your will in everything,which is our sanctification: *Si consurrexistis cum Christo : quæ sursum sunt quærite, ubi Christus est in dextera Dei sedens: quæ sursum sunt sapite, non quæ super terram. If you be risen with Christ, seek the things that are above, where Christ is sitting at the right hand of God. Mind the things that are above, not the things that are upon the earth.* (Col 3:1-2)

On Friday night during the Octave of Easter, I concentrated on the Gospel where You made magnificent promises to your disciples: *Undecim autem discipuli abierunt in Galileam in montem ubi constituerat illis Jesus And the eleven disciples went into Galilee, unto the mountain where Jesus had appointed them.* (Mt 28:16)

You chose to teach them before ascending into heaven from this mountain where, upon seeing You, they adored You: *quidam autem dubitaverunt; but some doubted.* (Mt 28:17b) Because love and fear prevailed, these poor disciples were fearful on seeing Him whose death in ignominy and shame, they had witnessed upon a mountain, but was now alive and glorious. The Gospel states that You approached these poor frightened ones to reassure them: *Et accedens Jesus locutus est eis, dicens: Data est mihi omnis potestas in cælo et in terra: euntes (1211) ergo docete omnes gentes: baptizantes eos in nomine Patris, et Filii, et Spiritus sancti: docentes eos servare omnia quæcumque mandavi vobis: et ecce ego vobiscum sum omnibus*

JEANNE'S ORIGINAL DRAFT

diebus, usque ad consommationem sæculi. And Jesus coming, spoke to them, saying: All power is given to me in heaven and in earth. Going therefore, teach ye all nations: baptizing them in the name of the Father and of the Son and of the Holy Spirit. Teaching them to observe all things whatsoever I have commanded you. And behold I am with you all days, even to the consummation of the world. (Mt 28:18-20)

When your illuminations elevated my sprit, You appeared to me upon a mountain where You were incomparable beauty, invested in whiteness, for You are the candor of eternal light. After You, I saw a multitude of people of all nations ascending this mountain to approach You. You allowed them to proceed with such marvelous lightness that they seemed to be walking upon the clouds. As they were thus ascending, all were engrossed in their duties and occupations. Among these various nations, You allowed me to see different persons of both sexes from Roanne. Their contemplation and activity were acceptable to You, because these were meant to please You. You were carrying a standard or a white banner, Divine Incarnate Word, and leading all these people as their head and as though in love with them. (1212)

I learned that one of these persons had gone up to You, Divine Love, but I did not know her name. Two days later, I received a letter from Father Trilliard of your Society, delivered to me by Father Gibalin. In it, he informed me that he had assisted at the illness and death of my cousin, Mademoiselle Defétière. She had entreated him to inform me about her confidence in and friendship for me. He added that her life and her death were held in a great odor of sanctity in Roanne. I had known this during my sojourn in Roanne during our conversations that always were about your kingdom and your glory, my Divine Savior.

Although married to a mortal man through obedience, this dear cousin has won the victory after all her struggles. In early morning, meaning her childhood, she had given her heart to You and to no one else. She possessed her husband and children in You and for love of You, who had disposed her to practice charity. (1213) Entrusting herself to your love, she took the remedies

AUTOBIOGRAPHY

JEANNE'S ORIGINAL DRAFT

prescribed for her, although they caused her more suffering than relief according to what she told me. However, she was very glad to suffer and thus go see You soon. Her heart and mine were united in You, and we were separated only in body. As I previously stated, I left Roanne on September 8, 1658. Yet our hearts dwelt in their center which is You, Divine Incarnate Word, our love and our treasure.

After this demonstration of your goodness toward my birthplace, I was not surprised at all on the birth of your Blessed Mother upon feeling so much resistance when I left church. It was there that I had received the very first grace; that is, baptism and the other sacraments, with a great profusion of illuminations and delight. You reminded me about what You had given me to understand on the Feast of Saint Lucy when I was still in my father's home. I also recalled that, just as Saint Lucy and Saint Agatha had brought lustre upon the city of Syracuse and Catane, Roanne was greatly favored by your goodness for being the place where I have received so many graces. (1214) It was your good pleasure to allow it to share in your splendors, because You are good to me, and You reward whoever tends to love me and wish me well for love of your exuberant love toward me.

On the Saturday during the Octave of Easter, You were the candor of eternal light and the image of his goodness for me. On seeing You, I see your Father who loves me through goodness and draws me to You. You lead me to Him through your love, your Holy Spirit, who breathes wherever He wills and as He wills, especially when You pray to your Father to send Him to us through your merits to console us for your absence which is worse than hell. During it, the soul that loves You undergoes a different kind of hell than that of the damned, because it suffers while it loves You, whereas those unhappy souls despise You. They want the mountains and hills to fall upon them and conceal them from your face which shows just indignation. (1215)

However, the loving soul, enveloped in darkness for reasons known to You but not to it, yearns to see You. It says: *Emitte lucem tuam et veritatem tuam. Send forth thy light and thy truth.* (Ps 42:3a) Stretch

JEANNE'S ORIGINAL DRAFT

forth your omnipotent hand and take me under your protection. Through mercy, dear Love, conceal me in your sacred side. If acceptable to You, let me say with the Apostle, St. Thomas: *Dominus meus et Deus meus. My Lord and my God.* (Jn 20:28b) You have called me from the abyss of worries to the abyss of joy, from darkness to light. Without tempting You nor being forward, may I enjoy salutary favors from your kindness and divine visits. Grant me the honor of ascending in company with all your faithful ones to the Mount of Olives when, by your own power, You ascend above all the heavens, drawing my heart after You. You assure it that You will dwell in it until the consummation of everything secular and mortal, allowing me to live your divine life. Should I have to descend, may I dwell in the Cenacle with this holy company in constant prayer that I may receive the Paraclete there whom You have promised to give us forever. (1216) I hope for everything from You, my magnificent Benefactor. These sentiments are mine through your goodness, and I unceasingly look for You by my desires to possess You always through faith, begging You to elevate me in You through hope, and to transform me into Yourself through charity: *Qui manet in charitate, in Deo manet, et Deus in eo. He that abideth in charity abideth in God, and God in him.* (1 Jn 4:16b)

Whoever possesses God, possesses everything by having You. I see myself lost in You and dead to myself. Also, after the loving descent of your Spirit of Love, You let me understand that You wanted me hidden in humility like the grain of wheat and that I should die to everything that is not You. I was not to be disturbed by any contempt or rejection either now or in the future. No one knows your Father nor You in the interior workings You operate in those You choose to sanctify. You dwell in these high clouds; even though they are all mercy and truth, your unknown paths are not meant for everyone. You manifest your secrets and mysterious purposes to few persons on earth. Just as You sent your Evangelical Prophet, You also send others to blind those who see with their eyes and make deaf those who hear with their ears, and think with their hearts. (1217) You want souls to be faithful, just as David was, in accordance with your own heart. David observed your will in everything and, after the anointing, was persecuted as soon as he was extolled

JEANNE'S ORIGINAL DRAFT

by the daughters of Israel. He underwent persecution from King Saul even to Simei, his subject, who obstinately injured and offended him. Yet that was little compared with what Absalom, his own son, did to him by stopping Abisai, *filius Sarviæ: Quid mihi et vobis est filii Sarviæ? Dimittite eum, ut maledicat: Dominus enim præcepit ei ut malediceret David: et quis est qui audeat dicere, quare sic fecerit? Abisai, the son of Sarvia: What have I to do with you, ye sons of Sarvia? Let him alone and let him curse: for the Lord hath bid him curse David. And who is he that shall dare say, Why hath he done so?* (2 Sam 16:10)

As Samuel's mother Anne said: The Lord humbles and vivifies. He allows souls to go toward hell and rescues them from it when He wants them to follow the paths that He knows will lead them to Him. With the Prophet-King, He says to you: *In terra deserta, et invia, et in aquosa, sic in sancto apparui tibi, ut viderem virtutem tuam et gloriam tuam. In a desert land, and where there is no way and no water: so in the sanctuary have I come before thee, to see thy power and thy glory.* (Ps 62:3) (1218)

CHAPTER CLXVIII

St. John Baptist's joyous Feast in the one who provides us with milk. On the Feast of the Visitation, 34 years had passed since I had left my father's house. The altar charcoal is totally pure, shiny and heat-giving. Saint Teresa founded as many paradises of delight as she established monasteries. The Feasts of St. Magdalen, St. James, St. Anne and St. Ignatius of Loyola 1659.

I adored You in your Sacrament of Love on the day of your holy Feast

JEANNE'S ORIGINAL DRAFT

and its whole Octave. I said to You, my Divine Love: *Dominus regit me, et nihil mihi deerit: in loco pascuæ ibi me collocavit. The Lord ruleth me: and I shall want nothing. He hath set me in a place of pasture.* (Ps 22:1-2) I will remain there with You on your throne and table of grace and goodness where You show me your splendors. At the zenith of your love, You nourish me splendidly by your delights and illuminations.

On the Feast of the birth of your Precursor and my patron, You prompted me to call it "the feast of the joy of many", according to what Gabriel told his father Zacharias. (1219) Since You allowed me to rejoice therein, I shared in your joy, which was most pleasing to your Divine Father. He regarded You as the sun at the coming of which this aureole, heralded by heavenly lights, then faded and withdrew to Limbo on the day of his beheading.

On the Feast of the Apostle who found nothing satisfying in this world and spoke freely to You, I used his words in telling You in the name of all your daughters: *Domine, ad quem ibimus? verba vitæ æternæ habes. Lord, to whom shall we go? Thou hast the words of eternal life.* (Jn 6:69) Whatever is not You means nothing to us and cannot satisfy us. We believe and trust in You, Divine Love. Whoever speaks to You strengthens our resolve to accept You as the only Son of the Living God, Incarnate Word, our love and our peace. We would choose to be crucified with our head downward to be able to raise our eyes to heaven as did the one who told you that, since You know all things, You were not unaware of the fact that he loved You with an inexpressible love, just as You wanted him to do. (1220) He said to You: *Command what You wish and give us whatever is pleasing to You.*

I thought about the spirit of the one, who is all collateral, delivered from his body's mortality and flying up to heaven as soon as his head shed rivulets of milk upon earth to nourish all the children he had begotten through the word of your powerful truth. I yearned for this holy milk to live the life he had received from You, who were his life. Through his intercession, it could also be mine. I gently said: *Mihi enim vivere Christus est, et mori lucrum; For to me, to live is Christ: and to die is gain.* (Phil 1:21) Although prompted by two

JEANNE'S ORIGINAL DRAFT

desires, I awaited or trusted for the moment from your bountiful mercy that your power possesses. For the souls You have entrusted to me: *Coarctor autem e duobus: desiderium habens dissolvi, et esse cum Christo, multo magis melius: permanere autem in carne. But I am straitened between two: having a desire to be dissolved and to be with Christ, a thing by far the better. But to abide still in the flesh is needful.* (Phil 1:23-24) (1221)

On the Feast of the Visitation of your incomparable Mother, I remembered that, thirty-four years earlier, I had left my father's house to begin the mission entrusted to me by You and your Blessed Mother for your glory and the salvation of many. I said to You: Dear Love, in thirty-three years and several days, You finished your course. *Heu mihi, quia incolatus meus prolongatus est! Woe is me, that my sojourning is prolonged!* (Ps 119:5a) Lord, do you want me to abide longer among the people of Cedar, which means sadness? How could I rejoice there when I am so imperfect? How hard it is to put up with myself, and I make bold to tell You that this life is hard.

On July the fourteenth, the Seraphic Doctor filled me with joy by his ardors. I prayed to him to place the coal from the altar upon the lips of all hearts that would make them totally pure, resplendent and ardent. This had led him to know his love and his weight, for he had desired Him to be placed in his mouth, unless He entered there Himself. This He could do, for He is the Angel of the Great Council, the God of the living and the dead. He could make this zealous doctor be the support and consoler of everyone, defending and maintaining his Order against its persecutors. (1222) He also composed marvelous poetry that provides great solace for the sinful faithful. It moves the living to pray devoutly for the souls that yearn to see You, my God, and be delivered from their bonds to be able to fly to You like doves in the niches of your Sacred Wounds, Divine Savior. Washed in this precious milk, their eyes could reside near the rivulets of immortality as dearest spouses: *Oculi eius sicut columbæ super rivulos aquarum, quæ lacte sunt lotæ, et resident juxta fluenta plenissima. His eyes as doves upon brooks of waters, which are washed with milk, and sit beside the plentiful streams.* (Cant 5:12) By your goodness, when they see You, they become like what they love.

JEANNE'S ORIGINAL DRAFT

On July 20th, after a bad headache during part of the night, my spirit, which also suffered, considered the words of the Apostle St. James. He declared that assiduous prayer is powerful for obtaining everything from your merciful goodness. (1223) I thought of what is said about Rebecca's prayer: *Elias homo erat similis nobis passibilis: et oratione oravit ut non plueret super terram, et non pluet annos tres, et menses sex. Et rursum oravit: et cælum dedit pluviam, et terra dedit fructum suum. Elias was a man passible like unto us: and with prayer he prayed that it might not rain upon the earth. And it rained not for three years and six months. And he prayed again. And the heaven gave rain: and the earth brought forth her fruit.* (Jas 5:17-18)

I recalled that the Church included him in the martyrology, and that the members of his Order celebrated his feast as their Father and holy Founder. I prayed to my good angel and all the others to greet him for me wherever he might be according to the opinion commonly held. In spirit, I greeted him in the earthly paradise, asking You, my Divine Love, to prompt him to pray to You for me and to open heaven for me that seemed closed and made of bronze. A loving tenderness made my heart overflow so that my eyes became two fountains of tears for more than two hours. (1224) From this man of fire, You had received the sacrifice I offered, converting my eyes into canals where You made two rivulets serve as a miraculous antiperistasis to redouble your flames upon the altar of my heart. There it could be consumed as a holocaust, the wood and stone, everything that might serve You by making a spiritual consumption to show that You are my true God.

On noting that I was troubled by this life because of my own imperfections and the persecutions aimed against me, You removed my torpor by arousing my spirit. Through the power of the Sacred Bread, the Bread of the strong— not cooked upon ashes, but in the divine and human furnace—I was to find the courage to ascend to You through prayer. After different paths along which You sent my spirit, You allowed me to go along the Jordan, like another Eliseus, following my all-zealous Elias whom your angels, in the figure of a burning chariot have taken from this earth with your consent. (1225) You let

JEANNE'S ORIGINAL DRAFT

me understand that this chariot had entered the earthly paradise through the East. The Cherubim did not oppose this. His flaming sword was not meant to arrest the chariot of fire and flame nor those that directed the man who lived in fasting and prayer. The place of happiness in this world had to surrender. After the days of John the Baptist, the kingdom of heaven underwent violence. Since the days of Elias, the angels believed him to be worthy of their celestial glory. The guardians of the earthly paradise, the first kingdom on earth where Adam and Eve were king and queen before the sin resulting from their greed and presumption of being like You, my God, were banished from it because of these two sins, the source of all evil. Your holy Prophet Elias had been lodged there after he had fasted. (1226) Through a real sentiment of his nothingness, he declared that he was no better than the rest of mankind. In fact, he acknowledged himself to be weaker, upon seeing himself vanquished by the persecutions of a woman. In a short time, dogs would eat her flesh and drink her blood in the land or field of Jezrahel where Naboth's vineyard was located. You let me understand marvels about this great man Elias in the Paradise of Eden. Proportionately speaking, I knew a young woman who has been so profoundly elevated that she has heard secrets spoken *quæ non licet homini loqui; which it is not granted to man to utter.* (2 Cor 12:4) She dealt with the angels about this, asking them to visit St. Elias often. She wanted him to pray to You for her, my Divine Love, and the great Saint Teresa, worthy daughter of that great saint. On earth she established as many paradises of delight as the monasteries she founded by her reform. I was not accepted there, despite my desire to be so. Being too weak in my unworthiness, I was refused before I thought of our plan. (1227) Your wisdom ordained it thus. May You be blessed in everything, my Divine Love.

On the Feast of your beloved Magdalen, You let me understand marvels about her magnificent love which You converted into ecstasy in Simon's home when You invited him to see how this marvelous woman, who seemed to be love personified, came to resemble the One she loved. You told me to call this Feast of St. Magdalen the day or feast of divine love because of her ardor which holily transformed her into You. Just as You are the mirror of the Majesty, she was a mirror that enraptured the angels. In proportion, they

JEANNE'S ORIGINAL DRAFT

desired to gaze upon her unceasingly, heeding what You told Simeon to contemplate everything she did to your holy feet. She was linked to them by her hair, yet continued to wash, kiss and dry them, because love cannot say: That is enough delight *(numquam satis; is never satisfied)*. (1228) It appeared that your soul was more in her whom You loved than in your body that it animated and than the ointment she poured upon your head in Bethany alleviating for You the most harsh, bitter sufferings You would choose to undergo on Calvary within a few days. You censured whoever did not approve the excess of her marvelous ointment and the debris of the expensive vessel or box that contained it. You said that she had performed an action that would be spread and preached about throughout the world.

On the Feast of St. James, I desired those who bear his name to be the supplantors of the world, the devil and the flesh. I begged him to fight for the Church so that her enemies might be vanquished and acknowledge You, Incarnate Word, our Love.

It was the Feast of Saint Anne, your beloved grandmother who conceived, bore and gave birth to the Queen of men and angels, the Empress of the Universe. She has provided your Eternal Father with an incomparable Daughter and You, my Divine Savior, with an unparalleled Mother, the Holy Spirit with an unequalled Spouse. (1229) She allowed me to share in the gift of grace according to her name. I wanted her to present me to You as she did in 1619 when I experienced the baptism of love that makes the soul one same thing with You, my merciful Redeemer.

On the Feast of the one who professed your greater glory in everything, the prudent Founder of your Society, my Divine Jesus, I received many favors through him. You let me understand that his feast should be called the feast of glory. David, your forefather, would be very content were he still on earth to see the fire-bearer Ignatius carry it everywhere. We could tell You joyfully: *Dominus regnavit; exultet terra; lætentur insulæ multæ. Ignis ante ipsum præcedet, et in circuitu inimicos eius. Illuxerunt fulgura eius orbis terræ; vidit, et commota est terra. The Lord hath reigned, let the earth rejoice:*

JEANNE'S ORIGINAL DRAFT

let many islands be glad. A fire shall go before him, and shall burn his enemies round about. His lightnings have shone forth to the world: the earth saw and trembled. (Ps 96:1b, 3-4)

I often said to him: Ignatius of Loyola, you possess the power. Please obtain from the Divine Essence that the vanquished and the conqueror may be together. As for our hearts, make and set them afire like furnaces. (1230)

CHAPTER CLXIX

St. Peter's chains. Our Lady of the angels. The resplendent Transfiguration of the Savior. The burning alive of Saint Lawrence. The sight of a rod made of aromatic wood. Communions during 40 years. Saint Bartholomew's Feast. The removal of the great Baptist and the baptism of the Savior, the ram prefigured by that of Isaac.

On the Feast of the chains of the Prince of the Apostles (1659), bound more by a spiritual love than the chains that bound his body, my soul—that in this life languished from troubles—yearned to be freed from anything that could detain it upon earth. Had an angel favored it by freeing it, giving my heart the wound of grace, it would have sung the triumph of loving freedom.

I followed the multitudes of angels who were accompanying their Lord and Lady in the church of the Portiuncula. (1231) They shared the marvelous indulgence of their magnificence with the great St. Francis for the salvation of the entire world if it could enter there. I received many graces from your

JEANNE'S ORIGINAL DRAFT

goodness and your Blessed Mother.

It was the Feast of your sublime Transfiguration, O beautiful One par excellence, whom the angels unceasingly desire to contemplate, and St. Peter wished to lodge or dwell in your tabernacles with the law and the Prophets. He did not know what he was saying, forgetting the multitude further down that he was supposed to lead and assist to ascend higher. He possessed the keys to the kingdom. My soul adored You, telling You that it had no desire other than yours. Your Divine Father commanded it to listen to You speak from the excess of love and sufferings to be fulfilled in Jerusalem. It was satisfied to see only You. You chose to tell me that You make your Tabor wherever You manifest your glory, as You had already told me before I left Paris. (1232) You are faithful to souls that strive only to please You, consoling me for the afflictions I endured because of someone who before had consoled me with spiritual delight by conversation about your admirable marvels.

On the eve and day of the burning alive of Saint Lawrence, I almost continually shed tears as I ordinarily did. I offered them to him, saying that the apple of my eye spoke to him to report my troubles to You. Blessed Stanislaus had requested him to take a letter to your Blessed Mother that expressed his desires which she accepted. In the same way, I trusted that he would ask for favors and graces from the Mother and her Son.

On the Feast of the triumphant Assumption of your most August and Blessed Mother, I received very great blessings known to You. I cannot express them, for I feel so unworthy of them. (1233) After the sermon given by Father Gibalin, he told me that he was in a hurry to return to the College for the prayers being offered because of the King's vow.

When I left the confessional where I had listened to the sermon, I entered a little room nearby to cool off a bit. Your goodness told me: "*In me sunt vota tua; In me are vows to thee.* (Ps 55:12) Come, present them, my daughter. I will accept them with my Blessed Mother and all the saints." As I marveled at your goodness, I saw a rod of aromatic wood ascend and recalled: *Quæ*

JEANNE'S ORIGINAL DRAFT

est ista quæ ascendit per desertum sicut virgula fumi ex aromatibus myrrhæ, et thuris, universi pulveris pigmentarii? Who is she that goeth up by the desert, as a pillar of smoke of aromatical spices, of myrrh and frankincense, and of all the powders of the perfumer? (Cant 3:6) My spirit remained enraptured a long time, saying: My blessed goddess, who could not follow you, ardent sun, or certainly die upon losing you. (1234)

On the Feast of St. Bernard, I wanted to draw into my heart the bouquet of myrrh that he passionately loved. He said that your death was the death of his death; that, to allow him to live, You had chosen to die.

On the Octave of the glorious Assumption of your august and Blessed Mother, I endeavored to thank You for the inestimable grace You had given me in 1620, thirty-nine years earlier, counting year by year, of my beginning to receive daily Communion. I entreated your entire heavenly court to offer You all the Sacred Hosts received daily through obedience and love in thanksgiving for your magnificent liberality toward me. I said to You: "You have nurtured my soul with this daily bread for 40 years less one, which has already begun, so that I count the part as the whole. (1235) You have given me more favors than to your Hebrew people, because the manna You gave them was but the figure of the one You have given and still give me through pure goodness. I beg You to let all these Communions be for your glory and my salvation." I recalled what You had told me to report to Father Jean de Villars and Father Pival, then the rector of the College in Roanne: "My daughter, tell these priests that, just as I let the manna rain down daily upon my people (these are your own words), I want you to receive Communion daily. This fine and holy rector saw great difficulties in this, according to his reasoning. Father Bartholomew Jacquinot, provincial of the province of Lyons, came to Roanne. After hearing my general confession and becoming informed of your goodness toward me, he told me that he felt inspired to give me Holy Communion every day, as is recorded above. (1236) He would write his opinion to the Father General. This he did in the very same year, 1620, on the Octave of the Assumption of your Blessed Mother, who favored me in a way that cannot be expressed in this world.

JEANNE'S ORIGINAL DRAFT

On the Feast of your Apostle, Saint Bartholomew, You blessed me with favors according to your customary magnificence. I adored You in your immensity and simplicity. I reflected upon You as the greatest and the smallest, according to the declaration of this great Apostle. I begged him to adore You, deprived of everything, even of his own skin for love of You. I thanked You for the grace You deigned to grant me on a certain day when the Church proposes to us the vocation of the Apostles. You wanted me to lead a great number of souls and daughters to You. They were to be yours through a new Institute, under your banner, revering your Name, your Person and all your mysteries. (1237)

Divine Beloved, what yearning filled my heart on the Feast of our loving Father, Saint Augustine. He had loved You through your own Heart, having lost his own for You. Or perhaps, my Divine Love, You had taken it from him through love and grace in this passionate combat where, nevertheless, one finds You and, in You, eternal life.

At night, on the Feast of the Beheading of the great Baptist, greatest Savior, You chose to engage me for several hours about the mysteries of his life and death. You made me understand: "My daughter, at my baptism, John told Me with a veritable oath of humility: *Ego a te debeo baptizari, et tu venis ad me! I ought to be baptized by thee, and comest thou to me?* (Mt 3 :14). I answered him: *Sine modo: sic enim decet nos implere omnem justifiam. Suffer it to be so now. For so it becometh us to fulfil all justice.* (Mt 3:15) (1238)

"Having listened respectfully to the divine command, he baptized Me, after which I hurriedly emerged from the river; the heavens opened, the Holy Spirit, who is as swift as I am, descended in the form of a dove. He hovered over my head, and my Eternal Father declared from the heights of heaven: *Hic est filius meus dilectus, in quo mihi bene complacui. This is my beloved Son, in whom I am well pleased.* (Mt 3:17)

"He led me into the desert where I was to be tempted by the devil by three

JEANNE'S ORIGINAL DRAFT

temptations that he would propose to Me. I won and was triumphant over the flesh, the world and him. Angels were sent to serve me. Knowing that John had been taken captive and arrested, I left Nazareth in Galilee: *In Capharnaum maritima, in finibus Zabulum et Nephthalim: ut adimpleretur quod dictum est per Isaiam Prophetam. He came and dwelt in Capharnaum, on the sea coast, in the borders of Zabulon and of Nephthalim; that it might be fulfilled which was said by Isaias the prophet.* (Mt 4:13b-14) I had already begun to preach and to show that I am the true light for the people seated in darkness. (1239)

"My daughter, John's imprisonment and beheading had a purpose. He witnessed to what he had declared about Me: 'I must decrease, and He must increase. I must be removed, and He must become important, not only in the manner of dying, as explained by the eagle among the doctors.' John was beheaded, and Jesus was crucified, but to arrest the error of the people: *Et cogitantibus omnibus in cordibus suis de Joanne, ne forte ipse esset Christus. And all were thinking in their hearts of John, that perhaps he might be the Christ.* (Lk 3:15)

"This incredulous people, who tended toward idolatry, would have adored him had they seen Me crucified and had John lived longer than I. Michael's struggle with the demon over the body of Moses showed that it had been concealed by divine Wisdom to prevent it from being adored as God. John would have been regarded as the Messias, despite any explanation given them to prevent this. In spite of any authentic confession made to them about my divinity, his disavowal would have been attributed to humility. (1240) Even though he worked no miracles, his austere manner of preaching convinced them that he was holier than the One whom the Father had sanctified and sent into the world as Savior and Redeemer. As though astounded, his own disciples told Him: *Rabbi, qui erat tecum trans Jordanem, cui tu testimonium perhibuisti, ecce hic baptizat, et omnes veniunt ad eum. Rabbi, he that was with thee beyond the Jordan, to whom thou gavest testimony: behold, he baptizeth and all men come to him.* (Jn 3:26)

JEANNE'S ORIGINAL DRAFT

"'No man could do what he does nor say what he says without having received this from heaven.' 'You will be witnesses regarding my declaration that I am not the Christ, but that I have been sent before Him. *Qui habet sponsam, sponsus est: amicus autem sponsi, qui stat, et audit eum, gaudio gaudet propter vocem sponsi. Hoc ergo gaudium meum impletum est. Illum oportet crescere, me autem minui. He that hath the bride is the bridegroom: but the friend of the bridegroom, who standeth and heareth him, rejoiceth with joy because of the bridegroom's voice. This my joy therefore is fulfilled. He must increase: but I must decrease.'* (Jn 3:29-30)

"John was very content to die before I did, thus going to Limbo as my Precursor. (1241) How intense was his joy in announcing to the holy Fathers there that I had been born six months in time after he was, but that he had acknowledged me to be born from all eternity amid the splendor of the saints. He added that he was unworthy to untie the strap of my sandals, to serve my Sacred Humanity. Once again, Abraham possessed the inconceivable joy of knowing that the Unique One, who was and is in the bosom of the Father of all eternity, was on earth, the ram prefigured by the one he had offered in Isaac's place. My divine joy was great in my humanity, which loves the divinity immeasurably more than all mankind or all the angels have loved, do love and will ever love It.

"As the Incarnate Word, I am with the Father and the Holy Spirit, equally jealous of the glory that is essentially due Us. (1242) This support of the most Sacred Humanity is immense, infinite. God Himself gave my Humanity an immense, infinite and divine joy to the degree that it was capable of being anointed by the oil of rejoicing above all pure creatures. Still, it was limited in my Humanity, there being no human subsistence, for it depended upon the Second Hypostasis of the Trinity. As the Word of God and the Word-God, I was and am greater than John the Baptist.

"My daughter, all the angels endured great assaults and extreme violence ever since the time of John the Baptist, upon seeing him elevated so high and

JEANNE'S ORIGINAL DRAFT

become so great in the opinion of mankind. (1243) They heard the praise and compliments that I personally declared about him, knowing that I am the truth that cannot deceive and that I do what I say, that I call things that do not exist into being. They were in constant admiration to the very day that he descended into Limbo and was received there as the Precursor and friend of the Bridegroom, and not the Bridegroom Himself, who was to come there as Redeemer in name and merit."

CHAPTER CLXX

The Feast of St. Giles and the Birth of the Blessed Virgin. Graces I have received and the illumination I have had about the most Reverend Father Cotton (1659).

I was marveling at the royal decision of the great St. Giles. He knew that serving your Divine Majesty is to reign. To live a supereminent life in solitude, he abandoned his country and the place he knew: *Sedebit solitarius, et tacebit, quia levabit super se. He shall sit solitary and hold his peace: because he hath taken it upon himself.* (Lam 3:28)

Your providence once sent this Prophet of fire a doe and, on another occasion, a raven. (1244) You look after the body when souls strive to love only You. You let me understand: "My daughter, direct your thought to Me. I will nourish you with my own delights. I am your bread and milk all the days of your mortal life." If You were not to give me this favor, Divine Love, which is very great, I would dare ask You to deliver me from this prison in order to be with your saints and, like them, to bless your holy Name forever.

JEANNE'S ORIGINAL DRAFT

The birth of her who enraptured men and angels and is the Mother of her Creator produced great joy for all creatures. She is the marvel of God Himself. Could I dare state that, by considering her among his ideas, unless He had been Sadoc sufficient unto himself, He would have felt a holy impatience to impart existence to her even before creating angels and mankind. The Eternal Father delights in the power He prepared for Her, the Son in the wisdom He could communicate to Her and the Holy Spirit in the goodness and love with which He would fill Her. The entire Blessed Trinity would regard Her as the fulfillment of its divine delight.

Divinely enlightened, David repeatedly prayed to dwell in the Lord's house and visit his temple so that he might there see his divine delight all the days of his life. My Divine Master, I would desire this for all eternity.

My august goddess (if I may be allowed thus to speak), may I have the same view and favor from your magnificent benevolence. Why not, since, upon exhorting me to offer myself to the most August Trinity for the establishment of the Order of your Son, our Incarnate Word, You told me: "My daughter, have no fear, He who performs marvels all alone will do this. Write about this to Father Cotton." (1245) This fine priest replied that he would speak to Monseigneur de Marquemont, Archbishop of Lyons, who was made a cardinal this very year in Rome. From there, he would go to heaven to receive the crown of glory due to the good works he had perseveringly fulfilled on earth. The Visitation Sisters are greatly obligated to him after their founder, Francis de Sales, who, adhering to the advice of this very wise, devout and enlightened archbishop and eminent cardinal, have become religious. Their Order has been confirmed and has multiplied in a marvelous way. The said Father Cotton died in a holy manner on the Feast of St. Joseph in 1626.

Having spoken to him several times when he passed through Roanne, I admired his great, innate gentleness. Because of it, he enabled the timid to confide in him, even though they had had no intention of alluding to their interior life. I acknowledge that he was the first priest to whom I revealed the magnificences with which the Divine Majesty has favored me. By divine

JEANNE'S ORIGINAL DRAFT

providence, I entered the confessional and, with no previous intention of doing so, related what occurred in my soul. His gentleness was a wonderful hook.

On January 13, 1625, when he arrived in Roanne, I remained praying, letting others see him first. During my prayer, I began to weep, because of the intimate delight of your love. You let me see an imaginary vision of a city set upon a high mountain, replete with towers, bastions and boulevards. Then I saw great silk nets which descended from heaven.

The next day, while I assisted at Holy Mass offered by Father Cotton, I understood: "This priest is the strong city, supplied with strong fortresses for its defense, the preservation of God's Church and the destruction of her enemies." (1246) The nets represented his holy, heavenly words, replete with kindness by which he attracts people, pulling them forth from the sea of sin and leading them to the port of grace. Anyone who went to him with subtlety and duplicity reaped no benefit from having done so. He possessed such a persuasive manner of speaking that he touched the hearts of those who listened to him so forcefully that I can affirm that these words of Cotton were cannons whose blows created breaches. A number of times when I spoke to him or attended his sermons, I experienced such impetuous assaults that it was difficult for me to withdraw through fear of being perceived. I was not always successful in doing so. Thus, I decided to ask God for the strength to penetrate and sustain his understandings without being inconvenienced. I asked the priest to pray to obtain this grace from God for me. He did so and obtained it from the divine goodness with liberality.

His great devotion to the Blessed Sacrament was obvious when he offered Holy Mass and exhorted the people. He was devoted to the Blessed Virgin, the Mother of God. He drew the hearts of all his penitents and listeners to these paths and necessary devotions. He exhorted souls to piety by charitable associations and through his charity. He associated me with him, telling me that Sister Marie de Valence and Mademoiselle De Conche were, too, and would be happy about this and that he would pray six times daily for me in particular. If he did so for me who did not deserve it, he did the same for

JEANNE'S ORIGINAL DRAFT

others. His charity extended to all the needs of his neighbor. (1247)

His humility was so deep that I am embarrassed to exaggerate my esteem for his term "humble" when he alluded to himself in his letters to me. He often taught me about devotion to St. Joseph and the Holy Family of Jesus and Mary. I desire and want this devotion to be especially recommended to all our daughters of our Order since, as our special intention, we profess to honor and imitate Jesus, Mary, Joseph, St. Joachim, St. Anne, St. Elizabeth, St. Zacharias, St. John the Baptist and the Evangelist and all the others belonging to the Holy Family of Jesus.

CHAPTER CLXXI

The graces and illuminations I received on the Feast of the Exaltation of your Holy Cross. About your Apostles and saints, my special teachers and protectors up to the Feast of All Saints (1659).

On the Feast of the Exaltation of your precious Cross, by a holy rapture, You elevated me up to You. You let me understand that, if I deeply esteemed and loved You alone, You would be everything to me in my superior part and all the powers of my soul would have the happiness of this supereminent, divine attraction, during which the soul belongs to You and You to it. (1248) It possesses every good thing that can be named, that is, your glory: *per modum transeuntes; in a transitory way : Et ego si exaltatus fuero a terra, omnia traham ad me ipsum. And I, if I be lifted up from the earth, will draw all things to myself.* (Jn 12:32)

JEANNE'S ORIGINAL DRAFT

During these blessed moments, the soul enjoys inexpressible delights in passing. It certainly would choose to be delivered from the prison of its mortal body to dwell in the happy land of the living, there eternally to please and contemplate You.

On the Feast of St. Thecla, I considered that she could rightfully declare, as did the Apostle about charity, that she could not be separated from her body because of its torments. Victorious, she appeared strong through your insurmountable assistance. Divine Love, You let me apply the words of the Prophet Hosea to her: "I will be your death, O death, and your sting, O hell, in order to master life by martyrdom. I do not fear your wrath. I shall live a few years to teach a number of people on earth about the angelic, heavenly life and will be invoked by the agonizing. I will assist them during their final passage. I will present them for their entrance into eternal life. Miraculous Virgin, obtain this favor for me on my last day, after I will have received Communion many times during my temporal life.

The charity and union of St. Cosmas and St. Damian in healing corporal ills as physicians prompted me to pray to these two saints to obtain from their charitable goodness perfect health and spiritual holiness. This is to go from visible to invisible things, from the natural to the supernatural. They have often accorded this to me.

The great doctor St. Jerome, who humbled himself during his mortal life to teach a little granddaughter of his great Saint Paula, was very willing to descend from on high in his immortal life to teach and interpret Sacred Scripture for the most imperfect of all creatures: (1249) *Qui autem docti fuerint, fulgebunt quasi splendor firmamenti; et qui ad justitiam erudiunt multos, quasi stellæ in perpetuas æternitates. But they that are learned shall shine as the brightness of the firmament: and they that instruct many to justice, as stars for all eternity.* (Dan 12:3)

The General of God's armies, his faithful servant par excellence, brings down his enemies even to the depths of the abysses with the lance of his divine

JEANNE'S ORIGINAL DRAFT

word, not to say the sword of fire from his mouth: *De ore eius gladius utraque parte acutus exibat. And from his mouth came out a sharp two-edged sword.* (Ap 1:16b) He deprived proud spirits of glory, distributing grace to the humble, weighing their merits, elevating them by holy rays until he filled the seats in the Empyrean. He let me enjoy heavenly blessings, allowing the sterile to dwell at times in the house of the children of joy. This is what prompted me to prescribe the Office of this great Archangel for our Order on the day of his Feast. It was observed from the year 1626 to 1631. I really want it to be continued so as to request him to champion your Order on earth, Divine Incarnate Word, just as in heaven he upheld your side against the spirits who rebelled against your will.

On the Feast of St. Francis, the copy of the crucified Original, he allowed me to experience his loving thoughts, molding me to the delightful sorrows of the King of lovers, Love itself. O, my God, my All! As I repeat these fervent, holy words of my father, St. Francis, I pray incessantly: O my God, my God, You are everything to me! *Be me*, my God, my All, in time and eternity and elevate me to You at the final moment of my life! (1250)

Dionisius, divinitus stillatus; Dionysius, holily distilled united and filled me with the graces of the One in whom the fullness of the divinity corporeally dwells. His being and majesty are better expressed by negation than by affirmation. His profound immensity is known and penetrated by Him alone. This thought enraptured me, taking me out of myself to take up my abode in Him. He taught me this divine theology, because souls that are divinized both feel and see in the blessed darkness wherein Moses heard the divine commands: *Lex Domini immaculata, convertens animas; Testimonium Domini fidele, sapientiam præstans parvulis. The law of the Lord is unspotted, converting souls: the testimony of the Lord is faithful, giving wisdom to little ones.* (Ps 18:8)

On the Feast of the Evangelist St. Luke, who, with marvelous confidence, was so blessed to be able to paint the Mother of the Most High who taught and entrusted to him all that occurred in the angelical and celestial embassy

JEANNE'S ORIGINAL DRAFT

where God became Man and the Man-God by a divine dispensation, I was elevated to understand this most ineffable Incarnation. However, in a number of notebooks, I have already declared what here I could only report with stammering, after giving the legitimate excuse of the Prophet who had been sanctified in his mother's womb: *A, a, a, Domine Deus, ecce nescio loqui, quia puer ego sum. Ah, ah, ah, Lord God, behold, I cannot speak, for I am a child.* (Jer 1:6)

I will not expand on this discourse, but declare, using the words of the Virgin Mother: *Ecce ancilla Domini, fiat mihi secundum Verbum; Behold the handmaid of the Lord: be it done to me according to thy word.* (Lk 1:38b) I withdrew with the angel: *Et dicessit ab illa angelus; And the angel departed from her.* (Lk 1:38c) The Holy Spirit came upon her, and the power of the Most High overshadowed her during the adorable interaction of this marvelous incarnation: *Quod enim in ea natum est, de Spiritu Sancto est. That which is conceived in her is of the Holy Ghost.* (Mt 1:20c) (1251)

On the Feast of the holy Apostles, St. Simon and St. Jude, relatives of the Word made Flesh and providers for all the saints, your divine goodness astounded me deeply by having me say what St. Jude expressed to You at the Supper: "Why do You grant me so many favors, manifesting Yourself to me with so much love and profusion meant for a high degree of perfection? *Domine, quid factum est, quia manifestaturus es nobis teipsum, et non mundo? Lord, how is it that thou wilt manifest thyself to us, and not to the world?*" (Jn 14:22b)

Ineffable goodness, what graces I received from your divine love on the Feast of All Saints. It made me say and repeat with admiration things that I was unable to express: *O quam gloriosum est regnum in quo cum Christo gaudent omnes Sancti, amicti stolis albis sequuntur Agnum quocumque ierit! O how glorious is the kingdom where all the Saints rejoice with Christ; clothed in white robes, they follow the Lamb wherever He goes!* (Antiphon: Vespers for All Saints)

JEANNE'S ORIGINAL DRAFT

At the Transfiguration, St. Peter yearned to remain for all eternity upon the mountain, contemplating a sample of your Majesty's glory that was shown to five persons. Your Body was still passible, and in a few days it would be disfigured. Then, what rejoicing and exhilaration must transport all the saints who enjoy the plenitude and immense happiness that the divine goodness enables them to possess. By your light, they see all the light of the divine splendor. They are inebriated by the torrent of your beauty. (1252)

CHAPTER CLXXII

A rapture I experienced on the Feast of St. Andrew. St. Xavier's love and the Immaculate Conception. The radiant night of the birth of our Divine Beloved.

On the Feast of the most great St. Andrew, one of the two first disciples of your divine and loving wisdom: *Erat autem Andreas, frater Simonis Petri, unus ex duobus qui audierant a Joanne, et secuti fuerant eum. And Andrew, the brother of Simon Peter, was one of the two who had heard of John and followed him,* (Jn 1:40) I experienced the ineffable delights of wonderful happiness with which Incarnate Wisdom feted these privileged and favored ones. I do not know if my rapture resembled that of the Queen of Sheba at the sight and sound of the marvelous wisdom of King Solomon who was but the figure of our divine and most loving Savior: *In quo sunt omnes thesauri sapientiæ et scientiæ absconditi. Quia in ipso inhabitat omnis plenitudo divinitatis corporaliter. In whom are hid all the treasures of wisdom and knowledge. For in him dwelleth all the fulness of the Godhead corporeally.* (Col 2:3, 9)

JEANNE'S ORIGINAL DRAFT

Since I was invited to share in the holy satisfaction of these two blessed disciples, I could only admire and praise the One who surpasses Solomon. He spoke, not to his servants, but to his friends, communicating his human and divine splendors to them.

On the Feast of the Apostle of Japan and the Indies, I exclaimed privately: *Satis est Domine; It is enough, Lord!* As I contemplated him in ecstasy, his face ablaze like that of the Seraphim, he opened his robe to envelop all people on earth with the love that filled him, thinking that its circumference could not contain the ardor of his great heart which was made for You. It could be filled only by You, my God and my All. I will be satisfied when your glory will appear to me and fill me with your immense charity. This prompts me to tell You that the world is too small to serve You properly. You created it and have loved it so much as to give your only Son to save it personally. He is the Eternal Word, the image of your goodness, the figure of your substance, the splendor of your glory. *Portansque omnia verbo virtutis; Upholding all things by the word of his power.* (Heb 1:3c) (1253)

On the Feast of the Immaculate Conception of her whom all generations declare blessed, I greeted her as Daughter of the Father, Mother of the Son, Spouse of the Holy Spirit, and Temple of the Most Blessed Trinity. You enraptured me, three divine hypostases in the excess of fervor by three holy ecstasies while I contemplated her as my Queen, my august one, my most just and totally holy Mother, excellent in body, heart and spirit. Her love was perfect and stronger than death.

On the eve of your marvelous and excellent birth, preparing us with divine and human graciousness in blessing through the most exalted words of all mankind, You told us: *Hodie scietis quia veniet Dominus et salvabit nos: Videbitur gloria eius. This day you shall know that the Lord is coming, and will save us: You shall see his glory.* (Antiphon, Vigil of Christmas) By its magnificent light, his glory enveloped the shepherds: *Et ecce angelus Domini stetit juxta illos, et claritas Dei circumfulsit illos. And behold an angel of the Lord stood by them and the brightness of God shone round about them.* (Lk 2:9a)

JEANNE'S ORIGINAL DRAFT

This light adorned them like heavenly courtiers bearing the livery of the Unique One who is forever born from the bosom of the Father and, in this light that is brighter than day, enters from the bosom of his Mother into mine with ineffable gentleness. It enables me to experience that the delights of the right hand of the Father exist on earth through the benignity of the Word. This maternal heart told me: *Apparuit benignitas et humanitas; Benignity and Humanity appeared.* (1254)

CHAPTER CLXXIII

The pain caused by the Circumcision and that my Divine Love allowed me to feel keenly the displeasures that certain persons caused me, removing from me the one I needed.

On the Feast of the Circumcision 1660, deprived of my secretary, I found this deprivation to be harder than Abraham did the sending away of (1254) Agar and Ishmael at your command and that of Sara. These two persons were neither necessary nor useful for the Father of multitudes: *Abraham pater excelsus, Abraham pater multitudinis. Abraham, mighty father; Abraham, father of multitudes.* Your most mighty, gentle wisdom gently and strongly disposed the spirit of this Father of believers to obey Sara whom he could call his lady, just as she called him her lord, being his companion. By your prudent wisdom, she was Abraham's mistress in everything that he was and possessed. Profoundly enlightened by your divine illuminations, the Evangelical Prophet sends the faithful to each of them to draw from them and imitate their perfections. As their children, we should imitate and resemble them.

I would say that it was the year 1633 when this secretary saw that I had a

JEANNE'S ORIGINAL DRAFT

terrible flux from my eyes that prevented me from writing and making a good copy of what I so painfully recorded. She prayed to great St. Joseph that, through his charitable pity, she might be enabled to imitate my writing easily and thus make a perfect copy of what I did, for her letters were round like that of experts. Apparently he heard her prayer, because, in a few days, she wrote so perfectly that she could really imitate my writing which she could easily read. Before this, it was only with great difficulty that she could do so. She was the only one to be so dedicated to this work or relief ever since the year 1633. I could not dictate without first personally writing things out by hand, that had a hard time following the understanding that instructed and enlightened me. Due to my poor eyes, from this time on my writing became harder to read, and no one would have been able to do so had she not made a good copy first. (1255) Those who have taken her away from me will see, in your presence, my Divine Teacher, that one must not tempt You to do miracles unnecessarily and that, whatever You have joined to reproduce You, in a spiritual and holy way, should not be separated. Unite me to You, Divine Beloved, so perfectly that I may always be totally yours, and that You may eternally be all mine.

CHAPTER CLXXIV

The court of Bethlehem. The temple of the divinity where it is perfectly adored. The purification of the Virgin and an apparition of the soul of the late Duke of Orleans (1660).

The court of Bethlehem is more magnificent than that of the Empyrean, since the Divine Dauphin has princes of blood as courtiers and because Zacharias, the Virgin and St. Joseph are present there, admiring and adoring all his divine and human marvels. The divinity is visible and adored by three

AUTOBIOGRAPHY

JEANNE'S ORIGINAL DRAFT

hierarchies: the nine choirs of angels who are spirits, assisting and serving in the stable; the most Sacred and Divine Humanity is adored by those in heaven and those on earth. This Dauphin adores his Divine Father who, until the Incarnation, had been adored only by the angels and mankind. (1256) In the stable, a God adores God. Without any injustice, this tiny Child may claim equality with the Divine Father.

On the Feast of the Purification, the Court of Bethlehem went to the Temple. The Virgin, living temple of the Lord; this Son, Sacred Temple that is both divine and human, the temple of the divinity and God Himself wherein the Father was adored in spirit and in truth by the true Adorer who is the desire of the eternal hills; three divine hypostasis awaited and desired his acts of adoration, if I may thus express myself and say that they are the eternal hills. They are divine; they are God.

On February 12th, the Eve of Brandon's Day [First Sunday in Lent], I left church to go to the kitchen to care for my daughters who assured me that I had spent more than two hours at prayer. You raised my spirit to You in the presence of the two Sisters who accompanied me, my Sister Catherine Fleurin and my Sister Marie Chaut. They waited until I was able to speak and eat. In the evening, between 9 and 10 o'clock, they questioned me to learn what had happened to me and what I had learned during this rapture. I felt that your wisdom ordered me to tell them that one of the King's sons had come to thank me for the prayers I had offered God for him ever since the year he had been in trouble and was accused before His Majesty so as to be prevented from inheriting the throne. He thanked me also for my reply to the late Cardinal of Lyons in the Lyons Hotel in Paris, which was then near the port of Bussy. His Eminence had told me that he wondered what had happened to the Cardinal Duke, his brother, and whether or not You, my Divine Oracle, did not speak to me about that. I told him that his brother was not Joab.

He then requested me to explain, because that was an enigma. "Monseigneur, Joab thrust three lances into Absalom's heart. (1257) That fact overwhelmed David, as you know better than I do, Monseigneur, for he had insisted that, even though his son Absalom was a rebel, his life was to be

JEANNE'S ORIGINAL DRAFT

spared. When Joab learned that the latter was dangling from a tree, trapped there by his hair, he asked the one who had witnessed this why he had not pierced him through. Then he personally carried out what the soldier refused to do in obedience to the king, the father of this rebellious son. If the Cardinal Duke were to have the Duke of Orleans killed in the state he was in, this death would signify the third lance and designate him to be a rebel. He really would become converted, for he loved the king, and I assured him that God loved him more than David loved Absalom. After that, the Cardinal Duke, having heard his brother, had the Duke of Orleans summoned. He married a princess who was according to God's heart. At his home, there was someone who guided the prince to devotion. Thus, he was impressed by the preface recited by the priest at Mass for Passion Sunday that mentions that sin causes men to die by the tree, that You had chosen to die upon the tree of the Cross to save mankind by the adorable wood, that You had changed the curse into a blessing, the death of sin into the life of grace. What had drawn the prince to love things contrary to your law, drew him to observe it and have his court be called *the holy court at Blois*.

In this vision, after acknowledging to me his gratitude and joy upon being on the way to salvation, his blessed soul was assured of eternal happiness. He let me understand that life in this world is but a breath. He said: "This life means very little, and no one should become attached to it." (1258) He then refrained from speaking and left me in deep peace, without informing me whether he was in Purgatory or had already left it. I did not even remember to ask him about this. My enraptured soul marveled at your wisdom and goodness in its obligation to you for having inspired me to pray for the salvation of this blessed prince. Monsieur de Boissac, of happy memory, was overjoyed when I assured him about the foregoing. He said to me: "I will no longer complain about the limited good I will leave behind, nor my small fortune which belongs to Him, but I praise God that my master Gaston is numbered among the chosen ones." Madame Charrin of Lyons was present there on the last day of the year 1660 and will join me in praising your most merciful goodness and kindness.

JEANNE'S ORIGINAL DRAFT

CHAPTER CLXXV

My gratitude to God for the election of St. Matthias and daily meditations on the Gospel during Lent.

On the Feast of St. Matthias, who has always been favorable toward me, I admired the condition of the saints in him in both the divine and human light, the God-Man betrayed and sold by a most unfortunate Apostle. I thanked the incarnate wisdom for this election and considered the prayer made by the primitive Church, the first assembly after the exodus of St. Peter which was marvelous: (1259) *Et statuerunt duos. Joseph, qui vocabatur Barsabas, qui cognominatus est Justus, et Mathiam. Et orantes dixerunt: Tu Domine, qui corda nosti omnium, ostende quem elegeris ex his duobus unum, accipere locum ministerii huius, et apostolatus, de quo prævaricatus est Judas ut abiret in locum suum. Et dederunt sortes eis, et cecidit sors super Mathiam, et annumeratus est cum undecim Apostolis. And they appointed two: Joseph, called Barsabas, who was surnamed Justus, and Matthias. And praying, they said: Thou, Lord, who knowest the hearts of all men, shew whether of these two thou hast chosen to take the place of this ministry and apostleship, from which Judas hath by transgression fallen, that he might go to his own place. And they gave them lots: and the lot fell upon Matthias. And he was numbered with the eleven apostles.* (Acts 1:23-26)

The faithful Matthias, possessing as much humility as love, accepted this blessed appointment, making up for all the infidelities of the deceiver. He was the twelfth one, thus enshrining in the heart of the most august Virgin Mary the crown of joy that will be seen in glory by all the elect. Who among mortals has understood the affliction of this Mother of Sorrows? It was a pitiless sword that pierced her soul. Her Son, the Man of Sorrows, declared that Judas and the pontiffs were more responsible for his death than Pilate who condemned Him to the torture of the Cross.

JEANNE'S ORIGINAL DRAFT

1660

Wednesday
1

During the holy time of Lent, since I was unable to observe it and was obligated to break it, I usually felt sad. This was because I had heard in the Preface of Holy Mass that it elevates the soul, draws down the favors of heaven and enriches it by virtue. I felt empty of all this, overwhelmed by faults and imperfections. This made me lament unceasingly; I am the daughter who acknowledges my spiritual poverty.

Thursday
2

Then, hoping against hope, I said to You: Lord, I am not worthy of your magnificent visits, but say the word of grace, and my soul will be alleviated. (1260) If it is not relieved of the weight that retains it in its own misery, I do not deserve to have You think of me.

Friday
3

But You are my mercy. Remove from my heart anything that is not You. Enable me to love those who make me suffer, that I may assist their salvation.

Saturday
4

Deliver me from the waves and various agitations that trouble us on the sea of this life or this world. My dear Divine Savior, tell all the powers of my soul and heart: *Confidete, ego sum, nolite timere. Have a good heart. It is I. Fear not.* (Mk 6:50) My gentle Jesus, come to me and calm the winds and tempests.

Sunday
5

Lead me into the desert by your good Spirit, helping me to overcome every temptation and all my enemies.

Monday
6

Through charity, may I bear and practice all works of spiritual and corporal mercy, and may I say as do all your elect: *Venite benedicti Patris meis. Come, ye blessed of my Father.* (Mt 25:34)

JEANNE'S ORIGINAL DRAFT

Tuesday 7	Enter your temple and expel from it all the buyers and sellers; consecrate it anew by your indwelling, through your prayers and merits. May all my innocent desires cry out to You: *Hosanna filio David. Hosanna to the son of David.* (Mt 21:9)
Wednesday 8	Desiring to listen to the One who is more powerful than Solomon and to fulfil the will of his Heavenly Father, I consider myself as being allied to the Divine Savior in a triple alliance as daughter, sister and mother. (1261)
Thursday 9	By emerging from the confines of self-love, I pray to You, as the Son of David, to take pity upon this little puppy by allowing crumbs to fall, through your natural pity, in contrast to those who trouble me. You strengthen me in faith that draws me closer to You in confidence.
Friday 10	Through grace, cleanse me in the pool of your charity, merciful Savior, and save me from all evil, fault and pain. Command me to take up my pallet and to sin no more.
Saturday 11	Raise me up by your divine election and separate me from earthly things that are an obstacle to my prayer. *Intret oratio mea, in conspectu tuo. Inclina aurem tuam ad precem meam, Domine. Let my prayer come in before thee: incline thy ear to my petition.* (Ps 87:3)
Sunday 12	Divine Savior, through your inexpressible goodness, let me be transformed into You and see only You, as I listen to your divine Word by order of your Divine Father.
Monday 13	*In corde meo abscondi eloquia tua, ut non peccem tibi. Thy words have I hidden in my heart, that I may not sin against Thee.* (Ps 118:11) Never leave me alone; may I always do your holy will according to your good pleasure.

JEANNE'S ORIGINAL DRAFT

Tuesday
14

Be my only Master, my Truth, my Way and my Life. May I humble myself in truth, and may I bless You in time and in eternity.

Wednesday
15

Let me understand the secret of your loving Passion. May I one day say: I know nothing in this life except my Jesus Crucified: *Mihi vivere Christus est, et mori lucrum. For to me, to live is Christ: and to die is gain.* (Phil 1:21)

Thursday
16

May I meditate on your law day and night. May I observe it, and may it always be at the center of my heart. May You be my weight and my love: *Benedictus qui confidit in Domino, et erit Dominus fiducia eius. Blessed is the man that trusteth in the Lord, and the Lord shall be his confidence.* (Jer 17:7) (1262)

Friday
17

My God, my Father and my Spouse, may I offer You all the old and new fruit of all time, blessing You with all your saints.

Saturday
18

Through your mercy, invest me with the robe of innocence and all the adornments of grace, in every way forgiving my sins of thought, word and deed: *Ab occultis meis munda me; et ab alienis parce servo tuo. From my secret ones cleanse me, and from those of others spare thy servant.* (Ps 18:13b-14a)

Sunday
19

Enlighten me and let my eyes behold You uninterruptedly. May I tell You with the holy Angels: *Oculi mei semper ad Dominum, quia evellet de laqueo pedes meos. Respice in me, et miserere mei; quia unicus et pauper sum ego. My eyes are ever towards the Lord: for he shall pluck my feet out of the snare. Look thou upon me, and have mercy on me; for I am alone and poor.* (Ps 24:15-16)

JEANNE'S ORIGINAL DRAFT

Expel the demons and may I bless your Name with that of your wonderful Mother who carried You, gave You birth and nourished You with her virginal, holy milk. May I hear your divine word and keep it within me. May it never return empty, but fulfill your will perfectly.

Monday 20

After I have been cleansed in the river of repentance as was Naaman in the River Jordan, may I receive You, my Divine Elias, *Deus Dominus, My God, my Lord.* Bless your mercies within me, that nurture me with You Yourself in your most august Sacrament, the wheat of the elect and the wine that engenders virgins.

Tuesday 21

Incarnate Word, our All in the Most Blessed Sacrament, dwell eternally among your daughters whom You have ordered me to assemble together for your glory and my salvation. Let them join me in praising You for all eternity. (1263)

Wednesday 22

Divine Love, fill our hearts; and, from the abundance of our hearts, may our lips speak and proclaim your praises. Eternal Father, in our hearts, plant the Tree of Life: your Son, the God-Man, whom we acknowledge to be the grafted Word who will personally save them: *In mansuetudine suscipite insitum verbum, quod potest salvare animas vestras. With meekness receive the ingrafted word, which is able to save your souls.* (Jas 1:21b)

Thursday 23

Divine Physician, deliver us from all our misfortunes and grant us your blessings. May we serve faithfully here below all our mortal lives, and may You give us lodging in heaven with You during all your eternal life.

JEANNE'S ORIGINAL DRAFT

Friday
24

O Lover par excellence, You are so weary and tired. Be seated in our hearts just as your favorite disciple saw You, and fill them with your love and the water that quenches our thirst and gushes forth to eternal life.

Saturday
25

Man of desire, sanctify your servant through your divine and human innocence. In your presence, may she always remain elevated to You and through You. May whatever is not God be nothing to her.

Sunday
26

Adorable Providence, raise me up to the mountain of perfection, making me disregard whatever is not God, for outside of You, everything is subject to inconstancy like the waves of the ocean.

Monday
27

Eternal Father, may the zeal of your house consume me, and may all the powers of my soul bless your holy Name. (1264) Let all creatures acknowledge and adore your Name and your love.

Tuesday
28

My good Master, *Doce me facere voluntatem tuam, quia Deus meus es tu. Teach me to do your will, for you are my God. (*Ps 142:10a) May your good Spirit lead me *in terram rectam. Propter nomen tuum, Domine, vivificabis me et qui tacet me; in the right land. For thy name's sake, O Lord, thou wilt quicken me in thy justice [and who makes me keep quiet]* (Ps 142:11a)

Wednesday
29

Be sanctified in us, and gather us from all nations on earth. Shower that clearest water upon us that cleanses us from all our stains. Give us your Holy Spirit who creates a clean, upright and new heart within us. By your divine power, open our hearts and eyes that, by seeing You here through the eyes of faith, we may adore You in spirit and in truth as the true Son of God.

JEANNE'S ORIGINAL DRAFT

Thursday 30	Lord of Prophets, visit all your daughters. Console the one who weeps over them and all her spiritual children. Make them faithful to your inspirations. May they and I, too, live a holy and divine life.

Friday 31	Friend of friends, call me powerfully and, through love, bid me to leave everything that is earth and mud. Unbind me from everything that could detain me in my lowliness; and let me show forth your loving delectation and the glory of your Divine Father who always answers You.

Saturday 32	Jesus, splendor of the Father's glory, be my unfading light. May I always follow You. My Divine Savior, never allow me to walk in darkness. Be with me, show me your ways and your paths. (1265) May I do your will in everything. Show me that You are my God; and, in accordance with your word and promises, bless me with all your blessings, making me your daughter who makes progress. I trust that my Mother was a real prophetess, since You inspired her to tell me that I would be Joseph.

You perfected her through great affliction. She suffered from sword, fire, water; she ought to be at rest. After her death, You allowed a number of people to see her with all the saints in grace and glory. I praise and thank You for this, my Lord and my All.

Sunday 33	Existing before and after Abraham, You are always adorable in your divine and human goodness. You chose to let me see your two births that are ineffable and let me participate in both of them. *Generationes eius quis enarrabo? Who shall declare his generation?* (Is 53:8b)

JEANNE'S ORIGINAL DRAFT

Monday 34	Divine Love, thank You for inviting me a number of times to drink from your living, dynamic waters and, by the law of charity, for making a fountain within me by giving me your Divine Spirit. May He eternally be my pure flame, my powerful, living fountain and my warming fire. By illuminating my charity, may He be my spiritual anointing. For lovers, everything is held in common.
Tuesday 35	O God, my God, when will You be recognized in your favors and adored by all nations? When will your own brothers and sisters believe in You and adore You in the unity of the Holy Spirit with a holy respect? (1266)
Wednesday 36	Shepherd of shepherds, defend us from the wolves, and, in everything, let us hear your voice and obey your holy, adorable will.
Thursday 37	Eternal Pontiff, after having allowed me to kiss your holy feet one hundred and fifty times daily, say that my sins are forgiven, granting me great love and a plenary indulgence.
Friday 38	Redeemer of mankind, who died for everyone, give me your life that I may live and die through and for love of You. It is the one necessary thing that I have yearned for and continue to desire always.
Saturday 39	The Prophet saw you upon a glorious throne: *In anno quo mortuus est rex Ozias, vidi Dominum sedentem super solium excelsum et elevatum; et ea quæ sub ipso erant replebant templum. In the year that king Ozias died, I saw the Lord sitting upon a throne high and elevated: and his train filled the temple.* (Is 6:1) Meanwhile, the Seraphim exclaimed: *"Holy, Holy, Holy is the Lord God of Hosts, plena est omnis terra gloria eius;*

JEANNE'S ORIGINAL DRAFT

all the earth is full of his glory." (Is 6:3)

Did I not hear the voice of your Divine Father who glorified You at the Jordan River by calling You his Beloved Son, and upon Tabor by testifying that You are his delight? Today You repeatedly receive the glory after You said to your Eternal Father: *Pater, clarifica nomen tuum. Venit ergo vox de cælo: Et clarificavi, et [iterum] clarificabo. Father, glorify thy name. A voice therefore came from heaven: I have both glorified and will glorify it again.* (Jn 12:28) At the same time, all who bless You, say to You: *Hosanna, benedictus qui venit in nomine Domini, rex Israel. Hosanna. Blessed is he that cometh in the name of the Lord, the king of Israel.* (Jn 12:13)

Divine Savior, the Evangelist said that, after all these marvels, You withdrew and concealed Yourself. Thus, Isaias has written: *Vere tu es Deus absconditus et salvator. Verily thou art a hidden God, the Savior.* (Is 45:15) (1267) It might be feared that You would no longer be welcome in Jerusalem that was unworthy of your visit, but where sin abounds through the wickedness of your enemies, through your goodness, You wanted grace to abound there even more by dying so as to give them your life.

Holy
Thursday

At about ten o'clock in the evening on Holy Thursday, I was on the altar step before You in your Sacrament, weeping bitterly with your angels of peace. You let me understand: "Daughter of Jerusalem, weep for yourself and your children. Your daughters fill you with distress. You are a Mother in Israel and my Deborah seated under the palm-tree of my victories, under my Cross. Pray for those who betray you and grieve you."

JEANNE'S ORIGINAL DRAFT

Good
Friday

The next day, having awakened quite early, I understood: "They have cast lots for my robe and have divided my clothes." I saw three dice. I was unaware of the plans of those who made me suffer by withdrawing far from your path.

Holy Church observes silence. I will keep it until the time that You order me to break it. Let my heart melt and tear like the temple veil that is shredded by rocks. Let my understanding be darkened as was the sun; and let me enter the tomb with You, after having accomplished your will in everything. Consume me by the flames of your Sacred Humanity; and let me cease being what I am to become what You are and what You want me to be. (1268)

JEANNE'S ORIGINAL DRAFT

CHAPTER CLXXVI

Easter Sunday and its Octave. The rejoicing of my heart because of the superabundant assistance and illuminations your love gave me.

On Easter Sunday (1660), I adored You and chanted your ineffable victory as the true Phoenix who had assumed your new life. Your tomb made You glorious, removing doubt from the weakness and timidity of our sex by two of the sixty strong ones who stand near your adorable, majestic couch: *In lectulum Salomon sexaginta fortes ambiunt ex fortissimis Israel: Omnes tenentes gladios, et ad bella doctissimi: Uniuscujusque ensis super femur suum propter timores nocturnos. Behold threescore valiant ones of the most valiant of Israel surrounded the bed of Solomon! All holding swords, and most expert in war: every man's sword upon his thigh, because of fears in the night.* (Cant 3:7-8)

Great Pope St. Gregory had said that heaven and earth listened when the angels Michael (*Quis sicut Deus; Who is like to God?*) and Gabriel (*vir Deus Dei; man of the Lord God*) spoke. They were the two who participated in everything referring to your glory in the Incarnation and all your mysteries, both divine and human. They were the most powerful leaders of your celestial princes in your armies, the princes who assist before your throne that is your bed of justice and peace. They fought in order to save mankind, as well as to exalt your glory. Abraham swore to Eliezer to obtain and take Rebecca home as a bride for his son Isaac: *Elieser Dei a Dei adjutorium posuit ergo servus manum sub femore Abraham domini sui, et juravit illi sermone hoc. The servant therefore put his hand under the thigh of Abraham, his lord, and swore to him upon this word.* (Gen 24:9)

While pouring out her tears and perfumes, Magdalen was courageous enough to go anoint You with her ointment. You allowed me to draw near

JEANNE'S ORIGINAL DRAFT

your adorable couch, surrounded by the sixty strong ones of Israel. I prayed You to order them immediately to Rome for the healing of the Holy Father, to sustain the one whom You have chosen to fill the office and possess St. Peter's chair with dignity. (1269) I immediately told this to Monsieur de Ville, official and substitute Vicar, as I have already briefly mentioned.

Without your superabundant light and most powerful, persevering aid, I could never describe my joy on *Quasimodo* Monday [Low Monday]. I spent all my time in rejoicing and *Alleluias* with great delight in your wonderful mysteries and mysterious wonders of snow and fire. Since I am unable to speak properly about this, the lips of the Most High will make up for my incapacity, giving glory to his praise.

Adorable One, am I still here in this life after having seen and heard these divine locutions? Incarnate Word, those who say that your discourses are so ravishing that they cannot help but marvel at You maintain that no one can speak as You do. Far from capturing You to place You in the power of your enemies, they themselves were captivated. Then they tasted and saw how loving and gracious You are toward your friends, since You inspire your enemies. (1270)

JEANNE'S ORIGINAL DRAFT

CHAPTER CLXXVIII[1]

The birth of St. John whom Jesus Christ canonized with his own lips. The three suns that entered my room. The King's marriage, and what I learned about the late Cardinal of Lyons. (1660)

It was the feast of the birth of the incomparable one among all those born of women, your miraculous Precursor, whom You canonized with your own lips. O Lord, You extend from one end to the other and unite the finite with the infinite: two natures in unity of Persons, subsistences and hypostases, without becoming separate from the Father who begets You before the day amid the splendor of the saints. Together with Him in one sole principle, You produce the unique flame, the love of two spirants who, under different forms, illuminates and fills all hearts. Unique in Himself, He multiplies his favors and graces outside of Himself without emerging from the source of origin, the fountain of the entire Divine Trinity, penetrating this Father and Son, just as He is penetrated by Them. Although distinctive, your three supports exist one within the other by your marvelous circumincession which I adore as your active and passive relationships, your immanent and immense emanations *ad extra, externally* and doing good *ad extra*. With the Seraphim, I exclaim to myself: *Holy, Holy, Holy*, begging them to conceal me with their wings or to let me be consumed by the flames of this kiss by using tongs to take from the altar a coal that incessantly burns in the heavenly Jerusalem, the Empyrean heaven that is illuminated by the face of God Himself, by these divine wheels that exist one within the other. Daniel, man of desire, pray for me; and you, holy Prophet Ezechiel *fortitudo Dei, strong one of God*. I am in a torrent of fire that can transform me into itself. (1271)

When, at the Trinsfiguration, St. Peter yearned to erect three tabernacles,

---

[1]There is no Chapter Number CLXXVII.

JEANNE'S ORIGINAL DRAFT

he did not know what he was saying: *Non enim sciebat quid diceret. For he knew not what he said.* (Mk 9:5) When I saw three suns enter my room, could I possibly speak about this? No, my God, with the Prophet Jeremias, I excuse myself. Should You command me to write, hold my hand; guide it as well as my tongue: *Lingua mea calamus scribœ velociter scribentis. My tongue is the pen of a scrivener that writeth swiftly.* (Ps 44:2) In your hands, they will be enabled to do anything You desire.

These three suns were Saint Zacharias, Saint Elizabeth, Saint John the Baptist who represented for me your Three Divine Persons. Saint Zacharias, was the husband of Saint Elizabeth and father of John the Baptist, just as she was his mother. Proceeding from them both, St. John symbolized for me the Holy Spirit whose dwelling-place he is and—in a wonderful, miraculous way—fills all three. This is because, enclosed within her womb, the sterile woman bears an infant; the mute one sings a canticle; the child reasons and adores its Creator. He performs his role as herald and precursor of the Savior. This God, hidden in his Virgin Mother, is revealed by Saint John's gestures and exhilaration when he heard Mary's greeting. He is the voice of the Incarnate and Increated Word within the virginal womb. He enlightens us amid the darkness, showing us the essential and eternal light. (1272) After these visits, I understood: *Per viscera misericordiœ Dei nostri: in quibus visitavit nos, oriens ex alto: illuminare his qui in tenebris et in umbra mortis sedent: ad dirigendos pedes nostros in viam pacis. Through the bowels of the mercy of our God, in which the Orient from on high hath visited us: To enlighten them that sit in darkness and in the shadow of death: to direct our feet into the way of peace.* (Lk 1:78-79)

My daughter, have confidence. The same goodness that promised you in 1627 that I would visit the Queen to give her a Dauphin who would be King, is the same that I send to visit you by these three suns. They are to provide you with the hope for a happy marriage that you requested of me together with multiple blessings. Have no doubt and do not remain silent about this. Let the prudence of persons who pretend to have humility blame you until my power confounds them by the confirmation of the truth. Your confidence incites my

JEANNE'S ORIGINAL DRAFT

clemency. These three suns that entered your room and that you saw also announce the joy and peace of the princes and of all France. Hope against hope; wait for the salvation of the one that seems to oppose you. The following words that are prophecies about the Pope and the King, will demonstrate, by miracle, the effects of your voice:

One night during the fifteen days of the Jubilee, in spirit I was taken to the chapel of the archbishopric in Lyons where I saw the late Cardinal. His head was uncovered, he was dressed in a purple robe, and the crown he bore had a halo. He came to me and presented me with the *Te igitur* of the Canon of the Mass, begging me to recite for him the part that I could. Respectfully, while kneeling, I received this canon from him with great politeness. Upon seeing that I did not do so immediately, he repeated his request. At daybreak, I entered our church. Since I was alone, I went up to the altar and prayed the *Te igitur* which I said for him except the words of the Consecration. (1273) After this, I arranged to have Holy Mass offered for his intention. While I was at prayer, he thanked me, letting me know that he had been very pleased to see me recite the entire content of this *Te Igitur*, asking You, my Eternal Priest, to pronounce the sacred words of the Consecration for your glory and to satisfy for everything he desired or that he might have omitted. I still pray to You for him with all the love and zeal that You give me for him, which has always been great, because You had given him to me as my pastor.

Since I did not have my secretary, I could not force myself to write except very little, because the flux from one eye had intensified. That is the reason that I sent back your words to You, conjuring You through your goodness that they might not return to You empty, but operate everything your charity desired of me. Your thoughts are as far from those of mankind as heaven is from earth. Fill me with your divine dew: *Rorate, cæli, desuper, et nubes pluant justum; aperiatur terra, et germinet Salvatorem, etc. Drop down dew, ye heavens, from above: and let the clouds rain the just. Let the earth be opened and bud forth a Savior.* (Is 45:8) (1274)

JEANNE'S ORIGINAL DRAFT

For each day of the week: first of all, in spirit, I enter the places marked herein:

Le lundi, dans une étable	*On Monday, in a stable*
Je vois Jésus tout aimable	*I see Jesus so amicable*
Que sa mère a enfanté	*Whom his Mother has borne*
Avec tant de pauvreté.	*In poverty so morne.*
Le mardi, entrant au temple	*On Tuesday, to the temple I go*
D'un grand amour je le contemple	*To contemplate Him lovingly; so*
Qui nous unit coeur à coeur	*Heart to heart, He unites us*
Et y triomphe des docteurs.	*And o'er the doctors is victorious.*
Le mercredi je repense	*On Wednesday, I then recall*
Ses pleurs et son abstinence	*His tears and his fasting all,*
Qui le rend dans un désert	*That in a desert made Him*
Victorieux de l'enfer.	*Vanquish hell and sin.*
Le jeudi à ses Apôtres	*On Thursday, to the Apostles*
Il se donne, et non aux autres,	*He gave Himself - not to others*
Et leur lave à tous les pieds	*Their feet He did gently lave;*
Je le prie de m'humiler. (1275)	*Give me humility, Lord, I pray.*
Le vendredi je soupire	*On Friday, how I yearn*
Sa passion et son martyre.	*For his Passion and death so stern;*
Pour t'aimer j'ai pris ta Croix	*To love You, I take up your Cross*
Alors j'entends ta douce voix.	*At which I hear your sweet voice.*
Le samedi, au sépulchre	*On Saturday, at the sepulchre*
Je regarde se beau lustre	*I see this beautiful Lustre*
Tout pâle et décoloré	*Completely pallid and discolored*
Et sa Mère éplorée.	*While his Mother mourns in sorrow.*

398

JEANNE'S ORIGINAL DRAFT

Le dimanche plein de gloire   *On Sunday, superbly glorious,*
Il emporte la victoire   *He is eminently victorious*
Au-dessus des ennemis   *O'er his enemies so false*
Qui en la Croix l'avaient mis.   *Who had placed Him on the Cross.*

par *J. de Matel*   **by** *J. de Matel*

INDEX

INDEX

Mission 109
Oratorians 41, 56, 65, 66, 131, 132, 210
Recollect Sisters 218
Sisters of Saint Elizabeth 273, 274
Sisters of the Antiquaille 274
St. Dominic 198
Theatine Fathers 146
Visitation Sisters 273, 371

P

Paradise 110, 264, 281, 282, 295, 334, 340, 341, 347, 362
Patent Letters 24
Priests
Abbé de Cerisy 3, 4, 5, 6, 8, 11, 21, 24
Abbé of St. Just 168, 228, 229, 254, 255, 273, 279, 287, 292
Father Brachet 24
Father Carré 24
Father Rudolph 140
Father Yvan 223
Gautery 135
Grenat des Anges 135
Monsieur Bernardon 18
Monsieur de Fléchère 274
Monsieur de la Piardière 38, 41, 57, 63, 67, 72, 92, 106, 109, 112, 113, 114, 131, 135, 136, 142, 143, 148, 149, 154, 161, 185, 190, 207, 210, 223, 224, 226, 228, 229, 323
Monsieur de la Salle 325
Monsieur de St. Just 287
Monsieur de Ville 229, 272, 394
Monsieur du Bousquet 49
Prior Bernardon 21

Prior of Croixil 20
Prior of Denicé 21, 32, 291, 301, 323
Saint Pierre 135
Prophet 91, 101, 116, 133
Purgatory 160, 382

Q

Queen
Marie de Medicis 279

R

Religious
Abbé de Cerisy 32
Augustinian Fathers 157
Capuchins 16, 17
Chartreux 9
Father Brachet 31
Father Carré 25, 32, 139, 145, 186, 197, 198, 210
Father Menam 66
Father Morin 56, 131, 132
Lucrecia de Bely 22, 55, 58, 59, 81, 63, 135, 184
Monseigneur de Langlade 198, 224
Monsieur Olier 135
Mother de Chantal 279
Mother Holy Spirit Nallard 54
Prior de Croixil 15, 22
Prior St. Robert 15
Sister Catherine Fleurin 381
Sister Catherine Richardon 57
Sister Conception 21
Sister Elie of the Cross 22
Sister Elizabeth Grasseteau 6, 16, 18, 22, 25, 29, 31, 32, 46, 53
Sister Françoise Gravier 22, 31, 32,